PERFORMANCE MEASUREMENT IN FINANCE

Butterworth-Heinemann Finance

QUANTITATIVE FINANCE SERIES

aims and objectives

- books based on the work of financial market practitioners and academics
- presenting cutting edge research to the professional/practitioner market
- combining intellectual rigour and practical application
- covering the interaction between mathematical theory and financial practice
- to improve portfolio performance, risk management and trading book performance
- covering quantitative techniques

market

Brokers/Traders; Actuaries; Consultants; Asset Managers; Fund Managers; Regulators; Central Bankers; Treasury Officials; Technical Analysts; and Academics for Masters in Finance and MBA market.

series titles

Return Distributions in Finance
Derivative Instruments: theory, valuation, analysis
Managing Downside Risk in Financial Markets: theory, practice and implementation
Economics for Financial Markets
Global Tactical Asset Allocation: theory and practice
Performance Measurement in Finance: firms, funds and managers
Real R&D Options

series editor

Dr Stephen Satchell

Dr Satchell is Reader in Financial Econometrics at Trinity College, Cambridge; Visiting Professor at Birkbeck College, City University Business School and University of Technology, Sydney. He also works in a consultative capacity to many firms, and edits the journal *Derivatives: use, trading and regulations*.

PERFORMANCE MEASUREMENT IN FINANCE

Firms, Funds and Managers

Edited by

John Knight

Stephen Satchell

BUTTERWORTH HEINEMANN

OXFORD AMSTERDAM BOSTON LONDON NEW YORK PARIS
SAN DIEGO SAN FRANCISCO SINGAPORE SYDNEY TOKYO

Butterworth-Heinemann
An imprint of Elsevier Science
Linacre House, Jordan Hill, Oxford OX2 8DP
225 Wildwood Avenue, Woburn MA 01801-2041

First published 2002

British Library Cataloguing in Publication Data
Performance measurement in finance: firms, funds and
managers. – (Quantitative finance series)
1. Rate of return – Evaluation 2. Portfolio management – Evaluation 3. Investment analysis 4. Investment advisors – Rating of 5. Investments – Econometric models
I. Knight, John II. Satchell, Stephen E.
332.6

Library of Congress Cataloguing in Publication Data
A catalogue record for this book is available from the Library of Congress

ISBN 0 7506 5026 5

Typeset by Laserwords Private Limited, Chennai, India
Printed and bound in Great Britain by Biddles Ltd *www.biddles.co.uk*

Contents

Preface

The purpose of this book is to bring together recent research on performance measurement, from both academic and practitioner perspectives. As in previous edited works by ourselves, we start with some survey chapters to allow readers to refresh their knowledge.

Before we describe the contents of this book, it is worth considering a number of themes in performance measurement that are of current interest. First, there are issues such as how to deal with complex multi-period portfolio returns where the assets may be derivatives and returns non-linear and non-normal. Second, there are issues to do with short performance histories; third, there are problems to do with benchmark failure as many indices have recently experienced unprecedented levels of entry and exit. Finally, there are deep issues connecting the volatility of markets to the use of benchmarks; if all managers are rewarded in the same way and are measured against the same yardsticks, we get herding behaviour and the possibilities of excess volatility and panic.

While the book does not claim to answer and resolve all the above questions and issues, it does address them.

The first chapter by Nathalie Farah deals with the financial theory relevant to performance measurement. Next, Guoqiang Wang discusses issues of econometrics and statistics associated with performance measurement.

Dr Emmanuel Acar and Andrew Pearson discuss the real-world problems associated with stochastic exposures, i.e. when portfolio weights are themselves random. Focusing on Value at Risk, they show how awareness of stochastic exposures/stochastic cash flow information can be incorporated into an improved performance measurement methodology.

Gaurav Amin and Dr Harry Kat use recent theoretical results to evaluate performance in hedge funds, their methodology is particularly suited to dynamic trading strategies.

Professor David Blake and Professor Allan Timmermann investigate the merits of different benchmarks used in the UK and USA. This is a research area of great topicality as indices such as the FT100 have recently been found wanting as a choice of benchmark.

Frances Cowell brings a practitioner's perspective onto the issue of performance evaluation via simulation and the methodology that lies behind a performance simulator.

Dr Soosung Hwang and Professor Mark Salmon use the theory of copulae and 14 UK investment trusts to analyse the non-linear dependency properties of standard performance measures. For those not familiar with copula theory, this is a powerful technique for modelling non-standard correlations.

Professor Bob Korkie, who has made many important contributions to performance issues in finance, has contributed two chapters. The first is a detailed case study of a Canadian investment company, Nesbitt Burns. The second, joint with Dr Turtle, is a theoretical paper addressing the changing opportunity set in an intertemporal context. This set is equivalent to the feasible mean-variance space in a one period world and hence one can measure performance by considering frontier slopes.

Dr Mark Lundin and Dr Stephen Satchell investigate performance issues in a long–short framework and advocate a particular measure of risk. Dr Emanuela Sciubbia presents an analysis of performance from the perspective of economic theory.

David Spaulding considers the important issue of how to calculate rates of return. His chapter contrasts various methods and demonstrates that the differences can be significant. Professor Ian Tonks, in the final chapter, presents an analysis of UK pension fund performance focusing on whether there is an optimal fund size.

John Knight and Stephen Satchell

Contributors

Emmanuel Acar works at Citibank as a Vice-President within the FX Engineering Group. He was previously (since 1990) a proprietary trader at Dresdner Kleinwort Benson, BZW, and Banque Nationale de Paris' London Branch. He has experience in quantitative strategies, as an actuary and from having done his PhD on the stochastic properties of trading rules.

Gaurav S. Amin graduated as a Bachelor of Commerce from the University of Mumbai, India. He holds an MBA from Narsee Monjee Institute of Management Studies, Mumbai, India, and an MSc (with Distinction) in International Securities, Investment and Banking from the ISMA Centre at the University of Reading, UK. He is currently pursuing a PhD degree at the ISMA Centre, doing research on hedge fund performance.

David Blake is Professor of Financial Economics at Birkbeck College in the University of London and Chairman of Square Mile Consultants, a training and research consultancy. Formerly Director of the Securities Industry Programme at City University Business School and Research Fellow at both the London Business School and the London School of Economics. His research interests include the modelling of asset demands and financial innovations, the investment behaviour and performance of pension funds and mutual funds, and pension plan design. He has published in major economics and finance journals in all these fields. He is author of numerous books on financial topics, the most recent of which is *Financial Market Analysis*.

Frances Cowell works in London for Vestek-Quantec, a subsidiary of Thomson Financial. Before joining Quantec in 1998, she was part of the Quantitative Investments team at Natwest Investment Management in Sydney, where she was responsible for domestic and international indexed equity portfolios and indexed balanced portfolios. Experience in applying quantitative solutions to domestic equity portfolios has enabled her to proceed to construct investment strategies combining physical assets and derivatives; exploiting inconsistent pricing between related instruments; and subsequently to design portfolios with pre-specified return and risk characteristics.

Nathalie Farah is a PhD candidate at the Faculty of Economics and Political Science at the University of Cambridge. She is researching in portfolio theory and performance measurement. She completed her MSc in Finance and Economics at the London School of Economics after obtaining her BA in Economics at the American University of Beirut, Lebanon. She plans to make a career in investment consulting.

Soosung Hwang is a Lecturer in Finance in the Faculty of Finance and the Deputy Director of the Financial Econometrics Research Centre, City University Business School, London. He is also an Honorary Research Associate of the Department of Applied Economics, Cambridge University. He received his PhD from Cambridge University and his research interests include finance, financial econometrics and forecasting.

Harry M. Kat is currently Associate Professor of Finance at the ISMA Centre Business School at the University of Reading. Before returning to academia he was Head of Equity Derivatives Europe at Bank of America in London, Head of Derivatives Structuring and Marketing at First Chicago in Tokyo and Head of Derivatives Research at MeesPierson in Amsterdam. Dr Kat holds MBA and PhD degrees in Economics and Econometrics from the Tinbergen Graduate School of Business at the University of Amsterdam. He is a member of the editorial board of *The Journal of Derivatives* and *The Journal of Alternative Investments* and has (co-)authored numerous articles in well-known finance journals such as *The Journal of Financial and Quantitative Analysis*, *The Journal of Derivatives*, *The Journal of Financial Engineering*, *Applied Mathematical Finance* and *The Journal of Alternative Investments*. His new book *Structured Equity Derivatives* was published in July 2001 by John Wiley & Sons.

Bob Korkie is Head of Investment Research and Risk Management at OPTrust. He is formerly Professor of Finance at the University of Alberta and has been a visiting professor in Austria, France, Turkey and the United States. He is an affiliate member of the Society of Financial Analysts, and principal of

RMK Financial Consulting. He has an undergraduate degree in Engineering, an MBA (both Saskatchewan) and a PhD (University of Washington). His research has been published in numerous financial journals and magazines.

Mark Lundin is the Head of Quantitative Research at Fortis Investment Management in Brussels. His interests and activities primarily involve the application of advanced techniques to investing in and trading the financial markets. Before joining Fortis, Mark was a Research Scientist at Olsen & Associates Research Institute for Applied Economics in Zurich where he developed real-time, high-frequency trading models and performed multivariate financial research. Mark is an ongoing external technical referee for *Risk Magazine* and an independent referee for *IEEE Transactions on Neural Networks in Financial Engineering*. He holds a PhD in Particle Physics from Université Louis Pasteur, Strasbourg, and a BS in Mathematics and Computer Science from the University of Illinois.

Andrew Pearson is currently Vice-President within the FX Analytics group at Citibank. Previously he worked as a quantitative analyst for Citibank FX Options Technology. His PhD was in Theoretical Physics at Imperial College, London.

Mark Salmon joined City University Business School in 1997 having previously been Professor of Economics and Chair of the Economics Department at the European University Institute, Florence. He had earlier held appointments at the University of Warwick, the Australian National University, the Bank of England and the London Business School and visiting appointments at Nuffield College Oxford, Princeton, Paris I Sorbonne, Aix-Marseille, Bordeaux IV and Illinois. He has served as a consultant to a number of city institutions and was recently a member of a 'Task Force' set up by the European Commission to consider exchange rate policy for the euro. He has been a member of the European Financial Markets Advisory Panel and has worked with the National Bank of Hungary on transition policies towards membership of the European Union. He currently acts as a consultant to the Bank of England. He is a Research Fellow of the Centre for Economic Policy Research associated with the International Macro and Finance Programmes and has published widely in journals such as *Econometrica*, *The Annals of Statistics*, *Journal of Econometrics*, the *Economic Journal*, the *Journal of Economic Dynamics and Control* and the *International Economic Review*. His most recent book is a graduate level textbook on Financial Econometrics.

Mark is also Deutsche Morgan Grenfell Professor of Financial Markets and Director of the Financial Econometrics Research Centre.

Emanuela Sciubba is Fellow of Newnham College and University Lecturer in Economics at the University of Cambridge. She was previously a research fellow at the Tinbergen Institute in Rotterdam and at Ente Einaudi (Bank of Italy) in Rome. She received an MA in Business and Economics from LUISS University in Rome and a PhD in Economics from the University of Cambridge. She has been invited to present her work at universities and research institutes all over Europe and in the United States. Her research interests and writings have covered a variety of topics in economic theory and finance, including evolutionary finance and the survival of portfolio rules, the role of asymmetric information in dynamic financial markets, the implications of relative performance for portfolio choices and asset pricing, the implications of relative performance for risky choices in banking and the effect of entry in the banking sector.

David Spaulding is President of The Spaulding Group, Inc., a Somerset, NJ-based consulting, publishing and research firm that provides services to the money management industry. He is the founder and publisher of *The Journal of Performance Measurement* and the author of *Measuring Investment Performance – Calculating and Evaluating Investment Risk and Return*, which was published by McGraw-Hill in August 1997. He is a member of the AIMR Performance Presentation Standards Implementation Committee (AIMR-PPS) and the Investment Performance Council Interpretations Subcommittee. Several of Mr Spaulding's consulting assignments have involved Performance Measurement and the AIMR Standards, including the development of a stand-alone composite maintenance and reporting system. In addition, he has helped clients comply with the AIMR-PPS and address other performance-related issues. His articles have appeared in *Wall Street & Technology*, *Traders Magazine*, *Pensions & Investments*, *Dow Jones Investment Advisor*, *Dow Jones Asset Management* and *Premier Review*. Before founding TSG, he was Vice-President and Director of Systems for SunAmerica Asset Management. There, he and his staff were responsible for significantly enhancing the firm's use of technology. This included the design and development of a performance measurement system.

Allan Timmermann is a Professor of Economics at the University of California, San Diego, and has previously held positions at Birkbeck College and the London School of Economics. He acquired his PhD from the University of Cambridge. Dr Timmermann has published extensively on topics related to financial economics and econometrics and is currently an associate editor of *Journal of Business and Economic Statistics*, *Journal of Economic Dynamics and Control* and *Journal of Forecasting*.

Ian Tonks is a Professor of Finance in the Department of Economics at the University of Bristol, where he is the director of pensions research in the Centre for Market and Public Organization. Previously he has held positions at the London School of Economics and the University of British Columbia. His research has focused on market microstructure and the organization of stock exchanges; directors' trading in the UK; fund manager performance; and the new issue market. He has undertaken consultancy work for a number of regulators and private sector organizations.

Harry Turtle is an Associate Professor of Finance in the College of Business and Economics at Washington State University. His research interests lie in the fields of international finance, investment management and other general topics in financial economics. His work has appeared, or is forthcoming, in numerous financial journals including the *Journal of Business and Economic Statistics*, *Journal of Financial Economics*, *Journal of Financial and Quantitative Analysis*, *Journal of Portfolio Management*, and *Management Science*.

Guoqiang Wang is currently working as a data analyst for the Hudsons Bay Company. He got his PhD degree in Economics at the University of Western Ontario. His research interests are in risk management, mutual fund performance and data analysis of large financial databases.

Chapter 1

The financial economics of performance measurement

NATHALIE FARAH

ABSTRACT

This chapter aims to provide insights into the different performance measures that have been constructed over the years with the aim of better evaluating and assessing the fund manager's abilities. Indeed, the finance literature has for some time been interested in this matter, first because superior ability and outperformance by definition contradict the efficient market hypothesis and second because there is a very important need to justify active management and the high fees that fund managers tend to charge. After reviewing various performance measures and techniques, it is clear that there are still many questions concerning the extent to which these measures apply in the real world.

1.1 INTRODUCTION

The quest for active portfolio managers who can deliver abnormal excess returns and beat a specified benchmark has been crucial for the portfolio management industry. Indeed, finding an accurate and reliable measure able to assess and compare the performance of various fund managers has been stimulating the finance literature for a long period.

Since the tremendous growth that the mutual and pension fund industry experienced – in the US, for example, over $5.5 trillion are currently managed by the mutual fund industry, with roughly $3 trillion managed in equity funds (Chen, Jegadeesh and Wermers, 2000) – there has been a great deal of attention directed towards portfolio performance measurement.

On the one hand, investors sought a method that could value the service rendered by active management and justify the fees and expenses they were paying. On the other hand, fund managers wanted to illustrate the importance of their role and justify why one should buy an actively rather than a passively managed portfolio.

Academic studies found this subject fascinating and tried to devise diverse methods to tackle the number of issues at stake: measuring any abnormal performance and assessing the superior ability of fund managers, examining whether there is any persistence in the performance of the actively managed funds, and finally constructing appropriate benchmarks that allow a genuine comparison between active and passive management. The importance of these issues lies in the fact that it is also a test of efficient market hypothesis: managers making abnormal returns contradict this crucial hypothesis.

Before presenting the various measures that the researchers have constructed over the years to answer these important questions, this review starts by defining some of the key concepts to performance evaluation, allowing the reader a better and easier understanding of the discussion that follows. Starting by distinguishing active and passive management, this chapter defines the activities and decisions a fund manager engages in, in order to generate abnormal performance. Understanding the intuition behind these processes is the first step towards grasping the methods developed to evaluate them.

In managing funds, two different techniques can be used: passive and active. Passive portfolio management entails what is commonly referred to as a 'buy-and-hold strategy', where the weights on the securities constituting the portfolio are set at the beginning of the investment period and are then held constant until the end, with only minor changes. The assumptions that lie behind passive portfolio management are market efficiency and homogeneity of expectations. Indeed, if markets are efficient, the fund manager cannot capitalize on any mispricing of securities and gain from actively trading them. Moreover, if all investors have homogeneous expectations, the fund manager cannot take advantage of any differences in the securities market expectations regarding returns and risk to generate abnormal performance from active trading (Blake, 1994).

In contrast, the assumptions behind active management are that markets are not 'continuously efficient' and that investors do have heterogeneous expectations regarding securities risk and returns. In fact, active managers believe that they have the ability both to obtain better estimates of the true securities' risk and return and to spot any mispricing of securities, making use of this to generate excess returns. As a result, managers frequently adjust their portfolio weights to follow different strategies and identify any opportunities to 'beat the market'. (Blake, 1994).

Active management, thus, demands the mastering of different skills needed to optimally perform the activities it requires: asset allocation, security selection and market timing. Indeed, as a first step, the fund manager must decide on the allocation of his portfolio across a number of broad asset classes, such as bond, shares, cash or any money-market securities. This is referred to as asset allocation and represents one of the fundamental and most important decisions in the management of the fund, since it not only dominates the performance of most portfolios (Blake, 1994), but also accounts for a large part of the variability in their return (Sharpe, 1992).

Once the proportions in each asset class have been chosen, the manager has now to decide on which particular securities to hold within each asset class. This is referred to as security selection. In this activity, the fund manager uses his assumptions and information about the market to take advantage of any mispricing[1] that he believes is occurring. Indeed, the fund manager accepts that 'most shares are fairly priced but a few are either underpriced or overpriced' (Blake, 1994) and uses the information he has about the mispricing to gain abnormal returns. If a manager does have superior ability and can identify the over- and/or underpriced securities then he can game on his skills and generate excess returns.

Furthermore, according to Jensen (1968), 'a manager's forecasting ability may consist of an ability to forecast the price movements of individual securities and/or an ability to forecast the general behaviour of security prices in the future'.

The first ability describes security selection skills while the second refers to the fund managers' ability to time the market.

An active fund manager engages in market timing by changing the beta of his portfolio over time, depending on his expectations about the market. For instance, if the fund manager has positive (negative) information about the market, he would increase (decrease) his portfolio's beta, aiming at capitalizing on his expectations. If the fund managers possess real superior forecasting abilities, then they would be able to provide the investors with excess abnormal returns.

Note that timing abilities can also be used if managers have expectations about stocks with certain characteristics. Indeed, if the fund manager believes that stocks with specific characteristics (size, book to market, etc.) are going to experience high returns, he could tilt his portfolio weights towards them, in an attempt to time those various stock characteristics.

---

[1]A mispricing of a security happens when for an informed investor its expected return (or risk estimate) is different from the market belief. If a security is underpriced (overpriced), it is expected to rise (fall) in price.

To summarize, the difference between selection and timing abilities can be described as follows: while selectivity mirrors the ability to choose investments that will do well relative to the benchmark portfolio, timing ability mirrors the ability to forecast the return of the benchmark portfolio (Grinblatt and Titman – hereafter referred to as GT – 1989b).

Assessing whether active managers have genuine superior abilities in completing these tasks, and whether the high fees and expenses that they charge are justified by those superior abilities in the form of excess returns, is the aim of the performance literature. Consequently, the literature has devised, over the years, several different performance measures that help determine these issues.

Having defined the terms and notions used in the performance evaluation world, this chapter will present next a literature survey of the variety of performance measures and techniques that have been constructed throughout the years to evaluate whether active managers have genuine superior abilities. The aim is to discover if active managers do actually possess superior information that could allow them to 'beat the market' and generate abnormal returns.

1.2 THE SHARPE RATIO

The first measure discussed is the Sharpe ratio (Sharpe, 1966), a very commonly used way to determine the excess return earned per unit of risk. It is formulated as follows:

$$SR_i = \frac{R_i - R_f}{\sigma_i} \tag{1.1}$$

where:

R_i is the mean return on fund i over the interval considered

R_f is the average risk free rate over the interval considered and

σ_i is the standard deviation of the return on fund i over the interval considered.

This ratio is a measure of 'reward per unit of risk' (Sharpe, 1966).

1.3 THE TREYNOR MEASURE

A similar measure to the Sharpe ratio is the Treynor measure (Treynor, 1965), which uses the systematic risk β_i of the fund as a measure of its risk instead of its standard deviation:

$$T_i = \frac{R_i - R_f}{\beta_i} \tag{1.2}$$

The Treynor measure adjusts the excess reward earned by the fund for its systematic risk, the capital asset pricing model's beta.

Next, this review moves to one of the most widely used measures in the empirical performance literature, the Jensen measure (Jensen, 1968, 1969).

1.4 THE JENSEN MEASURE

1.4.1 The theory and the aim behind the Jensen measure

Jensen (1968, 1969) created a measure of abnormal performance based on the CAPM model of Sharpe (1963, 1964), Lintner (1965) and Treynor (1961). This measure, however, allows for the abilities of the fund managers to be reflected by the inclusion of an intercept in the traditional equation:

$$\tilde{R}_{jt} - R_{Ft} = \alpha_j + \beta_j[\tilde{R}_{Mt} - R_{Ft}] + \tilde{u}_{jt} \tag{1.3}$$

where the error term $\tilde{u}_{jt}$ should be serially independent and $E(\tilde{u}_{jt}) = 0$.

This expression hence measures the deviation of the portfolio evaluated from the security market line. Particularly, it aims at picking up the manager's ability to forecast future security prices and thus at measuring his security selection skills.

The benchmark used to compute this measure is assumed to be mean-variant efficient from the perspective of an uninformed observer. Consequently, a passively managed fund is expected to generate a zero intercept, while an actively managed fund whose manager possesses some superior information or abilities is expected to generate a positive intercept. Note that various customized benchmarks such as style indexes or multiple-benchmarks models are used throughout the literature to calculate the Jensen alpha.

However, Jensen (1968) acknowledged that by making β_j stationary over time in the above model, his measure does not account for the manager's abilities to 'time the market'. Indeed, he affirms that a manager can easily change the risk level of his portfolio, in an attempt to 'outguess the market'.

Since the managers can possess two kinds of forecasting abilities, security selection and market timing, Jensen recognized the need for 'an evaluation model which will incorporate and reflect the ability of the manager to forecast the market's behaviour as well as his ability to choose individual issues'.

Consequently, assuming that the fund manager has a 'target' risk level that he wishes to maintain on average, Jensen (1968) modified the above model to include such forecasting abilities by expressing the portfolio's systematic risk at any time t as follows:

$$\hat{\beta}_{jt} = \beta_j + \tilde{\varepsilon}_{jt} \tag{1.4}$$

where:

β_j is the 'target' risk level which the portfolio manager wishes to maintain on average through time

$\tilde{\varepsilon}_{jt}$ is a normally distributed random variable that has a 0 expected value.

According to Jensen (1968), $\tilde{\varepsilon}_{jt}$ is 'the vehicle through which the manager may attempt to capitalize on any expectations he may have regarding the behaviour of the market factor $\tilde{\pi}$ in the next period'. Hence, if the fund manager has some positive expectations about the market, he can game on them by increasing the risk of his fund, i.e. by making $\tilde{\varepsilon}_{jt}$ positive. Jensen expresses this relationship more formally as:

$$\tilde{\varepsilon}_{jt} = a_j \tilde{\pi}_t + \tilde{w}_{jt} \tag{1.5}$$

where the error term is assumed to be normally distributed with a 0 expected value. A fund manager who possesses some forecasting ability will be characterized by a positive a_j.[2]

Replacing this in equation (1.3), Jensen (1968) obtains the following:

$$\tilde{R}_{jt} - R_{Ft} = \alpha_j + (\beta_j + \tilde{\varepsilon}_{jt})[\tilde{R}_{Mt} - R_{Ft}] + \tilde{u}_{jt} \tag{1.6}$$

The authors then affirm that the least squares estimator of $\hat{\beta}_j$, assuming that the forecast error $\tilde{w}_{jt}$ is uncorrelated with the market factor $\tilde{\pi}_t$, can be shown to be equal to:

$$E(\hat{\beta}_j) = \frac{\text{cov}[(\tilde{R}_{jt} - R_{Ft}), (\tilde{R}_{Mt} - R_{Ft})]}{\sigma^2(\tilde{R}_M)} = \beta_j - a_j E(\tilde{R}_M) \tag{1.7}$$

If $a_j = 0$, then this generates an unbiased estimate of the fund manager's selection abilities.

If a_j is positive, i.e. if the fund manager does have any forecasting ability, equation (1.7) shows that β_j will be biased downward and hence $\hat{\alpha}$ will be biased upward. As a result, Jensen (1968) concludes that if the fund manager possesses some superior ability, then this model will definitely give evidence of it since it tends to 'overstate their magnitude'.

1.4.2 The various caveats and problems that face the Jensen measure

Although the Jensen measure is widely used throughout the performance evaluation literature, it has been subject to many criticisms (Jensen, 1972 and Roll, 1978). The most important ones are related to:

---

[2]Jensen (1968) notes that a_j cannot be negative since this would be a sign of irrationality.

1. *Benchmark inefficiency*

The Jensen approach, being based on the CAPM model, necessitates the use of a benchmark to conduct the performance evaluation. This, however, has been pointed out to be the source of two problems. First, Roll (1978, 1979) claimed that the Jensen measure is not a genuine and reliable indicator of the true performance of a fund because of the lack of an appropriate benchmark with which to compute its beta. Indeed, many empirical studies demonstrated the mean-variance inefficiency of the CAPM benchmarks, showing that they exhibit various biases such as dividend-yield or size biases. Roll has also shown, along with many other researchers, that the Jensen measure can be sensitive to the choice of the benchmark, and thus can lead to the adoption of different conclusions, depending on the benchmark used.

2. *Timing ability*

Jensen (1972) showed that the Jensen measure, due to the bias in its estimate of the systematic risk of a market timing strategy, could provide biased conclusions about market timers and assign them negative performance. Indeed, successful market timing activities by the fund manager being evaluated can lead to 'statistical bias' in the Jensen measure, in that such a fund would generate negative performance numbers (GT, 1994).

To illustrate this point, GT (1989b) provided an example of such a situation. They assumed a case where an informed investor receives information about the market behaviour in the form of two 'signals': positive information indicates that the excess return on the benchmark will be above its unconditional mean at r_H and negative information indicates that it will be at point r_L, below the unconditional mean. This informed investor is also restricted to a choice between a high beta portfolio and a low beta portfolio as shown in Figure 1.1.[3]

If the investor is a 'market timer', he will be at point A (B) when he receives the positive (negative) signal, choosing the high (low) beta portfolio.

From the point of an uninformed investor, the risk of this strategy is measured by 'the slope of the dotted line', i.e. *higher* than either of the high- or low-beta portfolios. Furthermore, this figure plotted by GT (1989b) shows that the Jensen measure, represented by the intercept C of the dotted line, could assign a negative performance to a genuine superior investor, 'erroneously indicating that the informed investor is an inferior investor'.

3. *Separation of the selection and timing abilities*

Jensen (1972) observed that using equation (1.1) and information solely on the return data, it is quasi-infeasible to separate the security selection and timing

[3]These lines pass through the origin since GT (1989b) assume the benchmark is mean-variance efficient.

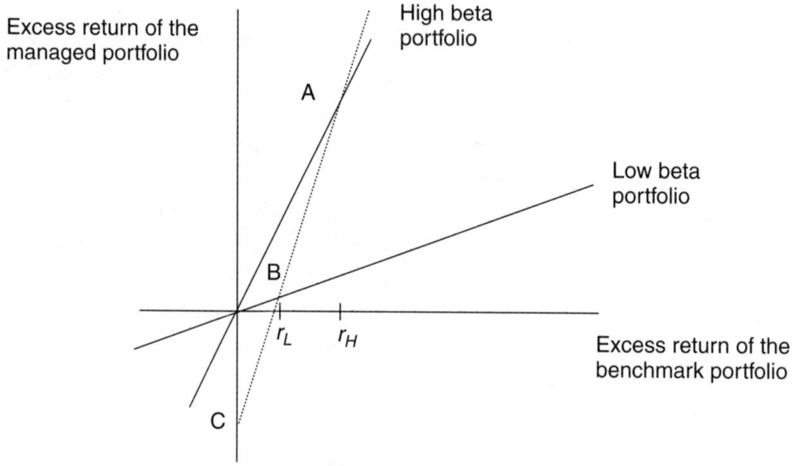

Figure 1.1 This graph illustrates the statistical bias in the Jensen measure, which can lead to biased conclusions about market timers

abilities' effect on performance. Indeed, according to him, in order to achieve this separation and measure the manager's timing abilities, one needs to know 'the market-timing forecast, the portfolio adjustment corresponding to that forecast and the expected return on the market'. Consequently, in his article, Jensen (1972) first makes two main assumptions: the market timer attempts to forecast the actual return on the market portfolio, and the forecasted return and the actual return on the market are assumed to have a joint normal distribution. Then he shows that under these assumptions, the correlation between the market timer's forecast and the realized return on the market can be used to measure the market timer's ability (Henriksson and Merton, 1981).

This problem is also described in Lehmann and Modest (1987) who discuss this issue and explain how it can be quite problematic. Indeed, Lehmann and Modest (1987) start with a K-factor linear model for securities returns and then express the following return generating process for N individual assets:

$$\underline{\tilde{R}}_t = B\underline{\tilde{R}}_{mt} + \underline{\tilde{\varepsilon}}_t \tag{1.8}$$

where:

$\underline{\tilde{R}}_{mt}$ is a $K \times 1$ vector of returns on the reference portfolios

B is the $N \times K$ matrix of factor sensitivities

$\underline{\tilde{R}}_t$ and $\underline{\tilde{R}}_{mt}$ denote excess returns above the riskless rate or zero-beta return where appropriate.

Consequently, they write the return on any mutual fund portfolio as

$$\tilde{R}_{pt} = \sum_{i=1}^{N} w_i(\underline{s}_t)\tilde{R}_{it} = \sum_{i=1}^{N} [w_i(\underline{s}_t)\underline{b}'_i\underline{\tilde{R}}_{mt} + w_i(\underline{s}_t)\underline{\tilde{\varepsilon}}_{it}] \tag{1.9}$$

where:

$w_i(\underline{s}_t)$ is the weight of the ith security in the portfolio at date t
$\underline{b}'_i$ is a $1 \times K$ vector consisting of the ith row of B
$\underline{s}_t$ is a vector of signals received by the fund manager for predicting $\underline{\tilde{R}}_{mt}$ and $\underline{\tilde{\varepsilon}}_t$.

Equation (1.9) can be reformulated as:

$$\tilde{R}_{pt} = \underline{\beta}'_{pt}\underline{\tilde{R}}_{mt} + \tilde{\varepsilon}_{pt} \tag{1.10}$$

where:

$$\underline{\beta}'_{pt} = \sum_{i=1}^{N} w_i(\underline{s}_t)\underline{b}'_i = \underline{\overline{\beta}}'_p + \underline{x}(\underline{s}_t)'$$

$$\tilde{\varepsilon}_{pt} = \sum_{i=1}^{N} w_i(\underline{s}_t)\underline{\tilde{\varepsilon}}_{it} \tag{1.11}$$

According to the authors, 'the elements of $\underline{\overline{\beta}}'_p$ are the target or average sensitivities of the fund to the K common factors, and $\underline{x}(\underline{s}_t)$ are the time t deviations from $\underline{\overline{\beta}}'_p$ selected by the manager in attempts to time factor movements. Similarly, if the manager possesses stock-selection ability, $\tilde{\varepsilon}_{pt}$ will not have a zero population mean'.

As a result, any change in $\underline{\beta}_{pt}$ will mirror the manager's timing abilities while $\tilde{\varepsilon}_{pt}$ will illustrate his security selection skills.

Now, to come back to the Jensen measure, Lehmann and Modest (1987) perform the usual security market line regression, the regression of $\tilde{R}_{pt}$ on $\underline{\tilde{R}}_{mt}$ (as in equation (1.10)):

$$E^*[\tilde{R}_{pt} \mid \underline{\tilde{R}}_{mt}] = \hat{\alpha}_p + \underline{\hat{\beta}}'_p\underline{\tilde{R}}_{mt} \tag{1.12}$$

where:

$$\hat{\alpha}_p = \left[\bar{\varepsilon}_p - \text{cov}\{\underline{x}'_t\underline{\tilde{R}}_{mt}, \underline{\tilde{R}}_{mt}\}' \sum_m^{-1} \underline{\overline{R}}_m + E\{\underline{x}'_t\underline{\tilde{R}}_{mt}\}\right]$$

$$\underline{\hat{\beta}}_p = \left[\underline{\overline{\beta}}_p + \sum_m^{-1} \text{cov}\{\underline{x}'_t\underline{\tilde{R}}_{mt}, \underline{\tilde{R}}_{mt}\}\right]$$

$$\bar{\varepsilon}_p = \sum_{i=1}^{N} \text{cov}\{w_i(\underline{s}_t), \tilde{\varepsilon}_{it}\}$$

$$\sum_m = E[\{\underline{\tilde{R}}_{mt} - \underline{\overline{R}}_m\}\{\underline{\tilde{R}}_{mt} - \underline{\overline{R}}_m\}']$$

$$\underline{\overline{R}}_m = E[\underline{\tilde{R}}_{mt}] \tag{1.13}$$

As for the notation, the authors use $E^*[X \mid Y]$ as 'the minimum-variance linear estimator of X given Y (i.e. the regression function)', $\underline{x'}_t$ as a 'shorthand' for $\underline{x}(\underline{s}_t)'$, $\text{cov}\{\underline{x'}_t\underline{\tilde{R}}_{mt}, \underline{\tilde{R}}_{mt}\}$ as the $K \times 1$ vector of the covariances between $\underline{x}'_t\underline{\tilde{R}}_{mt}$ and the K elements of $\underline{\tilde{R}}_{mt}$.

In this model, the coefficient $\hat{\alpha}_p$ denotes 'the usual Jensen performance measure'.

Using the above format, the authors conduct the following analysis:

- If the fund manager possesses no security selection skills and no timing abilities, i.e. $\bar{\varepsilon}_P = 0$ and $E\{\underline{x'}_t\underline{\tilde{R}}_{mt}\} = \text{cov}\{\underline{x'}_t\underline{\tilde{R}}_{mt}, \tilde{R}_{jt}\} = 0$ for all $j = 1, \ldots, K$, the Jensen measure will be equal to 0 and the above model will show no evidence of abnormal performance:

$$E^*[\overset{\leftrightarrow}{R}_{pt} \mid \underline{\tilde{R}}_{mt}] = \underline{\overline{\beta}}'_p\underline{\tilde{R}}_{mt} \tag{1.14}$$

- If the mutual fund manager 'possesses stock selection ability but no market-timing ability', the model will give evidence of some superior performance:

$$E^*[\overset{\leftrightarrow}{R}_{pt} \mid \underline{\tilde{R}}_{mt}] = \bar{\varepsilon}_p + \underline{\overline{\beta}}'_p\underline{\tilde{R}}_{mt} \tag{1.15}$$

  where $\bar{\varepsilon}_p \succ 0$ under mild restrictions.
- Finally, if managers possess both market-timing and security selection ability, the Jensen measure could turn out to be positive or negative depending on the terms in the above expression for $\hat{\alpha}_p$.

Hence, Lehmann and Modest (1987) conclude that 'the Jensen measure cannot be used to evaluate managers since $\hat{\alpha}_p$ could be positive even if the manager were both an unsuccessful stock picker and a perverse market timer and conversely could be negative if the manager were both a successful stock picker and a successful market timer'.

In conclusion, although the above studies and many others have shown that the Jensen measure can be associated with many problems, it is still widely used, in combination with other measures, in various empirical studies to assess abnormal performance.

1.5 THE TREYNOR–MAZUY MEASURE

In the traditional CAPM model, the return on a portfolio is a linear function of the return on the market portfolio. In their study, however, Treynor and Mazuy (1966) claim that for market timers, this should not apply. Indeed, according to them, market timers, being able to forecast market returns, will increase (decrease) their holdings of the market portfolio when the return on it is high (low). As a result, the relationship between the fund's return and the market return should not be linear and thus the authors propose that a quadratic regression could actually pick up any market timing ability. For Lehmann and Modest (1987), 'the basic idea was quite simple; market timers should make money when the market rises or falls dramatically, that is, when the squared return on the market is large', hence the inclusion of this extra term can be of great value.

To be more precise, the Treynor–Mazuy measure aims at picking any beta variation that is associated with the return on the benchmark:

$$\beta_j = \theta_1 + \theta_2(\tilde{R}_{Mt} - R_{Ft}) \quad \theta_2 \succ 0$$

Replacing this in equation (1.3) gives the following:

$$\tilde{R}_{jt} - R_{Ft} = \alpha_j + \theta_1[\tilde{R}_{Mt} - R_{Ft}] + \theta_2[\tilde{R}_{Mt} - R_{Ft}]^2 + \tilde{u}_{jt} \tag{1.16}$$

Selectivity abilities are picked up by the intercept of this regression while the product of θ_2 and the variance of the benchmark return captures timing ability (GT, 1994). Indeed, after studying this regression's slope coefficients, Jensen (1972) and Adamti *et al.* (1986) confirmed the relation between θ_2 and timing ability.

However, although the Treynor–Mazuy measure is a 'promising advance' by the fact that it can actually pick up timing abilities, it still faces the same problem as the Jensen measure: the inability to evaluate separately the effects of the security selection and timing abilities on funds' performance.

In effect, going back to the Lehmann and Modest (1987) model discussed above, this can be clearly demonstrated. For simplicity reasons, the authors consider the one-factor version of their model:

$$\tilde{R}_{pt} = \beta_{pt}\underline{\tilde{R}}_{mt} + \tilde{\varepsilon}_{pt}$$

and then write the 'associated' quadratic regression as

$$E[\tilde{R}_{pt} \mid \tilde{R}_{mt}, \tilde{R}^2_{mt}] = \alpha^*_p + b^*_{1p}\tilde{R}_{mt} + b^*_{2p}\tilde{R}^2_{mt} \tag{1.17}$$

Lehmann and Modest (1987) formulate the regression slope coefficients as:

$$\begin{aligned}
\begin{pmatrix} b_{1p}^* \\ b_{2p}^* \end{pmatrix} &= \left(\text{var}\begin{bmatrix} \tilde{R}_{mt} \\ \tilde{R}_{mt}^2 \end{bmatrix}\right)^{-1} \text{cov}\left[\tilde{R}_{pt}, \begin{pmatrix} \tilde{R}_{mt} \\ \tilde{R}_{mt}^2 \end{pmatrix}\right] \\
&= \begin{pmatrix} \sigma_m^2 & \sigma_{3m} \\ \sigma_{3m} & \sigma_{4m} \end{pmatrix}^{-1} \begin{bmatrix} \bar{\beta}_p \sigma_m^2 + \text{cov}(x_t, \tilde{R}_{mt}^2) \\ \bar{\beta}_p \sigma_{3m} + \text{cov}(x_t, \tilde{R}_{mt}^3) \end{bmatrix} \\
&= \begin{bmatrix} \bar{\beta}_p \\ 0 \end{bmatrix} + \frac{1}{\sigma_m^2 \sigma_{4m} - \sigma_{3m}^2} \begin{bmatrix} \sigma_{4m} & -\sigma_{3m} \\ -\sigma_{3m} & \sigma_m^2 \end{bmatrix} \begin{bmatrix} \text{cov}(x_t, \tilde{R}_{mt}^2) \\ \text{cov}(x_t, \tilde{R}_{mt}^3) \end{bmatrix} \\
&= \begin{bmatrix} \bar{\beta}_p \\ 0 \end{bmatrix} + \begin{bmatrix} \gamma_{1p} \\ \gamma_{2p} \end{bmatrix} \qquad (1.18)
\end{aligned}$$

where:

σ_{3m} and σ_{4m} are the skewness and the kurtosis of $\tilde{R}_{mt}$

$\bar{\beta}_p$ is the target β of the mutual fund.

They also express the intercept of the quadratic regression as:

$$\begin{aligned}
\alpha_p^* &= \bar{\varepsilon}_p + \bar{\beta}_P \bar{R}_m + \text{cov}(x_t, \tilde{R}_{mt}) - b_{1p}^* \bar{R}_m - b_{2p}^* \bar{R}_m^2 \\
&= \bar{\varepsilon}_p + \text{cov}(x_t, \tilde{R}_{mt}) - \gamma_{1p} \bar{R}_m - \gamma_{2p} \bar{R}_m^2 \qquad (1.19)
\end{aligned}$$

Using this formulation of the Treynor–Mazuy measure, the authors show the ability of this measure to detect timing ability. Indeed, if the manager possesses no timing abilities, then $\text{cov}\{x_t, \tilde{R}_{mt}^2\}$ and $\text{cov}\{x_t, \tilde{R}_{mt}^3\}$ will be equal to 0, which implies that in equation (1.19), $\gamma_{1p} = \gamma_{2p} = 0$ and hence, $b_{1p}^* = \bar{\beta}_p$, the target beta, and b_{2p}^*, the coefficient on $\tilde{R}_{mt}^2$, is equal to 0 signifying the absence of timing abilities.

In contrast, if the manager does possess timing abilities, then $\text{cov}\{x_t, \tilde{R}_{mt}^2\}$ and $\text{cov}\{x_t, \tilde{R}_{mt}^3\}$ will be different from 0, and hence, b_{2p}^* will also be non-zero, revealing the manager's timing abilities.

However, the authors also show that the Treynor–Mazuy measure is still not able to evaluate the separate effects of the manager's timing and selection abilities on performance, unless one imposes additional 'restriction on distribution and preferences'. In fact, they claim that even if in equation (1.18) $\text{cov}\{x_t, \tilde{R}_{mt}^2\} = 0$[4] and hence one can estimate the values of $\bar{\beta}_p$ and γ_{2p}, it is still impossible to distinguish the 'two sources of abnormal performance' in equation (1.19).

---

[4]Which implies that there is 'no co-skewness between the fluctuations in the fund beta and the return on the factor'.

To overcome this problem, Henriksson and Merton (1981) offered a solution consisting of two different tests, to be discussed next.

1.6 PARAMETRIC AND NON-PARAMETRIC TESTS OF MARKET TIMING ABILITIES

Using a model of market timing developed in Merton (1981), Henriksson and Merton (1981) developed two tests, a parametric and a non-parametric test, that aim at solving two crucial issues: detecting whether superior timing abilities do exist and measuring the separate effects of security selection and timing abilities on funds' performance. The non-parametric test, which assumes that the forecasts made by a market timer are observable, offers one main advantage: it does not need the CAPM framework. Indeed, according to the authors, this test does not 'require any assumption about either the distribution of returns on the market or the way in which individual security prices are formed'. Furthermore, this test takes into account the fact that the market timer may possess different skill levels in predicting up and down markets.

Now, when the market timer's forecasts are not observable, Henriksson and Merton (1981) propose an alternative test, the parametric test of forecasting ability. The latter, however, does require the additional assumption of a CAPM or a multifactor pricing model of securities prices.

This review starts with a brief description of the model of market timing forecasts developed in Merton (1981), which is followed by an exposition of the non-parametric and parametric tests developed in Henriksson and Merton (1981). In so doing, this review follows the notation and presentation used in Henriksson and Merton (1981).

1.6.1 The starting point: Merton (1981)'s model of market timing forecasts

In his model of market timing forecasts, Merton (1981) assumes that the market timer forecasts solely whether $Z_m(t) > R(t)$ or $Z_m(t) \leq R(t)$, where $Z_m(t)$ is the return on the market portfolio and $R(t)$ is the risk-free rate.

In fact, Merton (1981) defines $\gamma(t)$ as 'the market timer's forecast variable', which can take two values: 0 if at time $t - 1$ the market timer forecasted that in period t, $Z_m(t) \leq R(t)$ and 1 if he forecasted that at time t, $Z_m(t) > R(t)$.

As a result, the author formulates the *conditional probabilities of a correct forecast* as:

$$p_1(t) \equiv \text{prob}[\gamma(t) = 0 \mid Z_m(t) \leq R(t)]$$

and

$$p_2(t) \equiv \text{prob}[\gamma(t) = 1 \mid Z_m(t) > R(t)]$$

Merton (1981) ascertained that under the assumption that these conditional probabilities are independent of the magnitude of $|Z_m(t) - R(t)|$ and hence only rely on whether $Z_m(t)$ exceeds $R(t)$ or not, 'the sum of the conditional probabilities of a correct forecast, $p_1(t) + p_2(t)$, is a sufficient statistic for the evaluation of forecasting ability'.

In particular, Merton (1981) showed that this sum being equal to one, i.e. $p_1(t) + p_2(t) = 1$, is a necessary and sufficient condition for a market timer's forecast to have 'no value'. Consequently, he demonstrated that testing whether $p_1(t) + p_2(t)$ is equal to one or not is a test of a market timer's abilities, the null hypothesis of no forecasting abilities being $H_0{:}p_1(t) + p_2(t) = 1$, where $p_1(t)$ and $p_2(t)$ need to be estimated.

Now, using the above model of market timing forecasts, Henriksson and Merton (1981) constructed a non-parametric test of forecasting abilities for the case of observable market timer's forecasts.

1.6.2 The non-parametric test of forecasting abilities

To achieve their target, the authors started by constructing a methodology that 'determines the probability that a given outcome from [the] sample came from a population that satisfies the null hypothesis'. Indeed, Henriksson and Merton (1981) wrote the following expressions for $p_1(t)$ and $p_2(t)$,

$$p_1 = E\left[\frac{n_1}{N_1}\right] \quad \text{and} \quad 1 - p_2 = E\left[\frac{n_2}{N_2}\right]$$

where they defined N_1 as the number of observations where $Z_m \leq R, n_1$ as the number of successful predictions given $Z_m \leq R$, N_2 as the number of observations where $Z_m > R$ and finally n_2 as the number of unsuccessful predictions, given $Z_m > R$.

Next, using the null hypothesis, they obtained that:

$$E\left[\frac{n_1}{N_1}\right] = p_1 = 1 - p_2 = E\left[\frac{n_2}{N_2}\right]$$

which gives that:

$$E\left[\frac{n_1 + n_2}{N_1 + N_2}\right] = E\left[\frac{n}{N}\right] = p_1 \equiv p$$

where N is defined as the total number of observations and n as the number of times the market timer's forecast was $Z_m \leq R$.

As a result, given that under the null hypothesis, n_1/N_1 and n_2/N_2 have identical expected values and 'are both drawn from independent subsamples', Henriksson and Merton (1981) confirmed the need to estimate only one of the two expressions.

Combining the above analysis, the null hypothesis and Bayes' theorem, the authors derived the following expression for the probability that $n_1 = x$ given N_1, N_2 and n:

$$P(n_1 = x \mid N_1, N_2, m) = \frac{\binom{N_1}{x}\binom{N_2}{m-x}}{\binom{N}{m}} \tag{1.20}$$

where 'the market timer forecasts m times that $Z_m \leq R$ (i.e. $m = n$)... [and] he is correct x times and incorrect $m - x$ times (i.e. $n_1 = x$ and $n_2 = m - x$)'.

The expression in equation (1.20) led Henriksson and Merton (1981) to the conclusion that the probability distribution of n_1, which represents under the null hypothesis the probability distribution for the number of correct forecasts given that $Z_m \leq R$, is a 'hypergeometric distribution and is independent of both p_1 and p_2'. Hence, there is no need anymore to estimate the unconditional probabilities.

Given this result and the fact that in this case the market timer's forecasts are assumed to be known, Henriksson and Merton (1981) affirmed that it is now very easy to test the null hypothesis since all the variables necessary to achieve that aim are observable.

Consequently, the authors move on to the construction of confidence intervals for testing H_0. Following the distribution of n_1 fixed by the expression in equation (1.20), the authors first determined the 'feasible range' for n_1 as being:

$$\underline{n}_1 \equiv \max(0, n - N_2) \leq n_1 \leq \min(N_1, n) \equiv \bar{n}_1 \tag{1.21}$$

Next, the authors presented the confidence intervals of a standard two-tail test of the null hypothesis that rejects H_0 if $n_1 \geq \bar{x}(c)$ or if $n_1 \leq \underline{x}(c)$, where c is the probability confidence level and $\bar{x}$ and $\underline{x}$ are the solutions to the following equations:

$$\frac{\sum_{x=\bar{x}}^{\bar{n}_1} \binom{N_1}{x}\binom{N_2}{n-x}}{\binom{N}{n}} = \frac{(1-c)}{2}$$

and

$$\frac{\sum_{x=\underline{x}_1}^{x} \binom{N_1}{x}\binom{N_2}{n-x}}{\binom{N}{n}} = \frac{(1-c)}{2}$$

However, arguing that a one-tail test might be more appropriate to their model, the authors also presented the confidence interval of a one-tail test of the null hypothesis where H_0 is rejected if $n_1 \geq x^*(c), x^*(c)$ being the solution to

$$\frac{\sum_{x=x^*}^{\bar{n}_1} \binom{N_1}{x}\binom{N_2}{n-x}}{\binom{N}{n}} = 1-c$$

Noting that for small samples, the calculation of the above confidence intervals can be quite simple, the authors admitted that for large samples, however, things could get very complicated. To remedy for that, Henriksson and Merton (1981) pointed out that for large samples it is possible to 'accurately' approximate the hypergeometric distribution by a normal distribution whose mean and variance are the mean and variance of the hypergeometric distribution of equation (1.20):

$$E(n_1) = \frac{nN_1}{N}$$

and

$$\sigma^2(n_1) = \frac{[n_1 N_1 (N - N_1)(N - n)]}{[N^2(N-1)]}$$

Finally, as mentioned earlier, this test takes into account the fact the market timer might possess different skills in predicting up and down markets ($p_1(t) \neq p_2(t)$). Nonetheless, Henriksson and Merton (1981) accounted also for the case where one has reason to believe that the market timer might have the same skill in forecasting up and down markets, i.e. the case where $p_1(t) = p_2(t) = p(t)$.

In this situation, they formulated the null hypothesis of no forecasting abilities as $H_0: p(t) = 0.5$ and defined the distribution of outcomes drawn from a population that satisfies this null hypothesis as the following binomial distribution:

$$P(k \mid N, p) = \binom{N}{k} p^k (1-p)^{N-k} = \binom{N}{k} (0.5)^N$$

where k is the number of correct predictions and N is the total number of observations.

Hence, in their article, Henriksson and Merton (1981) provided a thorough analysis of timing abilities by offering a non-parametric test that helps determine whether such superior abilities do exist. Nevertheless, all the above discussion was conducted for the case where one assumes that the market timer's forecast can be observed. This is not, however, always the case.

1.6.3 The parametric test

Indeed, acknowledging that in many cases the market timer's forecasts are not part of the available information, Henriksson and Merton (1981) proposed also a parametric test that aims at overcoming this problem.

In effect, this alternative test does not necessitate that one observes the market timer's forecast but it does, however, require the assumption of a particular generating process for the securities' returns. The innovation of this test is that, using only the securities' returns data, not only does it allow the evaluation of a market timer's abilities but it also allows the separate measurement of the effects of selection and timing abilities on performance.

First, following the previous empirical studies, the authors assumed that the returns on securities can be described within the CAPM framework.

Next, they assumed that the market timer vary his portfolio's systematic risk depending on his forecast; more particularly, they supposed that the market timer has two target betas from which he can choose, conditional on whether he forecasted that $Z_m(t) \leq R(t)$ or not.

Denoting $\beta(t)$ as the portfolio's beta at time t, the authors formulated this model in the following manner: $\beta(t)$ is equal to η_1 when the market timer forecasts that $Z_m(t) \leq R(t)$ and to η_2 when he forecasts that $Z_m(t) > R(t)$.

Given that the market timer's forecasts are not observable, $\beta(t)$ is to be considered a random variable and the authors thus denoted its unconditional expected value b as:

$$b = q[p_1\eta_1 + (1-p_1)\eta_2] + (1-q)[p_2\eta_2 + (1-p_2)\eta_1]$$

where q is the unconditional probability that $Z_m(t) \leq R(t)$.

Now, defining the random variable $\theta(t) = [\beta(t) - b]$ as the 'unanticipated component of beta', Henriksson and Merton (1981) wrote the return on the forecaster's portfolio as:

$$Z_p(t) - R(t) = \lambda + [b + \theta(t)]x(t) + \varepsilon_p(t)$$

where $x(t) = Z_m(t) - R(t)$.[5]

Using the above equation, the authors showed that by performing a simple least squares regression analysis, they could measure 'the separate increments to performance' from the manager's selection and timing abilities.

Indeed, writing the regression specification as:

$$Z_p(t) - R(t) = \alpha + \beta_1 x(t) + \beta_2 y(t) + \varepsilon(t) \tag{1.22}$$

where $y(t) \equiv \max\ [0, R(t) - Z_m(t)] \equiv \min[0, -x(t)]$, $\hat{\beta}_2$ represents *the market timer's forecasting abilities* and $\hat{\alpha}$ *his selection abilities.*

After various calculations, Henriksson and Merton (1981) demonstrated that using this regression specification, the following could be derived:

$$p\lim \hat{\beta}_1 = \frac{\sigma_{px}\sigma_y^2 - \sigma_{py}\sigma_{xy}}{\sigma_x^2\sigma_y^2 - \sigma_{xy}^2} = b + \bar{\theta}_2 = p_2\eta_2 + (1 - p_2)\eta_1 \qquad (1.23)^6$$

and

$$p\lim \hat{\beta}_2 = \frac{\sigma_{py}\sigma_x^2 - \sigma_{px}\sigma_{xy}}{\sigma_x^2\sigma_y^2 - \sigma_{xy}^2} = \bar{\theta}_2 - \bar{\theta}_1 = (p_1 + p_2 - 1)(\eta_2 - \eta_1) \tag{1.24}$$

and

$$p\lim \hat{\alpha} = E(Z_p) - R - p\lim \hat{\beta}_1\bar{x} - p\lim \hat{\beta}_2\bar{y} = \lambda \tag{1.25}$$

Consequently, Henriksson and Merton (1981), using the regression equations (1.22), (1.24) and (1.25), offered a method that permits the estimation of the 'separate contribution' of security selection and market

[5]The authors also show that:

$$E(\theta \mid x) = \bar{\theta}_1 = (1 - q)(p_1 + p_2 - 1)(\eta_1 - \eta_2) \text{ for } x(t) \leq 0 \text{ and}$$

$$E(\theta \mid x) = \bar{\theta}_2 = q(p_1 + p_2 - 1)(\eta_2 - \eta_1) \text{ for } x(t) > 0$$

and thus $E(Z_p \mid x > 0) = R + (b + \bar{\theta}_2)E(x \mid x > 0) + \lambda$ and

$$E(Z_p \mid x \leq 0) = R + (b + \bar{\theta}_1)E(x \mid x \leq 0] + \lambda.$$

[6]Where according to the authors $p\lim \hat{\beta}_1 = E[\beta(t) \mid x(t) > 0]$.

timing to performance, a very important contribution to the performance evaluation literature.

Next, this review presents a performance evaluation method developed by Grinblatt and Titman (GT, 1989b) that tries to rise above some of the problems facing the earlier measures such as the Jensen measure.

1.7 THE POSITIVE PERIOD WEIGHTING MEASURE

In response to the timing related biases of the Jensen measure, GT (1989b) proposed a new measure, the Positive Period Weighting (PPW) measure, with the aim of overcoming these problems.

This new measure, of which the Jensen measure is shown to be a special case, is defined by the authors to be a weighted sum of the period by period excess returns of the portfolio being evaluated.

It is formulated as follows:

$$\alpha^* = \sum_{t=1}^{T} \tilde{w}_t \tilde{r}_{pt}$$

such as

$$\tilde{w}_t = w(\tilde{r}_{Et}, T)$$

$$p \lim \left[\sum_{t=1}^{T} \tilde{w}_t \tilde{r}_{Et} \right] = 0$$

$$|p \lim[T w_t]| > \infty$$

$$\sum_{t=1}^{T} \tilde{w}_t = 1$$

$$\tilde{w}_t > 0, \quad t = 1, \ldots, T$$

where $\tilde{r}_{pt}$ is the period t excess return of the portfolio being evaluated and $\tilde{r}_{Et}$ is the period t excess return on the efficient portfolio chosen as the benchmark.

In their article, GT (1989b) proved this measure to be very useful. Indeed, they showed that with the PPW, an uninformed investor would generate zero performance while an informed investor, with selectivity and/or timing abilities, would generate positive performance if 'the selectivity and timing information is independent and the investor is a positive market timer'.

Moreover, the authors pointed out that 'an interesting interpretation' of their measure would be to choose as weights the investor's marginal utilities.

In this case, α^* would measure the incremental change in an investor's utility from adding 'a small amount' of the evaluated portfolio's excess return to his 'unconditionally optimal' portfolio. In a subsequent paper, GT (1994) implemented this notion to test the sensitivity of performance to the different measures, using for weights the marginal utilities of an investor with a power utility function.

The results showed that the Jensen and Positive Period Weighting measures were almost identical irrespective of the benchmark used. However, the authors attributed this to the fact that 'most mutual funds fail to successfully time the market'. Indeed, they claimed that these two measures are substantially different for funds that succeed in timing the market and hence, according to GT (1994) 'for some purposes, employing the Positive Period Weighting measure in lieu of the Jensen measure could still be worthwhile'.

1.8 CONDITIONAL PERFORMANCE EVALUATION

In a new perspective, Christopherson, Ferson and Turner (1999) claimed that the previous studies 'rely upon *unconditional* performance measures, those whose estimates of future performance ignore information about the changing nature of the economy. Thus, unconditional measures can incorrectly measure expected excess return when portfolio managers react to market information or engage in dynamic trading strategies. These well-known biases make it difficult to estimate alpha and beta'.

This is mainly the intuition behind the notion of Conditional Performance Evaluation (CPE) supported by Ferson and Schadt (1996) and Ferson and Warther (1996) who recommend the CPE because it can generate more accurate expectations about excess return and risk. This is a due to the fact that this method 'implicitly assumes that a portfolio's alphas and betas change dynamically with changing market conditions' and that fund managers are able to respond to available information about market conditions by modifying the fund's alphas and betas (Christopherson, Ferson and Turner, 1999).

To present the methodology behind the CPE, this review follows the exposition of Christopherson, Ferson and Turner (1999).

First, the dynamic changes in the *beta* were incorporated in the traditional model by Ferson and Schadt (1996). Indeed, assuming that available public information, as measured by a vector of market information Z, is fully reflected in market prices, the authors proposed the following:

$$\beta_p(z_t) = b_{0p} + B'_p z_t \qquad (1.26)$$

where:

$z_t = Z_t - E(Z)$ is a normalized vector of the deviations of Z_t, from the unconditional means

B_p is a vector with the same dimension as Z_t, whose 'elements measure the sensitivity of the conditional beta to the deviations of the Z_t from their means'

b_{0p} is the 'average beta'.

As a result, equation (1.3) can be rewritten as:

$$r_{pt+1} = \alpha_p + b_{0p} r_{bt+1} + B'_p[z_t r_{bt+1}] + \mu_{pt+1} \tag{1.27}$$

and in the absence of abnormal performance, the *conditional alpha* α_P will be equal to zero.

Ferson and Schadt (1996) discovered that the term $z_t r_{bt+1}$, which can be interpreted as the covariance between the conditional beta and the conditional expected market return, given Z_t, is the origin of many significant measurement errors in the estimation of the unconditional alphas. Consequently, one can obtain more reliable estimates of the alphas from equation (1.27), by 'controlling' for this covariance (Christopherson, Ferson and Turner, 1999).

Next, the dynamic changes in the *alpha* of the fund are accounted for by Christopherson, Ferson and Glassman (1998) who proposed a similar model to Ferson and Schadt (1996). Their methodology expressed the conditional alpha as follows:

$$\alpha_{pt} = a_p(z_t) = a_{0p} + A'_p z_t \tag{1.28}$$

Consequently, the final modified version of the traditional model presented in equation (1.3) is:

$$r_{pt+1} = a_{0p} + A'_p z_t + b_{0p} r_{bt+1} + B'_p[z_t r_{bt+1}] + \mu_{pt+1} \tag{1.29}$$

This model allows the researcher to take into consideration the fact that investors do react to various market information by changing their portfolio's alphas and betas accordingly, hence incorporating the dynamic nature of the alphas and betas.

Comparing the conditional and unconditional alphas in an empirical setting, Christopherson, Ferson and Turner (1999) conclude that conditional alphas are better predictors of future performance and that using them 'can improve on the current practice of performance measurement'.

In the pursuit of even more accuracy in abnormal performance measurement, many studies tried to improve upon the model of securities returns with the aim of controlling and adjusting better for the risk of the funds. Next, this review discusses such attempts.

1.9 THE 4-INDEX MODEL OF PERFORMANCE EVALUATION

With the aim of constructing a more accurate measure of performance and examining whether past information can carry information about the future, Elton, Gruber and Blake (1996) developed a 4-index model in which they included the following indexes: the S&P Index, a size index, a bond index and a value/growth index.

Elton, Gruber and Blake (1996) justified their choice of the size index by relating to a previous study by Elton *et al.* (1993) where a 'failure to include an index of firm size as a risk index led to a substantial overestimate of the performance of funds that hold small stocks and an incorrect inference concerning average performance'. As for the value/growth index, the study used it in order to separate any performance due to the particular type of the fund from performance due to superior skills by the fund manager. Using Elton, Gruber and Blake (1996)'s notations, the model is the following:

$$R_{it} = a_i + \beta_{iSP} R_{SPt} + \beta_{iSL} R_{SLt} + \beta_{iGV} R_{GVt} + \beta_{iB} R_{Bt} + \varepsilon_{it} \qquad (1.30)$$

where:

R_{it} = the excess return on fund i in month t (the return on the fund minus the 30 day Treasury-bill rate)

R_{SPt} = the excess return on the S&P 500 Index in month t

R_{SLt} = the difference in return between a small-cap and a large-cap stock portfolio, based on Prudential Bache indexes in month t

R_{GVt} = the difference in return between a growth and a value stock portfolio, based on Prudential Bache indexes in month t

R_{Bt} = the excess return on a bond index in month t, measured by par-weighted combination of the Lehman Brothers Aggregate Bond Index and the Blume/Keim High-Yield Bond Index

β_{ik} = the sensitivity of excess return on fund i to excess return on index $k(k =$ SP, SL, GV, B)

ε_{it} = the random error in month t.

The intercept from this 4-index regression, a_i, is the basis of Elton, Gruber and Blake (1996)'s measure of risk-adjusted performance. Indeed, the authors used this intercept to calculate both a '1-year alpha' and a '3-year alpha', the method depending on which period is being considered.

In the first period, referred to as the 'selection period', Elton, Gruber and Blake (1996) used these two measures alternatively to select and rank the portfolios. They calculated the '1-year alpha' for a fund i at time t by regressing equation (1.30) over the previous 3 years, estimating the value of a_i, and then adding to it the average monthly residual of the previous 1 year.

On the other hand, the '3-year alpha' is calculated as just the value of a_i from regressing equation (1.30) over the previous 3 years.

In the second period, referred to as the 'performance period', Elton, Gruber and Blake (1996) calculated the relevant alpha by regression equation (1.30) over the full period, estimating the 'overall' value of a_i and then adding to it the average of the monthly residual over the performance period. However, if at some point in the period under consideration, the fund being studied merged or changed its name or policy, Elton, Gruber and Blake (1996) adopted the following procedure instead: 'the alpha in the performance period is a weighted average of the alpha and residuals on the selected fund through the month of the merger or policy change and the average alpha plus average residuals on the surviving funds for the remaining months in the evaluation period'. The authors did consider other rules but did not find any significant change in the results.

Using these performance measures to conduct their performance evaluation, Elton, Gruber and Blake (1996) discovered that both the 1-year and 3-year selection alpha signal future performance and that the information thereby obtained works for 'periods 3 years in the future as well as 1 year in the future'.

Hence, using the above method could help in detecting any persistence in fund mangers' superior skills.

1.10 CARHART'S 4-FACTOR MODEL

In the same spirit of the previous study, particularly in the context of choosing high performing funds and studying whether past performance is indicative of future performance, Carhart (1997) set up a 4-factor regression model which characterizes the fund by what is commonly called a '4-factor alpha'.

The target here is first to adjust for the risk of the portfolio due to its various characteristics such as size, investment objective or momentum style and then calculate whether there is any performance left that is related to the active manager's skill.

This model is described using Jain and Wu (2000)'s notations:

$$\begin{aligned} R_{it} - R_{ft} &= \alpha_{4i} + \beta_{1i}(R_{mt} - R_{ft}) + \beta_{2i} SMB_t + \beta_{3i} HML_t \\ &\quad + \beta_{4i}\ momentum_t + error_{it} \end{aligned} \tag{1.31}$$

where:

R_{it} = the return on fund i in month t

R_{ft} = the risk-free rate in month t

R_{mt} = the return on a market portfolio in month t

SMB_t = the return on portfolios of small minus large firms in month t
HML_t = the return on portfolios of high minus low book-to-market stocks in month t
$momentum_t$ = the rate of return on portfolios of high minus low momentum (prior 1-year return) stocks in month t.

Using differences in returns to measure the different characteristics such as size, value/growth and momentum has two advantages: first, there is almost no correlation between the indexes constructed in this manner and second it is easier to grasp the extent of the indexes' effect on risk-adjusted performance since they represent 'zero-investment portfolios'. (Elton, Gruber and Blake, 1996).

In conclusion, Carhart (1997)'s 4-factor alpha is an estimate of the net returns earned by the fund manager after adjusting for the fund's risk, which is done by controlling for its various characteristics.

1.11 RISK-ADJUSTED PERFORMANCE

Modigliani and Modigliani (1997) claimed that given the importance of evaluating the performance of fund managers without ignoring the risk factor, and given that the traditional methods such as the Jensen measure or the Treynor ratio that achieve this objective are not very easy to grasp by any average investor, there is a crucial need for developing a new performance measure that could deal with both these issues.

As a result, the authors 'propose an alternative measure of risk-adjusted performance (RAP) that is grounded in modern finance theory and yet easy for the average investor to understand'.

Indeed, Modigliani and Modigliani (1997) constructed a method that entails first adjusting the risk of the portfolio under consideration to the risk of the benchmark portfolio, calculating the returns on this 'risk-matched' portfolio and finally comparing the returns on this new portfolio to the returns on the benchmark.

To match the risk of the evaluated portfolio to the market portfolio, Modigliani and Modigliani (1997) used leverage, referring to it as 'a key tool in achieving optimal investment performance', to obtain the following equation:

$$RAP(i) = (\sigma_M/\sigma_i)\,(r(i) - r_f) + r_f \tag{1.32}$$

where:

$RAP(i)$ = the annualized risk-adjusted performance of fund i
σ_M = the annualized standard deviation of 'market' returns
σ_i = the annualized standard deviation of returns for fund i

$r(i) =$ the average annual return for fund i
$r_f =$ the annual risk-free return.

This equation implies that if the fund being studied is more (less) risky than the market portfolio, then the returns on the funds are 'scaled down (up)' (Lobosco, 1999).

The authors also reformulated this equation in order to obtain a risk-adjusted performance measure based solely on excess returns, *RAPA*:

$$RAP(i) - r_f = (\sigma_M/\sigma_i)(r(i) - r_f)$$

and hence,

$$RAPA(i) = (\sigma_M/\sigma_i)(r(i) - r_f) \tag{1.33}$$

The authors note that by examining equation (1.33) and comparing it to the Sharpe ratio (Sharpe, 1966) where

$$RAPA(i) = \sigma_M \left(\frac{r(i) - r_f}{\sigma_i}\right)$$

and

$$SR_i = \frac{r(i) - r_f}{\sigma_i}$$

one can notice that both measures will produce the same rankings, i.e. 'the portfolio that is best by the RAP criteria is also best by the Sharpe measure (and conversely)'. The only difference according to Modigliani and Modigliani (1997) is that their risk-adjusted measure gives results in basis points which is easier to understand.

Once the returns on the risk-matched portfolio are calculated, they are compared to the returns of the chosen benchmark in order to discover whether there is any risk-adjusted abnormal performance.

1.12 STYLE/RISK-ADJUSTED PERFORMANCE

Noting that the results obtained by using Modigliani and Modigliani (1997)'s *RAP* measure may not be generated by the superior abilities of the fund manager but the style mandate that he is following, Lobosco (1999) proposed a 'supplemental' measure to the *RAP* that tries to 'compensate for these style effects': the style/risk-adjusted performance measure (*SRAP*).

Indeed, since the *RAP* measure does not control for the style of the fund under evaluation, the performance results could be due to the particular style doing well or badly during the period of study and not to any management skills. But by controlling for the style, one can obtain 'a valuable additional perspective'.

Lobosco (1999) designed the following method to calculate the *SRAP* of fund i:

(a) Calculate Modigliani and Modigliani (1997)'s *RAP* of fund i: *RAP (i)*.
(b) Perform a Sharpe style analysis[7] calculation (Sharpe, 1992) to find the Sharpe style index corresponding to fund i.
(c) Calculate the *RAP* of this style index: *RAP (Sharpe style index of fund i)*.
(d) Finally calculate the relative *RAP* of fund i versus its Sharpe style index, which gives the style/risk-adjusted performance measure of fund i:

$$\text{Relative } RAP = SRAP = RAP(i) - RAP\ (\textit{Sharpe style index of fund i})$$

The risk-adjusted performance relative to the Sharpe style index is the style/risk-adjusted performance.

1.13 THE SHARPE STYLE ANALYSIS

According to Sharpe (1992), 'a passive fund manager provides an investor with an investment style, while an active manager provides both style and selection'. Hence, to evaluate the performance of a fund manager that is not related to the style mandate he is following, one needs to adjust and control for the style factor, i.e. the returns that reflect management skills would be 'the difference between the fund's return and that of a passive mix with the same style'.

In effect, to develop his style analysis, Sharpe (1992) used a regression equation that takes the form of an asset class factor model:

$$\tilde{R}_i = [\, b_{i1}\tilde{F}_1 + b_{i2}\tilde{F}_2 + \ldots + b_{in}\tilde{F}_n] + \tilde{e}_i \tag{1.34}$$

where:

$\tilde{R}_i$ represents the return on asset i
$\tilde{F}_j$ represents the value of the jth factor, $j = 1, \ldots, n$
$\tilde{e}_i$ represents the non-factor component of the return on asset i
b_{i1} through b_{in} represents the sensitivities of the fund's return to factors $\tilde{F}_1$ through $\tilde{F}_n$.

[7]The Sharpe style analysis will be discussed next.

Sharpe (1992) ascertained that one very important assumption here is that the factors are the only source of correlation among returns, i.e. the non-factor return for one asset ($\tilde{e}_i$) is assumed to be uncorrelated with that of every other ($\tilde{e}_j$).

Sharpe also noted that 'the terms in the brackets can be termed as the return attributable to style and the residual component as the return attributable to selection'.

Now, to find the style of a fund i, i.e. to perform the style analysis, Sharpe (1992) used quadratic programming to find the best set of asset class exposures (the b_{ij} values) that minimizes the variance of the unexplained returns $\tilde{e}_i$ where:

$$\tilde{e}_i = \tilde{R}_i - [\, b_{i1}\tilde{F}_1 + b_{i2}\tilde{F}_2 + \ldots + b_{in}\tilde{F}_n] \tag{1.35}$$

This is, however, subject to two constraints: the coefficients must lie between 0 and 1 and they have to sum to 1.

Once the b_{ij} values are solved for, they are used to form the style benchmark for the fund being evaluated.

To summarize, Lobosco (1999) described Sharpe style analysis as finding 'the weighted average of a set of market indexes that most closely tracks the returns of the portfolio being analysed'.

The next study to be discussed presented three different measures that aim at measuring the different aspects of a manager's performance.

1.14 THREE INNOVATIVE MEASURES THAT CAPTURE THE DIFFERENT FACES OF A MANAGER'S SUPERIOR ABILITIES

As discussed earlier, a successful active manager engages in various activities such as security selection and market timing, with the aim of showing his superior abilities by generating abnormal performance.

In order to assess those superior skills and benchmark them, Daniel *et al.* (1997) devised several measures that decompose funds' returns – after controlling for style – making it easier to detect any superior management skills. To achieve that, Daniel *et al.* (1997) developed also a new method to construct benchmarks, where 'the benchmark portfolios are matched to stocks on the basis of size, book-to-market and prior-year return characteristics'. According to Daniel *et al.* (1997), this is a 'more precise method of controlling for style-based returns than the method of decomposing performance with factor-based regressions used by Carhart (1997)' (Wermers, 2000).

The method used to construct these benchmarks and control for style is presented first, then the various performance decomposition measures will be discussed. This will be done using the notation and the exposition presented in Wermers (2000).

1.14.1 Defining the benchmarks

According to Daniel *et al.* (1997), the construction of their relevant benchmarks follows the next steps:

1. First, all stocks are ranked, at the end of each June, by their market capitalization.
2. Quintile portfolios are formed and then each quintile is further subdivided into book-to-market quintiles, based on their book-to-market data as of the end of December immediately prior to the ranking year.
3. Finally, each of the resulting 25 fractile portfolios is further subdivided into quintiles based on the 12-month past return of stocks through the end of May of the ranking year.

This ranking method generates 125 fractile portfolios, each possessing a distinct combination of size, book-to-market and momentum characteristics. This procedure is repeated at the end of June of each year. Next, value-weighted returns are computed for each of the 125 fractile portfolios, and the benchmark for each stock during a given quarter is the buy-and-hold return of the fractile portfolio of which that stock is a member during that quarter (Wermer, 2000).

Therefore, as Wermers (2000) summarizes it, 'the characteristic-adjusted return for a given stock is computed as the buy-and-hold stock return minus the buy-and-hold value-weighted benchmark return during the same quarter'.

Having presented the procedure behind the construction of the benchmarks used by Daniel *et al.* (1997) to compute their performance measures, this review presents next an exposition of the measures themselves.

1.14.2 Measuring the manager's selection abilities: the characteristic selectivity measure

The Characteristic Selectivity measure is an evaluation of the ability of the fund manager to select outperforming funds within stocks with same characteristics, i.e. it aims at answering the following question: after controlling for style, does the fund manager have selection abilities?

It is computed as follows in quarter t:

$$CS_t = \sum_{j=1}^{N} \tilde{w}_{j,t-1} \left(\tilde{R}_{j,t} - \tilde{R}_t^{b_{j,t-1}} \right) \tag{1.36}$$

where:

$\tilde{w}_{j,t-1}$ = the portfolio weight on stock j at the end of the quarter $t - 1$
$\tilde{R}_{j,t}$ = the quarter t buy-and-hold return of stock j
$\tilde{R}_t^{b_{j,t-1}}$ = the quarter t buy-and-hold return of the characteristic-based benchmark portfolio that is matched to stock j at the end of quarter $t - 1$.

Wermers (2000) pointed out the existence of one qualification with this measure: it accounts solely for the effect of three characteristics. There might be numerous more stock characteristics that could affect the performance evaluation results, leading perhaps to an over- or underestimation of the management's skills.

1.14.3 Measuring the manager's timing abilities: the characteristic timing measure

The second measure developed by Daniel *et al.* (1997) is one that aims at measuring the fund manager's ability to time stocks characteristics. It is referred to as the Characteristic Timing measure.

Indeed, according to Wermers (2000), the intuition behind this measure is that 'managers can generate additional performance if size, B/M or momentum strategies have time-varying expected returns that the manager can exploit by 'tilting' his portfolio weights towards stocks having these characteristics when the returns on the characteristics are highest'.

To quantify the manager's ability to exploit his timing skills, the Characteristic Timing measure is computed as follows during quarter t:

$$CT_t = \sum_{j=1}^{N} \left(\tilde{w}_{j,t-1} \tilde{R}_t^{b_{j,t-1}} - \tilde{w}_{j,t-5} \tilde{R}_t^{b_{j,t-5}} \right) \tag{1.37}$$

The first term is the quarter t return of the quarter $t - 5$ matching characteristic portfolio for stock $j\,(\tilde{R}_t^{b_{j,t-5}})$ (times the portfolio weight at the end of quarter $t - 5$) while the second is the quarter t return of the quarter $t - 1$ matching characteristic portfolio for stock $j\,(\tilde{R}_t^{b_{j,t-1}})$ (times the portfolio weight at the end of quarter $t - 1$).

Thus, 'a fund manager who increases the fund's weight on stock j just before the payoff to the characteristic of stock j is highest, will exhibit a larger CT measure' (Wermers, 2000).

1.14.4 Measuring the effectiveness and superiority of a manager's style mandate: the average style measure

The third and last measure proposed by Daniel *et al.* (1997) is the Average Style measure. It is designed to measure the returns earned by the fund manager as a result of the particular style mandate he was following.

It is computed as follows in quarter t:

$$AS_t = \sum_{j=1}^{N} \tilde{w}_{j,t-5} \tilde{R}_t^{b_{j,t-5}} \tag{1.38}$$

Examining the expression for the Average Style measure, we can see that it entails the following.

At time $t - 5$, Daniel *et al.* (1997) propose to match the stocks held by each fund being evaluated with its characteristic-adjusted benchmark, following of course the method described earlier. Then, the Average Style measure is computed as the sum over all stocks or funds of the product of the quarter t return on this benchmark portfolio and the quarter $t - 5$ portfolio weights. Wermers (2000) duly notes that 'by lagging weights and benchmark portfolios by one year, returns due to timing characteristics are eliminated'. Indeed, timing characteristics usually involve taking position within one year and not before.

Conducting an empirical application of these measures, Wermers (2000) discovered, by examining funds' gross returns over the 1976 to 1994 period and comparing them to the corresponding average return of the CRSP value-weighted index, that the difference is 1.3% per year: 0.75% of it can be attributed to stock-selection abilities, 0% to timing skills, and the final 0.55% to the style followed by fund managers. However, once he considers the net returns, the results change; indeed, the funds underperform a broad market index by 1% per year.

Next, Blake, Lehmann and Timmermann (1999) proposed a method that, instead of decomposing securities returns as earlier, decomposes portfolio weights in order to measure managers' superior abilities.

1.15 DYNAMICS OF PORTFOLIO WEIGHTS: PASSIVE AND ACTIVE MANAGEMENT

Blake, Lehmann and Timmermann (1999) undertook an innovative study that examines the performance of multiple-asset-class portfolios and assesses it in terms of market timing and security selection. Furthermore, they employed a new approach to decomposing portfolio weights changes and studying their dynamics, with the aim of finding a measure of 'the relative importance of passive and active management, both in the short and long run'.

1.15.1 Decomposing portfolio weights

As a first step, the authors used a simple decomposition, in the spirit of the work by Brinson, Hood and Beebower (1986), that pinpoints the causes of portfolio weights changes and as a first step applied it to the aggregate portfolio. Using Blake, Lehmann and Timmermann (1999)'s notation and exposition, weights must satisfy the following 'accounting identity':

$$W_{jt} \equiv W_{jt-1}(1 + r_{jt} + NCF_{jt}) \tag{1.39}$$

where:

- W_{jt} is the total holdings in asset class j at the end of month t across all funds in the sample
- W_t is the total holdings across all assets classes
- r_{jt} is the rate of return on UK pension funds' holdings of asset class j
- NCF_{jt} is the rate of net cash flow into that asset class during month t.

The expression of the portfolio weight of asset class $j\,(\omega_{jt})$ is thus:

$$\begin{aligned}\omega_{jt} &= \frac{W_{jt}}{W_t} \\ &= \frac{\dfrac{W_{jt-1}}{W_{t-1}}\left(\dfrac{W_{jt}}{W_{jt-1}}\right)}{W_t/W_{t-1}} \\ &= \omega_{jt-1}\frac{1 + r_{jt} + NCF_{jt}}{1 + \sum\limits_{k=1}^{M} \omega_{kt}(r_{kt} + NCF_{kt})}\end{aligned} \tag{1.40}$$

Now, taking log-differences,

$$\Delta \log(\omega_{jt}) = \log(1 + r_{jt} + NCF_{jt}) - \log\left[1 + \sum_{k=1}^{M} \omega_{kt}(r_{kt} + NCF_{kt})\right] \quad (1.41)$$

Thus, a close approximation of the above equation would be

$$\Delta \log(\omega_{jt}) \approx r_{jt} - r_{pt} + NCF_{jt} - NCF_{pt} \quad (1.42)$$

where:

r_{pt} is the value-weighted total return

NCF_{pt} is the value-weighted net cash flow into the total portfolio during month t.

Blake, Lehmann and Timmermann (1999) point out that the first term in the decomposition above, $(r_{jt} - r_{pt})$, measures the extent to which changes in aggregate weights are due to any differences in returns across assets while the second term, $(NCF_{jt} - NCF_{pt})$, measures the extent to which changes in aggregate weights are due to any 'shifts' in net asset cash flows across asset classes.

The importance of this decomposition lies in the fact that:

> shifts due to the 1st component arise from the passive investment strategy of 'buy-and-hold', reinvesting asset income in the same asset categories, and distributing any net inflows in the pension fund according to the *ex post* asset allocation. In contrast, revisions associated with the 2nd component result from the active strategy of rebalancing the portfolio by redirecting cash flows across asset groups. (Blake, Lehmann and Timmermann, 1999)

Blake, Lehmann and Timmermann (1999) also consider the fund-specific version of this decomposition. For fund i:

$$\Delta \log(\omega_{ijt}) \approx r_{ijt} - r_{ipt} + NCF_{ijt} - NCF_{ipt} \quad (1.43)$$

Subtracting the two equations from each other gives the following:

$$\begin{aligned}\Delta \log(\omega_{ijt}) - \Delta \log(\omega_{jt}) &\approx [(r_{ijt} - r_{ipt}) - (r_{jt} - r_{pt})] \\ &\quad + [(NCF_{ijt} - NCF_{ipt}) - (NCF_{jt} - NCF_{pt})] \\ &\equiv \psi_{ijt}\end{aligned}$$

According to the authors, this is a useful 'baseline' model in the form of a 'fixed effects dummy variable model' where '$\Delta \log(\omega_{jt})$ is a time effect across funds, and the composite residual on the right-hand side is a fund-specific effect with a nonzero mean'. Applying it to a sample data of 306 pension funds in the UK, the authors found that the model fits well on average. The model also shows evidence that in the long run individual funds exhibit a slow mean reversion towards a 'commonly changing strategic asset allocation' but in the short term they do tend to deviate from it.

1.15.2 Assessing the importance of active versus passive management

In addition, Blake, Lehmann and Timmermann (1999) made use of this simple decomposition by Brinson, Hood and Beebower (1986) to compare the importance of active versus passive management in explaining portfolio returns.

Indeed, using the equation above and assuming there are M asset classes, they wrote the following arithmetic identity:

$$\underbrace{\sum_{j=1}^{M} \omega_{ajt} r_{ajt}}_{\text{Total return}} \equiv \underbrace{\sum_{j=1}^{M} \omega_{njt} r_{njt}}_{\text{Normal return}} + \underbrace{\sum_{j=1}^{M} \omega_{njt}(r_{ajt} - r_{njt})}_{\text{Return from security selection}}$$

$$+ \underbrace{\sum_{j=1}^{M} (\omega_{ajt} - \omega_{njt}) r_{njt}}_{\text{Return from market timing}} + \underbrace{\sum_{j=1}^{M} (\omega_{ajt} - \omega_{njt})(r_{ajt} - r_{njt})}_{\text{Residual return}} \tag{1.44}$$

where:

ω_{njt} is the 'normal' or strategic asset allocation of a fund in the jth asset class at time t

ω_{ajt} is the actual portfolio weight

r_{njt} is the 'normal' portfolio return

r_{ajt} is the actual portfolio return

and the 'normal' return is the return on the benchmark that one wishes to use.

Blake, Lehmann and Timmermann (1999) discussed here two possible choices for the normal weights.

The first is by Brinson, Hood and Beebower (1986) and takes the following form:

$$\omega_{njt} = \frac{\sum_{t=1}^{T} \omega_{ajt}}{T} \tag{1.45}$$

for all t. According to this expression, the appropriate choice for the normal weights is the average portfolio allocation over the sample. Blake, Lehmann and Timmermann (1999) affirmed that this choice could work if the funds are in a state of equilibrium: they have reached their 'target portfolio decomposition' and they possess stationary long-run investment positions. However, this is very unrealistic since portfolio weights are non-stationary. To account for this factor, Blake, Lehmann and Timmermann (1999) proposed to include a trend in the weights, 'letting the normal portfolio weights increase (or decrease) linearly in time between the initial and terminal weights'.

Consequently, their measure of the 'normal' portfolio weights is the following:

$$\omega_{njt} = \omega_{aj1} + (t/T)\left(\omega_{ajT} - \omega_{aj1}\right)$$

The authors stress one important property of this measure: given that $\sum_{j=1}^{M}(\omega_{ajT} - \omega_{aj1}) = 0$, the normal portfolio weights have to lie between 0 and 1 at each point in time.

The next study tried to overcome the problems associated with the use of benchmarks in assessing portfolio performance by devising a method of performance evaluation that does not require the use of a benchmark.

1.16 THE PORTFOLIO CHANGE MEASURE

Most of the performance measures devised and utilized in the literature require the use of a benchmark. However, as discussed earlier, many studies have pointed to the various biases that the use of a benchmark could lead to, such as the sensitivity of the performance measures to the choice of the benchmark, the dividend-yield and size biases related to any CAPM and APT-based benchmarks, etc.

In an attempt to overcome these problems, GT (1993) realized that most of these measures forgo one important aspect of the portfolio under consideration: its composition. According to them, taking portfolio composition into consideration leads to a performance measure that does not necessitate the use of a benchmark and hence eliminates the bias that occurs when one is used. This idea originates from a paper by Cornell (1979), in which he proposed an alternative measure, the Event Study Measure. In their study, GT (1993) discuss the Event Study Measure and then construct a more advantageous way to achieve the same goal, the Portfolio Change Measure. The main value behind developing such a measure, according to the authors, lies in the fact that since it does not require the use of a benchmark, any evidence of abnormal performance that it discovers cannot be attributed to benchmark inefficiency.

The intuition lying behind these two measures is the positive correlation existing between an informed investor's portfolio weights and future returns. They both find the sum of the time series of these covariances to be an 'intuitive measure of performance' since it can be viewed as 'the difference between the realized return of the managed portfolio and its expected return conditioned on the portfolio manager being uniformed' (GT, 1993). However, according to GT (1993), the Portfolio Change Measure is characterized by two advantages: it is free from survivorship bias and statistical inferences are much easier to compute from it.

In effect, the Event Study Measure 'calculates the difference between the returns of assets when they are in the portfolio (the event period) with their returns at later dates (the comparison period). The basic idea is that the assets held by informed portfolio managers will have higher returns when they are included in the portfolio than when they are not included'. (GT, 1993).

The Portfolio Change Measure also takes into account the advantages that an informed manager has. In effect, according to the authors, the motivation behind their measure is that for an informed manager, there could exist a correlation between his portfolio holdings and future returns. This is because such a manager possesses a changing vector of expected returns and hence can use this to increase (decrease) his holdings of the assets whose expected returns have increased (decreased). For an uninformed manager, however, the correlation between his portfolio holdings and future returns would be zero since 'his vector of expected returns is constant over time'.

Both measures provide an estimate of the sum of these time series covariances between portfolio holdings and returns:

$$\mathrm{cov} = \sum_{j=1}^{N} \left(E[w_j R_j] - E[w_j]E[R_j] \right) \tag{1.46}$$

However, in order to separate and show the difference between the Event Study measure and their measure, the authors reformulated the above equation in two ways, the first being the 'foundation' of the Event Study measure while the second the 'foundation' for their measure:

$$\text{cov} = \sum_{j=1}^{N} E[w_j(R_j - E[R_j])] \tag{1.47}$$

and

$$\text{cov} = \sum_{j=1}^{N} E[(w_j - E[w_j])R_j] \tag{1.48}$$

The authors noted the major and crucial difference between the two measures: while the Event Study Measure necessitates an estimate of the unconditional return $E[R_j]$, the Portfolio Change Measure needs an estimate of the expected weight.

Affirming that these two identities hold at the sample covariance level as well, GT (1993) wrote the following:

$$s\ \text{cov}(w_j, R_j) = \frac{\sum_{t=1}^{T} w_{jt}(R_{jt} - \bar{R}_j)}{T} = \frac{\sum_{t=1}^{T} (w_{jt} - \bar{w}_j)R_{jt}}{T} \tag{1.49}$$

where:

s cov = the sample covariance between the weights and returns of asset j

w_{jt} = the portfolio weights at the beginning of the period t (with sample mean $\bar{w}_j$)

R_{jt} = the portfolio return from date t to date $t+1$ (with sample mean $\bar{R}_j$).

Examining these expressions, GT (1993) pointed out that using past returns to estimate expected returns and using future holdings to estimate expected holdings can result in obtaining a biased estimate of the covariance.[8]

Consequently, summing over all assets, they formulated the two performance measures in the following manner:

$$\text{Event Study measure} = \frac{\sum_{t=1}^{T}\sum_{j=1}^{N} [w_{jt}(R_{jt} - R_{j,t+k})]}{T} \tag{1.50}$$

[8]The authors offer an example to illustrate this claim in the case of the Event Study Measure: 'a contrarian strategy of picking stocks that have previously experienced a price decline induces a positive sample covariance between portfolio weights and returns since it picks stocks that tend to have downward biased sample means'.

and

$$\text{Portfolio Change measure} = \frac{\sum_{t=1}^{T}\sum_{j=1}^{N}[R_{jt}(w_{jt} - w_{j,t-k})]}{T} \tag{1.51}$$

where:

$R_{j,t+k}$, the period $t + k$ return for each asset, is assumed to proxy for its period t expected return in the Event Study Measure

$w_{j,t-k}$, the period $t - k$ portfolio holdings, is assumed to proxy for its expected holdings for the Portfolio Change Measure.

As mentioned earlier, GT (1993) advocated two advantages that their new measure has over the Event Study Measure. First, the computation of statistical test of significance is very easy and simple using their new measure. This is because the Portfolio Change Measure represents the 'average dollar returns of a zero-cost portfolio' which, under the null of an uninformed investor, are serially uncorrelated while 'using future returns as performance benchmark [in the Event Study Measure] induces serial correlation in the time series of returns'. Second, since the Event Study Measure uses future returns in its computations, it relies very much on the survival of the assets or funds held in its portfolio. The Portfolio Change Measure, in contrast, uses only past and current weights, and hence it is free of survivorship bias at all time.

However, GT (1993) do recognize that their analysis can be subject to two possible limitations. First, if the mean returns of assets are not constant over the period studied (as it was crucially assumed in this study), investors can 'game' on the two equations above. For instance, 'portfolios that include assets when their expected returns are higher than usual (perhaps because they are temporarily riskier) will realize positive 'performance' with the measures'. Second, if there exists an upward trend in the unconditional expected returns, then the Portfolio Change Measure can give evidence of positive performance even if the investor is uninformed.

The authors suggested that to assess the importance of these two problems, one can perform a regression where the returns on the zero-cost portfolio are the dependent variable and the returns on the different market indexes are the independent variables. If the bias in the Portfolio Change Measure is negligible, then one would expect the average systematic risk obtained from the above regression is to be 'close to 0'. They also suggest using the intercept from this regression as the performance measure, claiming that this performance measure will still be less subject to the benchmark biases than the traditional measures.

In the following discussion, this review discusses ways of studying some of the traditional behaviour of managers and their effect on funds' performance.

1.17 THE MOMENTUM MEASURES

Momentum investing refers to the tendency of some fund managers to trade based on past returns: they tend to purchase stocks that possess past high returns, 'past winners', and sell the stocks that possess low past returns, 'past losers'.

Many studies have examined this behaviour, finding various evidence of its existence in fund managers' investment decisions and of its effect on the performance of funds (see, for example, Jegadeesh and Titman (1993)).

In order to assess whether the evidence of abnormal performance in gross returns data they discovered in earlier studies[9] was actually due to superior manager abilities or just to following momentum strategies, Grinblatt, Titman and Wermers (1995) constructed a measure aimed at assessing the extent to which fund managers follow such a strategy and the effect this have on funds' performance. Indeed, Grinblatt, Titman and Wermers (1995) ascertained that:

> If either irrationality or agency problems generate these trading styles, then mutual funds that exhibit these behaviours will tend to push the prices of stocks that they purchase above their intrinsic values, thereby realizing lower future performance. However, if this type of behaviour arises because informed portfolio managers tend to pick the same underpriced stocks, then funds that exhibit these styles should realize high future performance.

To assess the importance of momentum investing in fund managers' behaviour, Grinblatt, Titman and Wermers (1995) offer the following momentum measure:

$$M = \frac{1}{T}\sum_{t=1}^{T}\sum_{j=1}^{N}(\tilde{w}_{j,t} - \tilde{w}_{j,t-1})\tilde{R}_{j,t-k+1} \quad (1.52)$$

where:

$\tilde{w}_{j,t}$ is the portfolio weight on security j at date t

$\tilde{R}_{j,t-k+1}$ is the return of security $j(j = 1, \ldots, N)$ from date $t-k$ to date $t-k+1$, the historical benchmark period.

The purpose of this measure is 'to measure the degree to which a fund manager tilts his portfolio in the direction of stocks that have experienced high

[9]Grinblatt and Titman (1989a) and (1993).

returns in some historical benchmark period, and away from stocks that have experienced low returns' (Grinblatt, Titman and Wermers, 1995).

However, in order to apply this measure to empirical data, Grinblatt, Titman and Wermers (1995) altered it in order to account for the fact that while data on portfolio weights are on a quarterly basis, the data on stock returns are monthly. Given that they possessed data for 41 quarters, the authors wrote the following expression for the momentum measure:

$$M = \frac{1}{120} \sum_{t=1}^{40} \sum_{i=1}^{3} \sum_{j=1}^{N} (\tilde{w}_{j,3t} - \tilde{w}_{j,3t-3}) \tilde{R}_{j,3t-3\ k+i} \tag{1.53}$$

Claiming that 'the most recent returns are probably of the greatest interest to portfolio managers', Grinblatt, Titman and Wermers (1995) studied the above equation for $k = 1$, referred to as 'lag-0 momentum' (L0M), and for $k = 2$, referred to as 'lag-1 momentum' (L1M).

Furthermore, for even more precise measuring, the authors decomposed each of the L0M and L1M measures into two parts: 'Buy L0M', 'Sell L0M', 'Buy L1M', 'Sell L1M', where 'a high Buy (Sell) L0M or L1M measure for a fund means that it bought winners (sold losers) strongly, on average' (Grinblatt, Titman and Wermers, 1995).

For instance,

$$\text{Buy L0M} = \frac{1}{120} \sum_{t=1}^{40} \sum_{i=1}^{3} \sum_{\tilde{w}_{j,3t} > \tilde{w}_{j,3t-3}} (\tilde{w}_{j,3t} - \tilde{w}_{j,3t-3})(\tilde{R}_{j,3t-3+i} - \bar{R}_j) \tag{1.54}$$

and

$$\text{Sell L0M} = \frac{1}{120} \sum_{t=1}^{40} \sum_{i=1}^{3} \sum_{\tilde{w}_{j,3t} < \tilde{w}_{j,3t-3}} (\tilde{w}_{j,3t} - \tilde{w}_{j,3t-3})(\tilde{R}_{j,3t-3+i} - \bar{R}_j) \tag{1.55}$$

Moreover, to cover another aspect of momentum measuring, its effect on portfolio trades, Grinblatt, Titman and Wermers (1995) constructed a 'turnover-adjusted L0M' (TAL0M):

$$\text{TAL0M} = \frac{1}{120} \sum_{t=1}^{40} \sum_{i=1}^{3} \frac{\sum_{j=1}^{N} (\tilde{w}_{j,3t} - \tilde{w}_{j,3t-3}) \tilde{R}_{j,3t-3+i}}{\sum_{\tilde{w}_{j,3t} > \tilde{w}_{j,3t-3}} (\tilde{w}_{j,3t} - \tilde{w}_{j,3t-3})} \tag{1.56}$$

This measure adds to the L0M measure since it can show evidence of 'extreme' momentum investing that the L0M cannot capture easily. Indeed, according to the authors, 'A mutual fund that trades very little, but buys high past extreme winners and sells past extreme losers, will have a very high TAL0M measure even though the unmodified L0M measure will be very small'.

The TAL0M measure was also expressed in the form of 'Buy TAL0M' and 'Sell TAL0M', for $\tilde{w}_{j,3t} > \tilde{w}_{j,3t-3}$ and $\tilde{w}_{j,3t} < \tilde{w}_{j,3t-3}$, respectively.

Applying these measures to data on quarterly holdings for 274 mutual funds between 1974 and 1984, Grinblatt, Titman and Wermers (1995) found small but statistically significant evidence of momentum investing, more evidence, however, of buying past winners than of selling past losers. This was even more corroborated by the results from the TAL0M and Buy TAL0M measures, which established that for their sample 'buying winners [was] the chief method of momentum investing'.

Next, to assess how much this behaviour of momentum investing affects the funds' performance, Grinblatt, Titman and Wermers (1995) used the performance measure (α) developed in their earlier study, GT (1993), for a lag $k = 4$ quarters. In effect, depending on the sign of the L0M and L1M measures, the authors split their sample of funds into momentum and contrarian investors and then study their performance.

The results showed that momentum strategies and performance are 'highly correlated': In contrast to the contrarian investors, the investors who had the tendency of buying past winners did earn abnormal performance.

1.18 THE HERDING MEASURES

Herding behaviour refers to the tendency of mutual funds to buy and sell the same stocks at the same time. This strategy could also have a crucial impact on funds' performance and must be differentiated from any evidence of superior skills by fund managers.

To measure funds' herding behaviour, Lakonishok, Schleifer and Vishny (1992) proposed the following equation, referred to by Grinblatt, Titman and Wermers (1995) as the 'Unsigned Herding Measure'[10]:

$$UHM_{i,t} = \left|p_{i,t} - \bar{p}_t\right| - E\left|p_{i,t} - \bar{p}_t\right| \tag{1.57}$$

where:

$p_{i,t}$ equals the proportion of funds, trading in stock i during quarter t, that are buyers

[10]We follow here the exposition and notation presented by Grinblatt, Titman and Wermers (1995).

$\bar{p}_t$ is the expected value of $p_{i,t}$ and is calculated as the mean of $p_{i,t}$ over all stocks during the quarter t. It represents thus, for the average stock, the proportion of funds trades during quarter t that are buys.

Furthermore, for more accurate assessment of whether the herding behaviour goes beyond random trading and whether it is stronger on the buy or sell side, Grinblatt, Titman and Wermers (1995) subdivided their data into two groups: 'Stock i during quarter t was considered to be a 'buy herding' stock-quarter if $p_{i,t} > \bar{p}_t$; similarly, stock 'sell herding' categorization occurred when $p_{i,t} < \bar{p}_t$'.

The results from Grinblatt, Titman and Wermers (1995)'s study showed that there is evidence of herding behaviour, but it is very small and not statistically significant. The authors offered two possible explanations for these findings: it might be due to the fact that the sample of investors considered in their study was too broad or to the fact that all quarters were considered even those with 'very little trading'. Indeed, the evidence of herding behaviour increased substantially when the study considered quarters with five or ten trades respectively.

Next, to construct their herding behaviour measure, Grinblatt, Titman and Wermers (1995) started by using the Unsigned Herding Measure (UHM) to develop a new measure that assesses the extent to which particular funds 'go with the crowd', the 'Signed Herding Measure' (SHM), which according to the authors 'provides an indication of whether a fund is 'following the crowd' or 'going against the crowd' in a particular stock during a particular quarter':

$$SHM_{i,t} = I_{i,t} \times UHM_{i,t} - E[I_{i,t} \times UHM_{i,t}] \tag{1.58}$$

where $SHM_{i,t} \equiv 0$ in the case where less than 10 funds traded stock i during quarter t.

Otherwise:

$I_{i,t} =$ 0 if $|p_{i,t} - \bar{p}_t| < E\,|p_{i,t} - \bar{p}_t|$
In this case, $SHM_{i,t}$ is also 0 since the stock-quarters show 'negative herding' – the proportion of buys is less than the expected proportion, i.e. less than the average.

$=$ 1 if $p_{i,t} - \bar{p}_t > E\,|p_{i,t} - \bar{p}_t|$ and the mutual fund is a buyer of stock i during quarter t or if $-(p_{i,t} - \bar{p}_t) \succ E\,|p_{i,t} - \bar{p}_t|$ and the fund is a seller, i.e. here, the fund trades with 'the herd'.

$= -1$ if $p_{i,t} - \bar{p}_t < E\,|p_{i,t} - \bar{p}_t|$ and the mutual fund is a seller of stock i during quarter t, or if $-(p_{i,t} - \bar{p}_t) \succ E\,|p_{i,t} - \bar{p}_t|$ and the fund is a buyer, i.e. here, the fund trades 'against the herd' in that stock.

The authors provided as well an explanation of the method behind calculating the second term in the above equation: $E[I_{i,t} \times UHM_{i,t}]$.

Indeed, they affirmed that under the null hypothesis of no herding, 'the number of trading funds that are buyers is binomially distributed'. Consequently, for stock i and quarter t, they proposed that

$$E[I_{i,t} \times UHM_{i,t}(p)] = \sum_{p:p-\bar{p}>E|p-\bar{p}|} (2p-1)UHM(p)\Pr(p) - \sum_{p:-(p-\bar{p})>E|p-\bar{p}|} (2p-1)UHM(p)\Pr(p)$$

where:
p = the proportion of funds trading in stock i in quarter t that are buyers
n = the number of funds trading in stock i in quarter t
$\bar{p}$ = the proportion of trading funds in the population that are buyers; it is calculated in the same manner as was earlier described for equation (1.57)

and where for the n discrete values that p can assume:

$$\Pr(p) = \binom{n}{np} \bar{p}^{np}(1-\bar{p})^{n-np}$$

To complete this analysis, Grinblatt, Titman and Wermers (1995) presented their measure of herding behaviour for an individual fund k; they construct it by replacing the SHM in equation (1.53), for $k = 1$:

$$FHM_k = \frac{1}{120}\sum_{t=1}^{40}\sum_{i=1}^{3}\sum_{j=1}^{N}(\tilde{w}_{j,3t} - \tilde{w}_{j,3t-3})SHM_{j,3t-3+i} \tag{1.59}$$

According to the authors, the intuition behind this measure goes as follows.

If this individual fund k exhibited herding behaviour in quarter t, i.e. it followed the crowd by buying or selling the same stock during that quarter t, FHM will have a positive increment in that quarter since it will then be equal to either:

- the product of a positive SHM (in the case where the herding behaviour of the crowd was manifested by collective buying in a given stock) and a positive difference in weights (since this particular fund did follow the crowd and revised his portfolio holding by buying that stock); or
- the product of a negative SHM (in the case where the herding behaviour of the crowd was manifested by collective selling) and a negative difference

in weights (since this particular fund did follow the crowd and revised his portfolio holding by selling that stock).

Now, if the individual fund k did not exhibit herding behaviour in quarter t, i.e. it did not follow the crowd in that quarter, FHM will have a negative increment in that quarter since it will be equal to either:

- the product of a positive SHM (in the case where the herding behaviour of the crowd was manifested by collective buying in a given stock) and a negative difference in weights (since this particular fund did not follow the crowd and revised his portfolio holding by selling that stock); or
- the product of a negative SHM (in the case where the herding behaviour of the crowd was manifested by collective selling) and a negative difference in weights (since this particular fund did not follow the crowd and revised his portfolio holding by buying that stock).

And so, 'funds that tend to buy (sell) when other funds are also buying (selling) will be characterized as herders by this measure' (Grinblatt, Titman and Wermers, 1995).

1.19 STOCKHOLDINGS AND TRADES MEASURE

Another approach to mutual fund performance measurement is to focus not on funds' returns or portfolio holdings but rather on the performance of the stocks held and actively traded by those funds.

As a matter of fact, Chen, Jegadeesh and Wermers (2000) claimed that the measures relying on the traditional approaches might not be powerful enough to find any evidence of superior management skills. However, in their opinion, 'active stock trades are expected to represent a stronger manager opinion than the passive decision of holding an existing position in a stock, since the latter may be driven by non-performance related reasons such as concern over transaction costs and capital gain taxes' and hence, studying the patterns and the performance of stocks held and traded by funds may reveal much more information about any abnormal performance earned by the managers' stock-picking abilities.

Consequently, Chen, Jegadeesh and Wermers (2000) proposed constructing measures that study the funds' holdings and trades of stocks and then using these measures to assess the funds' performances and to detect any superior management skills.

The intuition behind Chen, Jegadeesh and Wermers (2000)'s methodology goes as follows:

> If mutual funds have stock-picking skills, then stocks widely held by funds should outperform their benchmarks. Similarly, stocks that are newly purchased

> should outperform their benchmarks, while stocks that are newly sold should not outperform their benchmarks. On the other hand, if the average mutual fund manager has no talent for picking stocks, then one should find no relation between stock returns and the level of mutual fund holdings or trades.

Moreover, the authors examined the turnover level of the stocks held and traded by funds to detect whether any evidence of excess performance justifies a strategy of frequent trading.

1.19.1 A brief presentation of the different measures

To achieve that, the authors proposed first a measure of 'aggregate stock holdings' that aims at evaluating 'which stocks are most widely held by mutual funds at the end of a given quarter':

$$FracHoldings_{i,t} = \frac{Number\ of\ shares\ held_{i,t}}{Total\ shares\ outstanding_{i,t}}$$

Where:

$Number\ of\ shares\ held_{i,t}$ = the aggregate number of shares in stock i held at the end of quarter t by all mutual funds.

$Total\ shares\ outstanding_{i,t}$ = the total number of stock i shares outstanding as of that date.

This measure will be identical for all stocks if all funds were invested in the market portfolio; however, if funds are actively managed, then they will be characterized by different *FracHoldings* measures. Now, if managers do possess some stock-picking abilities, it should follow that the stocks with 'larger *FracHoldings* measures' are associated with 'higher future returns' than those with 'smaller *FracHoldings* measures'. (Chen, Jegadeesh and Wermers, 2000).

Next, Chen, Jegadeesh and Wermers (2000) proposed a measure of the 'aggregate trades of a stock by mutual funds' which they define as being 'the quarterly change in the *FracHoldings* measure for that stock'. For stock i, during quarter t, it is formulated as:

$$Trades_{i,t} = FracHoldings_{i,t} - FracHoldings_{i,t-1}$$

Here also, the authors affirmed that if fund managers do engage in active management, the *Trades* measure will be different across stocks.

Chen, Jegadeesh and Wermers (2000) pointed out that the *Trades* measure resembles the 'Portfolio Change Measure' developed by GT (1993). However, these two measures differ on two crucial points. First, contrary to the Portfolio

Change Measure, the *Trades* measure evaluates the net share trades by all funds. This constitutes a major difference since as the authors show 'if a small fund buys a stock, while a large fund sells the same number of shares of that stock, the Portfolio Change Measure will be positive... [whereas] the *Trades* will be 0'. Second, changes in portfolio holdings are not only caused by active management, but they also occur in the context of a passive strategy because of the natural variations in stock prices. The Portfolio Change Measure cannot distinguish between these two effects and hence can reflect both of them, leading it to be somewhat biased towards 'past winners'. In contrast, the *Trades* measure detects only the changes due to active trading and 'will not change when there are no net buys or sells by funds, in aggregate'.

Finally, Chen, Jegadeesh and Wermers (2000) examined 'the performance of stocks held and traded by funds with varying levels of portfolio turnover' to assess whether frequent trading is justified by abnormal returns. They use the CRSP definition[11] of turnover of fund k during quarter t:

$$Turnover_{k,t} = \frac{\min(Buys_{k,t}, Sells_{k,t})}{TNA_{k,t}}$$

where:

$Buys_{k,t}(Sells_{k,t})$ = the total value of stock purchases (sales) during year t by fund k

$TNA_{k,t}$ = the average total net assets of fund k during year t.

1.19.2 Applying the above measures to performance evaluation

To apply their newly constructed measures to the evaluation of funds' performance, Chen, Jegadeesh and Wermers (2000) started by constructing deciles based on the *FracHoldings* and *Trades* measures: stocks are ranked according to their *FracHoldings* and *Trades* respectively and then they are divided into deciles where decile 1 contains the 10% most widely held (or traded) stocks, decile 2 contains the next 10%, and so on.

Having ranked the stocks from the most widely held (traded) decile to the least widely one, Chen, Jegadeesh and Wermers (2000) performed various calculations that aim at analysing the characteristics, returns and performance of the holdings and trades of funds as well as assessing any stock-picking abilities by fund managers. They also identified stocks bought (Buys) and sold (Sells) by funds in order to detect any difference in their performance.

[11] According to Chen, Jegadeesh and Wermers (2000), this measure 'captures fund trading that is unrelated to investor inflows or redemptions' because 'this definition of mutual fund turnover uses the minimum of buys and sells, since the dollar value of the buys minus sells is equal to the net inflow (or outflow) of money from investors (controlling for changes in fund cash holdings)'.

Next, to evaluate the correlation between fund performance and turnover, the authors 'add new evidence to this issue by examining whether stocks held and traded by high turnover funds outperform stocks held and traded by low turnover funds'.

To achieve this target:

(a) They start first by ranking the funds at the end of a quarter according to their turnover level in the previous 'calendar' year.
(b) Then, the authors separate the funds into quintiles where the quintile with the highest turnover level is called 'high turnover funds' and the one with the lowest turnover level is referred to as 'low turnover funds'. The quintiles are reconstructed once per year.
(c) Finally, Chen, Jegadeesh and Wermers (2000) calculate the *FracHoldings* and *Trades* measures for each stock 'separately for high turnover and for low turnover funds'.

To evaluate the performance of these quintiles, the authors calculate unadjusted and characteristic-adjusted (following the methodology by Daniel *et al.* (1997) for all holdings Buys and Sells of high and low turnover funds.

The results show that stocks that are widely held do not outperform the ones that are not. Once trades are examined, it was shown that stocks that were 'recently bought' outperformed those that were 'recently' sold, but only for the first year after the trades were completed. In addition, the authors discovered that most of the persistence in performance is due to the momentum effect in stocks. Indeed, there was only very weak evidence of superior stock-picking abilities by fund mangers.

Finally, Chen, Jegadeesh and Wermers (2000) showed that the performance of high turnover funds possessed only 'marginally better stock selection skills' than the low turnover funds. Hence, frequent trading does not necessarily mean that fund managers possess genuine superior abilities; it could be only due to 'noise' trading.

1.20 CONCLUSION

This review has presented the reader with a wide presentation of the most important techniques developed over the years, which aim at thoroughly assessing funds' performance. All of these methods attempt to answer the crucial questions that prevail in the portfolio management industry: do some managers possess genuine superior abilities that can 'beat the market' and is their abnormal performance persistent?

However, the ability of theory to analyse real-world situations is clearly very limited. Most notions of performance relative to a benchmark are based on some assumptions of the theory of aggregation. In many cases, the assumptions are not appropriate. How to measure performance in a world that is dynamic and where there are qualitatively different investors (informed versus noise traders) seems a long way from the sort of analysis presented in this chapter. Indeed, most of these measures cannot account for the full spectrum of variables that determine the managers' performance in the real world, and thus performance measurement remains a very hot and debatable issue in the financial literature circle.

REFERENCES

Adamti, A., Bhattacharya, S., Pfleiderer, P. and Ross, S.A. (1986) On timing and selectivity, *Journal of Finance*, **41**(3), 715–730.

Blake, D. (1994) *Pensions Schemes and Pension Funds in the United Kingdom*, Oxford University Press.

Blake, D., Lehmann, B.N. and Timmermann A. (1999) Asset allocation dynamics and pension fund performance, *Journal of Business*, **72**(4), 429–461.

Brinson, G.P., Hood, L.R. and Beebower, G.L. (1986) Determinants of portfolio performance, *Financial Analysts Journal*, July/August, 39–48.

Carhart, M. (1997) On persistence in mutual fund performance, *Journal of Finance*, **52**, 57–82.

Chen, H., Jegadeesh, N. and Wermers, R. (2000) The value of active mutual fund management: an examination of the stockholdings and trades of fund managers, *Journal of Financial and Quantitative Analysis*, **35**(3), 343–368.

Christopherson, J.A., Ferson, W.E. and Glassman, D.A. (1998) Conditioning manager alphas on economic information: another look at persistence in performance, *Review of Financial Studies*, **11**(Spring), 111–142.

Christopherson, J.A., Ferson, W.E. and Turner, A.L. (1999) Performance evaluation using conditional alphas and betas, *Journal of Portfolio Management*, Fall, 59–72.

Cornell, B. (1979) Asymmetric information and portfolio performance measurement, *Journal of Financial Economics*, **7**(December), 381–390.

Daniel, K., Grinblatt, M., Titman, S. and Wermers, R. (1997) Measuring mutual fund performance with characteristic-based benchmarks, *Journal of Finance*, **52**, 1035–1058.

Elton, E.J., Gruber, M.J., Das, S. and Hlavka, M. (1993) Efficiency with costly information: a reinterpretation of evidence for managed portfolios, *Review of Financial Studies*, **6**, 1–22.

Elton, E.J., Gruber, M.J. and Blake, C.R. (1996) The persistence of risk-adjusted mutual fund performance, *Journal of Business*, **69**(2), 133–157.

Ferson, W.E. and Schadt, R. (1996) Measuring fund strategy and performance in changing economic decisions, *Journal of Finance*, **51**, 425–462.

Ferson, W.E. and Warther, V.A. (1996) Evaluating fund performance in a dynamic market, *Financial Analysts Journal*, **52**, 20–28.

Grinblatt, M. and Titman, S.D. (1989a) Mutual fund performance: an analysis of quarterly portfolio holdings, *Journal of Business*, **62**(3), 393–416.

Grinblatt, M. and Titman, S.D. (1989b) Portfolio performance evaluation: old issues and new insights, *Review of Financial Studies*, **2**(3), 393–421.

Grinblatt, M. and Titman, S.D. (1993) Performance measurement without benchmarks: an examination of mutual fund returns, *Journal of Business*, **66**(1), 47–68.

Grinblatt, M. and Titman, S.D. (1994) A study of monthly mutual fund returns and performance evaluation techniques, *Journal of Financial and Quantitative Analysis*, **29**(3), 419–444.

Grinblatt, M., Titman, S.D. and Wermers, R. (1995) Momentum investing strategies, portfolio performance, and herding: a study of mutual fund behavior, *The American Economic Review*, **85**(5), 1088–1105.

Henriksson, R. and Merton, R. (1981) On market timing and investment performance. II. Statistical procedures for evaluating forecasting skills, *Journal of Business*, **54**(4), 513–533.

Jain, P.C. and Wu, J.S. (2000) Truth in mutual fund advertising: evidence on future performance and fund flows, *Journal of Finance*, **55**(2), 937–958.

Jegadeesh, N. and Titman, S.D. (1993) Returns to buying winners: implications for stock market efficiency, *Journal of Finance*, **48**(1), 65–91.

Jensen, M. (1968) The performance of mutual funds in the period 1945–1964, *Journal of Finance*, **23**, 389–416.

Jensen, M. (1969) Risk, the pricing of capital assets, and the evaluation of investment portfolios, *Journal of Business*, **42**, 167–247.

Jensen, M. (1972) Optimal utilization of market forecasts and the evaluation of investment portfolio performance, *Mathematical Methods in Investment and Finance*, G.P. Szego and Karl Shell (eds), Amsterdam, North Holland.

Lakonishok, J., Schleifer, A. and Vishny, R.W. (1992) The structure and performance of the money management industry, *Brookings Papers: Microeconomics*, 339–379.

Lehmann, B.N. and Modest, D.M. (1987) Mutual fund performance evaluation: a comparison of benchmarks and benchmark comparisons, *Journal of Finance*, **42**(2), 233–265.

Lintner, J. (1965) The valuation of risk assets and the selection of risky investments in stock portfolios and capital budgets, *Review of Economics and Statistics*, February, 13–37.

Lobosco, A. (1999) Style/risk adjusted performance, *Journal of Portfolio Management*, Spring, 65–68.

Merton, R.C. (1981) On market timing and investment performance. I. An equilibrium theory of value for market forecasts, *Journal of Business*, **54**(July), 363–406.

Modigliani, F. and Modigliani, L. (1997) Risk-adjusted performance, *Journal of Portfolio Management*, Winter, 45–54.

Roll, R. (1978) Ambiguity when performance is measured by the securities market line, *Journal of Finance*, **33**, 1051–1069.

Roll, R. (1979) A reply to Mayers and Rice, *Journal of Financial Economics*, **7**, 391–400.

Sharpe, W. (1963) A simplified model for portfolio analysis, *Management Science*, Fall, 277–293.

Sharpe, W. (1964) Capital asset prices: a theory of market equilibrium under conditions of risk, *Journal of Finance*, **19**(4), 425–442.

Sharpe, W. (1966) Mutual fund performance, *Journal of Business*, **39**, 119–138.

Sharpe, W. (1992) Asset allocation: management style and performance measurement, *Journal of Portfolio Management*, Winter, 7–19.

Treynor, J.L. (1961) Toward a theory of the market value of risky assets, unpublished manuscript.

Treynor, J.L. (1965) How to rate management of investment funds, *Harvard Business Review*, **43**, January/February, 63–75.

Treynor, J.L. and Mazuy, F. (1966) Can mutual funds outguess the market?, *Harvard Business Review*, **44**, 131–136.

Wermers, R. (2000) Mutual fund performance: an empirical decomposition into stock-picking talent, style, transaction costs, and expenses, *Journal of Finance*, **55**(4), 1655–1695.

Chapter 2

Performance evaluation: an econometric survey

GUOQIANG WANG

ABSTRACT

In this chapter, we present a survey of the various econometric methods used in the literature of performance evaluation. We discuss the statistical properties of various performance measures such as Sharpe ratio, Jensen's alpha and Treynor index, and compare these measures with Morningstar's risk-adjusted rating. This chapter also explores the relationship between performance measurement and portfolio efficiency, and analyses regression-based test procedures for performance difference. The various methods used to classify mutual funds' style and the empirical results of mutual fund from non-US nations are also examined.

2.1 INTRODUCTION

Performance evaluation (or measurement) has been a central concern in finance since the 1930s, when Cowles (1933) published his work 'Can stock market forecasters forecast?'. Recently, this topic has become even hotter. For example, the whole of the September 2000 issue of the *Journal of Financial and Quantitative Analysis* was contributed to performance measurement. It is not a surprise given the dramatic growth of the mutual fund industry. Now trillions of dollars are invested in all kinds of assets worldwide by institutional portfolio managers. From a social perspective it is important to know whether these investors as a group add value to the portfolios they manage or whether they merely generate wasteful transaction costs through their active management. At the micro level it is important to know how to select a portfolio manager with the ability to add value to the portfolio he manages. Performance evaluation seeks to address both of these issues. In particular, it studies whether superior returns can be generated by active managers who are better able to collect and interpret information that helps forecast securities returns. No matter which perspective is assumed in the research, certain econometric methods have to be applied to mutual fund data in order to detect any abnormal performance and their causes.

While there exist a few excellent surveys on performance evaluation, for example Ippolito (1993) and Grinblatt and Titman (1995), they have a different emphasis rather than the econometric one, which is our central concern in this survey.

Ippolito (1993) documented the empirical results of US mutual fund performance over a 30-year period (1962–1991). During the first half of this period, starting with the publication of Jensen and Sharpe's classical work on mutual fund performance, most research showed that mutual funds underperformed common market indexes. And it is commonly believed that mutual fund investment performance is consistent with the original version of the efficient market hypothesis that expenditures on research and trading are wasted because securities prices already reflect all available information. However, most of the empirical studies over the second half of this period contradict the hypothesis that funds' fees and expenses are wasted. They are generally consistent with the hypothesis that mutual funds are sufficiently successful in finding and implementing new information to offset their expenses. The results fit neatly into a modified version of the efficient markets hypothesis, which takes account of the simple proposition that information is not free. It is worth pointing out here that different empirical findings about performance result from different samples of mutual fund data and the econometric methods employed.

Grinblatt and Titman (1995) is the most comprehensive and incisive survey up to now on performance evaluation. Their concern is more about the foundation of modern financial economics underlying performance evaluation. The research on performance evaluation coincided with the inception of modern asset pricing theory. Jensen and Sharpe's work was based on the Capital Asset Pricing Model (CAPM). Later multi-factor pricing models or Arbitrage Pricing Theory (APT) took shape in the 1970s, and a large amount of research based on APT followed in the 1980s. Due to the unavoidable error of misspecification of any theoretical model, researchers have pursued more robust performance measures which can substantially reduce or eliminate the need of a benchmark model. To achieve this goal, more or less, the data about the funds' portfolio weights must be available. Once again, the issue of data and econometric methods come into play.

In this survey, we try to fill the gap created by the lack of a comprehensive and up-to-date summary of econometrics employed in the literature of performance evaluation. In section 2.2, the statistical properties of different performance measures, e.g. Sharpe ratio and Treynor index, are discussed. In section 2.3, a more elaborate point, mutual funds style, is explored. It is not enough to study the mutual funds in general, as the universe of mutual funds is centred on a few clusters of portfolios with similar characteristics and performance patterns. The so-called Style Analysis has become more and more popular these days and will be studied in this section. The empirical results of mutual fund performance in different countries besides the US are summarized in section 2.4 to show that performance evaluation is data-oriented. Section 2.5 concludes.

2.2 STATISTICAL PROPERTIES OF PERFORMANCE MEASURES

Mutual fund performance measures are typically based on one or more summary statistics of past performance. Measures that attempt to take risk into account incorporate a measure of historical return and a measure of historical volatility or loss. A fundamental question arises naturally associated with investment decisions; whether the statistics derived from past performance have at least some predictive content for future performance. Although there is ample evidence that past performance measures are highly imperfect predictors of expected future return, both practitioners and academics are inclined to adopt the assumption that statistics from historical frequency distributions are reliable predictors of corresponding statistics from a probability distribution of future returns, in other words, portfolio returns should follow a stationary distribution.

There are three general classes of two parameter performance measures dependent on their definition of risk. The first class includes performance measures based on total risk (volatility) of return, the Sharpe ratio (1966) and its variation belong to this category. The second class is comprised of measures based on systematic risk (beta or covariance) of return, Treynor's index (1965) and Jensen's alpha (1964) are the two most prominent examples. The third class does not require a measure of risk, for example the Cornell (1979) procedure which computes the sample mean return prior to the test period and computes the sample mean's prediction errors in the test period. Due to the unpopularity of the third class of measures, this survey will concentrate on the study of the first two classes.

2.2.1 Single comparison: Sharpe ratio, Treynor index and Jensen's alpha

Suppose we have a portfolio, i, with a return R_i. We also observe a benchmark portfolio, denoted by m, with return R_m. Let the excess return be given by $r_i = R_i - R_m$, and $\bar{r_i}$ be the sample mean excess returns. The Sharpe ratio is defined by

$$sh = \frac{\bar{r_i}}{s_i} \tag{2.1}$$

where s_i is the sample standard deviation of r_i. This ratio captures the expected excess return per unit of risk measured by volatility of excess returns. As a measure of risk, volatility is appropriate for quadratic utility or multivariate spherically symmetric returns. However, since sh is not defined relative to any particular data generating process, it has wider applicability.

Due to the use of excess returns instead of returns themselves, it is important to appreciate that the Sharpe ratio always refers to the differential between two portfolios. We can think of this differential as reflecting a self-financing investment portfolio, with the first component representing the acquired asset and the second reflecting the short position – in cash or in some other asset – taken to finance the acquisition.

In the case of i.i.d. normal returns, Miller and Gehr (1978) show that (2.1) is a biased estimator and

$$\frac{\Gamma\left(\frac{n-1}{2}\right)}{\Gamma\left(\frac{n-2}{2}\right)}\left(\frac{2}{n-1}\right)^{\frac{1}{2}}\left(\frac{\bar{r_i}}{s_i}\right) \tag{2.2}$$

is the unbiased estimator that can be employed in its place. Using a Taylor series expansion and assuming normality, Jobson and Korkie (1981) use the result,

$$E\frac{[\bar{r_i}]}{s_i} = \left(1 + \frac{3}{4T} + \frac{100}{128T^2}\right)\frac{\mu_i}{\sigma_i} \tag{2.3}$$

to construct a better estimator

$$\left(1 + \frac{3}{4T} + \frac{100}{128T^2}\right)\frac{\bar{r_i}}{s_i} \tag{2.4}$$

and show empirically that (2.4) approximates (2.2) to three significant figures even when the sample size T is as low as 12. Further, under these conditions, the asymptotic distribution of (2.4) is normal

$$N\left(\frac{\mu_i}{\sigma_i}, \frac{1}{T}\left(1+\frac{\mu_i^2}{2\sigma_i^2}\right)\right) \tag{2.5}$$

from which confidence intervals and hypothesis tests can be derived.

If one wishes to measure performance relative to a systematic measure of risk, it is essential first to establish a benchmark model against which performance should be measured. The Treynor index (Treynor, 1965) makes explicit use of the estimated systematic risk (beta) derived from the empirical version of the traditional CAPM,

$$r_{it} = \alpha_i + \beta_i r_{mt} + \varepsilon_{it} \tag{2.6}$$

where r_{it} and r_{mt} are fund and market excess return, respectively. Specifically, performance is measured by

$$Tr_i = \frac{\bar{r}_{it}}{\widehat{\beta}_i} \tag{2.7}$$

so that excess returns are divided by a systematic risk measure when evaluating performance. It is well known that $\widehat{\beta_i} = \frac{s_{im}}{s_m^2}$ in the CAPM, where s_{im} is the sample covariance between portfolio i and market portfolio, m, s_m^2 the variance of market portfolio. Similar to the case of the Sharpe ratio, Jobson and Korkie (1981) derived an approximation of unbiased estimator for the Treynor index,

$$E(Tr_i) \approx \left[1+\frac{1}{T}\left(\frac{1}{\rho_{im}^2}-1\right)+\frac{1}{T^2}\left(1-\frac{4}{\rho_{im}^2}+\frac{3}{\rho_{im}^4}\right)\right]\frac{\mu_i\sigma_m^2}{\sigma_{im}} \tag{2.8}$$

where ρ_{im}^2 is the true correlation between portfolio i and market portfolio, m. And the asymptotic distribution of the Treynor index may be derived as

$$Tr_i \sim N\left(\frac{\mu_i\sigma_m^2}{\sigma_{im}}, \frac{1}{T}\left\{\sigma_i^2+\mu_i^2\left(1-\frac{1}{\rho_{im}^2}\right)\right\}\frac{\sigma_m^4}{\sigma_{im}^2}\right) \tag{2.9}$$

While the asymptotic results are valid, they may be poor in small samples. Pedersen and Satchell (2000) derived the cumulative distribution function of the Treynor index, and thus obtained very accurate interval estimates of this index.

Based on a similar asset pricing model underlying the Treynor index, Jensen's alpha is the arithmetic difference of the portfolio's return from its expected return. In the case of the CAPM (2.6), Jensen's alpha is simply defined as the intercept term $\hat{\alpha}$.

$$\hat{\alpha} = r_{it} - \hat{\beta}_i r_{mt} \tag{2.10}$$

Consequently, its properties can be deduced by standard linear regression techniques and are well known. Fabozzi and Francis (1977) consider Jensen's alpha in a log-linear CAPM model, but concluded that the change in model specification did not change the estimate of $\hat{\alpha}$ significantly. Conner and Korajczyk (1986) examine the econometric properties of Jensen's alpha when the underlying model is a general APT. Given the standard assumptions of the multiple linear regression model such as the non-correlation between the regressors and error terms, and a multi-normally distributed error term, a consistent estimator of α can be generated from both APT and CAPM.

Since Jensen's classical work in the 1960s, Jensen's alpha has become one of the most influential performance measures. One reason for its popularity is that it is easily computed by finding the intercept in a linear regression. Second, Jensen's alpha can be interpreted as the difference between the return of the measured portfolio and the return of a passive portfolio consisting of beta units of the benchmark excess returns. Hence it explicitly puts the actively managed funds and passively managed funds such as index funds into comparison, which is one of the central topics in performance measurement.

The application of Jensen's alpha requires the specification of a benchmark, which turns out to be one of the most controversial issues in performance measurement. Up to now, the well-received performance benchmark proposed in the literature include:

1. Equally-weighted index.
2. Value-weighted index.
3. Price-weighted index.
4. Fama and French's 3-factor portfolio.
5. Carhart's 4-factor portfolio.
6. Grinblatt and Titman's 8-portfolio benchmark.
7. Ferson and Schadt's conditional expectation model.

A great amount of empirical research has concluded that the benchmark does matter in evaluating performances – see the summaries by Grinblatt and Titman (1995).

Only the first two moments of return – mean and variance are taken into account in the CAPM model, and the same is true of the above performance measures. If return distributions are asymmetric and investors value skewness, those measures may not be adequate. To alleviate the problem that may be associated with asymmetric rates of return, several researchers have developed other performance measures based on higher moments. For example, Ang and Chua (1979) constructed an excess return index using the three moment CAPM developed by Kraus and Litzenberger (1976). This index incorporates investors' preference for positive skewness of returns. Prakash and Bear (1986) developed a composite performance measure incorporating skewness based on the Kraus and Litzenberger skewness preference model. The Prakash and Bear measure has the desirable property of reducing to the Treynor index in the absence of skewness.

Stephens and Proffitt (1991) generalized the Prakash and Bear performance measure to account for any number of moments. The Stephens and Proffitt methodology is essentially the same as that of the Prakash and Bear except the Stephens and Proffitt measure was developed from Rubinstein's (1973) n parameter pricing model rather than from Kraus and Litzenberger's three moment CAPM. The Stephens and Proffitt measure reduces to the Prakash and Bear measure in the two moment case. Stephens and Proffitt (1991) apply their measure to evaluate the performance of 27 internationally diversified mutual funds. They note that higher moment performance measures seem to be appropriate for evaluating international mutual fund portfolios, as they empirically find that the distributions of fund returns are not symmetric.

2.2.2 Industry practice: Morningstar's risk-adjusted rating

In the financial markets of United States, the most popular performance measure is neither the Sharpe ratio nor Jensen's alpha, rather the 'risk-adjusted rating' (RAR) produced by Morningstar Inc. The popularity of Morningstar's measure justifies a separate subsection in this survey to discuss its property. To calculate its ratings, Morningstar first classifies funds into one of four categories: domestic equity, international equity, municipal bond and taxable bond. For each category, more narrow peer groups are defined. In mid-1997, for example, there were 20 domestic equity categories, nine international equity categories, five municipal bond categories and ten taxable bond categories. The risk-adjusted rating (RAR) is calculated by subtracting a measure of the fund's relative risk (*Rrisk*) from a measure of its relative return (Rr_i):

$$RAR = Rr_i - Rrisk_i \tag{2.11}$$

$$= \frac{r_i}{Br_{g(i)}} - \frac{risk_i}{Brisk_{g(i)}} \tag{2.12}$$

Each of the relative measures in (2.7) for a fund is computed by dividing the corresponding measure for the fund by a denominator that is used for all the funds in a specified peer group, which will be explained later. Morningstar computes four sets of star ratings: the first three cover the last 3, 5 and 10 years, but the most popular (overall) measure is based on a combination of the 3-, 5- and 10-year results.

Morningstar's measure of a fund's return is the difference between the cumulative value obtained by investing \$1 in the fund over the period, VR_i, and the cumulative value obtained by investing \$1 in US T-bills, VR_b.

$$r_i = VR_i - VR_b \tag{2.13}$$

The denominator used to calculate the relative returns is obtained through two steps. First, the returns for all the funds in a group, $g(i)$, are averaged. If the result is greater than the increase in value that would have been obtained with T-bills, the group average is used. Otherwise, the growth in value for T-bills is used. Thus,

$$Br_{g(i)} = \max\{E_{i \in g(i)}[r_i], VR_b - 1\} \tag{2.14}$$

and

$$Rr_i = \frac{r_i}{Br_{g(i)}} \tag{2.15}$$

To measure a fund's risk, Morningstar first computes the fund's excess return (ER) for each month by subtracting the return on a short-term T-bill from the fund's return. Next, it converts all the positive monthly excess returns to zeros. Finally, it takes a simple mean of the resulting 'monthly losses' and reverses the sign to give a positive number. Thus,

$$risk_i = -E_t[\min_t\{ER_{it}, 0\}] \tag{2.16}$$

The result is defined as a measure of the fund's 'average monthly loss'. The base used to calculate the relative risk for all the funds in a group is simply the average of all the risk measures for the funds in that group:

$$Brisk_{g(i)} = E_{i \in g(i)}[risk_i] \tag{2.17}$$

Morningstar ranks the RARs for all the funds in a peer group. Funds that fall in the top 10% of the resulting distribution receive five stars; those in the next 22.5% get four, the next 35% get three, the next 22.5% get two, and the bottom 10% get one.

Unfortunately, the properties of RAR statistics are complex, and it is impossible to derive their distribution analytically even if the funds' returns are assumed to be i.i.d. normal cross-sections and over time. Because RARs represents the difference between two relative values, each of which can be considered to equal the result obtained by raising (one plus the geometric mean return) to the Tth power, where T is the number of months in the overall period, we can only approximate such statistics through some more traditional ones.

Rearranging equation (2.7) gives

$$RAR = \frac{1}{Br_{g(i)}}\left(r_i - \frac{Br_{g(i)}}{Brisk_{g(i)}} \cdot risk_i\right) \tag{2.18}$$

Note that $\frac{1}{Br_{g(i)}}$ and $\frac{Br_{g(i)}}{Brisk_{g(i)}}$ are the same for all the funds in a given group. From the perspective of investors in that group, the above two terms can be regarded as constants. Thus, the statistic property of RAR mainly depends on r_i and $risk_i$. To begin, consider return r_i. Denote G as the sample geometric mean return,

$$r_i = (1 + G_i)^T - (1 + G_b)^T \tag{2.19}$$

A close approximation for the geometric mean of a series is given by subtracting one-half of the sample variance s^2 from the sample arithmetic mean, A. Thus,

$$r_i \simeq \left(1 + A_i - \frac{s_i^2}{2}\right)^T - \left(1 + A_b - \frac{s_b^2}{2}\right)^T \tag{2.20}$$

Under the normal distribution, A and s^2 follow the normal and chi-square distribution, respectively, but we do not know the exact distribution of the term, $(1 + A - \frac{s^2}{2})^T$.

Letting $p(x)$ be the probability of the state of the world x and ER_{ix} be the excess return on fund i in state x, then $risk_i$ for fund i is defined as

$$risk_i = -\sum_x p(x) \cdot \min\{ER_{ix}, 0\} \tag{2.21}$$

Interestingly, this formula reminds us of the option pricing formula. Using a relationship given in Triantis and Hodder (1990), it can be shown that for a normal distribution, we can get a close formula for $risk_i$ which is very close to the Black–Scholes formula,

$$risk_i = s_i \cdot \phi(-z) - (A_i - R_b) \cdot \Phi(-z) \tag{2.22}$$

where

$$z = \frac{A_i - R_b}{s_i} \tag{2.23}$$

$$R_b = \text{the known risk–free interest rate} \tag{2.24}$$

$$\phi() = \text{the standard normal density function} \tag{2.25}$$

$$\Phi() = \text{the standard cumulative normal distribution function} \tag{2.26}$$

In short, RAR is a non-linear function of sample mean and variance. It is shown in Sharpe (1998) that the relationship between RAR and A_i is monotonic and close to linear in some given region ($A_i \in [3\%, 10\%]$, $s_i \in [10\%, 20\%]$).

Because Morningstar's measure does not assume any asset pricing model, we can compare it with the Sharpe ratio. Morningstar's measure is best suited to answer questions posed by an investor who places all of his or her money in one fund. The excess-return Sharpe ratio is best suited to answer questions posed by an investor who allocates money to one fund and also to borrowing or lending. When an investor decides to allocate his or her money into a portfolio of funds, neither Morningstar's measure nor the excess-return Sharpe ratio is an appropriate performance measure. The reason is simple: when evaluating the desirability of a fund in a multi-fund portfolio, the relevant measure of risk is the fund's contribution to the total risk of the portfolio. This contribution will depend on the fund's total risk and, more importantly in most cases, on its correlations with the other funds in the portfolio. Neither the Morningstar RAR measure nor the Sharpe ratio incorporates any information about correlations. Therefore, excessive reliance on either measure for selecting funds could seriously diminish the effectiveness of the resulting multi fund portfolio. Rather, Jensen's alpha can be utilized in the correlation case to be explained later.

In a recent study by Blake and Morey (1999), it is found that low ratings from Morningstar generally indicate relatively poor future performance. Second, there is little statistical evidence that Morningstar's highest-rated funds outperform the next-to-highest and median-rated funds. Third, Morningstar ratings, at best, do only slightly better than the alternative predictors in forecasting future fund performance.

2.2.3 Misspecification and errors-in-variables

Despite the popularity of Jensen's alpha, critics point to two faults, measurement error and specification error. Measurement error is due to benchmark error and error structures arising from non-synchronous trading. Previously, the errors resulting from non-synchronous trading appeared to be the most serious when securities were traded infrequently and at low prices so that price changes tend to occur in discrete intervals.

Recently, the opposite is the case, as funds trade much more frequently than before. Goetzmann, Ingersoll and Ivković (2000) address the bias associated with parametric measurement of market timing skill based on monthly returns when timers can make daily timing decisions. Simulations suggest that the standard parametric measure of timing skill is weak and biased downward when applied to the monthly returns of daily times. They proposed an adjustment that mitigates this problem without the need to collect daily returns. Even after adjustment, their empirical tests show that very few funds exhibit statistically significant timing skill.

Benchmark error has been identified by Roll (1978) and is still a contentious issue. Roll argued that according to CAPM, all portfolios should lie on the security market line, and any observed deviation (abnormal performance) may well be nothing but measurement error due to improper selection of the benchmark. He showed that two benchmark portfolios lying inside the mean-variance efficient frontier could reverse the rankings of a group of passive portfolios. On the other hand, a benchmark portfolio that is mean-variance efficient cannot distinguish between passive portfolios. Passive portfolios, like all securities, lie on the security market line in this case.

Statistically, benchmark error is a version of the errors-in-variables problems and is due to using incorrectly measured variables or proxy variables in regression models. Several approaches can be employed to correct for the errors-in-variables problems and to obtain consistent estimates and their standard errors. These approaches include grouping methods, direct and reverse regression methods and methods with latent variables, which have been summarized in Maddla and Nimalendran (1996). In the performance literature, Rahman, Fabozzi and Lee (1991) applied direct and reverse regression methods to derive upper and lower bounds for Jensen's alpha based on CAPM. However, the extension to APT proves to be hard and requires further research.

Specification error, on the other hand, arises from adopting the wrong functional form in the model. Failure to use the correct functional form may result in bias in estimating the parameters of the model. A recent study by Kothari and Warner (1998) pointed out the misspecification in performance measurement could be astonishing. They calculated standard mutual fund performance measures, using simulation procedures combined with random and random-stratified samples of NYSE and AMEX securities and then tracking simulated fund portfolios over time. These portfolios' performance is ordinary, and well-specified performance measures should not indicate abnormal performance. Regardless of the performance measure used, there are indications of abnormal fund performance, including market-timing ability, when none exists.

Fabozzi, Francis and Lee (1980) employed Box and Cox's transformation technique to correct the potential misspecification in CAPM. Jagannathan and Korajczyk (1986) proposed two methods of testing the specification of performance measurement models, which explores the fact that the misspecification most likely causes a non-linear relation between fund returns and regressors in model (2.6). The first test is the White (1980) test on linearity that involves looking at the difference between the OLS and WLS parameters. The second test is to include additional variables (specifically, non-linear transformations of some of the regressors). If the model is linear, then the regression coefficient on the additional variables should be close to zero. Neither test was reported to have higher relative power in this chapter.

2.2.4 Performance measurement and portfolio efficiency

Most empirical studies of fund performance indicate that both outperformance and underperformance are common phenomena. Given this, it is natural to ask whether the difference in performance is statistically significant. There are two ways to test this proposition: the first test, which has been well documented in Grinblatt and Titman (1995), is to test whether the past performance of a mutual fund is a good indicator of its future performance. The second is to simultaneously estimate the regression models for each fund return and to jointly test the restriction that their Jensen's alphas are equal to each other.

$$H_0\colon \alpha_1 = \alpha_2 = \ldots = \alpha_k \tag{2.27}$$

This test does not quantify differential performance. It merely rejects or fails to reject the hypothesis that all funds have the same risk-adjusted returns. However, this test relates closely to the issue of portfolio efficiency and has profound implications for optimal portfolio selection.

To set the stage, define r_{it} the fund return, $i = 1, \ldots, N$, $t = 1, \ldots, T$. Each fund return is modelled by a CAPM-like regression model,

$$r_{it} = \alpha_i + \beta_i r_{mt} + \varepsilon_{it} \tag{2.28}$$

It is assumed that the disturbances ε_{it} are independent over time and jointly normally distributed, each period, with mean zero and non-singular cross-sectional covariance matrix Σ, conditional on the vector of market returns r_m. If we modify (2.27) a little bit

$$H_0\colon \alpha_1 = \alpha_2 = \ldots = \alpha_k = 0 \tag{2.29}$$

this is exactly the null hypothesis about the efficiency of the benchmark portfolio m in the system of (2.28). To test hypothesis (2.29), Gibbons, Ross and Shanken (1989) derive the F-statistic with degrees of freedom N and $T - N - 1$, which equals $(T - N - 1)N^{-1}(T - 2)^{-1}$ times the Hotelling T^2 statistic

$$Q = T\hat{\alpha}'\hat{\Sigma}^{-1}\hat{\alpha}/[1 + \bar{r}_m^2/s_p^2] \tag{2.30}$$

where $\bar{r}_m^2$ and s_p^2 are the sample mean and standard deviation of market excess return; $\hat{\alpha}$ is the N-vector of OLS intercept estimates and $\hat{\Sigma}$ is the unbiased estimate of Σ, computed from cross-products of OLS residuals divided by $T - 2$.

In the language of performance measurement, $\hat{\alpha}$ and $\bar{r}_m/s_p$ are the sample Jensen's alpha and Sharpe ratio. These interpretations of tests for mean-variance efficiency in terms of performance measures can be found in Gibbons, Ross and Shanken (1989), and Jobson and Korkie (1982, 1984, 1989). More interestingly, the Hotelling T^2 statistic can easily be interpreted as the percentage increase in squared Sharpe ratios scaled by T. As Q in equation (2.30) equals

$$T[sh(*)^2 - sh(m)^2]/[1 + sh(m)^2] \tag{2.31}$$

where $sh(*)$ is the sample Sharpe ratio with maximum squared value over all portfolios. Examining the numerator of (2.31), other things being equal, the larger the F-statistic is, the lower is the squared Sharpe ratio for benchmark portfolio m in relation to the maximum squared sample ratio. Thus, the F-statistic is large when m is much worse performing than *ex post* minimum variance portfolio.

From equation (2.31), the F-statistic is distributed, under the alternative, as non-central F with non-central parameter

$$\lambda = T[s\hat{h}(*)^2 - s\hat{h}(m)^2]/[1 + s\hat{h}(m)^2] \tag{2.32}$$

In this context, $s\hat{h}(m)$ may be viewed as a constant, and hence the non-central parameter in (2.32) is just the population counterpart of the sample statistic, Q, in (2.30). Under the null hypothesis that m is a minimum-variance portfolio, m attains the maximum squared *ex ante* ratio. In this case, λ equals zero and we have a central F distribution as earlier. In other words, there is no difference in performance among all the funds if the benchmark portfolio is mean-variance efficient.

In order to implement the F-test, the residual covariance matrix $\hat{\Sigma}$ must be invertible, which requires that N be at most equal to $T - 2$. Analysis in Gibbons, Ross and Shanken (1989) suggest that much smaller values of N should be used in order to maximize power, however. That is related to the fact that the number of covariances that must be estimated increases rapidly with the number of assets. Grinblatt and Titman (1989) obtain a similar conclusion.

Given the OLS estimates of the regression parameters in (2.6) and the initial mean-variance efficient portfolio of the benchmark m, it is straightforward to determine the new optimal portfolio weights – see DeRoon and Nijman (2001). The new optimal portfolio weights are determined by the vector of Jensen's alphas, the Sharpe ratio of the benchmark and the covariance matrix of the residuals of the OLS regression of r_i on each element of the efficient benchmark portfolio m. If there is only one fund, its weight in the new optimal portfolio will increase with the fund's Jensen's alpha.

2.3 MUTUAL FUNDS STYLE

Today's investors face the large and growing number of mutual funds available in the financial marketplace. For example, by reading fund names equity funds range from 'aggressive growth' funds holding low-dividend, high-growth stocks to 'income' funds seeking high-dividend equities. However, it is not enough to determine the funds style from their name and/or objective statement. Style analysis of mutual funds is an important tool to help investors to characterize differences between funds, and has received considerable attention from both the financial practitioners and academics.

2.3.1 Mutual fund misclassification

Mutual fund classes are one way for investors searching for the 'right' fund to simplify their decision making. In addition to allowing investors to tailor their choice of mutual funds to their own risk-acceptance levels and income needs, the classification system also allows financial institutions, mutual fund data vendors and individual investors to rate objectively the performance of mutual funds within their respective categories, thus avoiding comparisons between apples and oranges.

Classification systems for US equity funds group most funds according to either their investment objectives, such as the growth, or the type of assets in which they concentrate their investments, as in the case of small-capitalization funds. For example, in Morningstar's classification system, the objective dimension consists of value, blend and growth while the asset dimension includes large, medium or small capitalization.

Under the present classification system, many equity funds exhibit behaviour that is inconsistent with that of their class. DiBartolomeo and Witkowski (1997) regress a fund's returns against the returns of the various objective indices and classify the fund as belonging to the objective group whose index provides the best fit. The objective group indices are equal weighted returns of all funds in that objective group. The process of fund classification and objective indices calculation is iterated until every objective index consists of funds that are actually classified into that objective group. Their results suggest that 9% of all equity funds are seriously misclassified and another 31% are somewhat misclassified. Two factors emerge as the most likely reasons for misclassification:

1. The ambiguity of the current classification system.
2. Competitive pressures in the mutual fund industry and compensation structures that reward relative performance.

Mutual funds managers can game on benchmark assets by investing in securities that are not in accordance with their stated investment objective or style.

Brown and Goetzmann (1997) focus on the question of whether fund classifications are useful in providing benchmarks for evaluating historical fund performance and in explaining differences in future returns among funds. Like DiBartolomeo and Witkowski (1997), they conclude that the current classification system is inefficient in answering these questions. For instance, growth funds typically break down into several categories that differ in composition and strategy. Monte Carlo simulations on out-of-sample data show that this misclassification has a significant effect on investors' ability to build diversified portfolios of mutual funds. They propose a generalized style classification method, a variation on the switching regression technique, in which funds are assigned to style classes based on the sensitivity of their returns to eight factors selected by the authors.

Indro *et al.* (1998) examine a sample of 770 actively managed funds in a recent 3-year period. Their results indicate that style consistency is far from the norm for many funds. Funds that changed both style strategies were the worst-performing group. Funds that changed one strategy did no better than style-consistent funds, where performance was also not uniform. Compared to the S&P 500, value-large-cap stock funds were the most mean-variance efficient style-consistent funds.

Chan, Chen and Lakonishok (1999) also provide some examples of inconsistent styles. Particularly, funds with poor past performance are more likely to change styles. When funds deviate from the benchmark they are more likely to favour growth stocks with good past performance. Other evidence suggests that growth funds have better style-adjusted performance than value funds. These results are not sensitive to style identification procedures.

Besides using historical fund returns, Kim, Shukla and Tomas (2000) employ discriminant analysis and classify funds based on their attributes (characteristics, investment style and risk/return measures). They find that the stated objectives of more than half the funds differ from their attributes-based objectives, and over one-third of the funds are severely misclassified. However, contrary to the reports in the financial press, they do not find that mutual funds are gaming their objectives, i.e. deviating from their stated objectives to earn a higher relative performance ranking.

2.3.2 Return-based style analysis

In order to avoid misclassification, Sharpe (1988, 1992) has proposed an econometric technique to determine the mutual fund's investment style which only requires a time series of historical fund returns. This technique involves a constrained regression that uses several asset classes to replicate the historical return pattern of a portfolio. The basic econometric framework is the following:

$$r_{it} = \alpha_i + \beta_{i1} f_1 + \beta_{i2} f_2 + \ldots + \beta_{iK} f_K + \varepsilon_{it}, \quad i = 1, \ldots, M \qquad (2.33)$$

where r_{it} denotes the mutual fund i return at time t, f_k is the asset class factor, β_{ik} is a factor loading that expresses the sensitivity of the fund return to the factor-mimicking portfolio return f_k. Compared with the standard least squares estimation, we impose two extra constraints on parameters βs:

$$\sum_{j=1}^{K} \beta_{ij} = 1, \quad \forall i \qquad (2.34)$$

$$\beta_{ij} \geq 0, \quad \forall i, j \qquad (2.35)$$

The constraints are imposed to enhance an intuitive interpretation of the coefficients. First to interpret the coefficients as style weights within a portfolio, the coefficients (factor loadings) are required to add up to one. Second, coefficients should be positive to reflect the short-selling constraints most fund managers are subject to. A quadratic programming technique is proposed to derive point estimates for the style weights. The ultimate idea is to check whether the estimated style weights correspond with the targeted investment style of the mutual fund.

A crucial ingredient that may heavily affect the outcome of return-based style analysis is the choice of appropriate factors. While Sharpe (1992) uses a detailed 12-asset class factor model, simpler models often yield more sensible results, for instance in Lobosco and DiBartolomeo (1997). This is because many routinely selected factor-mimicking market indexes are highly correlated and often are prima facie likely to be linear combinations of other indexes. Thus the following prerequisites should be met before any reliable results can be obtained. First, the factors should be mutually exclusive. Second, they should not be linear combinations of other factors. A way to control for this possible problem is to look at cross-correlations and standard deviations. If correlations between specific factors are too high, we could consider dropping some of them to diminish multi-collinearity problems.

Another shortcoming in Sharpe's style analysis is the fact that only point estimates of the style exposure have been reported, ignoring the information that is available in the distribution of the parameter estimates. A practical reason is that the style weights need to meet particular constraints and deriving their distribution is not a straightforward task. Lobosco and DiBartolomeo

(1997) use the jackknife technique to isolate the portion of one market index's returns that are independent of the other market indexes used in the style analysis. Then the approximate standard deviation of style weights can be derived using Taylor's expansion, which increases with the standard error of the style analysis, and decreases with the number of fund returns and the independence of one market index from the other market indexes used in the style analysis. Monte Carlo simulation, verifies the efficacy of their procedure to some degree.

Similarly, Otten and Bams (2000b) proposed a technique that is a combination of the Kuhn–Tucker algorithm and Monte Carlo simulation. The principle behind the Kuhn–Tucker algorithm lies in the treatment of the inequality constraints on the style weights (coefficients). When a particular constraint is non-binding then its estimator is equal to the OLS estimator. When the particular constraint is binding then its estimator is equal to the Lagrange estimator. Beforehand it is not known which constraints will be binding and which will be non-binding. Therefore the estimators for all possible combinations of binding and non-binding restrictions are considered and the combination that leads to the lowest residual sum of squares and also meets all constraints leads to the optimal estimate. Empirical tests on a sample of UK equities funds demonstrate that the number of misclassified funds decreases by about 50% if the statistical significance of these style deviations is taken into account.

Unfortunately, the above methods are valid only in the special case in which none of the true style coefficients are zero or one, and there are often cases in practice where zero or unit coefficient values appear plausible. Kim, Stone and White (2000) apply recently developed results for obtaining confidence intervals in constrained regression and the Bayesian approach to the constrained normal linear regression model, to obtain statistically valid asymptotic precision measures for style coefficients, regardless of their true values. Monte Carlo simulation demonstrates that the finite sample property of asymptotic measures is reasonably satisfactory.

A more profound debate is whether all the constraints imposed in Sharpe's style analysis are reasonable. The portfolio and positivity constraints imposed by style analysis are useful in constructing mimicking portfolios without short positions. Such mimicking portfolios can be used, e.g., to construct efficient portfolios of mutual funds with desired factor loadings if the factor loadings in the underlying factor model are positively weighted portfolios. Under these conditions style analysis may also be used to determine a benchmark portfolio for performance measurement. Attribution of the returns on portfolios of which the actual composition is unobserved to specific asset classes on the basis of return-based style analysis is attractive if moreover there are no additional cross-exposures between the asset classes and if fund managers hold securities that on average have a beta of one relative to their own asset class. On the other hand, DeRoon, Nijman and Horst (2000) argue that if such restrictions are not met, and in particular if the factor loadings do not generate a positively weighted portfolio, the restrictions inherent in return-based style analysis distort the outcomes of standard regression approaches rather than improve the analysis. For example, whether the optimal weights of the portfolios with desired exposure are inconsistent or not depends on which regression is used, constrained or unconstrained.

Besides the return-based style analysis, there exists another approach, the so-called characteristics-based style analysis which uses actual portfolio constituents as input. One example is Daniel *et al.* (1997). They develop benchmarks based on the characteristics of stocks held by the portfolios that are evaluated. Specifically, the benchmarks are constructed from the returns of 125 passive portfolios that are matched with stocks held in the evaluated portfolio on the basis of the market capitalization, book-to-market and prior-year return characteristics of those stocks. Based on these benchmarks, 'Characteristic Timing' and 'Characteristic Selectivity' measures are developed that detect, respectively, whether portfolio managers successfully time their portfolio weights on these characteristics and whether managers can select stocks that outperform the average stock having the same characteristics. Their results show that mutual funds, particularly aggressive-growth funds, exhibit some selectivity ability, but that funds exhibit no characteristic timing ability.

Because up-to-date holdings of mutual funds are often not available, characteristics-based style analysis is not so popular as return-based style analysis.

2.4 INTERNATIONAL EMPIRICAL RESULTS OF PERFORMANCE

Most performance measurement models were developed from US data. In order to mitigate any data mining bias and ensure an objective assessment of these theories, it is a valuable exercise to study managed funds in other countries. So far, there have been many empirical studies on mutual funds in non-US nations.

Blake and Timmerman (1998) used a large sample containing the complete return histories of 2300 UK open-ended mutual funds over a 23-year period to measure UK fund performance. They found some evidence of underperformance on a risk-adjusted basis by the average fund manager, persistence of performance and the existence of a substantial survivor bias. Similar findings have been reported for US equity mutual funds. New findings not previously documented for non-US markets include evidence that mutual fund performance varies substantially across different asset categories, especially foreign asset categories. They also identified some new patterns in performance related to the funds' distance from their inception and termination dates: underperformance intensifies as the fund termination date approaches, while, in contrast, there is some evidence that funds (weakly) outperform during their first year of existence.

Dahlquist, Engström and Söderlind (2000) studied the relation between fund performance and fund attributes in the Swedish market. Performance is measured as the alpha in a linear regression of fund returns on several benchmark assets, allowing for time-varying betas. The estimated performance is then used in a cross-sectional analysis of the relation between performance and fund attributes such as past performance, flows, size, turnover and proxies for expenses and trading activity. The results show that good performance occurs among small equity funds, low fee funds, funds whose trading activity is high and, in some cases, funds with good past performance.

Horst, Nijman and de Roon (1998) found that Dutch mutual funds mainly investing in Netherlands equity show relative outperformance of the passive portfolio of indices reflecting the mutual fund's investment style. Moreover, the same group of funds provide an extension of the mean-variance efficient investment set for Dutch investors, even after taking short sales restrictions into account, indicating that a domestic market effect might be present.

Otten and Bams (2000a) gave an overview of the European mutual fund industry and investigated mutual fund performance using both unconditional and conditional asset-pricing models. The performance of European equity funds is investigated using a survivorship bias controlled sample of 506 funds from the five most important mutual fund countries: France, Germany, Italy, the Netherlands and the United Kingdom. This is done using the Carhart (1997) 4-factor asset-pricing model with factor-mimicking portfolio for size, book-to-market and stock price momentum. The overall results suggest that European mutual funds, and especially small cap funds, are able to add value, as indicated by their positive after cost alphas. If management fees are added back, four out of five countries exhibit significant outperformance at an aggregate level. Finally, they detected strong persistence in mean returns for funds investing in the UK. The strategy of buying last year's winners and selling last year's losers yields a return of 6.08% per year, which cannot be explained by common factors in stock returns.

Hallahan and Faff (1999) examined the market timing ability of a segment of the Australian investment fund industry, namely, equity trusts, over the period 1988–1997. The approach followed involves running both quadratic excess returns market model and dual-beta excess returns market model regressions. In addition, some specification tests are applied. The results suggest that for their sample over the period examined, there is little evidence of market timing ability. Further, there is no clear dominance of one market timing model over the other. They did find, however, that a cubic market model specification does fit the data quite well for nearly one-third of their sample.

Recent empirical evidence has suggested that the Japanese mutual fund industry has underperformed dramatically over the past two decades. Conjectured reasons for underperformance range from tax-dilution effects to high fees, high turnover and poor asset management, which are challenged by Brown *et al.* (1998). They show that this underperformance is largely due to tax-dilution effects and not necessarily to poor management. Using a broad database of funds which includes investment trusts closed to new investment, it is concluded that once an instrument for the time-varying tax-dilution exposure is included in a factor model, there is little evidence of poor risk-adjusted performance. A style analysis of the industry demonstrates that managers appear to pursue tax-driven dynamic strategies.

From the above empirical results of fund performance in other developed countries, it seems that the methodology developed mainly for US mutual funds can be readily passed on to studying data from developed countries. This is not a surprise as modern financial theory originated from developed financial markets which become more and more integrated and similar.

2.5 CONCLUSION AND FUTURE RESEARCH

The purpose of this survey is to summarize the econometric methods employed in the literature of performance measurement. The most often used technique is linear regression, from the single regressor case of CAPM to the multi-regressor case of APT and other linear factor pricing models. A great amount of valuable insights about mutual fund performance have been gained from these simple models.

On the other hand, even though regression is one of the most mature area in econometrics, its application in performance measurement is still limited. The statistical property of performance measures and style weights are more asymptotic than in terms of small sample. This is a huge deficiency given that usually only monthly fund returns are available to academics. Even for 10-year periods, there are only 120 observations which are extremely small compared to the frequency of other financial time series.

Non-parametric methods may also be worth exploring. Only few papers discuss non-parametric analysis of performance measurement. Pesaran and Timmermann (1994) show that the Henriksson–Merton (1981) test of market timing is better interpreted as an exact test of independence within a 2×2 contingency table in which the column and row sums are fixed. Considering the serious misspecification issues found in parametric performance models, more similar research should be done.

Undoubtedly, performance evaluation is a data-oriented and -intensive exercise. In the early days, fund returns were the only input of the performance evaluation models. Now, a full set of fund characteristics is also available, such as its portfolio holding, tenure, management fee, trading frequency, and so on. There has been some work on incorporating all this fund information to determine fund performance, by using different data mining techniques such as decision tree and meta analysis. Due to the scope of this survey, they will be covered in a future update.

REFERENCES

Ang, J.S. and Chua, J.H. (1979) Composite measures for the evaluation of investment performance, *Journal of Financial and Quantitative Analysis*, **14**, 361–384.

Blake, D. and Timmermann, A. (1998) Mutual fund performance: evidence for the UK, *European Finance Review*, **2**, 57–77.

Blake, C.R. and Morey, M.R. (1999) Morningstar ratings and mutual fund performance, *Journal of Financial and Quantitative Analysis*, **35**, 451–483.

Brown, S. and Goetzmann, W. (1997) Mutual fund styles, *Journal of Financial Economics*, **43**, 373–399.

Brown, S., Goetzmann, W. Hiraki, T. Otsuki, T. and Shiraishi, N. (1998) The open-end Japanese mutual fund puzzle, NBER Working Paper 6347.

Carhart, M. (1997) On persistence in mutual fund performance, *Journal of Finance*, **52**, 57–82.

Chan, L.K.C., Chen, H.L. and Lakonishok, J. (1999) On mutual fund investment styles, working paper, NBER.

Connor, G. and Korajczyk, R. (1986) Performance measurement with the arbitrage pricing theory: a new framework for analysis, *Journal of Financial Economics*, **15**, 374–394.

Cornell, B. (1979) Asymmetric information and portfolio performance measurement, *Journal of Financial Economics*, **7**, 381–390.

Cowles, A. (1933) Can stock market forecasters forecast?, *Econometrica*, **1**, 309–325.

Dahlquist, M., Engström, S. and Söderlind, P. (2000) Performance and characteristics of Swedish mutual funds, *Journal of Financial and Quantitative Analysis*, **35**, 409–423.

Daniel, K., Grinblatt, M., Titman, S. and Wermers, R. (1997) Measuring mutual fund performance with characteristic-based benchmarks, *Journal of Finance*, **52**, 1035–1058.

DeRoon, F. and Nijman, T. (2001) Testing for mean-variance spanning: a survey, *Journal of Empirical Finance*, **8**, 111–155.

DeRoon, F. Nijman, T. and Horst, J.R. (2000) Evaluating style analysis, working paper, Tilburg University.

DiBartolomeo, D. and Witkowski, E. (1997) Mutual fund mis-classification: evidence based on style analysis, *Financial Analysts Journal*, Sept./Oct., 32–37.

Fabozzi, F. and Francis, J. (1977) Stability tests for alphas and betas over bull and bear market conditions, *Journal of Finance*, **32**, 1093–1099.

Fabozzi, F., Francis, J. and Lee, C. (1980) Generalized functional form for mutual fund returns, *Journal of Financial and Quantitative Analysis*, **15**, 1107–1120.

Gibbons, M., Ross, S. and Shanken, J. (1989) A test of the efficiency of a given portfolio, *Econometrica*, **57**, 1121–1152.

Goetzmann, W.N., Ingersoll, J. and Ivković, Z. (2000) Monthly measurement of daily timers, *Journal of Financial and Quantitative Analysis*, **35**, 257–290.

Grinblatt, M. and Titman, S. (1989) Mutual fund performance: an analysis of quarterly portfolio holdings, *Journal of Business*, **62**, 97–112.

Grinblatt, M. and Titman, S. (1995) Performance evaluation in *Handbook in Operations Research and Managements Science*, Vol. 9, *Finance*, Elsevier, 581–609.

Hallahan, T.A. and Faff, R.W. (1999) An examination of Australian equity trusts for selectivity and market timing performance, *Journal of Multinational Financial Management*, **9**, 387–402.

Henriksson, R.D. and Merton, R.C. (1981) On market timing and investment performance. II. Statistical procedures for evaluating forecasting skills, *Journal of Business*, **54**, 513–533.

Horst, J.R., Nijman, T. and DeRoon, F. (1998) Style analysis and performance evaluation of Dutch mutual funds, working paper, Tilburg University.

Indro, D.C., Jiang, C.X., Hu, M.Y. and Lee, W.Y. (1998) Mutual fund performance: a question of style, *Journal of Investing*, **7**, 46–53.

Ippolito, R. (1993) On studies of mutual fund performance, 1962–1991, *Financial Analyst Journal*, Jan./Feb., 42–50.

Jagannathan, R. and Korajczyk, R. (1986) Assessing the market timing performance of managed portfolios, *Journal of Business*, **59**, 217–235.

Jensen, M.C. (1964) The performance of mutual funds in the period 1945–1964, *Journal of Finance*, **23**, 389–416.

Jobson, J.D. and Korkie, B. (1981) Performance hypothesis testing with the Sharpe and Treynor measures, *Journal of Finance*, **36**, 889–908.

Jobson, J.D. and Korkie, B. (1982) Potential performance and tests of portfolio efficiency, *Journal of Financial Economics*, **10**, 433–466.

Jobson, J.D. and Korkie, B. (1984) On the Jensen measure and marginal improvements in portfolio performance: a note, *Journal of Finance*, **39**, 245–251.

Jobson, J.D. and Korkie, B. (1989) A performance interpretation of multivariate tests of asset set intersection, spanning, and mean-variance efficiency, *Journal of Financial and Quantitative Analysis*, **24**, 185–204.

Kim, M., Shukla, R. and Tomas, M. (2000) Mutual fund objective misclassification, *Journal of Economics and Business*, **52**, 309–323.

Kim, T.-H., Stone, D. and White, H. (2000) Asymptotic and Bayesian confidence intervals for Sharpe style weights, discussion paper, University of Nottingham.

Kothari, S. and Warner, J. (1998) Evaluating mutual fund performance, working paper, MIT.

Kraus, A. and Litzenberger, R.H. (1976) Skewness preference and the valuation of risk assets, *Journal of Finance*, **31**, 1085–1100.

Lobosco, A. and DiBartolomeo, D. (1997) Approximating the confidence intervals for Sharpe style weights, *Financial Analysts Journal*, July/Aug., 80–85.

Maddala, R. and Nimalendran, J. (1996) Errors-in-variables problems in finance, *Handbook of Statistics*, Vol. 14, North-Holland.

Miller, R.E. and Gehr, A.K. (1978) Sample size bias and Sharpe's performance measure: a note, *Journal of Financial and Quantitative Analysis*, **12**, 943–946.

Otten, R. and Bams, D. (2000a) European mutual fund performance, working paper, Maastricht University.

Otten, R. and Bams, D. (2000b) Statistical tests for return-based style analysis, working paper, Maastricht University.

Pedersen, C.S. and Satchell, S.E. (2000) Small sample analysis of performance measures in the asymmetric response model, *Journal of Financial and Quantitative Analysis*, **35**, 425–450.

Pesaran, M. and Timmermann, A. (1994) A generalization of the non-parametric Henriksson–Merton test of market timing, *Economics Letters*, **44**, 1–7.

Prakash, A.J. and Bear, R.M. (1986) A simplifying performance measure recognizing skewness, *The Financial Review*, **21**, 135–144.

Rahman, S., Fabozzi, F. and Lee, C. (1991) Errors-in-variables, functional form, and mutual fund returns, *Quarterly Journal of Economics and Business*, **31**, 24–35.

Roll, R. (1978) Ambiguity when performance is measured by the securities market line, *Journal of Finance*, **33**, 1051–1069.

Rubinstein, M.E. (1973) The fundamental theorem of parameter-preference security valuation, *Journal of Financial and Quantitative Analysis*, **8**, 61–69.

Sharpe, W.F. (1966) Mutual fund performance, *Journal of Business*, **39**, 119–138.

Sharpe, W.F. (1988) Determining a fund's effective asset mix, *Investment Management Review*, **2**, 59–69.

Sharpe, W.F. (1992) Asset allocation: management style and performance measurement, *Journal of Portfolio Management*, **46**, 7–19.

Sharpe, W.F. (1998) Morningstar's risk-adjusted ratings, *Financial Analysts Journal*, 21–33.

Stephens, A. and Proffitt, D. (1991) Performance measurement when return distributions are nonsymmetric, *Quarterly Journal of Business and Economics*, **30**, 23–41.

Triantis, A.J. and Hodder, J.E. (1990) Valuing flexibility as a complex option, *Journal of Finance*, **45**, 549–564.

Treynor, J.L. (1965) How to rate management of investment funds, *Harvard Business Review*, **43**, 63–75.

Wermers, R. (2000) Mutual fund performance: an empirical decomposition into stock-picking talent, style, transactions costs, and expenses, *Journal of Finance*, **55**, 1655–1696.

White, H. (1980) Using least squares to approximate unknown regression functions, *International Economic Review*, 149–170.

Chapter 3

Distribution of returns generated by stochastic exposure: an application to VaR calculation in the futures markets

EMMANUEL ACAR AND ANDREW PEARSON

ABSTRACT

Stochastic exposures are frequently encountered in the world of finance. For instance, corporate companies are faced with uncertain cash flows in a tendering situation. Active investors also change their exposure to the market according to their anticipations. In other words, the directional views are captured by the changing weights over the period. The market timing ability is best rendered by the performance returns, which are the result of the by-product between the stochastic exposure and the market returns. Our goal here is not to forecast the excess returns generated by active timers but rather to highlight the commonality of uncertain exposure and its effect on Value at Risk calculations, both theoretically and empirically, in the futures markets. Examples of stochastic weights are chosen from popular strategies used by traders. They encompass both discrete and continuous distributions of cash flows. Raw calculations using the absolute value of end of day positions grossly underestimate Value at Risk. The error is largest at the 99% confidence level, where it is the most needed, because of lack of historical information. Considering instead that profits and losses follow a normal distribution provides more accurate calculations. However, treating the cash flow as a stochastic variable has the potential to improve further Value at Risk calculations. In the case of continuous exposures, the improvement is marginal and subject to the perfect knowledge of the distribution of market returns.

In the case of simple discrete exposure(s), the distribution of the uncertain cash flow can be worked out *ex ante* using analytical results independent of the underlying markets. We show that incorporating such information drastically improves Value at Risk calculations.

3.1 INTRODUCTION

When market risk is calculated, it gives the loss in value of a portfolio over a given holding period with a given confidence level. This calculation assumes that the composition of the portfolio does not change during the holding period. However, variable exposures are frequent in the world of finance and real life examples can be found within corporations, banking or asset management. Corporate companies are faced with uncertain cash flows in a tendering situation. Imagine a company that plans to make a bid of a specified amount of units in a foreign currency to acquire another firm domiciled in the foreign country. It may not be desirable for the takeover company to hedge the potential currency exposure. Indeed if the takeover is not accepted the optimal strategy retrospectively was to do nothing. However, if the takeover was certain full hedging should have been recommended. Takeover-contingent foreign exchange call options have been priced (Kwok, 1998: 104–107). A more general problem consists in modelling the uncertain cash flows such that an optimal hedging strategy can be designed *ex ante*. Brown and Toft (2001) derive optimal hedging strategies using vanilla derivatives (forwards and options) and custom 'exotic' derivative contracts for a value-maximizing firm that faces both price and quantity risks. They find that optimal hedges depend critically on price and quantity volatilities, the correlation between price and quantity, and profit margin.

Within banking, Jorion (2001) notes that traders change positions actively during the trading day whereas Value at Risk (VaR) is measured over a one-day horizon assuming that the current positions are 'frozen' over that time span. Despite this, he observes that empirical results for eight large banks indicate that on a quarterly basis VaR measures offer strongly significant predictions of the variability of trading revenues. Berkowitz and O'Brien (2001) independently compare, for a sample of six large dealer banks, daily VaR data as reported to regulators against subsequent trading profits. They find that VaR estimates tend to be conservative; that is, too high. The problem acknowledged in both papers is that the profits and losses refer to broad trading income including both the revenues generated by market-making activities and proprietary trading. The income generated by the purchase and sales of trading instruments on behalf of clients tends to be smoother than proprietary directional bets. A good illustration is provided by the Bankers Trust 1994 annual report reproduced in Chew (1996: 210). On the one hand, the statistical significance of the trading profits reported in both papers, Jorion (2001) and Berkowitz and O'Brien (2001), tend to be extremely high as measured by the T-statistics which roughly vary between 3.8 and 22. On the other hand, a pure directional bet is considered as very successful when the T-statistic reaches 2. This can be seen by studying the performance of alternative investments over long periods of time (see Managed Account Reports[1]). Although interesting, studies on banking profits can be difficult to interpret. Indeed, a too high VaR estimate may reflect a change of management policy rather than a methodology issue. Implementing corrective actions when directional losses start to develop is not uncommon.

Within asset management, there is a growing literature which modelizes the effect of stochastic weights within portfolios. Directional trading rules are typical examples of strategies affecting the distribution of return (Acar and Satchell, 1998). Extension of this work and its relevancy to hedge fund management has been investigated by Lundin and Satchell (2000). Generalization to active fund management and relative returns has been recently formulated in Hwang and Satchell (2001).

The purpose of this chapter is to highlight the direct effect of uncertain exposures on Value at Risk calculations both theoretically and empirically. Whereas corporations' cash flows are difficult to analyse for confidentiality reasons and banking profits are unfiltered, we have chosen to concentrate our examples on popular strategies used by active investors and directional traders. They encompass both discrete and continuous distributions of cash flows. The market timing ability is best rendered by the performance returns, which are the result of the by-product between the stochastic exposure and the market returns. Deans (2000) provides numerous examples of profit and loss calculation for backtesting. He especially recommends the use of profit and loss histograms to detect if the distribution is approximately normal, skewed, fat-tailed or if it has other particular features. This is why section 3.2 discusses the distribution of performance returns when the exposure is stochastic. Section 3.3 quantifies the implications for Value at Risk calculations. Section 3.4 illustrates trading returns in the futures markets. Section 3.5 summarizes our findings and proposes new avenues for future research.

3.2 DISTRIBUTION OF PERFORMANCE RETURNS

It is clear that no money manager or trader has control over the market returns denoted X. The best a trader can do is to time his entry and exit

[1] http://www.marhedge.com/

in the market via his exposure, labelled B (long, squared or short). In other words, the directional views are captured by the changing weights over the period. The market timing ability is best rendered by the performance returns $Z = BX$. Our goal here is not to forecast the excess returns generated by active timers but rather to quantify the risk taken by active money managers under the random walk assumption. Then we will assume no forecasting ability, which implies that active timing either based on discretion or trading rules cannot generate profits above and beyond the buy-and-hold returns. In statistical terms, this means that there is independence between the exposure B and the forthcoming returns X. Despite violating the inner purpose of using a forecasting strategy, the random walk assumption is nevertheless useful in giving us a proxy for VaR calculations. Indeed, it is critical for performance returns to include several different contributions other than those related to market risk measurement, namely leverage and timing.

We are interested in establishing the distribution of the performance returns resulting from the product of two independent random variables. B, the stochastic exposure, follows either a discrete or continuous distribution. X, the market returns, is supposed in this section to follow a normal distribution with mean μ_x and volatility σ_x .

3.2.1 Discrete exposure

Let's suppose that the exposure $B = \begin{cases} 0 & \text{with probability} \quad p_0 \\ b_1 & \text{with probability} \quad p_1 \\ b_2 & \text{with probability} \quad p_2 \\ \vdots & \\ b_n & \text{with probability} \quad p_n \end{cases}$

with $\sum_{i=0}^{n} p_i = 1,\ p_i \geq 0,\ i = 0, \ldots, n$ and $b_i \neq 0,\ i = 1, \ldots, n$

In this case, the performance returns $Z = BX$ satisfy:

$$\text{Prob}[Z < z] = \sum_{i=1}^{n} p_i \Phi\left(\frac{z - b_i \mu_x}{|b_i| \sigma_x}\right) \quad \text{if } z < 0$$

$$\text{Prob}[Z = 0] = p_0$$

$$\text{Prob}[Z < z] = p_0 + \sum_{i=1}^{n} p_i \Phi\left(\frac{z - b_i \mu_x}{|b_i| \sigma_x}\right) \quad \text{if } z > 0$$

where Φ is the cumulative function of a normal distribution $N(0, 1)$.

Two examples are given below. Their practical relevancy and economic justification are postponed to section 3.3.

$$B = \begin{cases} -1 & \text{with probability} \quad 0.363879 \\ -1/3 & \text{with probability} \quad 0.136121 \\ +1/3 & \text{with probability} \quad 0.136121 \\ +1 & \text{with probability} \quad 0.363879 \end{cases} \tag{3.1}$$

$$B = \begin{cases} 0 & \text{with probability} \quad 0.5 \\ 1 & \text{with probability} \quad 0.5 \end{cases} \tag{3.2}$$

3.2.2 Continuous exposure

If a trader follows a very large number of strategies, the resulting exposure may well be approximated by a normal distribution. This could also include the case of corporates tendering the markets. A good example is provided by the car industry where the sale of a car can be assimilated as a 'mini' tender to market. We still assume that the market returns X follow a normal distribution with mean μ_x and volatility σ_x and the exposure B follows a normal distribution with mean μ_b and volatility σ_b. Cornwell, Aroian and Taneja

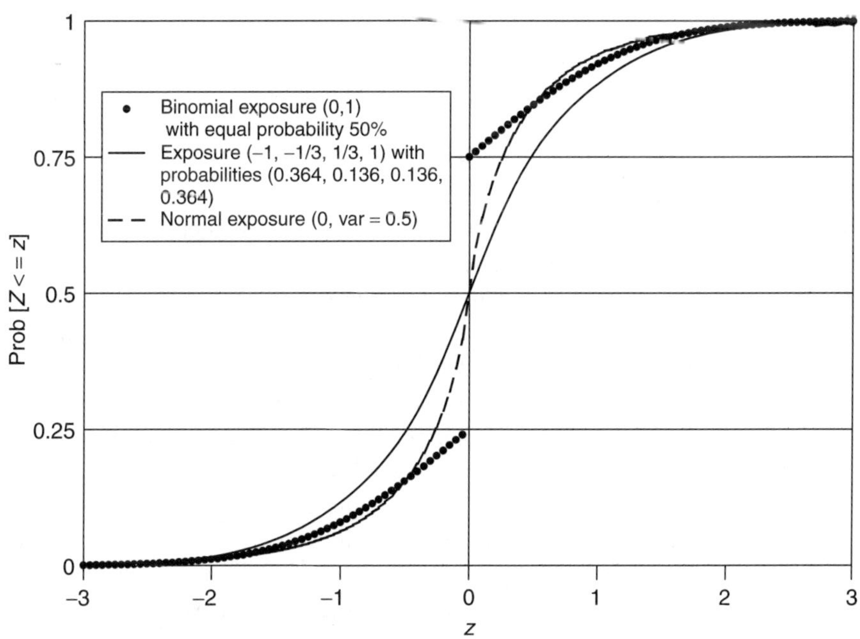

Figure 3.1 Cumulative function of performance returns

(1978) provide an algorithm to numerically evaluate the distribution of the product of two normal variables $Z = BX$. Their findings take into account possible non-zero correlation between the two variables B and X. It's worthwhile noting that when both $\mu_x = \mu_b = 0$, the variable Z is nothing else than the covariance between two normal variables over a sample of two observations. The exact distribution can be found in Johnson, Kotz and Balakrishnan (1995: 600, formula 36.120). When $\sigma_x = \sigma_b = 1$, this is a modified Bessel function of the second kind.

Figure 3.1 highlights the cumulative function of the Z variable for both types of exposure B: discrete as given by formulations (3.1) and (3.2), or normal with zero mean and variance equal to 0.5. This also assumes that the market returns follow a standardized normal distribution with mean zero and unit standard deviation.

3.3 IMPLICATIONS FOR VAR CALCULATIONS

The performance returns $Z = BX$ do not usually follow a normal distribution when the exposure B is stochastic even if the market returns, X, are generated by a normal distribution. This has potentially large implications on the way VaR is calculated. VaR is a single number estimate of how much a trader can lose due to the price volatility of the instrument he holds. VaR is usually reported at the 95% level of confidence meaning that there is only a 5% chance that the portfolio will fall by more than the VaR. Let's recall that the 'Exact' VaR at the critical level of α is given by the quantile c_α^E which is deduced from the equality $\text{Prob}[Z < c_\alpha^E] = 1 - \alpha$.

When the theoretical quantile is not known, risk managers tend to use either empirical estimates or crude calculations labelled as the normal assumption or raw method. With the normal assumption, the risk manager simply believes that the distribution of performance returns follows a normal distribution with mean zero and variance σ_z^2. Then the VaR at the critical level of α is equal to: $c_\alpha^N = \sigma_z\, q_{1-\alpha}$ where $q_{1-\alpha}$ is the $(1 - \alpha)$ quantile of a standardized normal distribution. For instance, if $\alpha = 95\%, q_{1-\alpha} = q_{5\%} = -1.645$. With the raw method, the risk manager calculates every day the VaR as being proportional to the market's exposure. Over long period of time and assuming constant market volatility, the average VaR is just: $c_\alpha^R = E(|B|)\, q_{1-\alpha}\sigma_x$.

VaR can always be formulated as a coefficient of proportionality to the underlying market volatility and that is the convention adopted in this chapter. If we look at an investor being exposed to the euro against dollar exchange rate and the underlying currency market's volatility is 10%, a VaR of −1.2 at a confidence level of 95% will mean that there is only a 5% chance that the portfolio will fall by more than −12% (= −1.2*10%).

Table 3.1 Analytical value at risk

Confidence	Basket exposure (1)			Binomial exposure (2)			Normal exposure (3)		
	Exact	Normal	Raw	Exact	Normal	Raw	Exact	Normal	Raw
95%	−1.49	−1.57	−1.35	−1.28	−1.47	−0.82	−1.13	−1.47	−0.93
96%	−1.60	−1.68	−1.43	−1.41	−1.58	−0.88	−1.26	−1.58	−0.99
97%	−1.74	−1.81	−1.54	−1.55	−1.72	−0.94	−1.43	−1.72	−1.06
98%	−1.92	−1.99	−1.68	−1.75	−1.91	−1.03	−1.68	−1.91	−1.16
99%	−2.20	−2.27	−1.90	−2.05	−2.19	−1.16	−2.11	−2.19	−1.31

Table 3.1 compares the three VaR, Exact, Normal and Raw, when the markets X follow a standardized normal distribution, with zero drift and unit variance, and the exposure B is stochastic as given by examples (1) to (3). It is interesting to note that the raw calculations systematically underestimate the true VaR because this fails to capture the stochastic nature of the exposure. The normal assumption is far less damaging but still systematically overstates risk especially when the exposure follows a continuous distribution. Note that approximating the performance returns by a normal distribution makes indistinguishable the binomial exposure of type (2) and the continuous exposure of type (3).

The Bank for International Settlements' requirement for calculation of regulatory capital is a 99% confidence interval (Basel Committee, 1996). In practice, most organizations use a confidence level of 95% or/and 99% for their in-house requirements (Hawkins, 2000). This is why the rest of this chapter will concentrate on only these two VaR numbers.

3.4 ACTIVELY TRADING THE FUTURES MARKETS

Futures contracts are probably the best financial markets to investigate the effect of stochastic weights. Low transaction costs allow high frequency of trades. The ability to short the market is also a key feature of active timers. We have chosen to restrain ourselves to the currency markets for the numerous real life examples of uncertain exposure which can be found there: active hedging, technical trading and tendering situations, among others. We now detail the trading process and dataset used to illustrate both discrete and continuous exposures.

3.4.1 Discrete exposure

According to Managed Account Reports, a tracking agency which reports the performance of alternative investments, most of the futures funds are managed by systematic traders (around two-thirds) while discretionary traders constitute the remainder. Systematic traders primarily rely on trading programmes or models that generate buy and sell signals.

The simplest rule of this family is the single moving average which says: when the rate penetrates from below (above) a moving average of a given length m, a buy (sell) signal is generated. If the current price is above the m-moving average, then it is left long, otherwise it is held short. Lequeux and Acar (1998) recall that most commodities trading advisers (CTAs) do not trade a single strategy but rather allocate capital to a few. The authors then show that single moving averages of length 32, 61 and 117 can be used to replicate the portfolio of trading rules followed by CTAs. Furthermore, Acar and Lequeux (2001) work out the exposure's probability under the assumption of a normal random walk without drift using well-known results on orthant probabilities. They find that there is a 36.3879% chance that the price is above (or below) three moving averages, therefore generating a long (short) position of $+(-)100\%$. There is a 13.6121% chance that the price is above only two moving averages out of three, corresponding to a long position of $33.33\% = (2-1)/3$. There is also a 13.6121% chance that the price is above only one moving average out of three, implying a short position of $-33.33\% = (1-2)/3$. If a proprietary trader or currency fund manager applies this portfolio of trading rules in the futures markets for which underlying returns are denoted X, he will exhibit performance returns $Z = BX$ where B is given by equation (3.1).

An even simpler example of discrete stochastic exposure is given by an active currency overlay programme. For the sake of clarity, we consider a yen-based investor being long of dollar assets. The benchmark is unhedged. Then a forecasting strategy is used to predict the dollar against yen move. This could be based on technical trading rules or on exogenous information such as fundamental variables. The only thing we know is that up and down forecasts are expected with equal probability.[2] Then if a long dollar position is triggered, the investor sticks to its unhedged benchmark. On the other hand, if a short dollar position is generated, the investor decides to hedge his position and therefore buy the Futures contracts, quoted in reciprocal terms, which earns returns X for the period. In other words, the relative performance or excess returns over the benchmark is simply equal to $Z = BX$ where B is given by equation (3.2).

[2]For illustrative purposes we have used the single moving average of length 117 days to generate the signals. Under the normal random walk without drift assumption, the VaR numbers should remain the same as long as buy and sell signals are generated with the same probability. It is only if the trading rule generates significant profits that the VaR number is likely to be different (smaller).

Table 3.2 Daily returns 21 July 1983 to 15 February 2001

Currency contracts	EUR	JPY	GBP	CHF	CAD
Average	0.0004%	0.0027%	0.0066%	−0.0040%	−0.0010%
Standard deviation	0.712%	0.726%	0.683%	0.778%	0.298%
Skewness	0.16	0.71	0.07	0.17	−0.24
Kurtosis	2.20	8.00	3.68	2.03	4.61
Minimum	−3.31%	−4.21%	−4.48%	−3.99%	−2.25%
Maximum	4.83%	8.27%	4.55%	4.97%	1.99%

Table 3.2 displays the summary statistics of the daily futures contracts. The first available contract has been chosen and rollover implemented on the day before last expiration. More precisely, we study the main five contracts: euro (Eur), Japanese yen (Jpy), pound sterling (Gbp), Swiss franc (Chf), and Canadian dollar (Cad). All these contracts are quoted in reciprocal terms; that is, dollar value of one foreign currency unit. Prior to 10 December 1999, the Deutschmark futures contracts had been used as a proxy for the euro.

Figures 3.2 to 3.7 provide VaR estimates for both trading strategies as a function of the methodology being used. All the results have been standardized by the underlying market volatility such that they can be compared. Our goal here is not to assess how easy or difficult it is to predict market volatility but rather assuming the market volatility to be known, what are the consequences of stochastic exposure? In addition to the empirical estimate, we indicate the

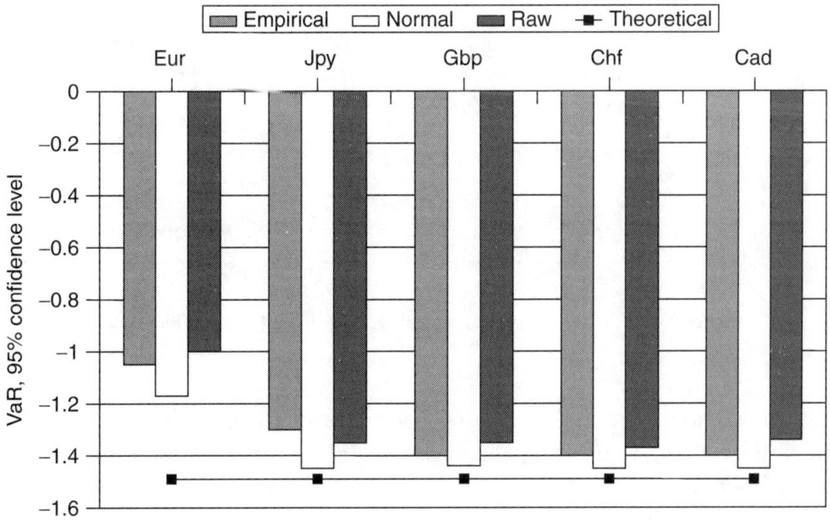

Figure 3.2 Basket of moving averages, 95% confidence level

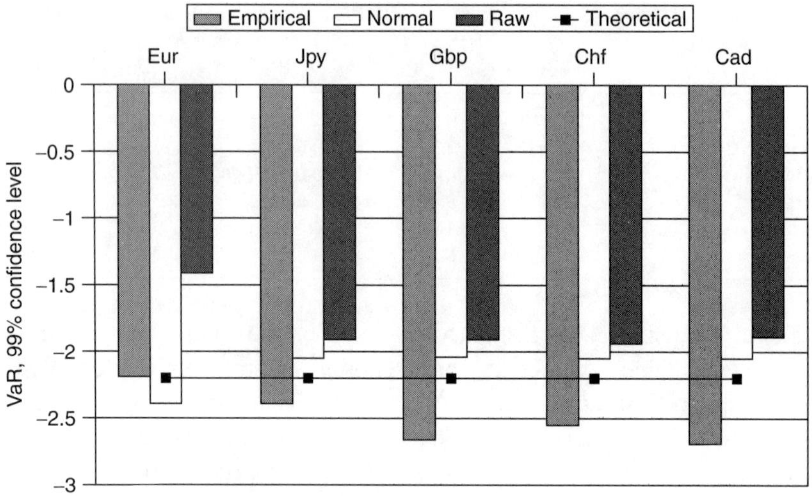

Figure 3.3 Basket of moving averages, 99% confidence level

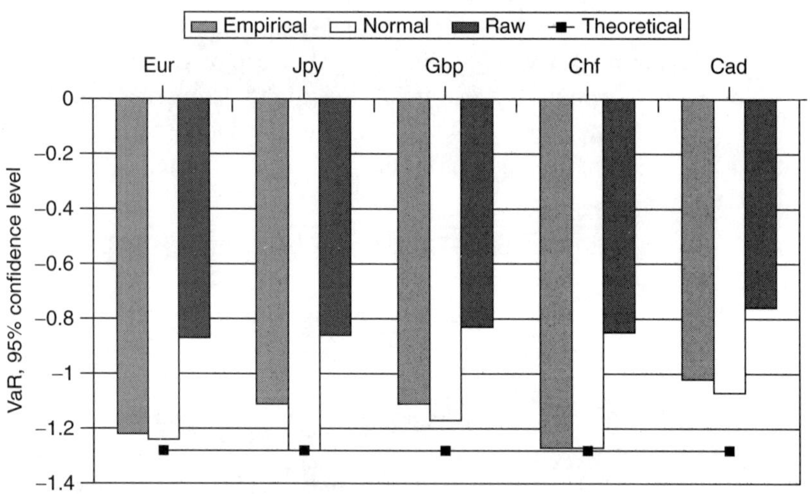

Figure 3.4 Binomial overlay, foreign currency base, 95% confidence level

raw calculations, the assumption of normal profits and losses as well as the theoretical distribution of the stochastic weights. The latter approach outperforms the others at the 99% confidence level and it is increasingly obvious the more the distribution of profits and losses departs from the normal assumption (binary weights). The raw calculations uniformly underestimate risk.

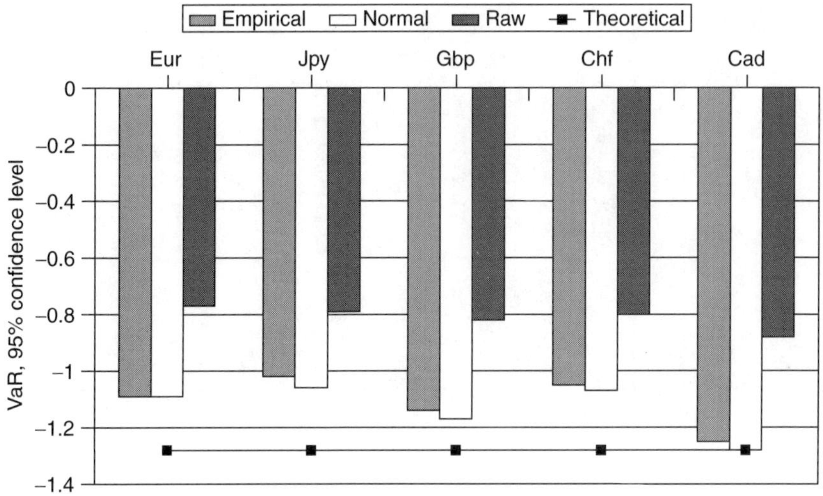

Figure 3.5 Binomial overlay, US dollar currency base, 95% confidence level

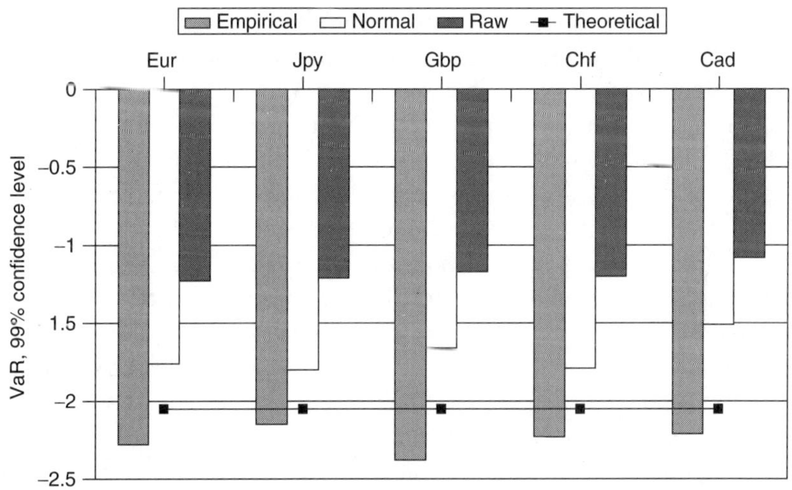

Figure 3.6 Binomial overlay, foreign currency base, 99% confidence level

3.4.2 Continuous exposure

Sometimes, traders combine technical trading rules with their fundamental view of the markets and the resulting trading process can no longer be formalized. In other words these money managers do not follow a predetermined forecasting strategy but rather watch a multitude of indicators including chartism, economics and flows. Then they might decide to leverage their

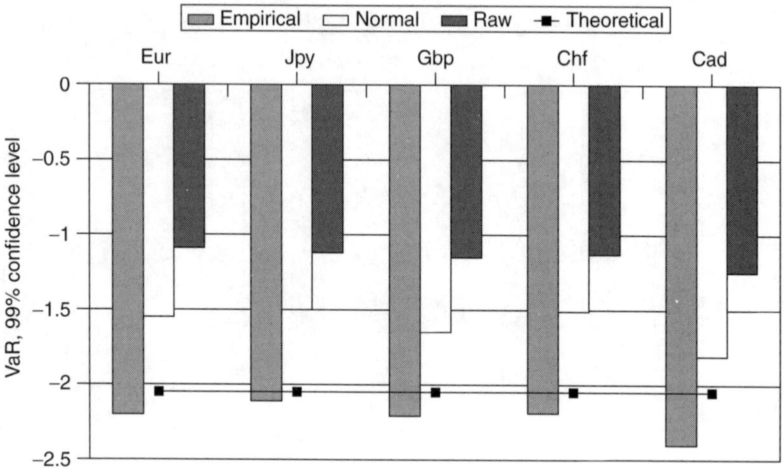

Figure 3.7 Binomial overlay, US dollar currency base, 99% confidence level

positions according to the cumulative score reached by adding the individual output/exposure initiated by each of the variables. A good proxy may well be provided by the commitments of traders' reports.[3] All of a trader's reported futures positions in a commodity are classified as commercial if the trader uses futures contracts in that particular commodity for hedging as defined in the Commission's regulations. Then we may see the total net commercial position as an aggregate of individual overlay programmes. The non-commercial activity regroups, among others: proprietary traders, commodity trading advisers and commodity pool operators,[4] many of whom apply some kind of trading rules. Therefore this will encompass a complex generalization of trend-following strategies. Table 3.3 indicates summary statistics on the net (long minus short) positions of both commercial and non-commercial traders reported on a weekly basis. The euro contract is not reported because for over a year the Deutschmark contract was traded in parallel rendering difficult the interpretation of individual volume. Compared to previous simulations, we added the Australian dollar contract. Distributions are rather normal with very little skewness and kurtosis. Such a cash flow is therefore best modelled by continuous stochastic exposures.

The VaR generated by the open positions of both commercial and non-commercial traders are indicated in Figures 3.8 to 3.11. All the figures have been standardized by dividing by the product of market and quantity volatility.

[3]http://www.cftc.gov/cftc/cftccotreports.htm

[4]Statistics breaking down non-commercial positions have been analysed in the crude oil, heating oil and gasoline futures markets (Weiner, 1999).

Table 3.3 Weekly net positions 30 September 1992 to 27 March 2001

	Jpy		Gbp*		Chf		Cad		Aud	
	Non commercial	Commercial	Non commercial	Commercial	Non commercial	Commercial	Non commercial	Commercial	Non commercial	Commercial
Average	−13,966	22,075	−414	1,053	−6,024	10,281	−2,009	−4,451	−472	436
Standard deviation	21,248	30,523	13,060	19,609	14,981	22,143	13,388	18,493	4,693	7,654
T-statistic	−13.85	15.24	−0.66	1.11	−3.47	9.78	−3.16	−5.07	−2.10	1.19
Minimum	−66,697	−62,162	−40,297	−54,307	−52,472	−59,113	−38,022	−69,983	−10,202	−29,916
Maximum	53,902	87,361	43,779	52,210	44,644	60,386	45,809	40,667	20,329	14,800
Kurtosis	−0.12	−0.48	0.17	−0.56	−0.04	−0.56	0.57	0.38	2.43	1.26
Skewness	0.41	−0.50	0.18	−0.19	0.13	−0.31	0.25	−0.38	0.71	−0.55

*Starting date = 26 January 93.

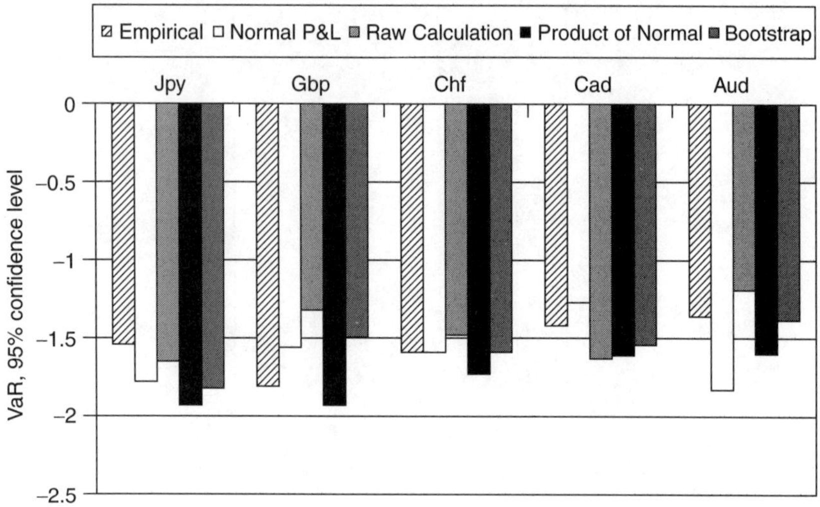

Figure 3.8 Non-commercial positions, 95% confidence level

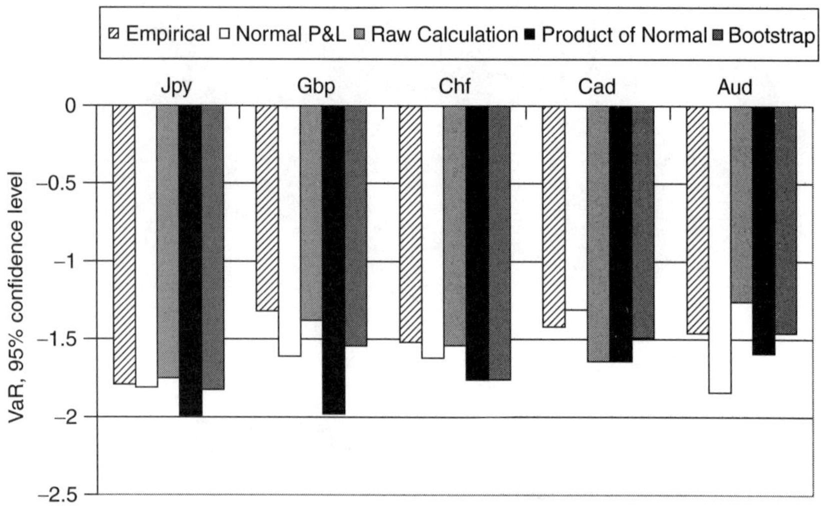

Figure 3.9 Commercial positions, 95% confidence level

Empirical values give the quantiles actually observed whereas the raw and normal profit and loss illustrate alternative VaR calculations as explained in section 3.3. 'Product of Normal' stands for the exact quantile value under the assumption that both market and exposure follow independent normal distributions with known means and variances. To understand how the shapes of individual distributions, flows and markets, affect the overall VaR, we used

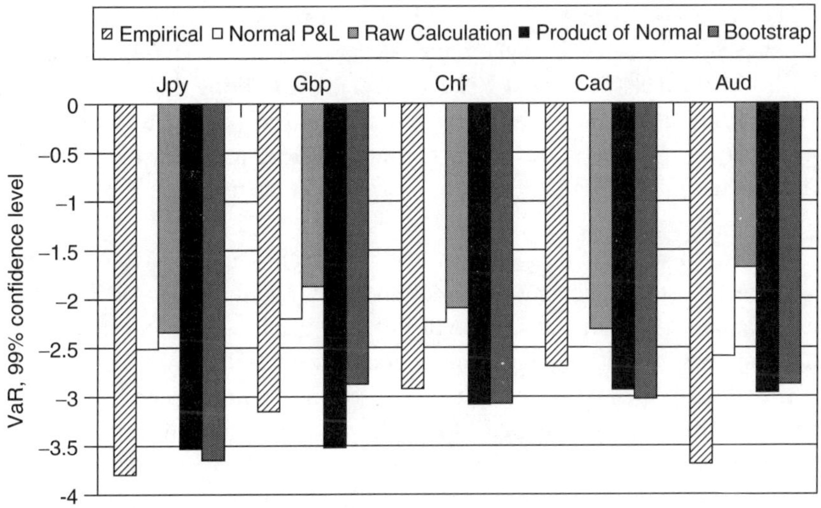

Figure 3.10 Non-commercial positions, 99% confidence level

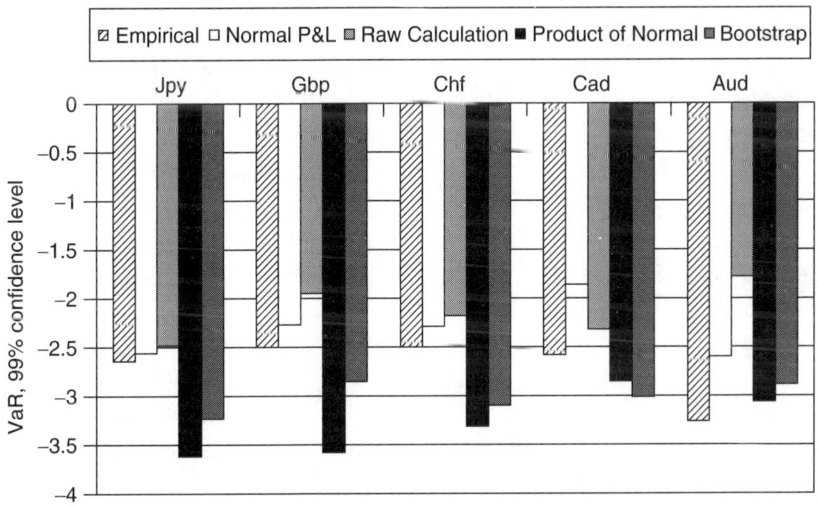

Figure 3.11 Commercial positions, 99% confidence level

a bootstrap methodology. Both flows and market returns were bootstrapped without replacement and independently. The VaR was then averaged over 200 similar simulations. These results are given for purpose of completeness only since they are only marginally closer to the empirical observations. This may well be due to the 'insight' nature of the bootstrap methodology and could exhibit little predictive power.

The raw methodology as expected by our theoretical results underestimates the true VaR. At the 99% level, empirical VaR are on average 60% higher than the crude estimates and up to 100% (higher). Considering that the profits and losses follow a normal distribution provides mixed results: underestimation of risk at the 99% level, reversing to slight overestimation at the 95% level. The product of two normal distributions tends to overestimate risk across the board.

Whereas it is clear that the raw methodology is unacceptable, choosing between the other calculations is not straightforward. When the number of observations is low, the tails of the distribution cannot be easily estimated and the 'empirical' quantiles may be inaccurate given the lack of historical information. It may then be tempting to suppose that the profits and losses follow a normal distribution and extrapolate the corresponding quantile. Standard deviation of returns requires far fewer observations to be properly measured than extreme quantiles. In other words, the confidence interval of the standard deviation estimator is a lot smaller than the extreme quantiles. The analytical results assuming that both market and exposure follow a normal distribution are also attractive but this supposes that the parameters are known. In real life such a methodology will require the estimation of four parameters against one for the normal assumption of profits and losses. It is therefore possible that degree of accuracy is inversely related to the number of parameters having to be estimated.

3.5 CONCLUSION

The purpose of this chapter has been to highlight the existence of uncertain exposure and its effect on Value at Risk calculations both theoretically and empirically in the futures markets. In many instances such as active trading or tender's situations, the exposure itself is uncertain. Raw calculations using the absolute value of end of day positions grossly underestimate value at risk. The error is the largest at the 99% level, where it is the most needed because of lack of historical information. Considering instead that the profits and losses follow a normal distribution provides more accurate calculations. However, treating the cash flow as a stochastic variable has the potential to improve further Value at Risk calculations. Very often, exposure is uncertain and cannot be easily modelled *ex ante*, or requires a large number of parameters to achieve a sufficient fit. In that instance, the difficulty in precisely estimating the parameters specifying the uncertain exposure may well overcome the potential gains. Nevertheless this chapter has shown that there are real life cases where the exposure follows a simple discrete distribution and parameters can be accurately estimated *ex ante*. The clearest example has been given by the use of popular trading rules. In that case, the distribution of the uncertain exposure can be worked out using analytical results independent of the underlying markets. Incorporating such information improves drastically VaR calculations while reducing the degrees of freedom. The results are especially conclusive when using the Bank for International Settlements' requirement of a 99% confidence interval. The rarer the extreme events, the harder it will be to make accurate predictions using empirical observations. The importance of theoretical modelling grows the closer the confidence interval is to 100%.

ACKNOWLEDGEMENTS

We would like to thank Stephane Knauf for useful discussion on the relevance of uncertain exposures within corporate treasuries and Eu-Jin Ang for helpful comments

REFERENCES

Acar, E. and Satchell, S.E. (1998) The portfolio distribution of directional strategies, in E. Acar and S.E. Satchell (eds), *Advanced Trading Rules*, Butterworth-Heinemann, Oxford, 103–111.

Acar, E. and Lequeux, P. (2001) Pursuing the debate on active currency management, *Journal of Alternative Investment*, Spring, **3**(4), 9–28.

Basel Committee on Banking Supervision (1996) Supervisory framework for the use of 'Backtesting' in *Conjunction with the Internal Models Approach to Market Risk Capital Requirements*, Basel, Switzerland: BIS, No. 22.

Berkowitz, J. and O'Brien, J. (2001) How accurate the Value-at-Risk models at commercial banks, working paper, Board of Governors of the Federal Reserve System.

Brown, G.W. and Toft, K.B. (2001) How firms should hedge, working paper, University of North Carolina.

Chew, L. (1996) *Managing Derivative Risks: The Use and Abuse of Leverage*, Wiley, London.

Cornwell, L.W., Aroian, L.A. and Taneja, V.S. (1978) Numerical evaluation of the distribution of the product of two normal variables, *The Journal of Statistical Computation and Simulation*, **7**(2), 123–132.

Deans, M. (2000) Backtesting, in M. Lore and L. Borodovsky (eds), *The Professional's Handbook of Financial Risk Management*, Butterworth-Heinemann, Oxford, 261–289.

Hawkins, I. (2000) Choosing appropriate VaR model parameters and risk-measurement methods, in M. Lore and L. Borodovsky (eds), *The Professional's Handbook of Financial Risk Management*, Butterworth-Heinemann, Oxford, 111–151.

Hwang, S. and Satchell, S.E. (2001) VaR versus Tracking Error, the strengths and weaknesses of two performance measures, in E. Acar (ed.), *Added Value in Financial Institutions, Risk or Return?*, Pearson, UK, 13–28.

Johnson, N.L., Kotz, S. and Balakrishnan, N. (1995) *Continuous Univariate Distributions*, Volume 2, Wiley, New York.

Jorion, P. (2001) How informative are Value-at-Risk disclosures, working paper, University of California at Irvine.

Kwok, Y.K. (1998) *Mathematical Model of Financial Derivatives*, Springer-Verlag, Singapore.

Lequeux, P. and Acar, E. (1998) A dynamic index for managed currencies funds using CME currency contracts, *European Journal of Finance*, **4**(4), 311–330.

Lundin, M. and Satchell, S.E. (2000) The long and the short of it, *Risk Magazine*, August, 94–98.

Weiner, R.J. (1999) Sheep in wolves' clothing? Speculators and price volatility in petroleum markets, working paper, George Washington University.

Chapter 4

A dynamic trading approach to performance evaluation

GAURAV S. AMIN AND HARRY M. KAT

ABSTRACT

In this chapter we introduce explicit dynamic trading strategies as a tool for performance evaluation. The advantage of using dynamic trading strategies for benchmarking is that this can be done without having to make any assumptions about fund return distributions. As a result, unlike traditional performance measures, the proposed method can be applied to funds with normal as well as non-normal return distributions. Applying the proposed method to 13 different hedge fund indices over the period May 1990–April 2000, we find 12 of the 13 indices to be inefficient on a stand-alone basis, with the average efficiency loss amounting to 3%. The same hedge fund indices score much better when seen as part of an investment portfolio though. Due to their weak relationship with the index, seven of the 12 hedge fund indices classified as inefficient on a stand-alone basis are capable of producing an efficient payoff profile when mixed with the S&P 500.

4.1 INTRODUCTION

Performance evaluation deals with the question whether investment managers are able to generate a superior risk-return trade-off for their investors, i.e. whether fund managers offer investors value for money. Although typically advertised as such, there is no good reason to expect this to be the case. Fund managers may all be experts in their field, but the presence of certain special skills does not guarantee superior performance. The opportunity costs of potentially poor diversification across assets as well as through time, the transaction costs incurred and the management fees charged, all have to be borne by the investor. The question therefore is not whether fund managers have special skills *per se*, but whether they have enough skill to compensate for all these costs, which can be very substantial. Only in that case can we speak of truly superior skill and performance.

Answering the above question is not easy since it requires the construction of a performance benchmark that tells us what classifies as 'normal' and what does not. Since the 1960s, a respectable number of authors have worked on this problem. Building on the asset pricing model in fashion, they derived benchmarks which are now known as the 'Sharpe ratio' and 'Jensen's alpha', for example. Later work concentrated specifically on the question whether investment managers are any good timing the ups and downs of the market. With only a limited set of historical returns available, this is a very hard question to answer, even with the large econometrical toolkit nowadays available.

All benchmarks developed so far suffer from the same drawback: they require explicit assumptions about the return generating process. Typically, they require fund and index returns to be normally distributed. In the early days of performance evaluation, when investment managers followed traditional long-only, non-leveraged, non-mechanical strategies, this was not an unrealistic assumption. Over the past 20 years, however, this has changed. Nowadays, more and more managers use options and/or follow some explicit dynamic trading strategy, like portfolio insurance, for example. It is well known that this yields return distributions that are far from normal.

In this chapter we present a performance benchmark that does not require any assumptions about the return generating process. It deals with normal distributions and any other type of distribution in exactly the same way. We apply the proposed evaluation procedure to the returns of 13 hedge fund indices over the period May 1990–April 2000. Hedge funds follow highly dynamic trading strategies and make extensive use of derivatives. This produces highly non-normal return distributions which makes them an interesting test case.

4.2 TRADITIONAL PERFORMANCE MEASURES

Practitioners typically use either one of two performance measures: the Sharpe ratio and Jensen's alpha.[1] The first measure was introduced in Sharpe (1966) and is calculated as the ratio of the average excess return and the return standard deviation of the fund in question. As such it measures the excess

[1] An extensive bibliography on performance evaluation can be found on www.stern.nyu.edu/~sbrown/performance/bibliography.html

return per unit of risk. The benchmark value is the Sharpe ratio produced by the relevant market index. Theoretically, the Sharpe ratio derives directly from the CAPM. Assuming all asset returns to be normally distributed (or, less plausible, that investors have mean-variance preferences), the CAPM tells us that in equilibrium the highest attainable Sharpe ratio is that of the market index. A ratio higher than that therefore indicates superior performance.

The alpha measure was introduced in Jensen (1968) and equals the intercept of the regression given by:

$$(R_h - R_f) = \alpha + \beta(R_i - R_f) + e_h \tag{4.1}$$

where R_h is the fund return, R_f is the risk-free rate and R_i is the total return on the relevant market index. Alpha measures the excess return that cannot be explained by a fund's beta. An alpha higher than zero indicates superior performance. Like the Sharpe ratio, Jensen's alpha is deeply rooted in the CAPM and therefore relies heavily on the assumption of normally distributed returns. According to the CAPM, in equilibrium all (portfolios of) assets with the same beta will offer the same expected return. Any positive deviation therefore indicates superior performance.

It is important to note that, although both stemming from the CAPM, both measures take a different perspective when looking at fund performance. The Sharpe ratio implicitly assumes that investors invest in nothing else than the fund in question, i.e. it evaluates fund performance on a stand-alone basis. Alpha, on the other hand, evaluates fund performance in a portfolio context by incorporating the correlation characteristics of the fund in the evaluation (via the fund beta). A fund with a Sharpe ratio higher than that of the market index will also have a positive alpha. The reverse need not be true, however, i.e. underperformance on a stand-alone basis does not necessarily imply underperformance in a portfolio context.

The above performance benchmarks both assume that fund returns are normally distributed, which in many cases is not a bad assumption. However, what happens if fund returns are not normally distributed? Suppose we had a stock index, like the S&P 500, for example, with a monthly price return that was normally distributed with an expected value of 1.24% (14.88% per annum) and a volatility of 3.59% (12.43% per annum). These estimates were obtained from monthly S&P 500 data over the period May 1990–April 2000. The index is worth \$100 and pays a continuous dividend yield of 2.65% per annum. The risk-free rate is 5.35%. This yields a Sharpe ratio for the index of 0.28. According to the Black–Scholes (1973) option pricing model, an ordinary at-the-money call on the index with one month to maturity would cost \$1.55. Now suppose we bought the index and wrote the call. Writing the call eliminates all upside potential but retains all downside risk. In return, we receive \$1.55 for the call. Creating this payoff profile requires no special skills. However, this is not the conclusion one would draw from the portfolio's alpha and Sharpe ratio. By writing the call, alpha goes up from zero to 0.34 and the Sharpe ratio rises from 0.28 to 0.42. This is purely the result of the changed shape of the return distribution though. By giving up all upside, the monthly standard deviation drops from 3.59% to 1.67%. The expected return drops as well, but this is partially compensated by the option premium that is received. As a result, the Sharpe ratio goes up. Although the above is just a simple example, it makes it painfully clear that traditional evaluation methods may very easily reach the wrong conclusion when dealing with a non-normal distribution.[2]

4.3 A NEW PERFORMANCE MEASURE

To evaluate the performance of funds with a non-normal return distribution correctly, the entire distribution has to be taken into account. Ideally, this should be done without having to make any prior assumptions regarding the type of distribution. The performance measure we propose in this chapter does exactly that. It is based on the following reasoning. When buying a fund participation, an investor acquires a claim to a certain payoff distribution. If we wanted to investigate whether a fund manager had any superior investment skills the most direct line of attack would therefore be to re-create the payoff distribution that he offers to his investors by means of a dynamic trading strategy in stocks and bonds and compare the cost of that strategy with the price of a fund participation. If the manager in question indeed had superior skills, the strategy should be more expensive than the fund participation. Of course, the same payoff distribution can be generated in many different ways. The critical issue is therefore to find the strategy that does so most efficiently, i.e. at the lowest cost. We will return to this shortly, but first we will explain the proposed procedure.

Having collected monthly return data on the fund to be evaluated, the first step is to use these returns to create an end-of-month payoff distribution, assuming we invest \$100 at the beginning of the month. The same is done for a well-diversified market index. We do not make any assumptions about the distribution of fund returns. We do, however, explicitly assume the index

---

[2]Bookstaber and Clarke (1985) discuss the shortcomings of mean-variance analysis when used to evaluate the performance of optioned portfolios. Over the years there have been several *ad hoc* attempts to solve this problem. Only recently, Leland (1999) has developed a skewness adjustment that has a sound theoretical basis in the early work of Rubinstein (1976).

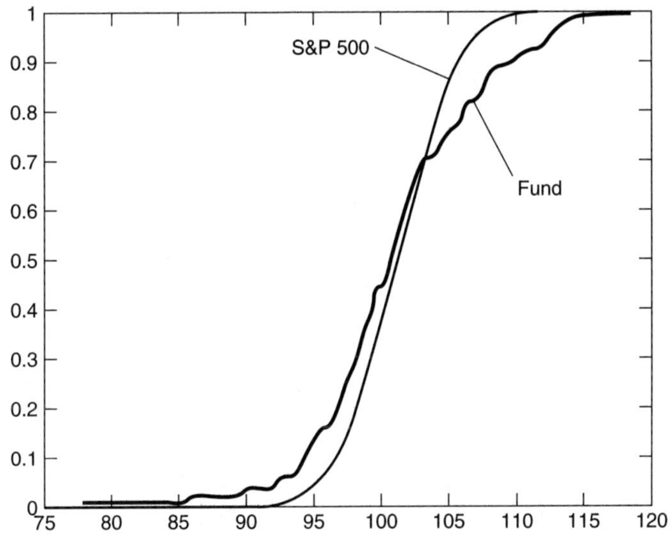

Figure 4.1 Cumulative probability distribution
This figure shows the cumulative probability distribution of the end-of-month payoff of a fund and the S&P 500 (excluding dividends). S&P 500 returns are assumed to be normally distributed.

to be normally distributed. The reason for this will become clear later. An example of the resulting cumulative distributions can be found in Figure 4.1.

The next step is to construct a payoff function that, in combination with the index distribution, yields exactly the same end-of-month payoff distribution as produced by the fund. Since there are many functions that will map one distribution into the other, we make the additional assumption that the payoff function must be a path independent non-decreasing function of the index value at the end of the month. There is a special reason for this, which we will discuss later. Under the latter assumption, constructing a payoff function is quite straightforward. Suppose that the fund distribution told us there was a 10% probability of receiving a payoff lower than 100. We would then look up in the index distribution at which index value X there was a 90% probability of finding an index value higher than X. If we found $X = 95$, the payoff function would be constructed such that when the index ended at 95 the payoff would be 100. Next, we would do the same for a probability of 20%. If the fund distribution told us there was a 20% probability of receiving a payoff lower than 110 and the index distribution said there was a 80% probability of finding an index value higher than 100, the payoff function would be constructed such that when the index ended at 100 the payoff would be 110. This procedure is repeated until we get to 100%. An example of a typical payoff function (using steps of 0.2% instead of 10% as in the above example) can be found in Figure 4.2.

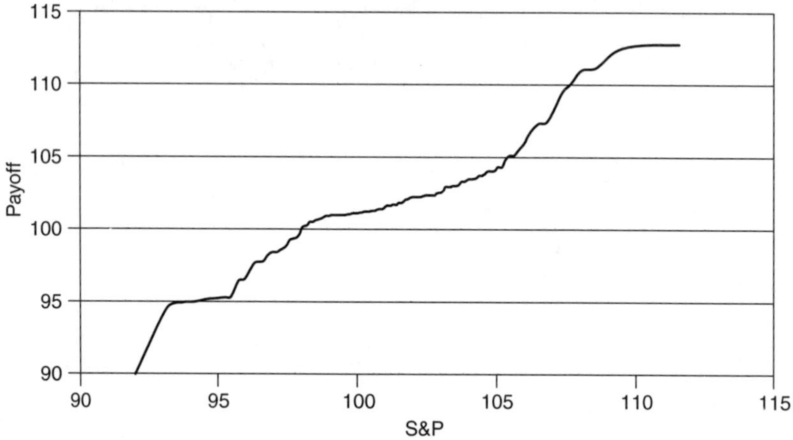

Figure 4.2 Payoff function
This figure shows an example of a payoff function resulting from the mapping procedure discussed in section 4.3. Given the S&P 500 distribution, this payoff function implies the same payoff distribution as the fund in question.

The third step consists of finding the initial investment required by the self-financing dynamic trading strategy, trading the index and cash, that generates the above payoff function. This is no different from what is usually done to price derivatives contracts. We can therefore use standard derivatives pricing technology and calculate the price of the derived payoff function as the discounted risk neutral expected payoff. Since the payoff is not a neat function, however, we will have to do so using Monte Carlo simulation instead of a more elegant analytical or numerical technique. The easiest approach is to assume we live in the world of Black and Scholes (1973), which explains why in step 2 we assumed index returns to be normally distributed. Having constructed a payoff function, we can in that case generate end-of-month index values using the discretized and risk neutralized geometric Brownian motion given by

$$S(t+\delta t) = S(t)\exp\left(\left(r - q - \tfrac{1}{2}\sigma^2\right)\delta t + \sigma\sqrt{\delta t}\varphi\right) \tag{4.2}$$

where $S(t)$ is the starting value of the index, r is the risk-free rate, q is the dividend yield on the index, σ is the index volatility, δt is the time step (one month) and φ is a random variable with a standard normal distribution. From the index values thus generated we subsequently calculate the corresponding payoffs, average them and discount the resulting average back to the present at the risk-free rate to give us the price of the payoff function in question. If the price thus obtained is higher than \$100, we take this as evidence of superior performance and the other way around.

The above efficiency test has a solid theoretical foundation in the work of Cox and Leland (2000) and the payoff distribution pricing model of Dybvig (1988a, 1988b). Cox and Leland showed that in the world of Black and Scholes (1973) all path dependent strategies are inefficient in the sense that the same payoff distribution can also be obtained by a path independent strategy, but at lower costs. In addition, from Dybvig (1988a, 1988b) we know that any investor who maximizes expected utility and prefers more money to less will want his wealth at the end of his investment horizon to be a monotonic non-increasing function of the state-price density. Investment strategies that do not have this feature will be inefficient, i.e. stochastically dominated by other strategies. In the world of Black and Scholes (1973) with a positive risk premium the state-price density is a decreasing function of the terminal value of the index. This means that for a strategy to be efficient, final wealth must be a monotonic non-decreasing function of the terminal index value. Intuitively, this is a plausible result. A non-decreasing payoff will be positively correlated with the index. As a result, the rebalancing trades required by the strategy generating that payoff will tend to be relatively modest, which serves to keep trading costs down. In short, *what we use as a benchmark is the cost of the cheapest self-financing dynamic trading strategy that generates the same payoff distribution as the hedge fund in question*. By doing so we test whether a hedge fund manager has sufficient skill to compensate not only for transaction costs and management fees (which simply do not exist in a Black–Scholes world), but also for the inefficiency costs of potentially poor diversification across assets as well as through time.

We are not the first to approach performance evaluation from a contingent claims perspective. Glosten and Jagannathan (1994) approximate mutual fund payoffs by a portfolio consisting of the index and a limited number of ordinary index calls. Agarwal and Naik (2000) show that simple option strategies are able to explain a significant part of the variation in hedge fund returns over time. Fung and Hsieh (2001) show that the returns from trend following strategies are similar to those from lookback straddles. Finally, Mitchell and Pulvino (2001) find that the returns from risk arbitrage strategies are very similar to the results from writing ordinary put options. All these authors link fund payoffs with specific option payoffs. Our efficiency test, however, does not do so. Apart from requiring the payoff to be a path independent non-decreasing function of the index, it is fully determined by the empirically observed distribution of fund returns.

4.4 SAMPLING ERROR

Because the available dataset will always be limited, the efficiency test will be confronted with a sampling error. Since we do not make any assumptions about the nature of the distributions involved, a formal study is problematic. We can, however, obtain a good indication of the possible extent of the error by studying the efficiency test's application on a payoff function that we know to be efficient, such as the index plus short call package discussed earlier in section 4.2, for example. Since the payoff of this package is hampered neither by transaction costs or management fees nor by inefficient diversification, the test should produce a value of exactly 100. If we had only a limited number of observations available, however, this need not always be the case.

To investigate the extent of the possible error we generated 120 end-of-month index values (corresponding with 10 years of data) and calculated the corresponding payoffs from the index plus short call package, as before assuming monthly index returns to be normally distributed with a mean of 1.24% (14.88% per annum) and a standard deviation of 3.59% (12.43% per annum), and a monthly dividend yield of 0.22% (2.65% per annum). Next, we applied the efficiency test to the 120 payoff values thus obtained, assuming the S&P 500 to follow a geometric Brownian motion with a volatility equal to the above standard deviation and a drift equal to the difference between the risk-free rate and the above dividend yield. The former was set equal to the 10-year historic mean of the 3-month USD LIBOR rate (5.35%). We repeated the above procedure 20,000 times. A frequency distribution of the annualized error, i.e. the difference between the actual test result and 100, can be found in Figure 4.3.

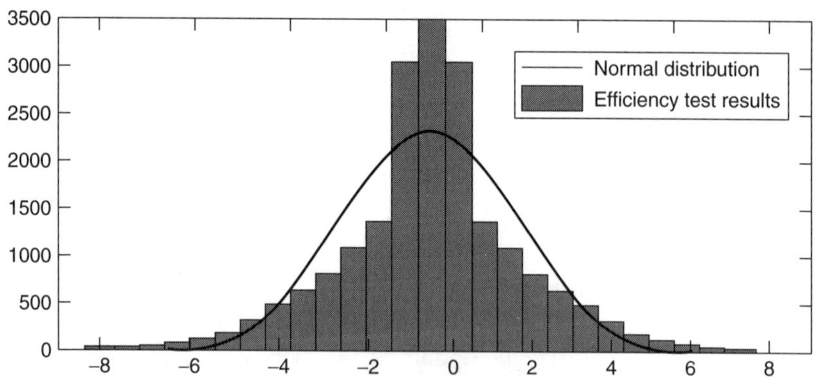

Figure 4.3 Sampling error

This figure shows the frequency distribution of the annualized errors from performing the efficiency test on a combination of the index and a short at-the-money call. To calculate the errors we first sampled 120 end-of-month index values and calculated the corresponding payoffs from the combination. Subsequently, we applied the efficiency test to these data and calculated the sampling error as the difference between the test result and 100. To obtain the frequency distribution shown, this procedure was repeated 20,000 times. The normal distribution shown has the same mean (−0.05) and standard deviation (2.14) as the sampling error distribution.

Figure 4.3 shows that with only 120 observations the efficiency test may produce an error that significantly differs from zero. The error distribution, however, has a high peak around zero, meaning that, compared to a normal distribution, there is a relatively high probability of a small error. In addition, Figure 4.3 shows that the efficiency test is unbiased. The average error is −0.05. We repeated the above analysis for a number of other (efficient) payoff profiles as well, which yielded similar results.

4.5 HEDGE FUNDS AND HEDGE FUND RETURNS

A hedge fund is a pooled investment vehicle that is privately organized, administered by professional investment managers, but not widely available to the public. Due to their private nature, hedge funds have fewer restrictions on the use of leverage, short-selling and derivatives than more regulated vehicles such as mutual funds. This allows for investment strategies that differ significantly from traditional non-leveraged, long-only strategies. As we will see, due to the special nature of the investment strategies adopted by hedge fund managers, hedge fund returns tend to exhibit a high degree of non-normality. It is therefore interesting to see what our test has to say about the efficiency of hedge funds and whether this is any different from what traditional benchmarks would tell us.

Hedge funds are a very heterogeneous group. There are, however, a number of 'ideal types' to be distinguished. Zurich Capital Markets, which is the source of the data we will use, uses the following main and subcategories:

Global: International
Funds that concentrate on economic change around the world and pick stocks in favoured markets. Make less use of derivatives than macro funds (see below).

Global: Emerging
Funds that focus on emerging markets. Because in many emerging markets short-selling is not permitted and without the presence of futures markets, these funds tend to be long only.

Global: Established
Funds that look for opportunities in established markets.

Global: Macro
These funds tend to go wherever there is a perceived profit opportunity and make extensive use of leverage and derivatives. These are the funds that are responsible for most media attention.

Event Driven: Distressed Securities
Funds that trade the securities of companies in reorganization and/or bankruptcy, ranging from senior secured debt to common stock.

Event Driven: Risk Arbitrage
Funds that trade the securities of companies involved in a merger or acquisition, typically buying the stocks of the company being acquired while shorting the stocks of its acquirer.

Market Neutral: Long/Short Equity
This category makes up the majority of hedge funds. Exposure to market risk is reduced by simultaneously entering into long as well as short positions.

Market Neutral: Convertible Arbitrage
Funds that buy undervalued convertible securities, while hedging all intrinsic risks.

Market Neutral: Stock Arbitrage
Funds that simultaneously take long and short positions of the same size within the same market, i.e. portfolios are designed to have zero market risk.

Market Neutral: Fixed Income Arbitrage
Funds that exploit pricing anomalies in the global fixed income (derivatives) market.

Fund of Funds: Diversified
Funds that allocate capital to a variety of hedge funds.

Fund of Funds: Niche
Funds that invest only in a specific type of hedge funds.

With the industry still in its infancy and hedge funds under no formal obligation to disclose their results, gaining insight in the performance characteristics of hedge funds is not straightforward. Fortunately, many hedge funds release monthly return information to attract new and accommodate existing investors. These data are collected by a number of parties that, among others, use them to calculate a number of hedge fund indices. In what follows we use the indices calculated by Zurich Capital Markets over the period May 1990–April 2000.[3] All these 13 indices are equally weighted and correspond with the fund classification discussed earlier. The 13 indices considered are listed below with the number of funds included as of April 2000 between brackets: Event Driven (106), Event Driven: Distressed (45), Event Driven: Risk

Table 4.1 Hedge funds index return characteristics[a]

	Mean (%)	Median (%)	Maximum (%)	Minimum (%)	Std. dev. (%)	Skewness	Kurtosis	Jarque–Bera
S&P 500	1.4594	1.7237	12.0853	−11.1118	3.6460	−0.2373	1.0581	19.9825*
GL EST	1.5176	1.4950	9.4000	−9.4200	2.6817	−0.4860	5.2187	29.3373*
GL EMER	1.2913	1.0550	19.3300	−26.2500	4.9667	−1.0786	11.2347	362.3179*
MKT ARB	1.2417	1.1100	14.1300	−4.7800	2.1551	4.3819	27.2839	3332.556*
EVENT DIST	1.2068	1.3650	6.0500	−9.2200	2.1938	−0.9483	6.5708	81.7394*
GL MACRO	1.1863	0.6650	8.6100	−5.3600	2.1264	0.7830	4.8976	30.2674*
GL INTL	1.1669	1.3600	7.9200	−10.1500	2.0618	−1.1506	9.9069	265.003*
EVENT-DRIV	1.1162	1.1350	4.7400	−5.6100	1.2454	−1.3217	10.3978	308.5748*
EVENT RISK	1.0768	1.0750	4.6800	−6.9100	1.3404	−1.6370	12.6030	514.6788*
FUND DIV	0.9558	1.0000	6.1500	−6.4200	1.4860	−0.6267	8.4144	154.4364*
FUNDOFFUND	0.9130	0.8850	4.5000	−6.4000	1.3809	−1.1858	9.0826	213.1098*
MKTNEUTRAL	0.9124	0.9500	2.3400	−0.6100	0.4348	−0.0557	4.4526	10.6118**
FUND NICHE	0.8827	0.8750	5.9300	−5.8700	1.5453	−0.2789	7.0183	82.2909*
MKT LONG	0.8682	0.8500	2.7600	−1.0300	0.4962	0.3005	5.4686	32.2763*

*Significant at 1%.

**Significant at 5%.

[a]This table shows the mean, median, maximum, minimum, standard deviation, skewness, kurtosis and the results of the Jarque–Bera (1987) test calculated from the monthly returns of 13 hedge fund indices and the S&P 500 over the period May 1990 to April 2000. The hedge fund indices are: Event Driven (EVENT-DRIV), Event Driven: Distressed (EVENT DIST), Event Driven: Risk Arbitrage (EVENT RISK), Fund of Funds (FUNDOFFUND), Fund of Funds: Niche (FUND NICHE), Fund of Funds: Diversified (FUND DIV), Global: Emerging (GL EMER), Global: Established (GL EST), Global: International (GL INTL), Global: Macro (GL MACRO), Market Neutral (MKT NEUTRAL), Market Neutral: Long/Short (MKT LONG) and Market Neutral: Arbitrage (MKT ARB).

Arbitrage (61), Fund of Funds (265), Fund of Funds: Niche (232), Fund of Funds: Diversified (33), Global: Emerging (85), Global: Established (245), Global: International (34), Global: Macro (58), Market Neutral (231), Market Neutral: Long/Short (109), and Market Neutral: Arbitrage (122).

Table 4.1 provides information on the monthly return characteristics of the S&P 500 and the 13 hedge fund indices over the 10-year period studied. The S&P 500 return is a total return, i.e. it includes dividends. All returns use continuous compounding. The return distribution of most hedge fund indices appears to be highly skewed. The last column in Table 4.1 shows the results of the Jarque–Bera (1987) test for normality, which confirms that *for none of the index return distributions normality is a satisfactory approximation.*

4.6 EVALUATION OF HEDGE FUND INDEX PERFORMANCE

The above results clearly indicate that hedge funds generate non-normal returns. Correct evaluation of hedge fund performance requires a performance measure that takes this into consideration. First, however, we take a look at the results that one would obtain if one used traditional performance measures to detect superior performance.

Using monthly total return data from May 1990 to April 2000, we calculated the alphas and Sharpe ratios of the S&P 500 and the 13 hedge fund indices. We used three-month USD LIBOR as a proxy for the risk-free rate and the S&P 500 as the relevant market index. The results can be found in Table 4.2. Eleven indices show significant positive alphas. Twelve indices generate a Sharpe ratio higher than that of the S&P 500. We also plotted the means and standard deviations of the 13 indices in traditional mean-standard deviation space together with a number of other equity, bond and commodity indices. The results can be found in Figure 4.4. From this graph it is clear that most of the hedge fund indices combine a relatively high mean return with a relatively low standard deviation. In terms of mean and standard deviation, the hedge fund indices are definitely more attractive than the other indices, which is in line with the message from these indices' alphas and Sharpe ratios.

Next, we applied our efficiency test to the monthly returns of the 13 hedge fund indices, using the same S&P 500 parameter values as in section 4.4. Note again that over the period studied the *ex post* risk premium has been relatively high, which potentially allows for significant inefficiency costs. The evaluation results can be found in Table 4.3. *Twelve of the 13 indices show signs of inefficiency* with the average efficiency loss on these 12 indices amounting to 3.00% per annum. With an average efficiency loss of 4.15%, the three fund of

Table 4.2 Traditional performance measures hedge fund indices[a]

	Alpha (%)	Sharpe ratio
S&P 500	0.0000	0.2796
MKT ARB	0.7443*	0.3720
GL EST	0.5445*	0.4018
EVENT RISK	0.5357*	0.4751
GL MACRO	0.4998*	0.3510
EVENT-DRIV	0.4713*	0.5429
EVENT DIST	0.4591*	0.3495
GL INTL	0.4501*	0.3526
MKTNEUTRAL	0.4319*	1.0865
MKT LONG	0.3901*	0.8629
FUND DIV	0.3283*	0.3471
FUNDOFFUND	0.2971*	0.3425
FUND NICHE	0.2464	0.2865
GL EMER	0.1965	0.1714

*Significant at 1%.

[a]This table shows the alphas and Sharpe ratios of 13 hedge fund indices based on monthly return data from May 1990 to April 2000. The hedge fund indices are: Event Driven (EVENT-DRIV), Event Driven: Distressed (EVENT DIST), Event Driven: Risk Arbitrage (EVENT RISK), Fund of Funds (FUNDOFFUND), Fund of Funds: Niche (FUND NICHE), Fund of Funds: Diversified (FUND DIV), Global: Emerging (GL EMER), Global: Established (GL EST), Global: International (GL INTL), Global: Macro (GL MACRO), Market Neutral (MKT NEUTRAL), Market Neutral: Long/Short (MKT LONG) and Market Neutral: Arbitrage (MKT ARB).

funds indices make an important contribution to this figure. Excluding the latter, the average efficiency loss drops to 2.61%. Obviously, this is a completely different conclusion than what traditional performance measures tell us, which underlines the importance of incorporating the whole return distribution in the evaluation process.

To gain insight into the sensitivity of the above results for outliers we removed the top and bottom 2.5% of the return observations, leaving 114 instead of 120 monthly returns. The overall results did not change much. The correlation between the results from 120 observations and 114 observations was 0.94. To see how sensitive the above results are for the choice of reference index, we performed the same exercise using the Dow Jones Industrial (DJI) index instead of the S&P 500. The DJI is substantially different from the S&P 500. The former is made up of only 30 stocks, while the latter contains 500. In addition, instead of being value-weighted like the S&P 500 and most other major stock market indices, the DJI is one of the few price-weighted indices in the world. Using

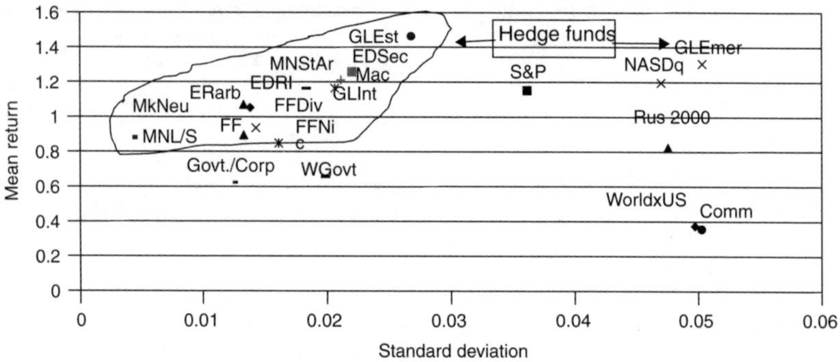

Figure 4.4 Mean-standard deviation plot

This figure plots the 13 hedge fund indices as well as some other market indices into mean-standard deviation space. All parameter estimates are based on monthly return data from May 1990 to April 2000. The hedge fund indices are: Event Driven (EDRI), Event Driven: Distressed (EDSec), Event Driven: Risk Arbitrage (Erarb), Fund of Funds (FF), Fund of Funds: Niche (FFNic), Fund of Funds: Diversified (FFDiv), Global: Emerging (GLEmer), Global: Established (GLEst), Global: International (GLInt), Global: Macro (Mac), Market Neutral (MkNeu), Market Neutral: Long/Short (MNL/S) and Market Neutral: Arbitrage (MNStAr). The other indices are: S&P 500 (S&P), Nasdaq (NASDq), Russell 2000 (Rus 2000), Morgan Stanley World index excluding US (WorldIdxUS), and Goldman Sachs Commodities index (Comm).

Table 4.3 Hedge fund index efficiency[a]

	Efficiency yearly
EVENT DIST	−2.8685
EVENT RISK	−1.1157
EVENT-DRIV	−1.6807
FUND DIV	−3.6614
FUND NICHE	−4.8756
FUNDOFFUND	−3.9225
GL EMER	−7.2672
GL EST	−0.7388
GL INTL	−2.4846
GL MACRO	−3.0333
MKT ARB	0.1380
MKT LONG	−2.4836
MKTNEUTRAL	−1.8591

[a]This table shows the annual (monthly times 12) efficiency loss (−) or gain (+) of 13 hedge fund indices based on monthly return data from May 1990 to April 2000. The hedge fund indices are: Event Driven (EVENT-DRIV), Event Driven: Distressed (EVENT DIST), Event Driven: Risk Arbitrage (EVENT RISK), Fund of Funds (FUNDOFFUND), Fund of Funds: Niche (FUND NICHE), Fund of Funds: Diversified (FUND DIV), Global: Emerging (GL EMER), Global: Established (GL EST), Global: International (GL INTL), Global: Macro (GL MACRO), Market Neutral (MKT NEUTRAL), Market Neutral: Long/Short (MKT LONG), and Market Neutral: Arbitrage (MKT ARB).

the DJI as our reference index, the results again did not change very much. The correlation between the S&P 500 results and the DJI results was 0.99.

By construction, our mapped payoffs are heavily correlated with the index. In reality, however, the relationship between hedge fund and stock market returns is rather weak. For example, over the period studied the average correlation between the S&P 500 and the individual hedge funds in the Zurich database was only 0.29. The efficiency test used so far does not take this into account as it aims only to replicate the hedge fund indices' payoff distributions and not their correlation profile. If we were to introduce an explicit correlation restriction into the efficiency test, i.e. require our trading strategies to replicate not only the indices' payoff distributions but also their correlation with the index, the hedge fund indices would come out better as the additional restriction would make our replication strategies more expensive. Unfortunately, technically this is much easier said than done. We therefore decided on the following procedure.

First, we formed portfolios of hedge fund indices and the S&P 500, with the fraction invested in hedge funds ranging from 0% to 100% in 1% steps. Subsequently, we ran the same efficiency test as before on these portfolios' 120 monthly returns while checking for the existence of a combination of hedge fund index and S&P 500 that offers a risk-return profile that cannot be obtained with a mechanical trading strategy at a lower price. Roughly speaking, this procedure tests whether the relationship between the hedge fund indices and the S&P 500 is sufficiently weak to make up for the efficiency loss observed on a stand-alone basis. Table 4.4 shows for every hedge fund index, the highest efficiency value achieved and the mix at which this occurs. From Table 4.4 we see that when mixed with the S&P 500, seven of the 12 indices that were found to be inefficient on a stand-alone basis are able to produce an efficient payoff profile, i.e. a payoff profile that cannot be obtained otherwise at a better price. In all seven cases the most efficient mix consists of around 20% hedge fund index and 80% S&P 500. The above strongly suggests that the main attraction of hedge funds lies not in their stand-alone risk-return properties but in their weak relationship with other asset classes. From an efficiency point of view, hedge funds should therefore not be held in isolation but always in combination with other assets.

4.7 CONCLUSION

In this chapter we have introduced dynamic trading strategies as a tool for performance evaluation. Because the method does not make any assumptions about fund return distributions, it can be applied to funds with normal as well as non-normal return distributions. The test appears to be unbiased, while

Table 4.4 Hedge funds index portfolio efficiency[a]

	Maximum efficiency	Investment in S&P 500
EVENT DIST	0.2790	79%
EVENT RISK	0.3142	81%
EVENT-DRIV	0.1936	78%
FUND DIV	0.0000	100%
FUND NICHE	0.0000	100%
FUNDOFFUND	0.0000	100%
GL EMER	0.3844	83%
GL EST	0.7331	82%
GL INTL	0.3475	81%
GL MACRO	0.1363	78%
MKT ARB	0.6032	77%
MKT LONG	0.0000	100%
MKTNEUTRAL	0.0000	100%

[a]This table shows the efficiency test results on portfolios constructed by investing in varying proportions in the hedge fund indices and the S&P 500. The second column shows the maximum efficiency level achieved. The third column gives the percentage to be invested in the S&P 500 to obtain that maximum efficiency level. The hedge fund indices are: Event Driven (EVENT-DRIV), Event Driven: Distressed (EVENT DIST), Event Driven: Risk Arbitrage (EVENT RISK), Fund of Funds (FUNDOFFUND), Fund of Funds: Niche (FUND NICHE), Fund of Funds: Diversified (FUND DIV), Global: Emerging (GL EMER), Global: Established (GL EST), Global: International (GL INTL), Global: Macro (GL MACRO), Market Neutral (MKT NEUTRAL), Market Neutral: Long/Short (MKT LONG) and Market Neutral: Arbitrage (MKT ARB).

with 120 observations sampling error risk does not seem to be prohibitively high. We applied the proposed method to 13 different hedge fund indices. On a stand-alone basis we found 12 of the 13 indices to be inefficient, with the average efficiency loss amounting to 3%. The hedge fund indices score much better when seen as part of an investment portfolio though. Due to their weak relationship with the index, seven of the 12 hedge fund indices classified as inefficient on a stand-alone basis are capable of producing an efficient payoff profile when mixed with the S&P 500. The best results are obtained when around 20% of the portfolio value is invested in hedge funds.

REFERENCES

Agarwal, V. and Naik, N. (2000) Performance evaluation of hedge funds with option-based and buy-and-hold strategies, working paper, London Business School.

Black, F. and Scholes, M. (1973) The pricing of options and corporate liabilities, *Journal of Political Economy*, **3**, 637–654.

Bookstaber, R. and Clarke, R. (1985) Problems in evaluating the performance of portfolios with options, *Financial Analysts Journal*, January–February, 48–62.

Cox, J. and Leland, H. (2000) On dynamic investment strategies, *Journal of Economic Dynamics and Control*, **24**, 1859–1880.

Dybvig, P. (1988a) Distributional analysis of portfolio choice, *Journal of Business,* **61**, 369–393.

Dybvig, P. (1988b) Inefficient dynamic portfolio strategies or how to throw away a million dollars in the stock market, *Review of Financial Studies*, **1**, 67–88.

Fung, W. and Hsieh, D. (2001) The risk in hedge fund strategies: theory and evidence from trend followers, *Review of Financial Studies*, **14**, 313–341.

Glosten, L. and Jagannathan, R. (1994) A contingent claim approach to performance evaluation, *Journal of Empirical Finance*, **1**, 133–160.

Jarque, C. and Bera, A. (1987) A test for normality of observations and regression residuals, *International Statistical Review,* **55**, 163–172.

Jensen, M. (1968) The performance of mutual funds in the period 1945–1964, *Journal of Finance*, **23**, 389–416.

Leland, H. (1999) Beyond mean-variance: performance measurement in a non-symmetrical world, *Financial Analysts Journal*, January–February, 27–36.

Mitchell, M. and Pulvino, T. (2001) Characteristics of risk and return in risk arbitrage, *Journal of Finance*, **56**, 2135–2175.

Rubinstein, M. (1976) The valuation of uncertain income streams and the pricing of options, *Bell Journal of Economics*, **7**, 63–72.

Sharpe, W. (1966) Mutual fund performance, *Journal of Business*, **39**, 119–138.

Chapter 5

Performance benchmarks for institutional investors: measuring, monitoring and modifying investment behaviour

DAVID BLAKE AND ALLAN TIMMERMANN

ABSTRACT

The two main types of benchmarks used in the UK are external asset-class benchmarks and peer-group benchmarks. Peer-group tracking is much more prevalent with pension funds and mutual funds than with life funds. However, the use of customized benchmarks that reflect the specific objectives set by particular funds is increasing. Benchmarks influence the type of assets selected and, equally significantly, the type of assets avoided. Peer-group benchmarks have a tendency to distort behaviour, particularly when combined with a fee structure that does not promote genuine active management. The outcome tends to be herding and closet index matching.

The main alternatives to peer-group benchmarks are: single-index benchmarks with time-varying coefficients, multiple-index benchmarks and fixed benchmarks. The first two alternatives have recently been discussed in the academic literature but have yet to catch on in the practitioner community.

There are also benchmarks based on liabilities. These are generally related to real earnings or consumption growth or to the discount rate on liabilities. Explicit liability-based benchmarking is currently not very common, but is likely to become so in the light of both the increasing maturity of pension funds, various regulatory and financial reporting developments, and the Myners Review of Institutional Investment. Liability-driven performance attribution explicitly takes the liabilities into account.

The US has similar external asset-class and peer-group benchmarks as the UK. Other countries tend to use fixed or bond-based benchmarks.

In conclusion, we find that benchmarks are important, but so are fee structures. They can either provide the right incentives for fund managers or they can seriously distort their investment behaviour.

5.1 INTRODUCTION

The issue of performance benchmarks for institutional investors has generated a great deal of controversy recently. Are they set too low, making them very easy to beat? Are they set too high, making them hard to beat unless fund managers take on excessive risks? Is the frequency of assessment against the benchmark (typically on a quarterly basis) appropriate for long-term investors? Do they introduce unintended (and undesired) incentives, such as the incentive for fund managers to herd together or to avoid holding securities (such as those of micro-cap, small-cap, unquoted or start-up companies) that are not included in the benchmark? How, if at all, should performance against the benchmark influence the fund manager's compensation. How should the fund's liabilities be taken into account when assessing the fund's performance. This chapter examines and assesses the benchmarks that are currently used by institutional investors in the UK. It also looks at possible alternatives to these benchmarks and briefly reviews what happens in other countries.

5.2 WHAT BENCHMARKS ARE CURRENTLY USED BY INSTITUTIONAL INVESTORS?

Performance benchmarks in the UK have been around since the early 1970s. They are an essential part of the investment strategy of any institutional investor and help both to define client/trustee expectations and to set targets for the fund manager. Benchmarks can be set in relation to liabilities and can therefore change if the liabilities change, say, as a result of increasing maturity. Benchmarks might also be influenced by regulations (e.g. a Minimum Funding Requirement[1] (MFR)), accounting standards (e.g. Financial Reporting Standard 17[2] (FRS17)), or client/trustee preferences (e.g. trustees might prefer

[1] Introduced in the UK by the 1995 Pensions Act and operating from 1997, but it was announced in the March 2001 Budget that it would be scrapped.

[2] Issued by the Accounting Standards Board in November 2000 and coming fully into force in June 2003.

to minimize the volatility of employer contributions into a pension plan than minimize the average level of employer contributions, given that, in final salary plans, the pension is funded on a balance of cost basis).

The benchmark, appropriately set, has important implications for how the actions of the fund manager are interpreted. An appropriate benchmark recognizes formally that the strategic asset allocation or SAA (i.e. the *long-run* division of the portfolio between the major categories of investment assets, such as equities, bonds and property) is a risk decision relative to the liabilities, rather than an expected return decision. In other words, the SAA, properly interpreted, is not an investment decision at all: instead it is determined largely by reference to the maturity structure of the anticipated liability cash flows. In contrast, the stock selection and market timing (i.e. tactical asset allocation) decisions are investment decisions and it is the fund manager's performance in these two categories that should be judged against the benchmark provided by the SAA.

5.2.1 Single-index benchmarks and peer-group benchmarks

The two main types of benchmarks used in the UK are external asset-class benchmarks and peer-group benchmarks. These benchmarks are used by both 'gross funds' (i.e. those without explicit liabilities) and 'net funds' (i.e. those, such as pension funds, with explicit liabilities). When external performance measurement began in the early 1970s, most pension funds selected customized benchmarks (which involved tailoring the weights of the external benchmarks to the specific requirements of the fund). Shortly after, curiosity about how other funds were performing led to the introduction of peer-group benchmarks. More recently, following the recognition that the objectives of different pension funds differ widely, there has been a return to customized benchmarks.

The WM Company,[3] for example, uses the following set of external benchmarks to assess the performance of the pension funds in its stable:

- UK equities: FTA All Share Index.
- International equities: FT/Standard & Poor World (excluding UK) Index.
- North American equities: FT/Standard & Poor North America Index.
- European equities: FT/Standard & Poor Europe (excluding UK) Index.
- Japanese equities: FT/Standard & Poor Japan Index.
- Asia – Pacific equities: FT/Standard & Poor Asia – Pacific (excluding Japan) Index.

[3]The WM Company is one of the two key performance measurement services in the UK, the other is CAPS (Combined Actuarial Performance Services).

- UK bonds: British Government Stocks (All Stocks) Index.
- International Bonds: JP Morgan Global (excluding UK) Bonds Index.
- UK index-linked bonds: British Government Stocks Index-linked (All Stocks) Index.
- Cash: LIBID (London Inter-Bank Bid Rate) 7-day deposit rate.
- UK Property: Investment Property Databank (IPD) All-Property Index.
- International Property: Evaluation Associates All Property Index (a US index to reflect the fact that most international property investments are held in the US).
- Total portfolio: WM Pension Fund Index (based on all the funds monitored by WM).

All these indices assume that income is reinvested (gross of tax) and the returns are calculated on a value- and time-weighted basis. These benchmarks have the virtues of being independently calculated and immediately publicly available. However, some of them (most notably cash and international equities and bonds) have weightings that can differ substantially from those of the pension funds. Some indices are subject to measurement problems, particularly the property indices. Further, the external benchmarks include only the securities of relatively large companies.

The WM Company also uses peer-group indices for pension funds:

- WM50 Index for very large funds.
- WM2000 Index for small and medium-sized funds.

These are designed to reflect the fact that UK pension funds have portfolio weights that can differ substantially from those of the external indices. For example, UK pension funds tend to have a higher weight in Europe and a lower weight in the US than a global market-weighted index (ex UK). They also reflect the fact that large (mainly mature) funds have a very different asset allocation from that of smaller (less mature) funds. Both sets of indices are gross of the following costs: transactions costs (dealing spreads and commissions) and running costs (management and custody fees, property security and insurance costs).

Peer-group tracking is less prevalent with life funds than with pension funds. WM has constructed a with-profits universe mainly as a result of the curiosity of life offices to know how competitors are performing, but acknowledges that the product range of life offices is too great to make meaningful peer-group comparisons. Most benchmarks for life funds are based on external indices. In comparison, peer-group comparisons are more common with unit trusts and are used for promotional purposes.

5.2.2 Evaluating the single-index benchmarks

How are they constructed?

The first question that must be asked with any external index-based benchmark is: how was it constructed? Suitable index-based benchmarks have to be constructed on a value- and time-weighted basis. This essentially means that the constituents of the index are weighted according to their market capitalizations and that the timing of reinvested income is not allowed to distort the measured return. Other types of indices such as price-weighted indices (which simply sum up the prices in the index regardless of market capitalization) and geometric indices (which simply multiply together the prices in the index regardless of the market capitalization) would not make suitable benchmarks. This is because it is impossible for any real-world portfolio to mimic the behaviour of either of these two indices. However, while it is impossible for a real-world portfolio to mimic, say, a geometric index, it would not be difficult for the real-world portfolio to beat this index: anyone who knows Jensen's inequality will understand why! (see Blake (2000: 590–591)).

Even with benchmarks constructed on a value- and time-weighted basis, there are practical considerations to take into account before using them to assess performance. First, benchmarks can be constructed without having to incur the kinds of costs that face real-world fund managers, such as brokers' commissions, dealers' spreads and taxes.

Second, the constituents of the benchmark change quite frequently. While this involves no costs for the benchmark, it involves the following costs for any fund manager attempting to match the benchmark. The deleted securities have to be sold and the added securities have to be purchased: this involves both spreads and commissions. In addition, when the announcement of the change is made, the price of the security being deleted tends to fall and the price of the security being added tends to rise and these price changes are likely to occur before any fund manager has the chance to change his portfolio. A bond index-based benchmark is even more expensive to beat: over time, the average maturity of a bond index will decline unless new long-maturing bonds are added to replace those that mature and automatically drop out of the index.

Third, the benchmark assumes that gross income payments are reinvested costlessly back into the benchmark on the day that the relevant stock goes *ex-dividend*. In practice no fund manager would be able to replicate this behaviour: dividends and coupon payments are not made until some time after the ex-dividend date, the payment is generally made net of income or withholding tax, there are commissions and spreads incurred when reinvesting income and the trickle of dividend or coupon payments that are received at different times are going to be accumulated into a reasonable sum before being reinvested. All these factors cause a tracking error to develop between the benchmark and any real-world portfolio attempting to match the benchmark, and leads to the real-world portfolio invariably underperforming the benchmark. So tracking error has to be recognized as an inevitable part of the process of fund management, both for active and passive strategies.

Why are they difficult to beat?

Apart from these practical considerations, there are other reasons why an institutional investor might find it difficult to beat an external index-based benchmark. First, there may be restrictions placed on fund managers which prohibit them from even attempting to match the index, let alone beat it. We can consider some examples. There can be trustee-imposed prudential limits on the maximum proportion of the fund that can be invested in a single security. For example, most trustees place a limit of 10% on the fund's investment in the shares of a single company. When the market weighting of Vodaphone in the FTSE100 index rose above 10% during 2000, fund managers were obliged to sell Vodaphone shares to bring their portfolios within the 10% limit and the FTSE100 index compilers were asked to introduce a new benchmark in the form of a 'capped' FTSE100 index that limits the weight of any security to 10%. As another example, some countries place regulatory limits on the holdings of certain securities by foreign investors: e.g. for national security reasons there might be limits on the foreign ownership of defence sector stocks.

Second, investors may not wish to be represented in some of the markets covered by the index. For example, a global emerging markets index would cover all continents, but investors might choose to avoid certain regions such as Africa, the Middle East or Russia.

Third, there is the so-called 'home country bias', the preference for securities from the home market. If UK pension funds were fully diversified on a global basis, they would hold less than 10% of their assets in the UK and more than 90% abroad. Yet UK pension funds which are the most diversified internationally of all the world's pension funds hold around 80% of their assets in the UK and only about 20% abroad.

Why should this be the case if the most diversified and hence the least risky portfolio possible is the global index? The only defensible answer to this question is that UK pension fund liabilities are denominated in sterling and, for liability matching purposes, pension fund managers select a high weight for sterling-denominated assets. It cannot really be justified on the grounds of risk. In the last 10 years, UK pension funds would have performed much better had they held the global index: although the Japanese market fell markedly, the rise in the US market more than compensated for this as well as outperforming the UK by a handsome margin (see, e.g., Timmermann and Blake (2000)).

Finally, even if an index is chosen as a benchmark, no index currently in use contains the shares and bonds of all the companies in the economy, although it should if it is to be an efficient index.

Why is there a bias against small companies and venture capital?

The external indices listed above contain the securities of only relatively large companies. This is a particularly important issue for new companies which find it difficult to obtain equity capital to finance their start-up or to expand in their early years. The gap in the provision of equity finance for small companies in the UK was first identified by the Macmillan Committee on Finance and Industry in 1931 (and is known as the 'Macmillan gap'). The Macmillan gap was still present when the Wilson Committee to Review the Functioning of Financial Institutions reported in 1980 and made these comments about pension funds:

> In law, their first concern must be to safeguard the long-term interests of their members and beneficiaries. It is, however, possible for fiduciary obligations to be interpreted too narrowly. Though the institutions may individually have no obligation to invest any particular quantity of new savings in the creation of future real resources, the prospect that growth in the UK economy over the next two decades might be inadequate to satisfy present expectations should be a cause of considerable concern to them. The exercise of responsibility which is the obverse of the considerable financial power which they now collectively possess may require them to take a more active role than in the past ... in more actively seeking profitable outlets for funds and in otherwise contributing to the solutions of the problems that we have been discussing. (Wilson (1980: 259–260)).

The pension funds' defence against this criticism rested on the argument that the costs of investing in small companies were much higher than those of investing in large companies. The reason for this is as follows. Small companies are difficult, and therefore expensive, to research because they are generally relatively new and so do not have a long track record. Also, their shares can be highly illiquid, and pension funds, despite being long-term investors, regard this as a very serious problem. Further, pension fund trustees place limits on the proportion of a company's equity in which a fund can invest. For example, a pension fund might not be permitted by its trustees to hold more than 5% of any individual company's equity. For a company with equity valued at £1 m, the investment limit is £50,000. A large pension fund might have £500 m of contributions and investment income to invest per year. This could be invested in 10,000 million-pound companies or it could be invested in 50 large companies. It is not hard to see why the pension fund is going to prefer the latter to the former strategy, even if it could find 10,000 suitable companies in which to invest.

Related to the criticism that pension funds are unwilling to invest in small companies is the criticism that pension funds have been unwilling to supply risk-taking start-up or venture capital to small unquoted companies engaged in new, high-risk ventures. Venture capital usually involves the direct involvement of the investor in the venture. Not only does the investor supply seed-corn finance, he also supplies business skills necessary to support the inventive talent of the company founder. This can help to reduce the risks involved. The reward for the provision of finance and business skills is long-term capital growth. The problem for pension funds is that, while they have substantial resources to invest, they do not generally have the necessary business expertise to provide the required support. Further, while venture capital investments only ever take up a small proportion of the total portfolio, they take up a disproportionate amount of management time. Also the performance in the early years can be poor. As a result, pension funds remain largely portfolio investors rather than direct investors. In other words, they prefer to invest in equity from which they can make a quick exit if necessary, rather than make a long-term commitment to a particular firm.

Not only do pension funds tend to avoid the risks of direct investment, they tend also to be risk-averse when it comes to portfolio investment. They seek the maximum return with the minimum of risk, and the investment managers of pension funds tend to be extremely conservative investors, devoid of entrepreneurial spirit. As G. Helowicz has pointed out, pension funds:

> do not have any expertise in the business of, or a commitment to, the companies in which they invest. Shares will be bought and sold on the basis of the potential financial return. It therefore follows that the potential social and economic implications of an investment decision have little influence on that decision. (Benjamin *et al.* (1987: 98))

The other main factor is the legacy of the great inflation of the 1970s and the stop-go policies of governments at the time. UK investors with highly cyclical venture capital investments experienced substantial losses during every 'stop' phase.

UK pension funds have in recent years responded to the above criticisms. For example, some of the larger funds have established venture capital divisions. But they invest only about one-tenth of what US pension funds invest as a proportion of assets: 0.5% of total assets in 1998 as against 5% in the

US, according to the British Venture Capital Association. The venture capital industry raised three times more funding in 1998 from overseas pension funds and insurance companies than from their UK equivalents: 37% of the total as against 13%. Moreover, most of the venture capital in the UK is used to finance management buy-outs in existing companies, rather than to finance green field site development.

Nevertheless, it appears to be the case that the 'statement of investment principles' and the 'statement on socially responsible investment' required by the 1995 Pensions Act have focused the attention of pension funds on these issues in a way that was absent before the Act. The same is likely to be true of the 'principles of institutional investment' that will be introduced following the Myners Report.[4] It is possible that establishing a suitable venture capital benchmark might help to promote pension fund investment in new start-ups as well. It certainly appears to be the case that behaviour soon follows measurement when a performance benchmark is established: very quickly, the benchmark changes from being a tool of measurement to a driver of behaviour.

5.2.3 Evaluating the peer-group benchmarks

What is the effect of peer-group benchmarks?

This question has recently been addressed by Blake, Lehmann and Timmermann (2000). They find that the answer depends to a large extent on the industrial organization of and practices within the fund management industry.

The UK fund management industry is highly concentrated, with the top five fund management houses accounting for well over 50% of the funds under management (it was as high as 80% in 1998). This contrasts with the US where the top five fund managers account for less than 15% of the market. There is also a much lower turnover of fund management contracts in the UK than in the US, implying that client loyalty can help smooth over periods of poor performance more effectively than in the US. In addition, there is a single dominant investment style in the UK (namely balanced multi-asset management), which contrasts with the much wider range of styles in the

[4]Myners (2001). The principles cover: effectiveness of decision making by well-informed fund trustees, clarity of investment objectives for the fund, adequacy of time devoted to the strategic asset allocation decision, competitive tendering of actuarial and investment advice services to trustees, explicit investment mandates for fund managers, shareholder activism, appropriate benchmarks, performance measurement of fund managers and advisers, transparency in decision making, publication of mandates and fee structures via the statement of investment principles, regularity of reporting the results of monitoring of advisers and fund managers.

US (e.g. value, growth, momentum, reversal, quant and single asset-class management).

Further, the remuneration of the fund manager typically depends solely on the value of assets under management, not on the value added by the fund manager and there is typically no reward for outperforming either the external or peer-group benchmark and no penalty for underperforming these benchmarks. However, the long-term success of any fund management house depends on its relative performance against its peer group. The large fund management houses in the UK have lost business in recent years not because of their poor *absolute* performance, but because of their poor *relative* performance.

These differences in industrial organization and practice have led to significant differences in investment performance between pension funds in the UK and US. Blake, Lehmann and Timmermann (2000) found that, during the 1980s and 1990s, the median UK pension fund underperformed the market index by a fairly small 15 basis point p.a., whereas the median US pension fund underperformed by a much wider margin of 130 basis points p.a.[5] At the same time, the dispersion of pension fund returns around the median was much greater in the US than in the UK (603 basis points for the 10–90 percentile range, compared with 311 basis points in the UK).[6] These results, illustrated in Figure 5.1, clearly indicate that genuine active fund management is much more prevalent in the US than in the UK: UK pension fund managers display all the signs of herding around the median fund manager who is himself a closet index matcher.

What role do fee structures play?

Fee structures appear to provide a disincentive to undertake active management in the UK, while relative performance evaluation provides a strong incentive not to underperform the median fund manager. While UK pension fund managers are typically set the objective of adding value, their fees are generally related to year-end asset values, not to performance. Genuine *ex ante* ability that translates into superior *ex post* performance increases assets under management and, thus, the base on which the management fee is calculated. However, this incentive is not particularly strong and active management subjects the manager to non-trivial risks.

The incentive is weak because the prospective fee increase is second order, being the product of the *ex post* return from active management and the management fee and thus around two full orders of magnitude smaller than

[5]The US results come from Lakonishok, Shleifer and Vishny (1992: 348).

[6]The US results come from Coggin, Fabozzi and Rahman (1993: 1051).

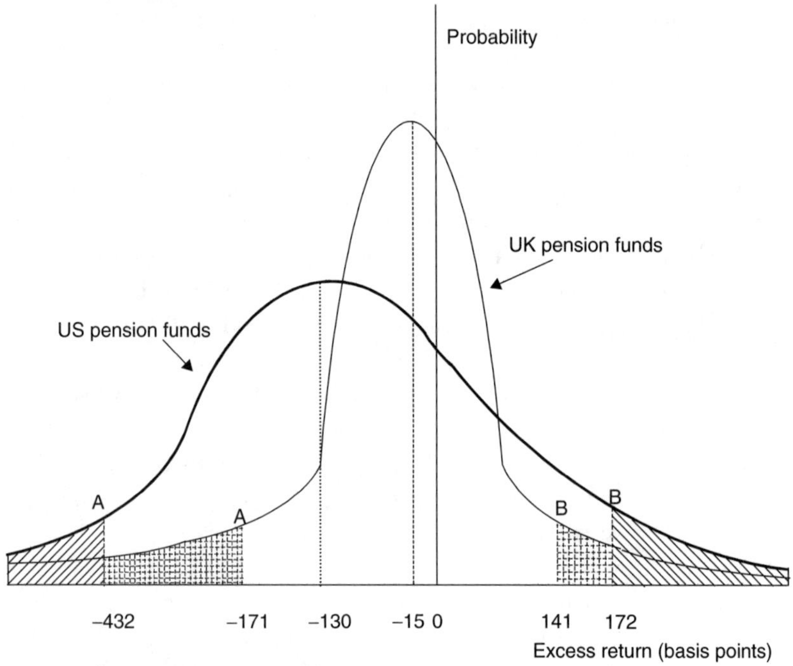

Source: Blake, Lehmann and Timmermann (2000).
Note: A = 10th percentile of funds; B = 90th percentile of funds

Figure 5.1 The dispersion of returns on UK and US pension funds in excess of the market index

the base fee itself. Moreover, the *ex post* return from active management of a truly superior fund manager will often be negative and occasionally large as well, resulting in poor performance relative to managers who eschewed active management irrespective of their ability. The probability of relative underperformance large enough to lose the mandate is likely to be at least an order of magnitude larger than the proportional management fee. Hence, the risk of underperformance due to poor luck outweighs the prospective benefits from active management for all but the most certain security selection or market timing opportunities.

How successful are active fund managers?

The next result concerns the active management abilities of UK pension fund managers, that is, their skill in outperforming a passive buy-and-hold strategy. There are two principal types of active management: security selection and market timing. Security selection involves the search for undervalued securities (i.e. involves the reallocation of funds within asset categories) and market timing involves the search for undervalued sectors (i.e. involves the reallocation of funds between sectors or asset categories).

Blake, Lehmann and Timmermann (1999) decomposed the median total return earned by pension fund managers into the following components:

Component	Percentage
Strategic asset allocation	99.47%
Security selection	2.68%
Market timing	−1.64%
Other	−0.51%
Total	100.00%

The most important task of pension fund managers is to establish and maintain the SAA and the decomposition reveals that, of the median total return over the sample period of 12.06% p.a., 12.00% p.a. (or 99.47% of the total) was due to this essentially passive activity. In terms of the active components, the average pension fund was unsuccessful at market timing, generating a negative contribution to the total return of −1.64%. Security selection was more successful, making a positive contribution to the total return of 2.68%. Even so, the overall contribution of active fund management at just over 1% of the total return (or about 12 basis points p.a.) is less than the annual fee that active fund managers typically charge (which range between 20 basis points for a £500m fund to 75 basis points for a £10m fund[7]).

Finally, the study by Blake, Lehmann and Timmermann (2000) found that above-average performance by a particular fund manager (so-called 'hot hands' in investment performance) was very short-lived: it rarely lasted more than a year. Studies of US fund managers have found persistence in performance extending out to two or three years, but no longer (Hendricks, Patel and Zeckhauser, 1993).

Is there a role for performance-related fees?

One way of providing appropriate incentives to those fund managers who believe that they can generate superior investment performance is to use performance-related investment management fees. In one example of this, the fee is determined as some proportion, f_1, of the difference between the fund's realized performance, g_t, and some benchmark or target, g_t^*, plus a base

[7] *Pensions Management* (September 1998).

fee to cover the fund manager's overhead costs, set as a fixed proportion, f_2, of the absolute value of the fund (V_t in period t):

$$\textit{Performance-related fee in period } t = f_1(g_t - g_t^*)V_t + f_2 V_t \qquad (5.1)$$

This would reward good *ex post* performance and penalize poor *ex post* performance, whatever promises about superior *ex ante* performance had been made by the fund manager. The fund would have to accept a reduced fee or even pay back the client if g_t was sufficiently below g_t^* (although the latter case generally involves credits against future fees rather than cash refunds).

Another possibility that is less extreme since it does not involve refunds is:

$$\textit{Performance-related fee in period } t = f_i V_t \qquad (5.2)$$

where f_i is the fee rate if the fund manager's return is in the ith quartile.

An example of this second type of fee structure is that of the Newton Managed Fund whose particular fee structure is listed in Table 5.1. Figure 5.2 illustrates how this fee structure might work in practice. The chart shows the distribution of fees payable to the manager of a middle-sized fund, based on a Monte Carlo simulation. The 90% confidence interval for the fees lies between 0.22 and 0.45% p.a., while there is a 25% chance that the fee will exceed 0.37% p.a. and a similar chance that it will be less than 0.31% per annum. A mean annual charge of 0.34% implies a total take of approximately 8.9% of the terminal fund value over an investment horizon of 25 years.

The level set for the target g_t^* will have important implications for the outcome. If the target is unrealistic and outside the range of performance expected by a skilled fund manager, the only way the manager can reasonably achieve the stipulated performance is by increasing the volatility of his investment strategy, i.e. by increasing risk. This is highly relevant in practice as some targets are very hard to achieve. Examples of these are: 'beat the median fund by 2 percentage points over a three-year rolling period', or 'be

Table 5.1 Newton Managed Fund

Quartile rank	Fund size		
	Up to £10m	£10–£50m	Above £50m
1st	0.94%	0.59	0.04
2nd	0.79	0.44	0.03
Median	0.69	0.34	0.02
3rd	0.59	0.24	0.01
4th	0.44	0.09	0.01

Source: Newton Fund Managers.

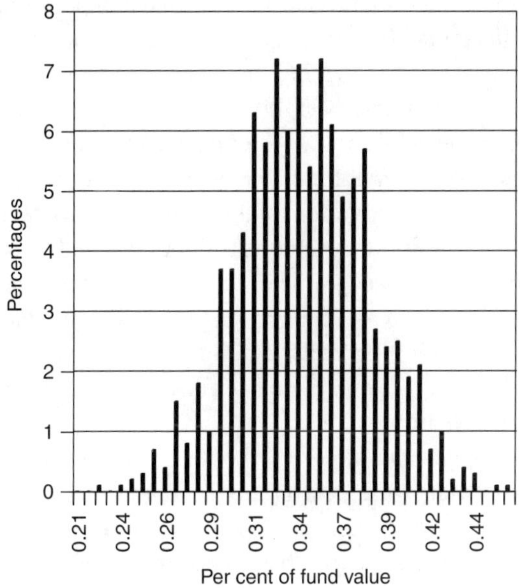

Note: The frequency diagram shows the annual distribution of performance-related fees in a fund with fees calculated according to the following performance scale:

Quartile rank	Fee (%)
1st	0.59
2nd	0.44
Median	0.34
3rd	0.24
4th	0.09

The Monte Carlo simulation assumes the following: a fund with a 25-year investment horizon, a distribution of returns which is normal with a mean of 9% p.a. and a standard deviation of 18%, and 1000 replications. Based on long-run returns reported in Credit Suisse First Boston's *Equity-Gilt Study* (2000), such a portfolio would be invested 35% in equities and 65% in bonds.

Figure 5.2 Frequency distribution of performance-related fees

in the upper quartile of performance'. There is an unconditional probability of 75% of failing to achieve the second target! Clients/trustees are beginning to accept that high targets will most likely be associated with greater volatility in performance, unless the client has *a priori* information that the fund manager is genuinely capable of delivering the target performance.

Clients/trustees are also beginning to accept that targets based on the peer-group median or peer-group distribution are very likely to distort fund manager behaviour. This is partly because the median performance is really an outcome rather than a target. Whereas a fund manager knows the composition of an external index prior to making his own investments and so knows how much he is overweight or underweight in different securities, he will not know for sure what the asset allocation of the median fund manager is until the end of the performance period. All fund managers will be in the same position and this provides a strong incentive for fund managers not to deviate too far from each other. Hence, we find that there is a tight distribution of fund managers around the median fund manager who, in turn, generates a performance little different from that of a passive index matcher. Those fund managers who beat the median fund by 2 percentage points over a three-year rolling period, or who end up in the upper quartile of performance, are therefore more likely to do so by chance than by skill.

All this suggests that the target g_t^* should be set in relation to an external benchmark rather than to a peer-group benchmark if clients/trustees wish their fund managers to pursue genuinely active fund management strategies. However, this makes quartile-based fee structures virtually impossible to implement, since information on the distribution of returns around the median value of the external index is not collected centrally.

It is particularly important for the fee rate to be symmetric about the target g_t^*, so that underperformance is penalized in exactly the same way that outperformance is rewarded. The worst possible fee structure from the client/trustee's point of view would be one that rewarded outperformance but did not penalize underperformance. An example of this would be:

$$\textit{Performance-related fee in period } t = \max[0, f_1(g_t - g_t^*)V_t] + f_2V_t \tag{5.3}$$

This particular fee structure would simply encourage the fund manager to take risks with the client/trustee's assets. If the fund manager's risk taking paid off, he would receive a large fee. If, on the other hand, performance was disastrous, the fund manager would still get the base fee. All the risk of underperformance (at least in the short term) therefore falls on the client/trustee.

How frequently should fund managers be assessed?

A final issue of importance concerns the frequency with which fund managers are assessed against the benchmark. Despite having very long-term investment objectives, the performance of pension fund managers is typically assessed on a quarterly basis. This is said to provide another disincentive from engaging in active fund management because of the fear of relative underperformance against the peergroup and the consequent risk that an underperforming fund manager will be replaced.

The frequency with which fund managers have their performance assessed ought to be related to the speed with which market anomalies are corrected. Suppose, as argued above, the benchmark has been set in relation to the SAA. Then it is the fund manager's performance in the two active strategies of stock selection and market timing that should be judged against the benchmark provided by the SAA. So the critical question is how long does it take for undervalued stocks to become correctly priced or for market timing bets to succeed? If financial markets are relatively efficient, then pricing anomalies should be corrected relatively quickly. This appears to suggest that a relatively short evaluation horizon is appropriate. To illustrate using a somewhat extreme example, if a market timing bet that involves, say, a significant underweighting of the US stock market, has not paid off after 10 years, then we might be tempted to say that the bet was a bad one.

However, two points speak against the use of relatively short evaluation horizons. The first has to do with time-variations in the investment opportunity set as represented by the relative expected returns and the conditional variances and covariances between the different asset classes. Many studies in the finance literature suggest that the first and second moments of returns on different asset classes vary systematically as a function of the underlying state of the world. Nevertheless, there is considerable uncertainty about how best to model such variations. But it seems reasonable to expect a successful market timing strategy to be linked to the ability to anticipate changes in the underlying economic state. This tends to evolve over fairly long periods of time, as exemplified by the 10-year expansion in the US economy up to 2000. If clients want fund managers to time swings in the business cycle, a long evaluation horizon would seem more appropriate.

The second justification for using a longer investment horizon is that performance is measured with so much noise that it is in effect impossible to assess true fund management skills based on a short performance horizon. Under reasonable assumptions,[8] it is possible to generate the following relationship between the length of the performance record and the power of the test for assessing fund management skills:

Power	Required data record
25%	3.5 years
50%	8 years
90%	22 years

[8]See the Appendix.

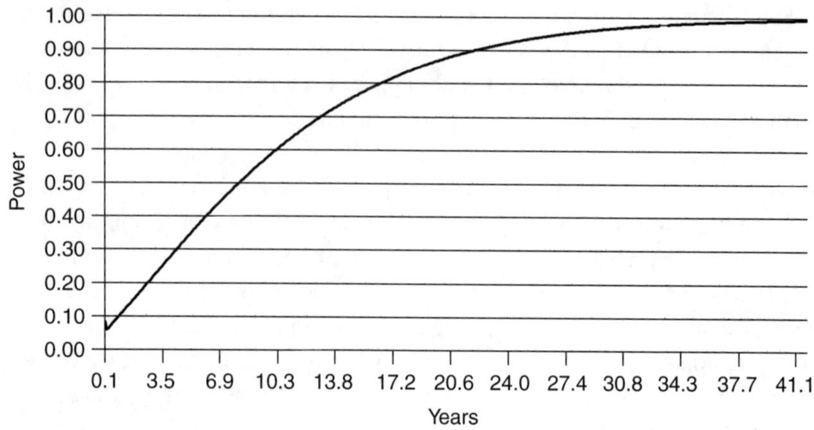

Source: See Appendix.

Figure 5.3 Power function – probability of correctly detecting abnormal performance

These figures are derived from Figure 5.3. The power of the test measures the probability of correctly rejecting the null hypothesis that the fund manager generates no abnormal performance. It is clear from the figures that it takes a long time to detect with reasonable confidence that the performance of the fund manager is abnormal. And this result is dependent on an unchanging investment opportunity set which is in itself an unlikely eventuality over a 22-year time horizon.

5.3 WHAT ARE THE ALTERNATIVES?

Recently, the academic literature has begun to investigate alternative benchmarks, based on extensions to the Capital Asset Pricing Model (CAPM). They help to identify the sources of any under- or outperformance by fund managers. There are also fixed benchmarks.

5.3.1 Single-index benchmarks with time-varying coefficients

The external benchmarks considered above are single-index benchmarks that can be justified by the CAPM, invented by Nobel prize winner Bill Sharpe and now one of the cornerstones of modern finance theory.

What is the CAPM?

The CAPM decomposes the expected return on a fund into two parts. The first is the return on a riskless asset such as Treasury bills: all professional investors should be expected to generate a return exceeding that on Treasury bills! The second is the additional return from taking on 'market risk'. This, in turn, has two components: the 'market risk premium' (otherwise called the 'excess return on the market' or the 'market price of risk'), and the 'quantity' of market risk assumed by a particular fund as measured by that fund's 'beta'.

The market risk premium is measured by the difference between the expected return on the market index and the risk-free rate. The principal market index in the UK is the FTA All Share Index and many equity fund managers have this index as their single-index benchmark. The historical long-run market risk premium for the UK is about 6% p.a.

The beta of a fund measures the degree of co-movement between the return on the fund and the return on the market index. Technically the beta is calculated as the ratio of the covariance between the returns on the fund and the market to the variance of the return on the market. It is also equal to the product of the standard deviation of the return on the fund and the correlation between the returns on the fund and the market. These are exactly the same formulae as the slope or beta coefficient in a time-series regression of the excess return on the fund on an intercept and the market risk premium, which explains how a beta coefficient is so named. If the standard deviation of the return on the fund or the correlation between the returns on the fund and the market are high, then the fund's beta will be high. The beta of the market index itself is unity. If the fund beta exceeds unity, the fund is more volatile than the market: a beta of 1.1 implies that the fund is 10% more volatile than the market so that if the market rises or falls by 20%, the fund will rise or fall by 22%.

The CAPM can be expressed as follows:

$$\begin{aligned} \textit{Excess return on fund} &= \textit{Alpha} + \textit{Beta of fund} \times \textit{Market risk premium} \\ &= \textit{Alpha} + \textit{Market risk of fund} \qquad (5.4) \end{aligned}$$

where the excess return on the fund is the difference between the realized return on the fund and the risk-free rate. The CAPM is illustrated in Figure 5.4.

If the excess return on the fund exceeds the market risk of the fund, then the fund has generated an above-average performance. The difference between the excess return on the fund and the market risk of the fund is called the fund 'alpha' (sometimes it is called the 'Jensen alpha' after its inventor). A successful fund manager therefore generates a positive alpha. However, it is important to recognize that a fund return exceeding the market index return does not necessarily imply a positive alpha. It is possible for a fund to take on a lot of market (i.e. beta) risk and generate a return higher than the market index return, but nevertheless generate a negative alpha: this would indicate that the market risk assumed by the fund manager was not fully rewarded.

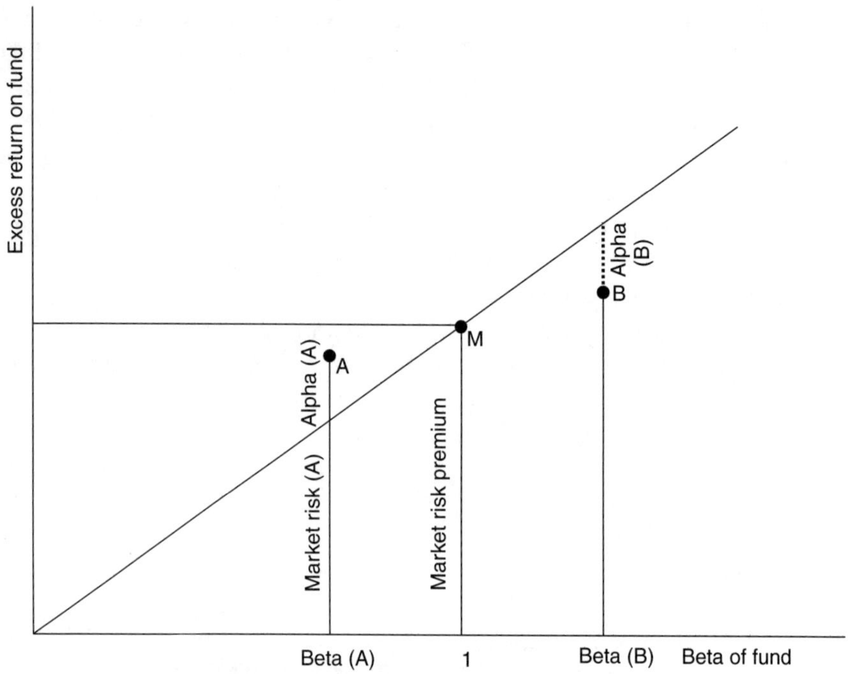

Source: Blake (2000: Fig.14.8); Note: M, excess return on the market index (which has a beta of unity), A – positive excess return of fund A, B – negative excess return of fund B.

Figure 5.4 The Capital Asset Pricing Model

This is the case for fund manager B in Figure 5.4: although B generated a return above that of both the market and fund manager A, A is a more successful fund manager.

How has the CAPM been extended?

This is how a single-index benchmark with constant coefficients for alpha and beta operates within the context of the CAPM. A recent development has been to make the beta coefficient of the CAPM time-varying, that is to allow for predictable time-variation in the beta coefficient on the grounds that fund managers should not be credited with using publicly available information concerning changes in investment opportunity sets when making their investment decisions (see Ferson and Schadt (1996); even more recently, Christopherson, Ferson and Glassman (1998) have extended this procedure to allow for time-varying alpha coefficients).

The beta coefficient is made a linear function of a set of predetermined variables: the lagged values of the short-term yield on T-bills, the long-term yield on government bonds and the dividend yield on an equity index such as the FTA All Share Index; these are all standard regressors with a long tradition in the literature on the predictability of stock returns. So the beta coefficient in this case is determined as follows:

$$\begin{aligned} \textit{Beta of fund} = {} & B(0) + B(1) \times \textit{T-bill yield lagged} \\ & + B(2) \times \textit{Government bond yield lagged} \\ & + B(3) \times \textit{Dividend yield lagged} \end{aligned} \tag{5.5}$$

When Blake and Timmermann (1998) substituted this beta equation into the CAPM equation above and applied it to UK unit trusts over the period 1972–1995, they found it raised the estimate of alpha for the UK balanced sector from −0.74 to −0.52. In other words it lowered the estimate of underperformance slightly for that sector. It made little difference to other sectors, however.

5.3.2 Multiple-index benchmarks

Another recent innovation has been the use of multiple-index benchmarks. For example, Elton *et al.* (1993) pioneered the use of a 'four-index' benchmark consisting of the excess return on large-cap stocks (i.e. a large-cap risk premium), the excess return on small-cap stocks (i.e. the small-cap risk premium), the difference between the returns on an equity growth index and an equity income index (i.e. a growth *minus* income factor) and the excess return on bonds (i.e. a bond risk premium). The multiple-index CAPM therefore becomes:

$$\begin{aligned} \textit{Excess return on fund} = {} & \textit{Alpha} + \textit{Beta}\ (1) \times \textit{Large-cap risk premium} \\ & + \textit{Beta}(2) \times \textit{Small-cap risk premium} \\ & + \textit{Beta}(3) \times (\textit{Growth}-\textit{Income}) \\ & + \textit{Beta}(4) \times \textit{Bond risk premium} \end{aligned} \tag{5.6}$$

Again, a successful fund manager will generate a positive alpha after taking into account these four factors. In other words, a successful active fund manager will be one who does more than simply buy a portfolio of large-cap stocks, small-cap stocks, growth stocks and corporate bonds.

A variation on this model has been applied to UK unit trusts by Blake and Timmermann (1998). For the UK Equity General sector, for example, they found the following three-index model for the sample period 1972–1995:

$$\begin{aligned} \textit{Excess return on fund} = {} & -0.16 + 0.86 \times \textit{Market risk premium} \\ & + 0.33 \times \textit{Small-cap risk premium} \\ & - 0.07 \times \textit{Bond risk premium} \end{aligned} \tag{5.7}$$

This indicates that after taking into account market risk, small-cap risk and bond risk, a typical unit trust from the UK Equity General sector generated a negative alpha (i.e. underperformed on a risk-adjusted basis) by 16 basis points p.a. on average.

The wider use of multiple-index benchmarks which include small-cap and micro-cap indices might well help to encourage institutional investors to consider their investments in these sectors more carefully since they would now have a specific reference point in the form of a performance benchmark.

5.3.3 Fixed benchmarks

Another possibility is to use a fixed benchmark. This in a sense is what was implied by the long-term financial assumptions of the MFR[9]:

- Rate of inflation – 4% p.a.
- Effective rate of return on gilts – 8% p.a.
- Effective rate of return on equities – pre-MFR pension age – 9% p.a.
- Effective rate of return on equities – post-MFR pension age – 10% p.a.
- Rate of increase of GMP under Limited Revaluation – 5% p.a.
- Rate of statutory revaluation for deferred benefits – 4% p.a.
- Rate of LPI increase in payment – 3.5% p.a.
- Rate of increase in post-1988 GMPs – 2.75% p.a.
- Rate of increase in S148 Orders – 6% p.a.
- The real rate of return on index – linked stocks is I where $(1 + I) = 1.08/1.04$.

The problem with fixed benchmarks is their arbitrary nature. Even if they are based on historical experience, there is no guarantee that they would provide accurate forecasts for the future. For example, the extraordinary performance of the UK stock market over the last quarter century has generated an equity risk premium approaching 10%. It would be highly inappropriate to use this figure to set a benchmark for equities over the next 25 years.

5.4 BENCHMARKS BASED ON LIABILITIES

5.4.1 Liability benchmarks

What are the key liability benchmarks?

The benchmarks considered so far, appropriately adjusted for the relevant universe, are suitable for any institutional investor without matching liabilities,

[9]See 'Current Factors for Use in MFR Valuation' in Guidance Note 27 of the Faculty and Institute of Actuaries, 1998, B27.11–12.

such as a defined contribution pension fund or a unit or investment trust. They are also used in practice by defined benefit pension funds which do have matching liabilities. However, it is important to consider explicit liability-based benchmarks. For example, the liabilities of a final salary pension plan depend on expected earnings growth; they also depend on other factors such as forecasts of life expectancy and the discount rate used for discounting liabilities.

One natural benchmark would therefore be earnings growth. A related benchmark might be GDP growth. Earnings growth and GDP growth are related in the long run, since the share of wages in national income does not trend significantly over time: in fact in long-run dynamic equilibrium, earnings growth and GDP growth will be the same. However, over the course of any business cycle, the growth rates in these two variables can differ substantially.

Another natural benchmark for pension funds would be the growth rate in consumption expenditure, since a pension plan's purpose is to finance consumption expenditure in retirement. Strictly speaking the weights for the consumption expenditure index should reflect the pattern of expenditure by the elderly, which might have a higher weight in medical expenses and a lower weight in foreign holidays, say, than younger more active cohorts of the population. Again in long-run dynamic equilibrium, the growth rates in GDP and consumption expenditure will be the same (otherwise the savings ratio will tend towards either zero or unity).

Why are they easy to beat?

A benchmark based on the growth rate of liabilities would be a fairly easy one to beat, since the returns on funds with a substantial weighting in equities tend to exceed the growth rate of liabilities whether measured by earnings growth, GDP growth or consumption growth. There is a good technical reason why this should be the case: it has to do with what is known as the 'dynamic efficiency' of the economy.[10]

It is possible for economies to accumulate too much productive capital (that is, the plant equipment and machinery used by workers to produce the goods and services that consumers wish to buy). As more capital is accumulated, its return falls: this is because the additional capital is being applied to increasingly marginal and less productive investment opportunities. When there is too much capital, the return falls below the growth rate of the economy. When this happens, the economy is said to be 'dynamically inefficient': everyone in the economy would be better off if there was less saving and investment and more consumption. With less investment, the capital stock falls (as depreciated

[10]See, e.g., Blanchard and Fischer (1989).

capital is not replaced) and the return on capital rises above the growth rate of the economy as measured by the GDP growth rate. When this happens, the economy is in a state of dynamic efficiency.

Most of the key economies in the world have been assessed as being dynamically efficient.[11] This means that, in such economies, the returns on financial assets such as equities (which represent claims on the capital stock) will on average exceed the growth rate of GDP, even though there will inevitably be some years when this does not happen. So a passive strategy of holding a broadly based equity portfolio will generate a return that is likely to exceed wage growth, GDP growth or consumption expenditure growth in most years.

How should future liabilities be discounted?

The discount rate for discounting future liabilities provides another possible benchmark if it is set independently of the return on the assets in the fund. Some asset-liability models use the weighted-average return on the assets in the fund as the discount rate for liabilities: obviously this could not be used as a benchmark. Others use the yield on long-term government or corporate bonds.

The 1995 Pensions Act's MFR norms, for example, used government bond yields to determine the present value of pensions in payment[12]:

> The current gilt yields to be used for valuing pensioner liabilities should be the gross redemption yield on the FT-Actuaries Fixed Interest 15 year Medium Coupon Index or the FT-Actuaries Index-linked Over 5 years (5% inflation) Index, as appropriate. In the case of LPI pension increases, either fixed-interest gilts with 5% pension increases or index-linked gilts with a 0.5% addition to the gross redemption yield should be used, whichever gives the lower value of liabilities. Similar principles should be applied for other pensions which are index-linked but subject to a cap other than 5%.

The justification for using a bond yield is that pensions-in-payment liabilities are less risky than equities and hence should be discounted at a lower yield. On the other hand, pensions-in-payment liabilities are not risk free, and so the discount rate should be higher than that on Treasury bills. This suggests that a bond yield provides an appropriate discount rate. The Faculty and Institute of Actuaries chose the above government bond yields to calculate pensions-in-payment liabilities under the MFR.[13]

---

[11] See Abel *et al.* (1989).

[12] See 'Current Factors for Use in MFR Valuation' in Guidance Note 27 of the Faculty and Institute of Actuaries, 1998, B27.11–12.

[13] The MFR allowed the accruing liabilities of active workers to be discounting using a weighted average of long-run gilt and equity yields, with the weights reflecting the asset mix in the fund.

However, for financial reporting purposes, the Accounting Standards Board requires, in FRS17, that all pension liabilities (including those relating to the accumulating liabilities of active members as well as pensions in payment) are valued using an AA corporate bond yield.[14]

Whichever particular bond yield is used, a fund with a heavy equity component is likely to beat a benchmark based on either government or corporate bond yields in most years, on account of the sizeable positive equity risk premium in the UK financial markets. On the other hand, since equity values are more volatile than those of bonds, there will also be a greater chance of producing periodic deficits in the fund.

Explicit liability benchmarking, although currently not very common, will soon become so for a number of reasons. First, there is the increasing maturity of pension funds: the crystallization of liabilities in terms of a specific stream of pensions-in-payment will inevitably move pension fund asset holdings towards bonds as the natural matching asset. Second, the financial reporting developments just mentioned will introduce a common liability benchmark for all schemes. Third, the replacement of the MFR with a scheme-specific funding standard, as announced by the government in March 2001 and recommended by the Myners Review (2001), will lead to the introduction of scheme-specific liability benchmarks.

5.4.2 Measuring the performance of pension funds using liability-driven performance attribution

'Liability-driven performance attribution' (LDPA) is the name given to the framework for analysing performance measurement and attribution in the case of asset-liability managed (ALM) portfolios, that is, portfolios whose investment strategy is driven by the nature of the investing client's liabilities.[15]

We can illustrate the LDPA framework using the following balance sheet for an asset-liability managed pension fund[16]:

Assets		Liabilities	
Liability-driven assets	A	Pension liabilities	L
General assets	E	Surplus	S

[14]This was the same yield chosen by the equivalent US accounting standard, FAS87.

[15]See Plantinga and van der Meer (1995).

[16]The components of the balance sheet are measured in present value terms. Also for simplicity of exposition, we assume that L relates to accrued past service; thus future contributions are excluded from the balance sheet: actuaries call this the 'accrued benefits method' of valuing pension liabilities.

Suppose that the 'pension liabilities' (L) generate a predetermined set of future cash outflows. The fund manager can meet these cash outflows by investing in fixed-interest bonds (A) with the same pattern of cash flows; these bonds constitute the 'liability-driven assets' (LDAs) in the balance sheet above.[17] Suppose that the pension fund 'surplus' (S) is invested in 'general assets' (E). These can be any assets matching the risk-return preferences expressed by the pension scheme's sponsor (e.g. equities). The surplus is defined as assets $(A + E)$ *minus* liabilities (L).[18] The return on the surplus is defined as:

$$r_S S = r_E E + r_A A - r_L L \tag{5.8}$$

where:
r_S = the rate of return on the surplus
r_E = the rate of return on the general assets
r_A = the rate of return on the liability-driven assets
r_L = the payout rate on the liabilities.

Both the pension liabilities and the liability-driven assets will be sensitive to changes in interest rates. Higher interest rates reduce the present value of pension liabilities. Similarly, higher interest rates reduce the value of fixed-interest bonds, since a given stream of fixed-coupon payments is worth less today when yields on alternative assets are higher.[19]

Assuming that interest rate risk is the only source of risk to this portfolio, we can use equation (5.8) to derive a decomposition of portfolio performance as follows. First, we rewrite the return on the general assets as:

$$r_E E = r_E S + r_E(E - S) \tag{5.9}$$

and the return on the liability-driven assets as:

$$r_A A = r_A L + r_A(A - L) \tag{5.10}$$

[17]If the pension liabilities are indexed to uncertain real wage growth or to future inflation then the liability-driven assets will be the assets most likely to match the growth rate in earnings or in inflation over the long term (e.g. indexed bonds, equities and property). But to keep the analysis simple, we assume that the cash flows on future pension payments are known.

[18]Following the 1986 Finance Act, the surplus in UK pension funds cannot exceed 5% of the value of the liabilities. Following the 1995 Pensions Act, the deficit in pension funds cannot exceed 10% of the value of the liabilities and must be reduced to zero within a maximum of ten years.

[19]It is theoretically possible to structure the liability-driven assets in such a way that the pension fund is immunized against interest rate movements. When this happens, the surplus will not respond to interest rate movements. Immunization is explained in Blake (2000: Chap. 14).

Then we can divide each side of (5.8) by S and substitute (5.9) and (5.10) to get the LDPA[20]:

$$\begin{aligned} r_s &= \frac{r_E S + r_E(E-S)}{S} + \frac{r_A L + r_A(A-L)}{S} - r_L \frac{L}{S} \\ &= r_E + \lambda(r_A - r_L) + \gamma(r_E - r_A) \\ &= r_E + \lambda(r_A - \bar{r}_A) + \lambda(\bar{r}_A - r_L) + \gamma(r_E - r_A) \end{aligned} \tag{5.11}$$

or:

Rate of return on the surplus = *Rate of return on the general assets*
+ *Rate of return on the LDAs due to security selection*
+ *Rate of return on the LDAs due to market timing*
+ *Rate of return from a funding mismatch*

where:

$\lambda = \frac{L}{S}$ = financial leverage ratio

$\gamma = \frac{L-A}{S} = \frac{E-S}{S}$ = funding mismatch ratio

$\bar{r}_A$ = the expected return on bonds when they are correctly priced on the basis of the spot yield curve (i.e. when the future coupon payments are discounted using the appropriate spot yields) (see, e.g., Blake (2000: Chap. 5)).

The four-component LDPA in (5.11) can be explained as follows:

1. The *rate of return on general assets* (r_E). This can be analysed using standard techniques, e.g. comparing performance against a pre-agreed peer-group or external benchmark, as outlined in sections 5.2 and 5.3 above.
2. The *rate of return on the liability-driven assets due to stock selection* in terms of, say, credit quality management or sector management. This follows because r_A is the actual return generated by the bonds chosen by the fund manager, whereas $\bar{r}_A$ is the benchmark return on the bonds if

[20] In the case where the surplus is exactly zero, the decomposition in (5.11) is not defined. The fund manager has just generated a sufficient return to meet the payout rate on liabilities. The LDPA in this case would be based on $r_L = r_E(E/L) + r_A(A/L)$ where (E/L) is the portfolio weight in general assets and (A/L) is the portfolio weight in liability-driven assets (see (5.8)).

they were correctly priced according to the spot yield curve: $(r_A - \bar{r}_A)$ is therefore the excess return arising from the stock selection skills of the fund manager.

3. The *rate of return on the liability-driven assets due to market timing*, that is, from choosing a portfolio of bonds with a maturity structure that differs from that of the underlying liabilities, thereby deliberately leaving the portfolio partially exposed to interest rate risk.
4. The *rate of return from a funding mismatch*, that is, from active management of the liability-driven assets such that part of this category is invested in riskier general assets such as equities.

We can illustrate the LDPA using an example. Suppose that a pension fund has the following balance sheet at the start and end of the year:

Assets	Start year	End year	Liabilities	Start year	End year
Liability-driven assets (A)	900	997	Pension liabilities (L)	1,000	1,107
General assets (E)	150	169	Surplus (S)	50	59
	1,050	1,166		1,050	1,166

We will assume that the liability-driven assets are bonds, while the general assets are equities (and that equities have no yield curve effect). The value of the liabilities is calculated as the present value of the liability cash flows using appropriate spot yields as discount rates. We have the following returns on the components of the balance sheet:

Component	Actual rate of return (%)	Benchmark rate of return (%)
Bonds	$r_A = 10.78$	$\bar{r}_A = 10.66$ (assumption)
Equities	$r_E = 12.67$	$\bar{r}_E = 13.30$ (assumption)
Liabilities	$r_L = 10.70$	

The actual rates of return are found by taking the difference between the end-of-year and start-of-year values as a ratio of the start-of-year values. The benchmark return on bonds is calculated in a similar way but based on start- and end-year present values of coupon payments using appropriate spot yields. The benchmark return on equities is simply the realized return on a relevant index, e.g. the FTA All Share Index.

Using equation (5.11) with $\lambda = L/S = 20$ and $\gamma = (L - A)/S = 2$ (using start-of-year values), the LDPA is determined as follows:

	Component		Return (%)
1.	General assets (r_E)		12.67
2.	Security selection ($\lambda(r_A - \bar{r}_A)$)		+2.40
3.	Market timing ($\lambda(\bar{r}_A - r_L)$)		−0.80
4.	Funding mismatch ($\gamma(r_E - r_A)$)		+3.78
		Total	18.05%

The total rate of return on the surplus of 18.05% is made up of 12.67% from the performance of the general assets, 2.40% from successful stock selection of the bond portfolio, 3.78% from a successful funding mismatch, and a loss of 0.80% from market timing. The security selection and market timing effects are magnified by a high leverage ratio (λ) of 20 (the minimum that is permissible since the surplus may not (in the long term) exceed 5% of liabilities), while the funding mismatch effect is magnified by a smaller funding mismatch ratio (γ) of 2. The positive net return of 1.60% from active fund management (i.e. the sum of the returns from security selection and market timing) and the positive net return from a funding mismatch help to generate a high surplus return. However, this cannot conceal the fact that the fund manager underperformed the benchmark in terms of general assets by 0.63%.

The LDPA therefore tells us a great deal about the investment skills of the pension fund manager when he or she is constrained on the liability side of the balance sheet. The only additional information that is required over the current performance measurement framework is as follows: the present value of the pension liabilities (as determined by the pension scheme's actuary), together with the payout rate on these, and the value of the liability-driven assets, together with a customized benchmark return on these.

5.5 WHAT HAPPENS IN OTHER COUNTRIES?

5.5.1 USA

Benchmarking is usually done on an asset class basis against well-known total return indexes. Thus the performance of domestic equity managers is assessed relative to the S&P 500 total return index, fixed-income managers relative to the Lehman aggregate, etc. The other kind of benchmarking is relative to the average within a peer group. Thus the average of all equity managers who subscribe to Lipper's performance service becomes the benchmark for all the managers in that 'universe'.

5.5.2 Japan

No definite benchmarks have been established yet in Japan. Tentatively, the annual rate of return from the Treasury bond (with a maturity in excess of 10 years) plus 0.1% is used, which is just equivalent to the investment performance from the Fiscal Investment and Loan Program.

5.5.3 Germany

There are four different pension vehicles in Germany.

(1) Direct commitments (book reserves)
Since there are no separate funds, there is no investment choice. Fifty-seven per cent of total occupational pension liabilities in Germany are financed through direct commitments.

(2) Support funds
There are no portfolio restrictions for support funds whatsoever. Instead, investment decisions are made solely by the employer. Therefore, there is either no communicated benchmark at all, or the employer selects the benchmark on a discretionary basis. There are more than 5,000 support funds in Germany but they account for only 8% of total pension assets.

(3) Direct insurance
Currently, the benchmark is 4% p.a. However, there is a public debate about whether this is too high since interest rates are currently low. Therefore, the government is considering lowering the benchmark to 3.5%. There are numerous direct insurance contracts in Germany and they account for 12% of total pension assets.

(4) Pension funds
Pension funds are the only vehicle where having a proper benchmark would make sense. However, pension funds are not required to make detailed information about their investment returns, etc. publicly available. This kind of information need only be disclosed to the regulator. Currently, there are 180 pension funds in Germany and they account for 22% of total pension assets.

5.5.4 Italy

Mixes of well-known indices like JPM bond and MSCI stocks in varying proportions. The exact benchmark of each pension fund is not made public. While it can be requested from the fund, this is a long process.

5.5.5 Chile

The benchmark is the average of the return of the other pension funds (AFPs). The use of market indices has been rejected because the local market benchmarks are of questionable applicability. Pension funds are subject to a number of investment constraints, not taken into account in the existing benchmark, e.g. the weights in the benchmark are changed every quarter but the pension funds invest with a very long horizon.

5.6 CONCLUSION

Performance benchmarks are important for three key reasons: they help to measure the investment performance of institutional fund managers, they provide clients/trustees with a reference point for monitoring that performance and they can also have the effect of modifying the behaviour of fund managers. But benchmarks are not the only factor of importance: fee structures also have a major impact.

At the same time, there needs to be a much greater understanding by clients/trustees of the nature of active fund management. At its simplest, an active portfolio can be interpreted as a passive portfolio plus a set of active side bets against the market. The passive component of the portfolio is the strategic asset allocation and, if the benchmark is set appropriately, the performance of the SAA should exactly match the benchmark. The active components should beat the benchmark if the fund manager's side bets are successful and it should be possible to assess this fairly quickly if financial markets are relatively efficient.[21]

A good benchmark combined with a suitable fee structure would therefore enable an above-average fund manager to deliver, on a systematic basis, superior investment performance without taking on excessive risks. The fact that the evidence indicates that fund managers cannot systematically deliver superior investment performance over extended periods is more an indication of the efficiency of financial markets than of the ineffectiveness of either the benchmark or the particular fee structure.

[21] Although we also showed that the noise generated by changing investment opportunity sets can make it difficult to assess genuine fund management skill over short horizons.

In addition, a good benchmark would be one that did not have built-in biases either in favour of or against particular asset classes. In particular, a dynamic financial system demands that there is no bias against start-up capital, and so a good benchmark would contain the appropriate market weighting in venture capital securities. A good benchmark might therefore be based on a multiple of indices that covers all the key asset categories as well as liabilities. In turn, a good fee structure has an appropriate performance-related element.

There are, of course, unsuitable benchmarks and fee structures. Peer-group benchmarks provide a strong incentive not to underperform the median fund manager, while fee structures based on the value of assets under management do not provide a particularly strong incentive to engage seriously in active fund management. We should not be surprised to find that the outcome is herding around the median fund manager who, in turn, is doing little more than match the index. In other words, this benchmark and fee structure have the effect of modifying the behaviour of the fund manager from that which was agreed with the client/trustee. This is rational behaviour by the fund manager since his long-term survival in the industry depends on his relative performance against other fund managers. But it is certainly not what the client/trustee intended. Similarly, a fee structure that awarded outperformance of a benchmark without penalizing underperformance would lead to the fund manager taking risks with the client/trustee's assets in a way that the client/trustee did not intend. As a final example, the maturing of net investors such as pension funds suggests that scheme-specific benchmarks that reflect the maturity of a particular scheme's liabilities become increasingly appropriate, while, correspondingly, those based on external or peer-group benchmarks become less so.

Benchmarks are important, but so are fee structures. They can either provide the right incentives for fund managers or they can seriously distort their investment behaviour.

5.7 APPENDIX: DERIVING THE POWER FUNCTION

Suppose a fund's monthly excess returns are generated by the equation:

$$R_t = \alpha + \beta R_{mt} + \varepsilon_t, \quad \varepsilon_t \sim N(0, \sigma^2)$$

where R_t is the excess return on the fund in period t, over and above the risk-free rate of return, β is its beta, R_{mt} is the excess return on the market portfolio in period t, ε_t is the residual in period t and α measures the fund's genuine ability to outperform. How long will it take for the trustees to detect with reasonable statistical reliability whether the fund produces abnormal performance? To answer this question, suppose that $\alpha = -0.1$ and it is known that $\beta = 1$ and $\sigma = 0.5$. For continuously compounded monthly returns data these parameter values correspond to a fund that underperforms the index by 1.2% per year while the idiosyncratic risk is 6% per year. Assuming that the size of the statistical test for the fund manager's ability to add value, p, is the standard 5%, we can illustrate the difficulty of conducting statistical inference about management skills by calculating the power function for a test of the null hypothesis:

$$H_0(\textit{no abnormal performance}): \alpha = 0$$

against the alternative hypothesis:

$$H_1(\textit{abnormal performance}): \alpha \neq 0$$

We do so by computing how many months of data are needed to ensure a 10, 25 or 50% probability of correctly identifying the fund's abnormal performance. The null hypothesis is rejected if:

$$|Z| \equiv \left| \frac{\bar{\alpha} - \alpha_0}{\sigma/\sqrt{n}} \right| > z_{1-p/2}$$

where $\bar{\alpha} = \sum_{t=1}^{n} (R_t - R_{mt})/n$ is the estimated mean performance and α_0 is the value of α under the null hypothesis of zero abnormal performance. $z_{1-p/2}$ is the $(1 - p/2)$ quantile of the distribution of the performance test statistic. The null is rejected if:

$$\bar{\alpha} < \alpha_0 - z_{1-p/2}\sigma/\sqrt{n}$$

or

$$\bar{\alpha} > \alpha_0 + z_{1-p/2}\sigma/\sqrt{n}$$

Otherwise it is accepted. Suppose that, under the alternative hypothesis, the fund manager's performance is α_1, so that $\bar{\alpha} \sim N(\alpha_1, \sigma/\sqrt{n})$. Then the rejection probability can be computed from:

$$\begin{aligned} P(\bar{\alpha} < \alpha_0 - z_{1-p/2}\sigma/\sqrt{n}) &= P\left(\frac{\bar{\alpha} - \alpha_1}{\sigma/\sqrt{n}} < \frac{\alpha_0 - \alpha_1 - z_{1-p/2}\sigma/\sqrt{n}}{\sigma/\sqrt{n}}\right) \\ &= P\left(Z < \frac{\alpha_0 - \alpha_1}{\sigma/\sqrt{n}} - z_{1-p/2}\right) \\ &= \Phi\left(\frac{\alpha_0 - \alpha_1}{\sigma/\sqrt{n}} - z_{1-p/2}\right) \end{aligned}$$

where $\Phi(\cdot)$ is the cumulative density function for a standard normal variate. Likewise, by symmetry of the normal distribution,

$$P(\bar{\alpha} > \alpha_0 + z_{1-p/2}\sigma/\sqrt{n}) = P\left(Z > \frac{\alpha_0 - \alpha_1}{\sigma/\sqrt{n}} + z_{1-p/2}\right)$$
$$= \Phi\left(\frac{\alpha_1 - \alpha_0}{\sigma/\sqrt{n}} + z_{1-p/2}\right)$$

For example, if $p = 0.05$ so that $z_{1-p/2} = 1.96$ and $\alpha_0 = \alpha_1 = 0$, then $P(Z < -2) = P(Z > 2) = 0.025$, so that the power of the test equals the size of the test at 5%.

However, if $\alpha_0 = 0$, $\alpha_1 = -0.1$, $\sigma = 0.5$, we get the following relation between power (the probability of correctly rejecting the null) and sample size:

$$\begin{aligned} P(Reject\ H_0|\alpha_1, \alpha_0, \sigma, n) &= Power(\alpha_1, \alpha_0, \sigma, n) \\ &= \Phi\left(\frac{\alpha_0 - \alpha_1}{\sigma/\sqrt{n}} - z_{1-p/2}\right) \\ &\quad + \Phi\left(\frac{\alpha_1 - \alpha_0}{\sigma/\sqrt{n}} + z_{1-p/2}\right) \\ &= P(Z < -1.96 + 0.2\sqrt{n}) \\ &\quad + P(Z < -1.96 - 0.2\sqrt{n}) \end{aligned}$$

This relationship is used to calculate the results in the main text.

REFERENCES

Abel, A., Mankiw, N.G., Summers, L. and Richard, J. (1989) Assessing dynamic efficiency, *Review of Economic Studies,* **56**, 1–19.

Benjamin, B., Haberman, S., Helowicz, G., Kaye, G. and Wilkie, D. (1987) *Pensions: The Problems of Today and Tomorrow*, Allen and Unwin, London.

Blake, D. (2000) *Financial Market Analysis*, Wiley, Chichester (especially, Chapters 5, 13 and 14).

Blake, D. and Timmermann, A. (1998) Mutual fund performance: evidence from the UK, *European Finance Review*, **2**, 57–77.

Blake, D., Lehmann, B. and Timmermann, A. (1999) Asset allocation dynamics and pension fund performance, *Journal of Business,* **72**, 429–461.

Blake, D., Lehmann, B. and Timmermann, A. (2000) *Performance Clustering and Incentives in the UK Pension Fund Industry*, Pensions Institute, London, June (www.pensions-institute.org).

Blanchard, O.J. and Fischer, S. (1989) *Lectures on Macroeconomics*, MIT Press, Cambridge, MA.

Christopherson, J., Ferson, W. and Glassman, D. (1998) Conditioning manager alphas on economic information, *Review of Financial Studies,* **11**, 111–142.

Coggin, T.D., Fabozzi, F.J. and Rahman, S. (1993) The investment performance of US equity pension fund managers: an empirical investigation, *Journal of Finance*, **48**, 1039–1055.

Elton, E., Gruber, M., Das, S. and Hlavka, M. (1993) Efficiency with costly information: a reinterpretation of evidence from managed portfolios, *Review of Financial Studies*, **6**, 1–22.

Ferson, W. and Schadt, R. (1996) Measuring fund strategy and performance in changing economic conditions, *Journal of Finance*, **51**, 425–462.

Hendricks, D., Patel, J. and Zeckhauser, R. (1993) Hot hands in mutual funds: short-run persistence of relative performance, *Journal of Finance*, **48**, 93–130.

Lakonishok, J., Shleifer, A. and Vishny, R.W. (1992) The structure and performance of the money management industry, *Brookings Papers: Microeconomics*, 339–391.

Myners, P. (2001) *Institutional Investment in the United Kingdom: A Review*, HM Treasury, London, March.

Plantinga, A. and van der Meer, R. (1995) Liability-driven performance attribution, *Geneva Papers on Risk and Insurance*, **20**, 16–29.

Timmermann, A. and Blake, D. (2000) *Determinants of International Portfolio Performance*, Pensions Institute, London, September (www.pensions-institute.org).

Wilson, Rt Hon. Sir H. (chairman) (1980) *Report of the Committee to Review the Functioning of Financial Institutions*, Cmnd. 7937, HMSO, London, June.

Chapter 6

Simulation as a means of portfolio performance evaluation

FRANCES COWELL

ABSTRACT

Conventional return and attribution analysis has some serious limitations, including:

- It has difficulty in distinguishing between chance and skill as the primary determinants of portfolio returns.
- It does not provide information about the investability or efficiency of the benchmark.
- It does not comprehensively quantify the impact of constraints.
- It does not easily quantify the contribution of mid-period transactions and market timing.
- It can only be applied to portfolios with completely transparent holdings.
- It does not facilitate 'what-if' analyses.
- Multi-period attribution analysis has limited validity because the investment opportunity set is subject to continuous change.

Simulation can address some of these shortcomings by using Monte Carlo selection to derive, from a given investment universe, a large, unbiased sample of portfolios that comply with given portfolio constraints and specifications. For any given performance measurement, such as return or tracking error, a distribution of outcomes can be obtained.

Simulations are carried out at the asset allocation level for a balanced portfolio of nine asset classes, comparing the distribution of returns obtained under unconstrained and two levels of constraints and allowing some inferences about the impact of constraints. A second set of simulations quantifies the impact of portfolio design on the observed tracking error of an international equity portfolio, allowing the conclusion that holding constraints designed to limit tracking error actually increase it. A third set of simulations tests the relationship between maximum number of stocks allowed on tracking error for a domestic equity indexed portfolio.

6.1 INTRODUCTION

Despite increasingly sophisticated techniques for portfolio return and attribution analysis, there remain limits to the inferences that can be drawn from the results they give. A single period attribution analysis, for example, can identify which relative imbalances contributed to return variation from benchmark, but cannot say with certainty whether those imbalances and the results to which they contributed were due to deliberate portfolio construction choices or the result, essentially, of luck. For investors choosing between investment managers and strategies, this lack of information can pose serious problems.

A positive active return can be achieved by an investment manager through either luck or skill. If the result is due to skill, the investor can reasonably conclude that this skill is likely to be repeated in future, and is therefore worth paying active management fees. If, on the other hand, the result is due mainly to chance, then subsequent active returns are as likely to be positive as negative and the investor will prefer either to invest in an indexed portfolio or to engage an investment manager who has demonstrated skill. Similar logic applies to selecting investment strategies. Observed positive returns to a strategy can be the result of either chance or strategy design and the ability to distinguish between the two is imperative for selecting a strategy that will yield positive results in the future.

Other aspects of portfolio performance that are often not adequately addressed by conventional return and attribution analysis include:

- The suitability and investability of the benchmark.
- The impact of constraints.
- The contribution of mid-period trading activity.

An important feature of a benchmark is that it should be investable. In other words, the investment manager should be able to buy all the assets in the benchmark in benchmark proportions without incurring excessive transactions costs. Not all benchmarks comply with this. Many investors work around this problem by using peer groups as benchmarks on the basis that, being actual portfolios, they are necessarily investable. Peer-group benchmarks have many merits, but suffer from the shortcoming that they encourage investment managers to conform to popular portfolio structures and can discourage active decision taking. For portfolios using non-peer-group benchmarks, a reasonable question to ask is whether the chosen benchmark is the most appropriate to the portfolio. A benchmark that is not fully investable will nearly always give exaggerated portfolio active returns and high tracking error. Conversely, attractive active returns that are attributed to skill on the part of the investment manager may simply be the result of the benchmark being 'easy to beat' given the universe of available investments. Most return and attribution analysis techniques do not add significant information about the relative investability or efficiency of the benchmark.

Related to the problem of benchmark selection is the vexed question of constraints. Many investors impose constraints on portfolio holdings as a means of containing risk. Often, however, the net effect of these constraints is merely to hamper the ability of the investment manager to achieve optimal diversification, resulting in increased risk for return or poor return for risk taken. Quantification of the impact on portfolio performance of holding and other constraints is very difficult using conventional return and attribution methods, since they can only quantify the marginal impact on assets actually constrained, without offering insight into how these constraints affect selection of the remainder of the portfolio.

Perhaps a more important limitation of conventional return and attribution analysis is the difficulty of quantifying the impact of mid-period trading activity. Comprehensive analysis of the contribution to portfolio return of trading activity requires analysis of each individual trade, itself necessitating the establishment and maintenance of an extensive database, including daily security prices and individual transaction details. Moreover, the resulting analysis, itself comprising large amounts of data, can be difficult to interpret.

Multiple period return and attribution analyses can often highlight persistent characteristics of a portfolio or management style and point to potentially significant patterns that could persist in future periods. But the validity of such analyses are usually limited because:

- Investment managers rarely employ precisely the same investment strategies over extended periods for actively managed portfolios.
- Even with a consistent approach to portfolio selection, changes in personnel within the investment management company mean that the range of skills and strengths within the company are subject to constant change, which is reflected in portfolio performance and often in investment policies.
- The investable universe is subject to continuous change as a result of new issues and privatizations, and as mainstream investors increasingly accept

new instruments, such as derivative instruments, exchange-traded funds and emerging markets securities.

- Data, tools and analysis techniques available to investment managers are continuously evolving, placing inevitable pressure on investment managers to upgrade and modify portfolio construction, analysis and monitoring techniques.
- Regulatory and tax environments are subject to continuous change, forcing investment managers to modify their approaches accordingly.
- Maintaining a reliable database of portfolio performance for the purpose of multiple period portfolio comparisons for even a moderately comprehensive range of investments is extremely difficult.

Portfolio return analyses therefore can usually span only a relatively small number of periods, so that the results obtained nearly always fail to meet any test of statistical significance or reveal persistent performance patterns.

The uncertainties implicit in traditional return and attribution analysis leave plenty of room for speculation by investors that persistent outperformance of benchmarks is due principally to luck or a particularly 'easy' mandate specification; and conversely claims by investment managers that persistently poor performance is the result of very tight or conflicting constraints. These are claims that are difficult to reliably support or refute using conventional return and attribution analysis.

Traditional attribution analysis cannot be applied to funds that do not regularly offer transparency of holdings to investors. Evaluation of such funds is limited to comparison with their stated benchmarks or with funds with similar stated investment objectives – comparisons of which may be of limited validity because of differences in objectives, focus, investment universe or constraints, and because there are often only a small number of similar portfolios available for comparison.

Conventional return and attribution analysis does not facilitate 'what-if' analyses, aimed at exploring the performance effect of changing various portfolio selection parameters, for example altering the scope of the investment universe and testing changes in hedging policy.

Moreover, these problems are all equally acute at the level of asset allocation for balanced portfolios and security selection for specialist sector portfolios.

6.2 OBJECTIVES OF SIMULATIONS

The objectives are:

- To distinguish portfolio outcomes that are due to chance from those resulting from deliberate investment choices and systemic biases in

portfolio construction; and from this to identify evidence of skill in portfolio construction.
- To determine the relative efficiency of the benchmark.
- To quantify the contribution to return of intra-period trading and market timing.
- To evaluate the impact of constraints and perform other 'what-if' analyses.
- To identify persistent strengths and weaknesses of an investment strategy over consecutive investment periods.

A partial solution can be obtained by means of simulation. The objective of this approach is to provide a large unbiased sample of portfolios, each selected from the same universe of investments and conforming to the same benchmark and other specifications as the target portfolio.

Thus a candidate portfolio might be assigned a single period performance p value of 0.86. Compared to the returns of 100 portfolios selected at random from the same investment universe and subject to the same constraints, the candidate portfolio would be expected to outperform 86 of them.

Altering portfolio selection parameters, for example to broaden or narrow the investment universe or modify constraints, can, by introducing a control, isolate the performance impact of the relevant parameters, facilitating 'what-if' analyses and thus adding insight into the forces affecting overall portfolio outcomes.

Comparing actual performance to a comparable buy-and-hold portfolio can quantify the impact of intra-period trading activity and market timing.

This approach is equally valuable for asset allocation within balanced portfolios and for security selection within specialist sector mandates.

6.3 METHODOLOGY

Each simulation is defined by an investment universe of assets, together with required constraints on portfolio holdings and imbalances, hedging policy, maximum and minimum number of assets, portfolio turnover, transactions costs and any other guidelines to which portfolio construction is subject. From the universe of assets a large number of portfolios are selected using a Monte Carlo sampling approach. Portfolios conforming to the constraints and specifications given are retained, while those not conforming are discarded. For each simulated portfolio are calculated a range of performance measurements, giving a distribution of outcomes. Actual portfolios and benchmarks are compared to the sample of portfolios selected at random.

6.4 ADVANTAGES OF SIMULATION

Applying simulation to the problem of performance evaluation presents a number of advantages.

1. Actual portfolio outcomes are compared to a large, unbiased sample of possible outcomes rather than a small number of actual 'peer' portfolios.
2. Sample selection is controlled so that the simulated portfolios are subject to exactly the same constraints and limitations as the actual portfolio. By contrast, the mandate specifications for 'peer' portfolios can differ in small but often important details.
3. The simulation of a random peer group for comparison avoids the judgemental and other biases inherent in live peer group comparisons.
4. By systematically altering or suppressing constraints and limitations, the marginal impact of each on simulation outcomes can be isolated, in effect providing a control, and thus providing the capability of conducting 'what-if' analyses.
5. Comparing actual portfolio outcomes with those from a 'buy-and-hold' equivalent can help quantify the impact of trading activity.
6. It can be applied to any portfolio of traded assets, and therefore is equally valid for asset allocation and security selection, including fixed interest.
7. Derivative, such as futures, options and swaps are easily incorporated into the simulation. Indeed, provided that the appropriate price data are available, there is no impediment to including any investment instruments, whether exchange-traded or over-the-counter.
8. Simulation requires slightly less data than conventional return and attribution analysis (mid-period transaction data are generally not required), and although greater computing resources are generally called for, most problems can be accommodated using a standard desktop computer.

6.5 EXAMPLES OF PORTFOLIO SIMULATION

To illustrate some of the potential applications, portfolio simulation is applied to four frequently occurring portfolio evaluation situations.

1. Simulations 1 and 2 compare the effectiveness of 1,000 and 5,000 unconstrained simulations for asset allocation for a portfolio comprising nine asset classes.
2. Simulations 3 and 4 evaluate the same nine-asset class portfolio with two sets of holding constraints.
3. Simulations 5, 6, 7 and 8 show the impact, in terms of return and tracking error, of a portfolio comprising only listed equity index futures contracts relative to global equities benchmark.
4. Simulations 9, 10 and 11 show the impact on the tracking error of a domestic indexed portfolio of constraining the maximum allowable number of stocks.

6.5.1 Single period tactical asset allocation

This is a typical short-term asset allocation problem with the benchmark set as the strategic asset allocation. Table 6.1 sets out portfolio and benchmark allocations, together with holding constraints and forecast returns for each asset class.

At the end of the first quarter the portfolio return is −3.59% compared to the benchmark of −3.48%, implying annualized returns of −13.61% and −13.21% for the portfolio and benchmark respectively, an annual active return of −0.40%.

Noting that the actual portfolio allocations are not very different from benchmark, the investor is interested to know if the constraints are inhibiting active return. A series of simulations was carried out to evaluate the performance impact of constraining relative portfolio allocations.

The first simulation, constraining only negative holdings, and applying 1,000 simulations, yields the results in Figure 6.1.

The mean of this distribution is −5.09% and the standard deviation is 3.00%. Given the non-normal shape of the distribution (the skew is 0.33 and the kurtosis is 2.29), it was decided to increase the number of simulations. Applying more simulations gives only a slightly more normal-looking result, as in Figure 6.2, which applies 5,000.

The mean of this distribution is −5.13% and the standard deviation is 3.03%, with a skew of 0.32 and kurtosis of 2.34.

Table 6.1 Portfolio, benchmark and expected returns

Asset name	Asset class	Portfolio holdings	Benchmark holdings	Expected return
JPM France Traded	French Composite Bonds	2.00%	5.00%	−3.00%
JPM Germany Traded	German Composite Bonds	2.00%	5.00%	−4.50%
JPM UK Traded	UK Composite Bonds	2.00%	5.00%	−2.50%
JPM US Traded	US Composite Bonds	2.00%	5.00%	−2.50%
CAC 40	French Equities	10.00%	10.00%	12.00%
DAX	German Equities	10.00%	10.00%	12.00%
FTSE All Share	UK Equities	25.00%	20.00%	18.00%
S&P 500	US Equities	45.00%	30.00%	25.00%
TOPIX	Japanese Equities	2.00%	10.00%	−4.50%
Portfolio expected return			17.81%	
Benchmark expected return			12.43%	
Expected active return			5.38%	
Expected tracking error			2.85%	

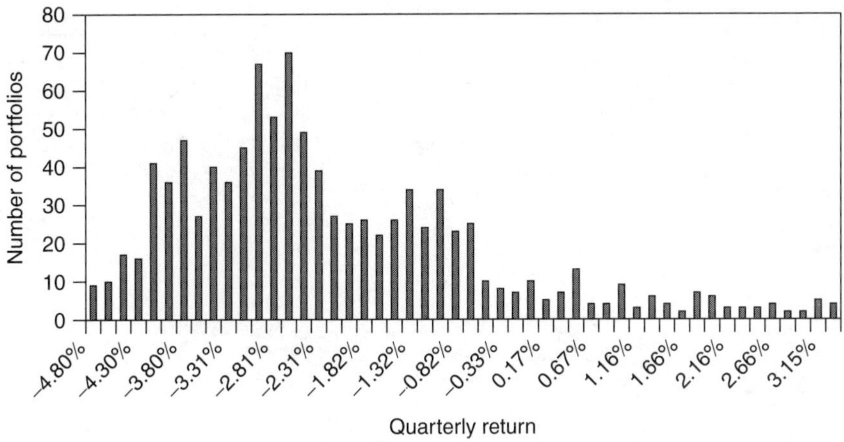

Figure 6.1 Asset allocation with 1,000 simulated portfolios

For this problem, it appears that 1,000 simulations are sufficient to give an indication of the distribution of all possible outcomes.

From this analysis, an interesting question to pose is: what portfolio characteristics yielded an active return of 10.0%? Examining an outlier portfolio can answer this question. A portfolio giving a quarterly active portfolio of 2.5% is set out in Table 6.2.

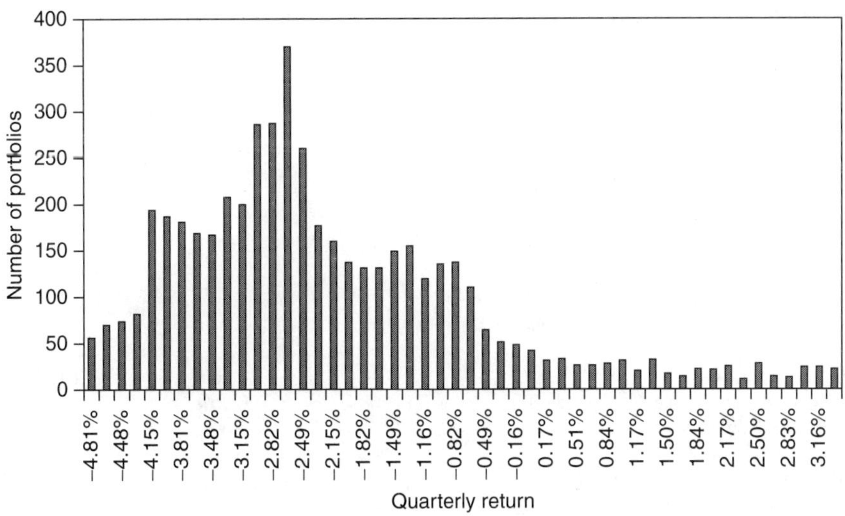

Figure 6.2 Asset allocation with 5,000 simulated portfolios

Table 6.2 Ten per cent Active return portfolio

Asset name	Asset class	Portfolio holdings	Benchmark holdings	Active holdings
JPM France Traded	French composite bonds	0.00%	5.00%	−5.00%
JPM Germany Traded	German composite bonds	10.93%	5.00%	5.93%
JPM UK Traded	UK composite bonds	2.26%	5.00%	−2.74%
JPM US Traded	US composite bonds	46.28%	5.00%	41.28%
CAC 40	French equities	0.71%	10.00%	−9.29%
DAX	German equities	0.00%	10.00%	−10.00%
FTSE All Share	UK equities	0.14%	20.00%	−19.86%
S&P 500	US equities	29.99%	30.00%	−0.01%
TOPIX	Japanese equities	9.71%	10.00%	−0.29%

With nearly half held in US Fixed Interest and a further 30% in US Equities, this portfolio challenges the principles of prudent diversification for a global portfolio. Its observed tracking error is 5.54% and its expected tracking error is 5.57%.

6.5.2 Asset allocation with holding constraints

Most investment managers would be reluctant to implement portfolios with such extreme allocations and risks. In fact many investors insist on imposing constraints to keep actual portfolio allocations reasonably close to benchmark. Table 6.3 shows typical holding constraints.

Imposing these constraints with 1,000 simulations gives the distribution of outcomes as shown in Figure 6.3.

The mean of the distribution is −3.11% and the standard deviation is 1.33%. It shows that the likelihood of achieving an active return of more than 1.5% is quite low. Applying looser constraints, as set out in Table 6.4, gives the results set out in Figure 6.4.

Table 6.3 Asset allocation with typical constraints

Asset name	Portfolio holdings	Benchmark holdings	Min. holding	Max. holding
JPM France Traded	2.00%	5.00%	0.00%	10.00%
JPM Germany Traded	2.00%	5.00%	0.00%	10.00%
JPM UK Traded	2.00%	5.00%	0.00%	10.00%
JPM US Traded	2.00%	5.00%	0.00%	10.00%
CAC 40	10.00%	10.00%	5.00%	20.00%
DAX	10.00%	10.00%	5.00%	20.00%
FTSE All Share	25.00%	20.00%	10.00%	30.00%
S&P 500	45.00%	30.00%	10.00%	50.00%
TOPIX	2.00%	10.00%	0.00%	20.00%

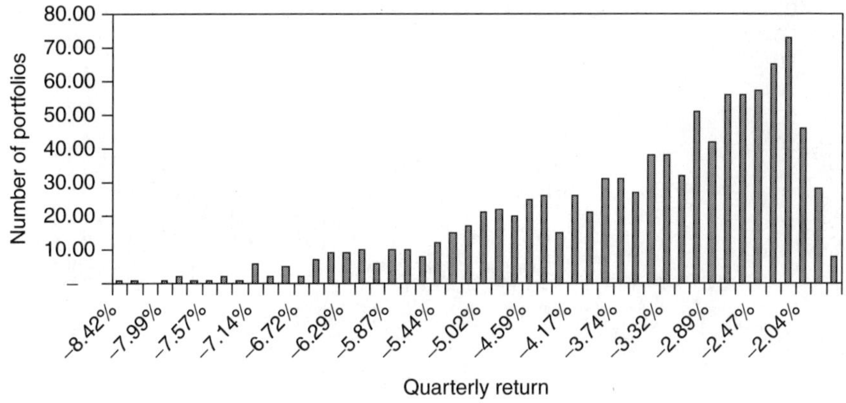

Figure 6.3 Asset allocation with typical constraints

This distribution has a mean of −2.96% and a standard deviation of 1.31%, suggesting that this relaxation of holding constraints is still insufficient to deliver the required active return.

Results

The results of Figures 6.1 to 6.4 are summarized in Table 6.5.

Conclusions

From this it can be concluded that the results given by 1,000 simulations are not greatly improved by extending this number to 5,000. It also can be concluded that, in this instance, the holding constraints are not the main source of disappointing returns, but appear to be contributing to both positive returns and increasing the likelihood of extreme returns.

Table 6.4 Asset allocation with relaxed constraints

Asset name	Portfolio holdings	Benchmark holdings	Min. holding	Max. holding
JPM France Traded	2.00%	5.00%	0.00%	15.00%
JPM Germany Traded	2.00%	5.00%	0.00%	15.00%
JPM UK Traded	2.00%	5.00%	0.00%	15.00%
JPM US Traded	2.00%	5.00%	0.00%	15.00%
CAC 40	10.00%	10.00%	0.00%	50.00%
DAX	10.00%	10.00%	0.00%	50.00%
FTSE All Share	25.00%	20.00%	5.00%	60.00%
S&P 500	45.00%	30.00%	5.00%	80.00%
TOPIX	2.00%	10.00%	0.00%	50.00%

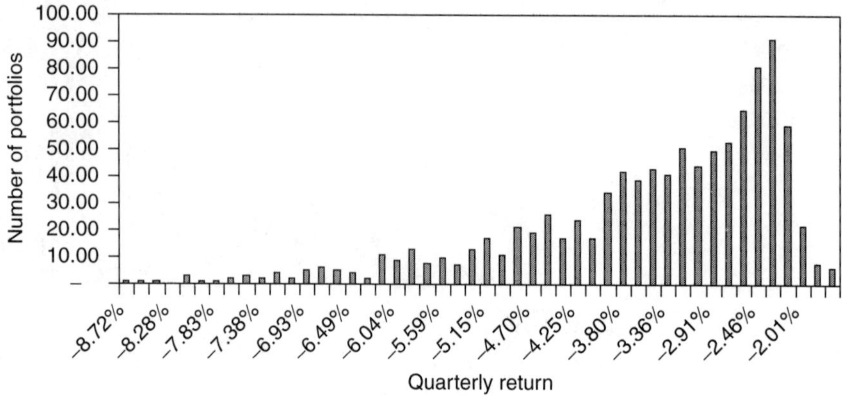

Figure 6.4 Asset allocation with relaxed constraints

6.5.3 International equity indexed portfolio invested using exchange-traded equity futures

Given the costs in terms of transactions, custodian and other administrative costs of investing in a diversified portfolio of international equities, many investors choose to replicate such a portfolio using mainly, or uniquely, futures and other derivative contracts. This approach has the advantage of significantly reducing the costs associated with international equity investing, an advantage that can be important in the case of a unitized portfolio where units are bought and sold frequently, necessitating purchases and sales of the assets held in the portfolio. The advantage of low transactions costs is offset by the disadvantage, as Figures 6.5 to 6.8 show, of significant return variation from benchmark, translating to an unavoidably high tracking error. In order to minimize this tracking error, the investment manager imposes constraints

Table 6.5 Evaluation of constraints on asset allocation

Simulation	Description	Number of simulations	Mean	Standard deviation	Skew	Kurtosis
1	Unconstrained quarterly return	1,000	−5.09%	3.00%	0.31	2.29
2	Unconstrained quarterly return	5,000	−5.13%	3.03%	0.32	2.34
3	Typical constraints quarterly return	1,000	−3.11%	1.33%	−0.95	3.33
4	Loose constraints quarterly return	1,000	−2.96%	1.31%	−1.22	4.24

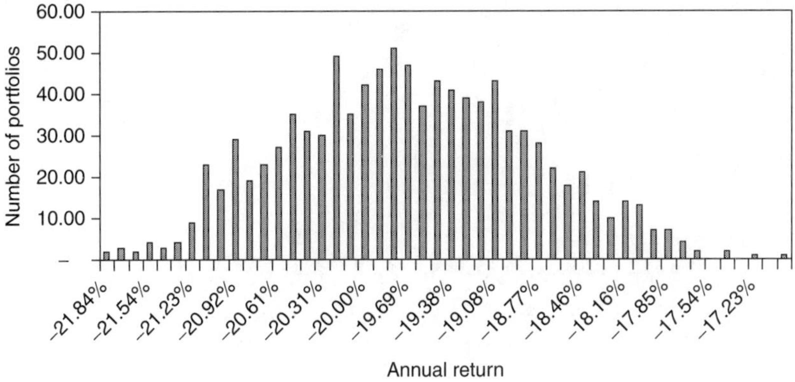

Figure 6.5 International equities with constraints on country allocations

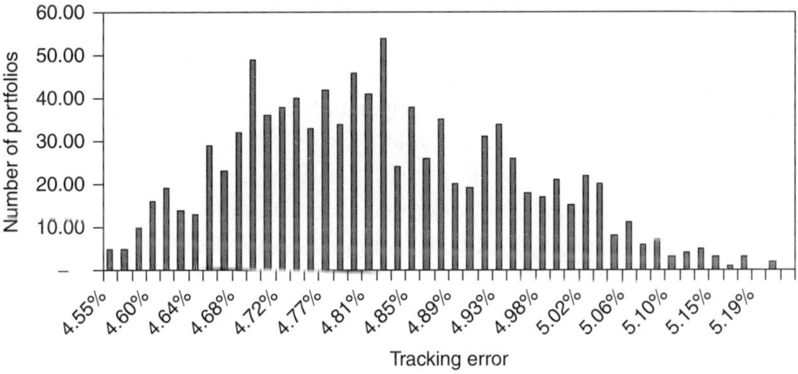

Figure 6.6 International equities with constraints on country allocations

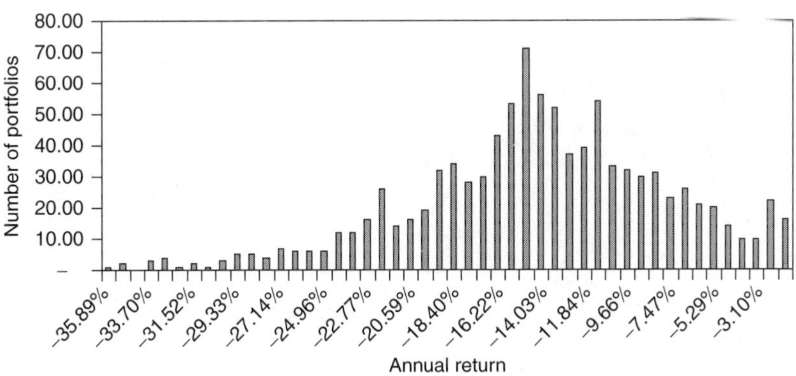

Figure 6.7 International equities unconstrained

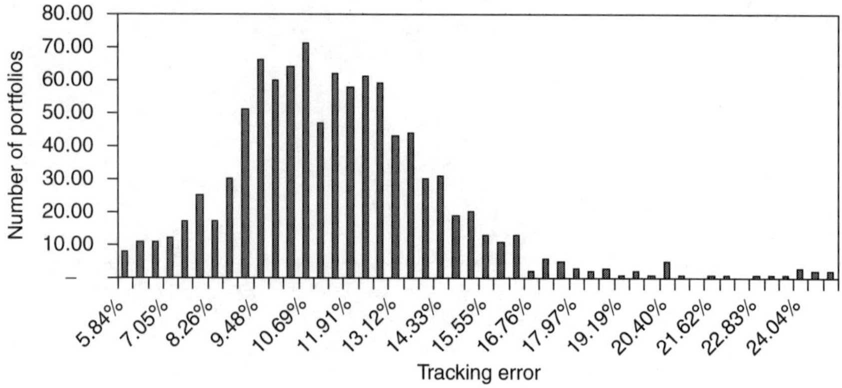

Figure 6.8 International equities unconstrained

on individual country allocations, keeping them close to the nominal country weights in benchmark.

For the period in question the portfolio returned −22.10% and the benchmark −21.26%. The investment manager uses simulations to show that this result is difficult or impossible to avoid. Figures 6.5 and 6.6 show return and tracking error respectively for the constrained portfolio, while Figures 6.7 and 6.8 show the same analysis with no holding constraints.

In Figure 6.5 the mean of this distribution is −19.73%, the standard deviation is 0.87%, with skew and kurtosis of 0.16 and 2.71, respectively. In Figure 6.6 the mean of this distribution is 4.81%, the standard deviation is 0.13%, with skew and kurtosis of 0.38 and 2.62, respectively.

With a mean tracking error of 4.81% the portfolio was unlikely to deliver index-like performance unless some of the constraints were relaxed. Figures 6.7 and 6.8 show return and tracking error with no limits on country allocation.

In Figure 6.7 the mean of this distribution is −14.26%, the standard deviation is 6.50%, with skew and kurtosis of −0.37 and 3.30, respectively. In Figure 6.8 the mean of this distribution is 11.45%, the standard deviation is 2.99%, with skew and kurtosis of 1.27 and 6.59, respectively.

Results

The results of Figures 6.5 to 6.8 are summarized in Table 6.6.

Conclusions

Figures 6.5 to 6.8 show that relaxing the constraints increased both the tracking error and the mean return, and made achieving index-like returns even more unlikely.

Table 6.6 Evaluation of constraints for international equities

Simulation	Description	Mean	Standard deviation	Skew	Kurtosis
1	Country holding Constraints annual return	−19.73%	0.87%	0.16	2.71
2	Country holding Constraints tracking error	4.81%	0.13%	0.38	2.62
3	Unconstrained annual return	−14.26%	6.50%	−0.37	3.30
4	Unconstrained tracking error	11.45%	2.99%	1.27	6.59

6.5.4 Domestic equity indexed portfolio with varying allowable maximum number of holdings

While classic domestic equities indexed portfolios often apply full replication to achieve index returns with very low tracking error, many investors prefer a sampling approach, which while increasing tracking error, can significantly reduce transactions costs, especially where the benchmark comprises a large number of stocks. The reasoning is sound enough, since the effect of tracking error on relative return can be either positive or negative, while the effect of transactions costs is always negative. The question is: how many stocks should the portfolio hold to achieve the best balance of tracking error and transactions costs. By quantifying the distribution of tracking error for various numbers of portfolio holdings, simulation can help, as shown in Figures 6.9 to 6.11.

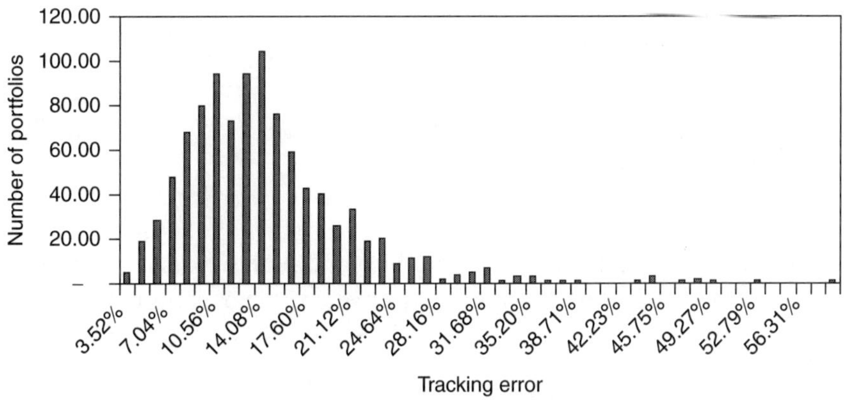

Figure 6.9 S&P 500 portfolio: 400 holdings allowed

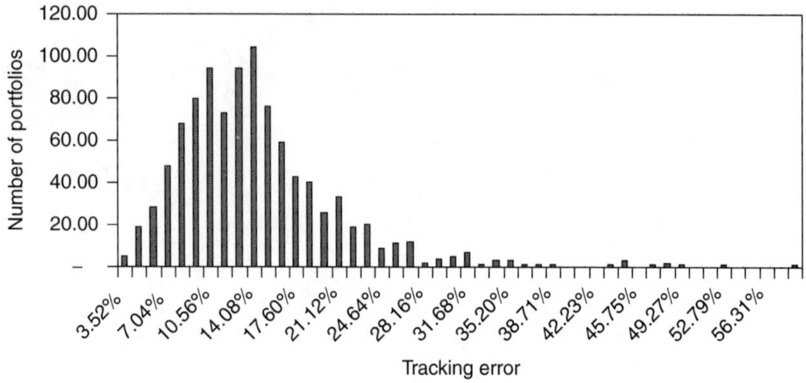

Figure 6.10 S&P 500 portfolio: 300 holdings allowed

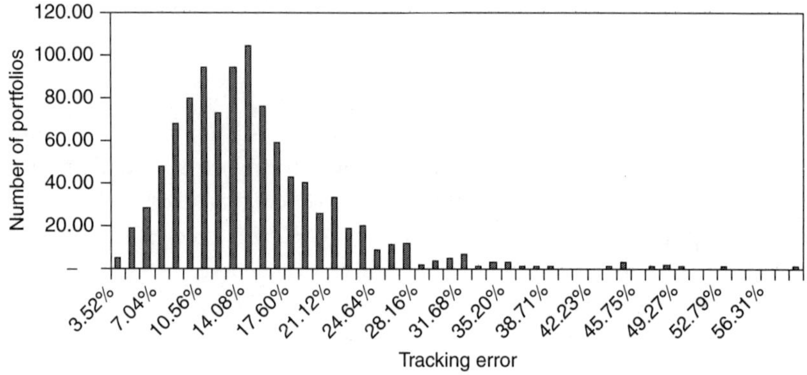

Figure 6.11 S&P 500 portfolio: 200 holdings allowed

In Figure 6.9 the mean of this distribution is 25.85%, the standard deviation is 4.85%, with skew and kurtosis of 2.57 and 16.3, respectively. In Figure 6.10 the mean of this distribution is 30.59%, the standard deviation is 6.94%, with skew and kurtosis of 2.66 and 14.29, respectively. In Figure 6.11 the mean of this distribution is 32.43%, the standard deviation is 6.79%, with skew and kurtosis of 2.81 and 10.63, respectively.

Results

Figures 6.9, 6.10 and 6.11 show that increasing the maximum number of allowable holdings does reduce tracking error, as summarized in Table 6.7.

Conclusions

Increasing the allowable number of stocks by itself reduces the mean tracking error achievable as well as the range of tracking errors likely, and so

Table 6.7 Maximum holdings and tracking error

Simulation	Description	Mean tracking error	Standard deviation	Skew	Kurtosis
9	400 stocks	26.85	4.85	2.57	16.30
10	300 stocks	30.59	6.94	2.66	14.29
11	200 stocks	32.43	6.79	2.81	10.63

potentially the accuracy of tracking error forecasts. However, simply allowing a large number of stocks does not by itself achieve low tracking error: this measure needs to be complemented with other constraints, such as direct tracking error constraints or appropriate holding constraints.

6.6 APPLICATIONS

6.6.1 Long–short simulation

The simplest form of simulation is a long-only portfolio benchmarked to a balanced or equity index; however, the same methodology can be applied to long–short or market neutral portfolios to evaluate active return. The technique can be very powerful for analysing and evaluating hedge funds, especially those investing in unlisted assets or derivatives. The potential value of simulation can be significant, particularly where the investment manager's remuneration is based on active return.

6.6.2 Multiple period simulations

The advantages of single period simulation can in some cases be extended to multiple period simulation. By augmenting the single period simulation inputs of investment universe, portfolio limitations, constraints and guidelines with trading and rebalancing rules, the simulation can generate a sample of multiple period portfolio outcomes highlighting, in addition to portfolio active return, tracking error and other characteristics, the range of portfolio turnover required to achieve given outcomes, and the related range of transactions costs.

Multiple period portfolio simulations can combine insights from portfolio analysis over time with the advantages of a large sample of possible outcomes within a period. The analysis therefore has the potential to highlight the strengths and weaknesses of an investment manager or investment strategy in different economic and market conditions. Because the time interval can be set to correspond with the history of a particular portfolio or strategy, or the tenure of a particular manager or analyst, simulating an investment strategy over time can provide a rigorous analysis that avoids the problems of discontinuity that plague real-life multiple period performance analyses.

6.6.3 Selection of metric

While the most obvious application of simulations is to compare portfolio returns with a sample of possible active returns, additional insight can often be derived by applying specialized metrics according to portfolio objectives. For example, when evaluating indexed portfolios, it is probably more appropriate to apply a tracking error metric to the analysis. Thus, for a given maximum number of assets, the distribution of tracking error can be derived, facilitating the evaluation of tracking performance, both *ex ante* and *ex post*.

Specialist portfolios, such as those designed to track growth and value indices, can be evaluated according to a style metric to show how the portfolio's exposure to a given style compares with all possible portfolios.

6.6.4 Solutions to practical problems

The ability to isolate the impact of portfolio constraints and other elements of portfolio construction, simulations can add considerable insight into the forces driving portfolio returns, specifically:

- *Benchmark evaluation* is facilitated by comparing the benchmark outcome with the distribution of random outcomes. This can quantify the amount of skill required to match or exceed benchmark outcomes with respect to the population of all possible outcomes. This can be especially powerful when investment management fees are determined by portfolio active return.
- *Constraint evaluation* can help quantify the extent to which holding and other constraints contribute to or hinder portfolio performance. Simulation can therefore help define the most effective and appropriate investment mandates.
- *What-if analysis* is greatly facilitated by allowing individual aspects of investment policy to be evaluated in isolation against a control.
- *Quantifying the impact of trading activity* is facilitated by comparing the buy-and-hold portfolio with the actual portfolio result and the distribution of all possible results. Similarly, estimation of the potential impact of transactions costs can be effected by varying the rate of transactions costs for each asset in the investment universe.
- *Performance comparison of non-transparent funds* can be assisted by applying simulation techniques whereby fund performance is compared to a random sample of all possible outcomes for the period. The additional

insight to be derived is particularly significant where traditional return attribution is prohibited by lack of portfolio holding information.

6.7 SUMMARY AND CONCLUSIONS

Portfolio simulation works by selecting a random sample of portfolios from a given investment universe to conform to given limitations and guidelines. The portfolios thus selected can then provide a meaningful comparison for real-life portfolios. Comparisons can be based on *ex post* active return, portfolio tracking error, portfolio style or any quantifiable portfolio characteristic. The metric can be chosen to meet the precise objectives of the analysis. These comparisons can help address some of the gaps left by conventional return and attribution analysis, specifically:

- By providing a large sample of comparable portfolio outcomes, simulation can help identify skill on the part of investment managers.
- Comparing the benchmark to the sample of portfolio outcomes can help determine the suitability and investability of the benchmark.
- By carrying out control simulations with and without portfolio constraints, their impact on portfolio performance can be quantified and 'what-if' analysis facilitated.
- Comparing actual portfolio outcomes to simulated buy-and-hold portfolios can help evaluate intra-period trading and market timing.

The potential benefits of single period simulation can be extended to multiple period, enabling evaluation of portfolios in a variety of market conditions. The methodology can be applied to any portfolio comprising traded assets, both exchange-traded and over-the-counter, including asset allocation, equity, fixed interest, futures, options, commodity and market-neutral portfolios.

The examples in this chapter show that simulation sometimes confirms expectations, as in Figures 6.5 to 6.8, but can often yield unexpected results, for example it can show that constraints designed to control risk may have little or no impact, as in Figures 6.3 and 6.4, or that, to be effective, portfolio guidelines need to be complemented with other portfolio construction parameters, as in Figures 6.9 to 6.11.

Chapter 7

An analysis of performance measures using copulae

SOOSUNG HWANG AND MARK SALMON

ABSTRACT

We have carried out a detailed comparison of the statistical properties, and the relationships between a set of five performance measures using 14 UK-based investment trusts over a sample period ranging from 1980 to 2001. Our results suggest very clearly that there is almost no difference between Jensen's alpha, the Treynor–Mazuy (TM) measure and the Positive Period Weighting (PPW) measure over our sample period and among our set of investment trusts. This would seem to indicate that there is no timing ability within these fund managers. The Sharpe ratio clearly provides different signals regarding performance than the other measures and is the only absolute measure in the set of measures we have considered. While simple correlation analysis suggests that there is a high degree of dependence between most of the measures we show that there is a lack of significant concordance between the Sharpe ratio and all the other measures. This reflects the inadequacy of correlation analysis with non-Gaussian data. We have also shown that the Sharpe ratio exhibits negative left tail area dependence with respect to Jensen's alpha, TM and PPW but is independent in the left tail, when poor performance is indicated, from the higher moment (HM) measure of Hwang and Satchell. Jensen's alpha, TM and the HM measure do not seem to show any significant asymptotic left tail dependency. All the measures appear to be asymptotically independent in their upper tail when good performance is indicated. These results are further refined by non-asymptotic quantile regression results which indicate finite sample dependency of the HM measure and Jensen's alpha throughout the body of their conditional distribution and in the left tail but not the upper tail.

7.1 INTRODUCTION

Studies of portfolio performance evaluation began in the 1960s along with the development of modern asset pricing theory. Treynor (1965), Treynor and Mazuy (1966) and Jensen (1968, 1969), for instance, used the CAPM to introduce portfolio performance measures. As finance theory developed so did performance measurement, for instance Connor and Korajczyk (1986) and Lehmann and Modest (1987) introduced APT-based measures, there are the positive period weighting measures of Grinblatt and Titman (1989), the intertemporal marginal rates of substitution-based measures of Glosten and Jagannathan (1994), the measures of Chen and Knez (1996) based on the law of one price and/or no arbitrage, and the higher moment measure of Hwang and Satchell (1998).

While the early CAPM-based performance measures have well-recognized deficiencies, in particular that they rest either on a false assumption that asset returns are normally distributed and thus distributed symmetrically or that investors have mean-variance preferences and thus ignore skewness, they still appear to be the most widely accepted for evaluating portfolio managers within the finance industry, see, for instance, the *AIMR Performance Presentation Standards Handbook* (1997). This would seem to deny the practical relevance of the theoretical arguments which led to the development of more refined measures, such as those indicated above. This chapter asks the simple question of whether or not this view is justified. We take a pragmatic approach by comparing several measures using times series of monthly returns for 14 UK-based investment trusts over a sample period running from January 1980 to February 2001.

Our objective on one level is crude and is simply to examine whether or not there are significant differences between the different performance measures and then, if so, in what states of the market they occur. We adopt a slightly different statistical approach to similar comparative exercises in that we are interested in determining where in the range of their potential values these measures are likely to provide different signals of performance or in other words when they are likely to be more dependent or independent of each other. They may, for instance, provide similar assessments when in their extremes but not when close to their average values – or vice versa. This we feel may be a critical practical concern for a fund manager uncertain as to which performance measure to adopt. Since the different measures represent different transformations of non-Gaussian return series we would expect to find that simple correlation analysis would be inadequate since it is only applicable in the context of elliptic distributions and even in that case only measures linear association.[1]

As an alternative we adopt the relatively recently developed theory of copula functions and associated dependency measures to examine more general forms of association between the different performance measures rather than just simply their normalized covariation. In particular we consider their concordance which enables us to consider general positive (or negative) dependency rather than simple linear association. We then examine the dependency between the performance measures as they take values in the tails of their distributions by asking the question: what is the probability that measure A will be beyond its 95th percentile given that measure B is also beyond its 95th percentile? In other words we quantify their tail area dependency given that this may be the most important area for many critical practical decisions. We then also examine, through bivariate quantile regressions, the significance of their association throughout the range of their distribution. Finally we demonstrate how copulae may be used as aggregator functions to combine different but statistically dependent performance measures into a single measure. Following the literature on forecast combination we may expect an increase in efficiency and a reduction in bias by combining performance measures as long as the dependence between the individual components is properly taken into account in constructing the aggregate.

In the next section we briefly introduce the performance measures used in this study; the Sharpe ratio, Jensen's alpha, the Treynor–Mazuy measure, the Positive Period Weighting measure, and a higher moment measure. We then compare these measures using data on the 14 investment trusts before introducing the notion of a copula and related dependency measures.

7.2 PERFORMANCE MEASURES

Several issues are of immediate importance when we seek to evaluate the performance of a portfolio although the relationship between the risk carried by the portfolio and the return is clearly paramount. Different concepts of risk, either relative or absolute, are employed and the notion of 'risk' itself may be measured more generally using quantiles than the traditional use of the second moment. Some measures such as Jensen's alpha calculate relative returns after considering the systematic risk of the portfolio in the CAPM

[1] More importantly in the context of performance evaluation perhaps is the fact that correlation is not independent of montone changes of the underlying data.

framework, while others such as the Sharpe ratio simply use the return and variance of the portfolio itself.

Another issue is the measurement of any superior timing ability as distinct from the stock selection ability in the fund manager. The difference between these two turns on whether private information lies in market aggregates or is firm-specific. For example, suppose that a fund manager has a portfolio which includes Microsoft. When he receives favourable information regarding Microsoft, he will increase his holding in Microsoft and this has nothing to do with the forecast of the market. Thus selectivity information is related to non-priced risk, while timing information is related to priced risk, see Grinblatt and Titman (1995) for a more detailed discussion on this topic. Another critical issue is the sensitivity to the choice of reference index and the need to select an efficient benchmark as again emphasized by Grinblatt and Titman (1994).

In the following section we briefly introduce the five performance measures we use below. Although the rationale and theoretical justification of these measures are to a degree different, empirically they may behave in a similar manner under many situations. How they differ in practice is a question of empirical evidence which we provide in the next section.

7.2.1 Traditional performance measures[2]

Treynor (1965) was the first to incorporate risk into a performance measure by considering the portfolio's rate of return with respect to the market rate of return. Jensen's (1968) extension is simpler and one of the most widely used in practice. Jensen's alpha, α_p^J, calculates the performance of a portfolio by measuring the deviation of a portfolio's return from the securities market line:

$$r_{pt} - r_f = \alpha_p^J + \beta_p(r_{mt} - r_f) + \varepsilon_{pt} \tag{7.1}$$

where r_{pt} represents the portfolio's return at time t, r_f is the risk-free rate, r_{mt} is the market return at time t, β_p denotes the systematic risk of the portfolio. Notice that Jensen's alpha is the expected excess return of the portfolio less the product of the expected excess return of the market portfolio and the portfolio's beta.

The second measure we use is the Treynor–Mazuy (TM) statistic introduced in Treynor and Mazuy (1966). For a portfolio manager with forecasting power, the return on the managed portfolio will not be linearly related to the market return. This arises because he will gain more than the market when the market return is forecast to rise and he will lose less than the market when the market

[2]Our objective here is not to provide a detailed theoretical comparison of the measures which can be found in a number of existing surveys but simply to provide the basis for the comparative analysis below.

is forecast to fall. Thus, his portfolio returns will be a concave function of market returns. Using the following quadratic model,

$$r_{pt} - r_f = \alpha_p + \beta_{1p}(r_{mt} - r_f) + \beta_{2p}(r_{mt} - r_f)^2 + \varepsilon_{pt} \tag{7.2}$$

Treynor and Mazuy (1966) showed how the significance of β_{2p} provides evidence of the overperformance of a portfolio. Admati *et al.* (1986) suggested conditions under which α_p in (7.2) can be interpreted as the selectivity component of performance (i.e. the ability to forecast the returns on individual assets) and $E(\beta_{2p}(r_{mt} - r_{ft})^2)$ interpreted as the timing component of performance (i.e. the ability to forecast market returns). The Treynor and Mazuy measure we use below is then given by

$$TM = \alpha_p + \beta_{2p}E((r_{mt} - r_f)^2) \tag{7.3}$$

The Sharpe ratio (SR) (Sharpe, 1966) is simply the reward per unit of variability:

$$SR = \frac{E(r_{pt} - r_f)}{\sigma_p} \tag{7.4}$$

where σ_p is the standard deviation of portfolio returns. The measure is simple, easy to understand and widely used.

The fourth measure we consider is the higher moment (HM) measure introduced by Hwang and Satchell (1998). Portfolio returns are invariably not normally distributed and higher moments such as skewness and kurtosis need to be considered to adjust for the non-normality and to a degree account for the failure of variance to measure risk accurately. In these cases, a higher moment CAPM should prove more suitable than the traditional CAPM and so a performance measure based on higher moments may also be more accurate than the measures outlined above. Assuming the validity of the three-moment CAPM and a quadratic return generating process of the form[3]:

$$r_{pt} - r_f = a_{0p} + a_{1p}(r_{mt} - r_f) + a_{2p}\{r_{mt} - E(r_m)\}^2 + \varepsilon_{pt} \tag{7.5}$$

we can define a performance measure of a portfolio under the three-moment CAPM as

$$a_p = \mu_p - \lambda_1\mu_m - \lambda_2(\beta_{pm} - \gamma_{pm}) \tag{7.6}$$

[3]Kraus and Litzenberger (1976) showed that the three-moment CAPM is consistent with the quadratic market model in (7.5).

where:

$$\lambda_1 = \frac{\gamma_m^2 \gamma_{pm} - (\theta_m - 1)\beta_{pm}}{\gamma_m^2 - (\theta_m - 1)} \tag{7.7}$$

$$\lambda_2 = \frac{\gamma_m \sigma_m}{\gamma_m^2 - (\theta_m - 1)} \tag{7.8}$$

with $\mu_p = E(r_{pt} - r_f)$, $\mu_m = E(r_{mt} - r_f)$, $\sigma_m = E[\{r_{mt} - E(r_{mt})\}^2]^{1/2}$, and

$$\gamma_m = \frac{E[\{r_{mt} - E(r_{mt})\}^3]}{\sigma_m^3}, \quad \theta_m = \frac{E[\{r_{mt} - E(r_{mt})\}^4]}{\sigma_m^4} \tag{7.9}$$

and

$$\beta_{pm} = \frac{E[\{r_{pt} - E(r_{pt})\}\{r_{mt} - E(r_{mt})\}]}{E[\{r_{mt} - E(r_{mt})\}^2]},$$

$$\gamma_{pm} = \frac{E[\{r_{pt} - E(r_{pt})\}\{r_{mt} - E(r_{mt})\}^2]}{E[\{r_{mt} - E(r_{mt})\}^3]} \tag{7.10}$$

Note that γ_m and θ_m are the skewness and kurtosis of the market returns, and β_{pm} and γ_{pm} are beta and coskewness, respectively. If the market returns are normal, then $\lambda_1 = \beta_{pm}$ and $\lambda_2 = 0$ and thus (7.6) is equivalent to Jensen's alpha.[4]

We also use the Positive Period Weighting (PPW) measure introduced by Grinblatt and Titman (1989). This measure is designed so that if selectivity and timing information are independent and the portfolio manager is a positive market timer, then the PPW measure assigns positive performance to stock selection ability and/or timing ability.[5] The PPW measure is obtained in two steps. First, we have to select a weighting vector $\{w_t\}_{t=1}^T$. The next step is to compute performance as a weighted average of the period-by-period portfolio excess returns:

$$\alpha_p^p = \sum_{t=1}^{T} w_t (r_{pt} - r_{ft}) \tag{7.11}$$

where $\sum_{t=1}^T w_t = 1$, and $w_t > 0$ for all t. Notice that $\sum_{t=1}^T w_t (r_{mt} - r_{ft}) = 0$ for the market portfolio. There are many sets of weights which satisfy these

[4]See Hwang and Satchell (1998) for detailed discussion of the properties of the higher moment performance measure.

[5]See Grinblatt and Titman (1989) for further discussion on the PPW measure.

conditions and we use weights derived from the marginal utilities of an uninformed investor with a power utility function, as in Grinblatt and Titman (1994).

The first three measures above may be classified as traditional performance measures and although they are widely used, there are problems with each of them. The Sharpe ratio, for instance, does not consider systematic risk which is the real risk in Markovitz's mean-variance world. On the other hand, a major problem with Jensen's alpha is that it can assign negative performance to a market timer because it is based on an upwardly biased estimate of systematic risk for a market-timing investment strategy; see Jensen (1972) for further discussion. The Treynor and Mazuy (TM) measure seems to be superior to the Sharpe ratio and Jensen's alpha in the sense that the timing and selectivity ability of portfolio managers can be decomposed. The higher moment performance measure also suffers from the same difficulties as Jensen's alpha but does account for non-Gaussianity. Notice that in the absence of market timing and with the assumption of normality, Jensen's alpha, the Treynor and Mazuy measure, the higher moment measure and the PPW measure are all expected to be identical. The empirical tests of Grinblatt and Titman (1994) and Cumby and Glen (1990) find that Jensen's alpha, the TM measure and PPW are indeed highly correlated. Hwang and Satchell (1998) showed, using emerging market data, that the higher moment measure can rank portfolios quite differently from the other measures when returns are not normal. As the AIMR performance presentation standards handbook (AIMR, 1997:90) states:

> The use of a variety of measures with an understanding of their shortcomings will provide the most valuable information because no one statistic can consistently capture all elements of risk of an asset class or a style of management.

However, as we discuss below, an aggregate measure, which properly accounts for the joint dependence between the constituent performance measures may well serve to compensate for the deficiencies in any one of the individual measures.

7.3 EMPIRICAL RESULTS

We now use data on the 14 UK investment trusts to consider how these five performance measures behave in practice under differing market conditions from January 1980 to February 2001. The FTSE All Share and three-month UK Treasury bill are used as the benchmark and risk-free return, respectively. This period is one of extraordinary growth in the index until 1999 with significant adjustments due to the crash of 1987 and following the Russian Crisis of August 1998.

We note that the choice of a benchmark portfolio is a critical issue in performance analysis. Roll (1978) suggested that the benchmark portfolio should be mean-variance efficient for uninformed managers, while it should be mean-variance inefficient for portfolio managers with forecasting ability. Our choice of the FTSE All Share Index as a benchmark portfolio may not satisfy these conditions, but this value-weighted market portfolio is the most widely used benchmark in empirical studies.

We first provide some statistical properties of the trusts and the benchmark returns and then the five performance measures are analysed for the entire sample period.

7.3.1 Data

Table 7.1 reports the basic statistical properties of the returns from our benchmark and the 14 UK investment trusts over the sample period. The monthly mean return ranges from 1.1% to 1.6% (13% to 19% in annual terms) with standard deviations between 4% and 8% (14% to 28% in annual terms). This performance is exceptionally high when compared with returns over longer horizons such as the last 100 years for US equities, see Cochrane (1997). Panel B of Table 7.1 also reports the same statistical properties when the 1987 market crash is excluded. As expected mean returns increase and standard deviations, skewness and excess kurtosis decrease. However, none of the returns are normally distributed, as indicated by the Jarque–Bera statistics, all showing a negative skew and leptokurtosis.

In panel C of Table 7.1, we report estimates of the correlations between the return series. As might be expected all the correlation coefficients are high and in particular all the correlations with the benchmark portfolio are larger than 0.5 and in fact except for four investment trusts they are all larger than 0.8. The correlations between the different investment trusts are also generally very high but we note that Invesco English & International Trust shows the lowest correlation with the benchmark portfolio and also with the other investment trusts.

7.3.2 Performance of the UK investment trusts for the entire sample period

We next calculate the five performance measures over the entire sample period; see Table 7.2. As in Grinblatt and Titman (1994) and Cumby and Glen (1990), we find that Jensen's alpha, TM and PPW, provide virtually identical results. For these three, the top five and bottom five investment

Table 7.1 Statistical properties of the benchmark portfolio returns and 14 UK investment trust returns

	Mean	STD	Skewness	Excess kurtosis	J & B statistics
A. 1987 market crash (October 1987) included					
FTSE All-share	1.352	4.866	−1.553	7.600	713.362*
Edinburgh Investment Trust (The) PLC	1.367	5.870	−1.099	5.065	322.652*
Fleming Mercantile Inv Trust PLC	1.373	5.707	−1.091	3.556	184.197*
Henderson Smaller Companies Investment Trust PLC	1.299	7.718	−0.783	3.824	180.752*
Govett Strategic Investment Trust PLC	1.198	6.940	−1.434	5.970	464.305*
City of London Investment Trust (The) PLC	1.543	5.939	−1.239	6.199	471.725*
Merchants Trust (The) PLC	1.458	6.158	−1.134	4.658	284.045*
Securities Trust of Scotland PLC	1.438	5.868	−1.320	6.232	484.823*
Fleming Claverhouse Inv Trust PLC	1.584	6.272	−0.853	3.286	145.014*
Murray Income Trust PLC	1.594	5.756	−0.955	3.858	196.065*
Dunedin Income Growth Inv Trust PLC	1.452	5.928	−0.862	4.551	250.698*
Temple Bar Investment Trust PLC	1.524	5.918	−0.911	3.515	165.887*
TR Property Investment Trust PLC	1.135	7.011	−1.018	3.972	210.903*
Throgmorton Trust (The) PLC	1.113	7.133	−0.547	2.943	104.342*
INVESCO English & International Trust PLC	1.209	8.372	−0.271	4.125	183.157*

Notes: A total number of 254 monthly log-returns from January 1980 to February 2001 has been used for the calculation.
*represents significance at 5% level.

B. 1987 market crash (October 1987) excluded					
FTSE All-share	1.479	4.434	−0.623	1.290	33.932*
Edinburgh Investment Trust (The) PLC	1.505	5.452	−0.398	1.051	18.321*
Fleming Mercantile Inv Trust PLC	1.485	5.428	−0.757	2.026	67.394*
Henderson Smaller Companies Investment Trust PLC	1.443	7.383	−0.475	2.809	92.718*
Govett Strategic Investment Trust PLC	1.357	6.476	−0.895	2.985	127.721*
City of London Investment Trust (The) PLC	1.692	5.454	−0.370	0.772	12.042*
Merchants Trust (The) PLC	1.598	5.751	−0.536	1.314	30.333*
Securities Trust of Scotland PLC	1.580	5.424	−0.593	1.933	54.230*
Fleming Claverhouse Inv Trust PLC	1.712	5.941	−0.418	1.246	23.731*
Murray Income Trust PLC	1.718	5.417	−0.442	1.255	24.858*
Dunedin Income Growth Inv Trust PLC	1.539	5.519	−0.144	0.678	5.714*
Temple Bar Investment Trust PLC	1.652	5.566	−0.379	0.737	11.791*
TR Property Investment Trust PLC	1.289	6.581	−0.479	1.092	22.236*
Throgmorton Trust (The) PLC	1.255	6.773	−0.098	1.062	12.300*
INVESCO English & International Trust PLC	1.312	8.226	−0.198	4.279	194.668*

Notes: A total number of 253 monthly log-returns from January 1980 to February 2001 except October 1987 has been used for the calculation.
*represents significance at 5% level.

(*continued overleaf*)

Table 7.1 *(continued)*

	FTSE All-share	Edinburgh	Fleming Mercantile	Henderson Smaller Companies	Govett Strategic	City of London Investment	Merchants Trust	Securities Trust of Scotland	Fleming Claverhouse	Murray Income Trust	Dunedin Income Growth	Temple Bar	TR Property	Throgmorton Trust	INVESCO
C. Correlation matrix for the market portfolio and 14 investment trust (1987 market crash included)															
FTSE All-share	1.000														
Edinburgh	0.888	1.000													
Fleming Mercantile	0.806	0.773	1.000												
Henderson Smaller Companies	0.770	0.755	0.806	1.000											
Govett Strategic	0.805	0.781	0.844	0.808	1.000										
City of London	0.878	0.833	0.741	0.703	0.760	1.000									
Merchants	0.865	0.845	0.731	0.656	0.746	0.860	1.000								
Securities Trust of Scotland	0.892	0.876	0.762	0.747	0.779	0.848	0.877	1.000							
Fleming Claverhouse	0.864	0.800	0.763	0.704	0.773	0.808	0.797	0.800	1.000						
Murray	0.840	0.827	0.716	0.648	0.727	0.848	0.875	0.852	0.783	1.000					
Dunedin Income Growth	0.845	0.842	0.717	0.626	0.729	0.822	0.858	0.823	0.827	0.823	1.000				
Temple Bar	0.852	0.794	0.698	0.616	0.707	0.838	0.852	0.817	0.793	0.832	0.821	1.000			
TR Property	0.702	0.648	0.665	0.602	0.685	0.710	0.689	0.667	0.600	0.646	0.641	0.653	1.000		
Throgmorton	0.756	0.678	0.794	0.755	0.786	0.714	0.662	0.707	0.714	0.661	0.644	0.687	0.637	1.000	
INVESCO	0.529	0.495	0.616	0.644	0.606	0.497	0.478	0.563	0.525	0.431	0.465	0.449	0.463	0.621	1.000

Notes: A total number of 254 monthly log-returns from January 1980 to February 2001 has been used for the calculation.

Table 7.2 Performance of 14 UK investment trust returns for the entire sample period

	Sharpe ratio	Rank	Jensen's alpha	Rank	Treynor–Mazuy	Rank	HM measure	Rank	PPW measure	Rank
Edinburgh	0.1016	9	−0.0245	9	−0.0177	9	0.0264	10	−0.0328	9
Fleming Mercantile	0.1055	8	0.0512	7	0.0638	6	**0.1442**	**4**	0.0525	6
Henderson Smaller Companies	0.0684	10	−0.1833	11	−0.1868	12	−0.2095	13	−0.1770	11
Govett Strategic	0.0616	11	−0.2415	13	−0.2152	13	−0.0472	11	−0.2446	13
City of London	**0.1300**	**2**	**0.1507**	**4**	**0.1605**	**2**	**0.2230**	**2**	**0.1417**	**4**
Merchants	0.1117	7	0.0523	6	0.0570	7	0.0870	7	0.0465	7
Securities Trust of Scotland	0.1137	6	0.0429	8	0.0563	8	**0.1416**	**5**	0.0360	8
Fleming Claverhouse	**0.1296**	**3**	**0.1665**	**2**	**0.1534**	**3**	0.0696	9	**0.1696**	**2**
Murray	**0.1431**	**1**	**0.2473**	**1**	**0.2495**	**1**	**0.2633**	**1**	**0.2423**	**1**
Dunedin Income Growth	**0.1149**	**5**	**0.0845**	**5**	**0.0844**	**5**	0.0836	8	**0.0792**	**5**
Temple Bar	**0.1274**	**4**	**0.1511**	**3**	**0.1447**	**4**	0.1041	6	**0.1538**	**3**
TR Property	0.0520	13	−0.2283	12	−0.1763	11	**0.1553**	**3**	−0.2295	12
Throgmorton	0.0479	14	−0.3042	14	−0.3103	14	−0.3494	14	−0.2953	14
INVESCO	0.0524	12	−0.0957	10	−0.0941	10	−0.0839	12	−0.0771	10

Notes: A total number of 254 monthly log-returns from January 1980 to February 2001 has been used for the calculation.
HM represents Hwang and Satchell's (1998) Higher Moment CAPM performance measure and PPW represents Positive Period Weighting measure by Grinblatt and Titman (1989). Jensen's alpha, Treynor–Mazuy, HM and PPW measures are multiplied by 100.

trusts are the same and the performance values are very similar. This provides indirect evidence that timing ability does not exist at least in these UK investment trusts.

However, the results for the Sharpe ratio show some differences from these three measures. The obvious difference being that the estimated Sharpe ratios are always positive, while the others are not. This arises essentially because the Sharpe ratio is not a relative performance measure given the performance of a benchmark and the positive values of the Sharpe ratio effectively reflect the positive performance in the benchmark portfolio over the sample period. In addition, measures such as Jensen's alpha and TM are based on non-diversifiable risk, while the Sharpe ratio is based on total risk. Despite these differences, generally the Sharpe ratio provides a similar pattern in the ranks of the investment trusts. Thus empirically, these results suggest that if we are only interested in ranks between the performance of the different portfolios, the Sharpe ratio, which is a simple and straightforward measure, may be good enough.

Finally, we can see that the HM measure provides quite different results; for example, TR Property which is ranked between 11th to 13th by the other measures is ranked 3rd by the HM measure. The statistical properties in Table 7.1 do not show any particular pattern in the returns of TR Property but the estimate of coskewness (γ_{pm}) for this investment trust is the smallest (−2.02) which implies that the HM measure for the trust will be increased.[6]

Several investment trusts appear to perform better using the HM measure, i.e. Edinburgh, Fleming Mercantile, Govett Strategic, City of London, Merchants, Securities Trust of Scotland, Murray Income and TR Property, while Henderson Smaller Companies, Fleming Claverhouse, Templer Bar and Throgmorton appear worse under the HM measure. Generally, investment trusts appear to perform better than the benchmark when the higher moment systematic risk such as the coskewness is taken into account. This suggests that the managers of these trusts maintain their portfolios better in the presence of large negative and positive shocks than can be explained in the mean-variance world.

So we suggest that when returns are normal and portfolio managers show no timing ability, then four measures, Jensen's alpha, TM, HM and PPW, are likely to provide very similar results. However, given the evidence for non-normality (as shown in Table 7.1) there are significant differences between the HM measure and the other three. These results are consistent with those

[6]Note that using the estimates of σ_m, γ_m, and θ_m in Table 7.1, we find that λ_2 is always negative. Thus for a given beta, any large negative coskewness will increase the value of the HM measure.

of Hwang and Satchell (1998) who found significant differences between the measures for highly non-normal emerging market returns. The slight differences between the three other measures, Jensen's alpha, TM and PPW, indirectly suggest that there is no significant timing ability shown by these portfolio managers.

7.3.3 Time varying properties of the performance of the UK investment trusts

The results in Table 7.2 do not show us how the 14 investment trusts perform over time and hence under different market conditions and this would seem to be operationally important since many organizations examine their performance on a daily and hence a dynamic basis. Are the ranks between the portfolios relatively stable or do they change over time as market conditions change? If we find that performance does not change dramatically over time then we could potentially construct a hedge portfolio with the portfolios and obtain excess returns.

The five performance measures are now calculated for each investment trust using rolling windows of 60 monthly returns. That is, the first value is calculated using the first 60 monthly returns, i.e. January 1980 to December 1984, and the second is obtained using the 60 monthly returns from February 1980 to January 1985, and so on. Using this approach, we obtain a time series for each performance measure that consists of 195 monthly observations from December 1984 to February 2001 for each investment trust.

Figure 7.1 provides examples of estimates of the five performance measures over time and Table 7.3 reports some statistical properties of the measures. First of all, the relationship between the performance measures can clearly vary quite widely over time. Note in particular that the Sharpe ratio can be seen generally to have noticeably moved down during the 1987 crash and then up with the UK's withdrawal from EMU in 1992, but for some trusts can be relatively unaffected by the Russian Crisis in August 1998.

The other relative measures, except the HM measure, do not generally show particularly large changes around the 1987 crash. Figure 7.1 indicates that the HM measure for Edinburgh shows a big downside movement around the 1987 crash while the other investment trusts show a much smaller reaction. This suggests that the HM measure does not always respond in the same way to negative (positive) shocks but it depends critically on the coskewness.[7] Over the entire sample period, TR Property performs better using the HM measure.

[7] The high ranking of *TR Property* with the HM measure in Table 7.2 can be seen in Figure 7.3b.

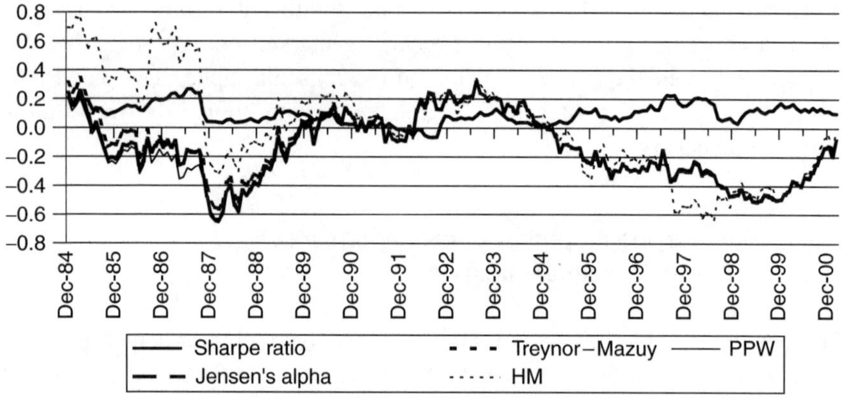

Figure 7.1a Edinburgh

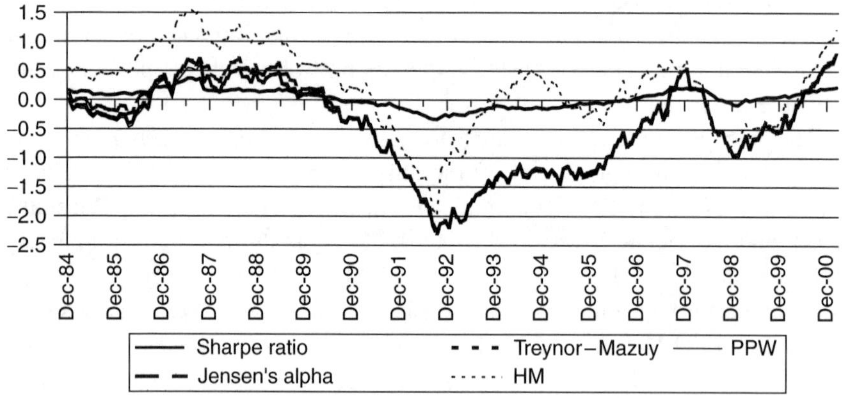

Figure 7.1b TR Property

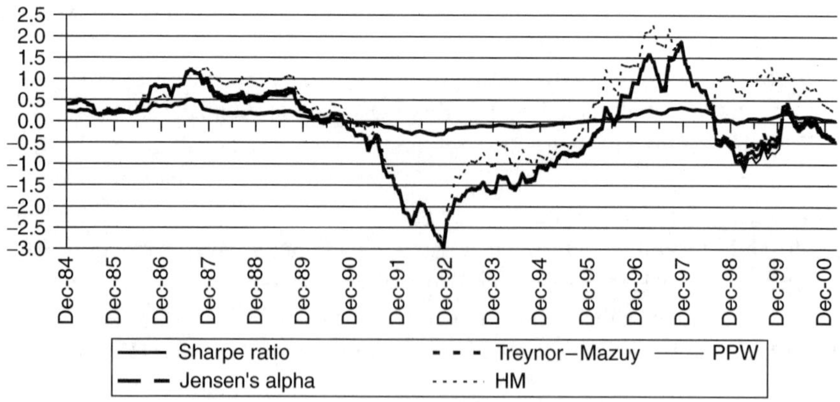

Figure 7.1c INVESCO English & International

Table 7.3 Statistical properties of performance measures for selected investment trusts

	Sharpe ratio	Jensen's alpha	Treynor–Mazuy	HM	PPW
A. Edinburgh					
Mean	0.095	−0.145	−0.125	−0.003	−0.158
STD	0.068	0.227	0.226	0.335	0.227
Skewness	0.221	0.009	0.048	0.248	0.055
Excess kurtosis	−0.199	**−0.896**	**−0.981**	−0.523	**−0.867**
Correlation matrix					
Sharpe ratio	1.000				
Jensen's alpha	−0.219	1.000			
Treynor–Mazuy	−0.205	0.990	1.000		
HM	0.112	0.670	0.725	1.000	
PPW	−0.266	0.994	0.979	0.593	1.000
Autocorrelations Lag 1	0.930	0.961	0.960	0.968	0.961
Lag 2	0.844	0.926	0.927	0.929	0.929
Lag 3	0.764	0.900	0.906	0.895	0.908
Lag 4	0.689	0.864	0.872	0.864	0.875
Lag 5	0.618	0.830	0.840	0.836	0.844
B. TR Property					
Mean	0.032	−0.471	−0.435	0.219	−0.477
STD	0.151	0.748	0.786	0.698	0.727
Skewness	−0.313	**−0.445**	**−0.436**	**−0.496**	**−0.473**
Excess kurtosis	−0.490	**−0.743**	**−0.820**	0.031	−0.661
Correlation matrix					
Sharpe ratio	1.000				
Jensen's alpha	0.958	1.000			
Treynor–Mazuy	0.951	0.997	1.000		
HM	0.816	0.830	0.837	1.000	
PPW	0.950	0.999	0.996	0.829	1.000
Autocorrelations Lag 1	0.984	0.985	0.987	0.975	0.984
Lag 2	0.965	0.969	0.972	0.947	0.967
Lag 3	0.940	0.950	0.956	0.918	0.947
Lag 4	0.913	0.929	0.937	0.885	0.924
Lag 5	0.882	0.902	0.913	0.846	0.897
C. Invesco					
Mean	0.083	−0.198	−0.169	0.239	−0.198
STD	0.175	1.011	1.014	1.042	1.004
Skewness	−0.153	**−0.528**	**−0.589**	**−0.851**	**−0.521**
Excess kurtosis	−0.415	−0.357	−0.323	0.431	−0.340
Correlation matrix					
Sharpe ratio	1.000				
Jensen's alpha	0.937	1.000			
Treynor–Mazuy	0.940	0.999	1.000		
HM	0.833	0.895	0.909	1.000	
PPW	0.933	0.999	0.996	0.881	1.000

(*continued overleaf*)

Table 7.3 *(continued)*

	Sharpe ratio	Jensen's alpha	Treynor–Mazuy	HM	PPW
Autocorrelations Lag 1	0.984	0.982	0.983	0.980	0.981
Lag 2	0.962	0.958	0.959	0.958	0.956
Lag 3	0.935	0.933	0.935	0.935	0.929
Lag 4	0.908	0.909	0.911	0.913	0.903
Lag 5	0.881	0.884	0.888	0.887	0.879

Notes: HM represents Hwang and Satchell's (1998) Higher Moment CAPM performance measure and PPW represents Positive Period Weighting measure by Grinblatt and Titman (1989). Jensen's alpha, Treynor–Mazuy, HM and PPW measures are multiplied by 100. The bold numbers represent significance at 5% level.

The statistical properties of the measures reported in Table 7.3 show little difference between Jensen's alpha, TM and PPW; the measures are either negatively skewed (Invesco), platykurtic (Edinburgh), or both (TR property). Figure 7.2 shows a typical example of the empirical kernel density estimates for the performance measures for the case of the TR Property Trust. The effectively common density shown by Jensen's alpha, TM and PPW can be compared with the distinctly different distributional shapes presented by

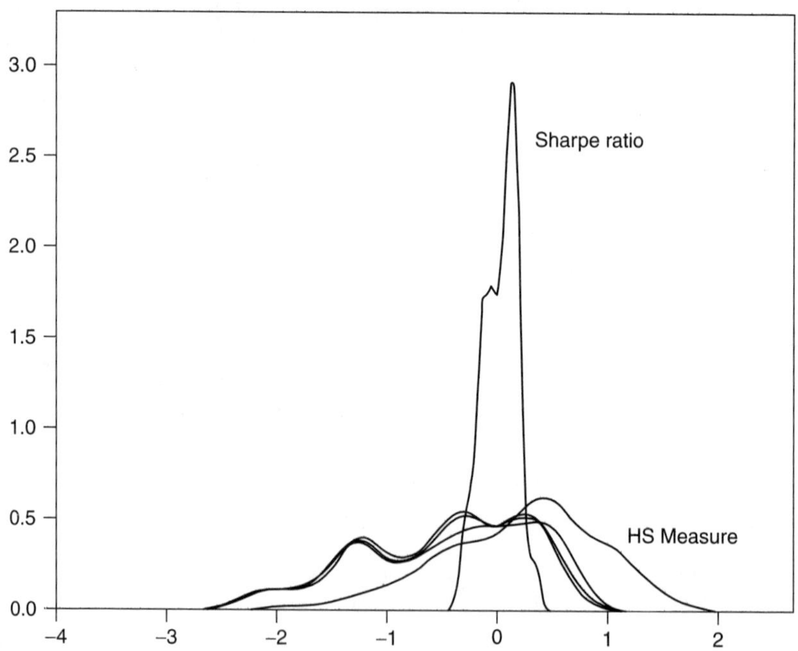

Figure 7.2 Kernel density estimates for the TR property trust

the Sharpe ratio and the HM measure. In addition, since they are highly autocorrelated and cross-correlated these measures move together over time and there really is relatively little difference between these three measures. The correlation matrices in Table 7.3 also show that in most cases the correlation coefficients between these three measures are larger than 0.99 although we have to be very wary of the utility of correlation as a measure of dependence given the apparent non-normal distribution of the performance measures. Once again, we find little evidence of timing ability in the investment trusts.

However, the statistics of the Sharpe ratio are again different from those of these three measures showing much less variation. For the Edinburgh Trust, the Sharpe ratio is not significantly correlated with any of the three measures nor the HM measure, while for TR Property and Invesco it is highly correlated with all the others. The estimates of skewness and excess kurtosis suggest that normality may be assumed only for the Sharpe ratio and even then only for a subset of the trusts. The HM measure is relatively less correlated with the three measures above with estimates of the cross-correlation coefficients generally less than 0.9.

Finally, we provide a comparison of the performance for eight investment trusts by performance measure in Figures 7.3a to 7.3c.[8] These plots show that there is no one investment trust which always performs better than the others. Murray Income Trust, which is the best among the 14 investment trusts for all five performance measures in Table 7.2, belonged to the top group during 1991 to 1995, but after 1997 this is no longer true. Since the ranking does not change rapidly, we could choose an investment trust which has performed well and expect it to perform well in the future if the horizon is relatively short. So there is some persistence in performance over time.

Figure 7.4 shows a typical multivariate scatter plot of the performance measures, in this case for the City of London Trust, and we can see the clear dependence structure. Jensen's alpha, Treynor and the PPW measures again essentially provide identical information over time whereas the other two measures, HM and SR, differ from these three in different ways.

Inspecting the time series plots in Figure 7.1 we can see the different patterns taken by the Sharpe ratio, Jensen's alpha and HM measures. First of all, while the HM measure behaves similarly to Jensen's alpha it seems to be more volatile than Jensen's alpha over time. The volatility in the HM measure supports the view that it is more sensitive to large shocks in the market than Jensen's alpha. In addition, the estimates of the HM measure are spread more

---

[8]Note that we only report results for Jensen's alpha among the set Jensen's alpha, TM and PPW since these three appear to show such little difference.

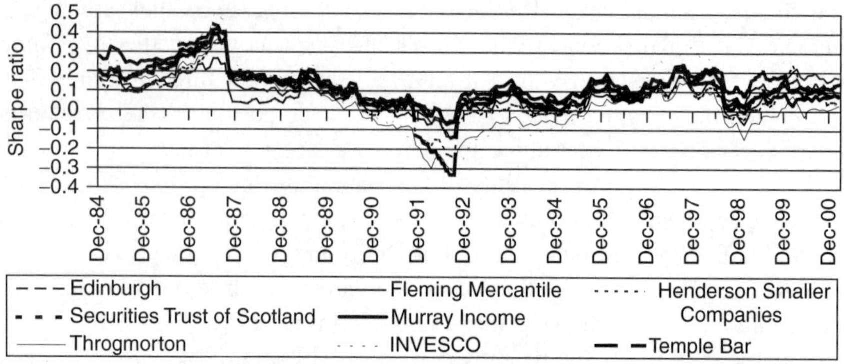

Figure 7.3a Sharpe ratios for the 14 UK investment trusts

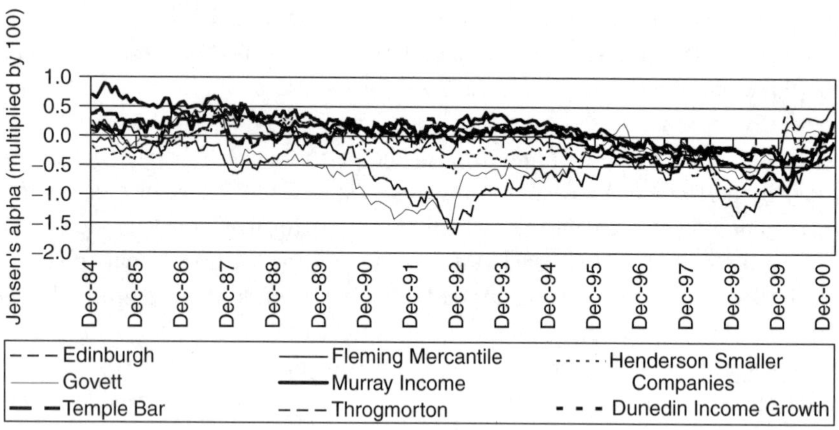

Figure 7.3b Jensen's alpha for the 14 UK investment trusts

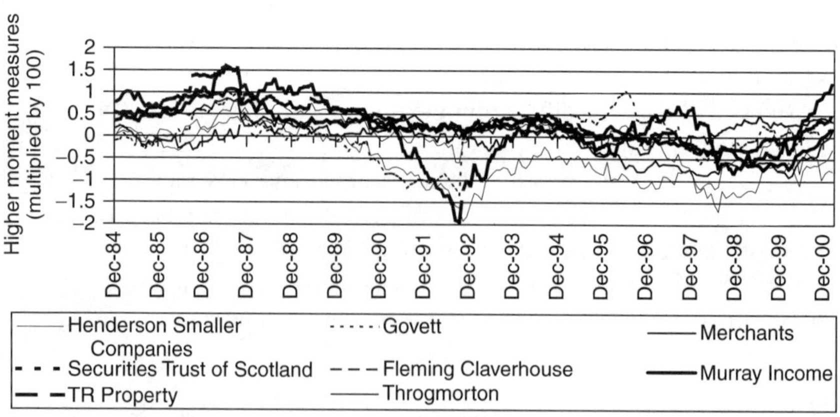

Figure 7.3c Higher moment measures for the 14 UK investment trusts

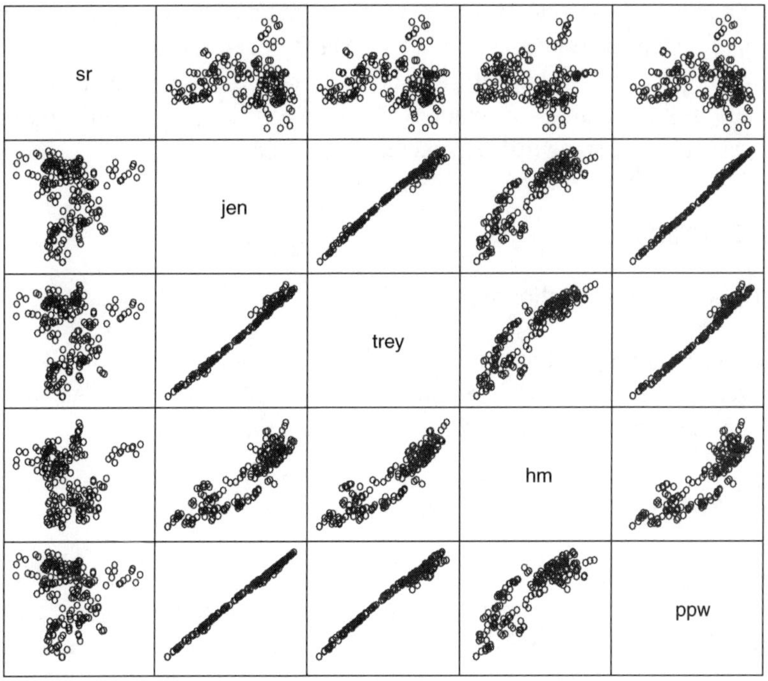

Figure 7.4 Multivariate scatter plot of performance measures for the City of London Trust

widely than those of Jensen's alpha which are in turn spread more widely than those of the Sharpe ratio.

The Sharpe ratio seems also to be sensitive to big market movements such as the market crisis of 1987, Sterling's withdrawal from EMU in 1992, the Russian crisis in 1998, etc. The effect of these episodes on the Sharpe ratio is stronger than on the other measures since all except the Sharpe ratio are relative measures and thus far less sensitive to jumps in the benchmark.

Interestingly, Jensen's alpha and the HM measure both show that these UK investment trusts performed well up to 1993, but soon after that point, the performance measures begin to show a dramatic decrease until 1999. If we assume that the betas of the investment trusts are very close to one, this means that during this period it became very difficult to outperform the benchmark. On the other hand, during the early sample period, i.e. early 1980s, beating the benchmark was probably easier than in late 1990s. However, these indications of performance relative to the benchmark portfolio cannot be seen in Sharpe ratio and the movement in Sharpe ratio roughly matches the UK market movement over the same period.

This fairly standard form of descriptive analysis of the patterns of behaviour identified above between the different performance measures can provide only casual insight. We need to move beyond correlation analysis to properly assess their interdependence given the non-Gaussianity of the performance measures shown in Figure 7.2. We now turn to consider how the use of copula functions can help us to quantify the relationships between the performance measures by assessing their statistical dependence more accurately.

7.4 COPULAE

7.4.1 A brief introduction to copulae

A copula is simply a function that links univariate marginals to their joint multivariate distribution or alternatively it is a joint distribution function with uniform marginals. Such a function is simply defined as follows:

$$C(u_1, u_2, \ldots, u_N) = \Pr[U_1 \le u_1, U_2 \le u_2, \ldots, U_N \le u_N] \qquad (7.12)$$

with $U_1, U_2, \ldots, U_N$ uniform random variables. Suppose we have a portfolio with N assets whose returns follow univariate marginal distribution functions $F_1(x_1), F_2(x_2), \ldots, F_N(x_N)$ then the copula will describe their joint distribution. The copula function C combines or couples the marginals together to give their joint density such that:

$$C(F_1(x_1), F_2(x_2), \ldots, F_N(x_N)) = F(x_1, x_2, \ldots, x_N) \qquad (7.13)$$

given the univariate marginal

$$F_i(x_i) = C(F_1(+\infty), F_2(+\infty), \ldots, F_i(x_i), \ldots, F_N(+\infty)) \qquad (7.14)$$

This follows directly from:

$$\begin{aligned}
&C(F_1(x_1), F_2(x_2), \ldots, F_N(x_N)) \\
&\quad = \Pr[U_1 \le F_1(x_1), U_2 \le F_2(x_2), \ldots, U_N \le F_N(x_N)] \\
&\quad = \Pr[F_1^{-1}(U_1) \le x_1, F_2^{-1}(U_2) \le x_2, \ldots, F_N^{-1}(U_N) \le x_N] \\
&\quad = \Pr[X_1 \le x_1, X_2 \le x_2, \ldots, X_N \le x_N] \\
&\quad = F(x_1, x_2, \ldots, x_N) \qquad (7.15)
\end{aligned}$$

Conversely, for a given multivariate distribution, there exists a copula function that links its marginals. Moreover Sklar (1959) proved that if the marginal distribution functions are continuous then we can be assured that the copula is unique.[9]

Since the multivariate distribution contains all the information that exists on the dependence structure between the variables, in our case the different performance measures, the copula must contain precisely the same information[10] and hence it captures exactly how the different performance measures are related to each other. Moreover since the copula is defined on the transformed uniform marginals it holds this information on dependence irrespective of the particular marginals of the underlying performance measures. So a simple procedure to analyse the multivariate distribution or dependence between the non-Gaussian performance measures would be to start by determining the marginal distribution relevant to each measure and then estimate the relevant copula from the data to give the multivariate distribution of the performance measures. Then given the estimated copula we can move to consider exactly where in their range spaces the different performance measures will provide different signals of portfolio performance. In other words where they may be jointly dependent or relatively independent.

Finance has traditionally assumed a multivariate Gaussian distribution for returns and in terms of copulae, this is equivalent to assuming that (i) the marginal density functions of each asset's return is Gaussian and (ii) that the copula that links univariate marginals is a particular copula, in fact a Gaussian copula. If we assume two random variables $X \sim N(0, 1)$, $Y \sim N(0, 1)$, with correlation coefficient $\rho(X, Y) = \rho$ and if their joint distribution is bivariate Gaussian, then $F(X, Y) = C_\rho^{\text{Gauss}}(\Phi(x), \Phi(y))$ with C_ρ^{Gauss} being the Gaussian copula such that for $(u, v) \in [0, 1]^2$:

$$C_\rho^{\text{Gauss}}(u, v) = \int_{-\infty}^{\Phi^{-1}(u)} \int_{-\infty}^{\Phi^{-1}(v)} \frac{1}{2\pi(1-\rho^2)^{1/2}} \times \exp\left(\frac{-(s^2 - 2\rho st + t^2)}{2(1-\rho^2)}\right) \mathrm{d}s\mathrm{d}t \tag{7.16}$$

However, if we chose $C \neq C_\rho^{\text{Gauss}}$, the joint distribution function $F(x, y) = C(\Phi(x), \Phi(y))$ will no longer be multivariate Gaussian but will still be a well-defined distribution. The Gaussian is one of a large number of parametric copula that could be used to join marginals and an important issue is the statistical identification of such copula. In the Gaussian copula considered here there is a single parameter, ρ, the correlation coefficient, that simultaneously

---

9 For a detailed discussion of copulae and their applications in statistics see, Joe (1997) or Nelsen (1999).

10 Since it cannot be held in the marginal distributions.

parameterizes the copula and the dependency between the variables. More general copulae may be parameterized or defined by several parameters and different measures of dependency may be expressed as different functions of these parameters. Measures of dependency need not necessarily be easily expressed as functions of these parameters but may instead be defined as functions of the copula map itself. A two parameter copula is, for example, given by

$$\begin{aligned} C(u, v; \theta, \delta) &= \{1 + [(u^{-\theta} - 1)^{\delta} + (v^{-\theta} - 1)^{\delta}]^{\frac{1}{\delta}}\}^{-\frac{1}{\theta}} \\ &= \eta(\eta^{-1}(u) + \eta^{-1}(v)) \end{aligned} \tag{7.17}$$

where $\eta(s) = \eta_{\theta,\delta}(s) = (1 + s^{\frac{1}{\delta}})^{-\frac{1}{\theta}}$ and the lower tail area dependency measure is $2^{-\frac{1}{\delta\theta}}$ and the upper tail area dependency measure is $2 - 2^{\frac{1}{\delta}}$ (which is independent of θ). More generally, having more than one parameter facilitates the measurement of different types of dependency.

A central result is that if the random variables $X_1, \ldots, X_n$ are independent then the copula function that links their marginal is the product copula:

$$C(F_1(x_1), F_2(x_2), \ldots, F_N(x_N)) = F(x_1)F(x_2)\ldots, F(x_N) \tag{7.18}$$

and tests for independence can be based on the distance of the empirical copula to this product copula. More generally the copula is a function defined over the range of the random variables when transformed into a uniform [0,1] space and hence we can examine the varying dependence structure throughout the entire range of the potential variation of the performance measures. This is in contrast to the use of a single number such as the correlation which is assumed to apply globally and to accurately measure a common degree and form of dependence throughout the entire range of values taken by the variables. This is an assumption which is only valid if the performance measures were distributed elliptically.

7.4.2 Measuring dependency using copulae

Let us start by briefly recalling the failure of correlation as a measure of association.

The inadequacy of correlation

The standard definition of the Pearson correlation coefficient is

$$\rho = \frac{\frac{1}{n}\sum_{i=1}^{n}(x_i - \bar{x})(y_i - \bar{y})}{\sigma_x \sigma_y} \tag{7.19}$$

with

$$\bar{x} = \frac{1}{n}\sum_{i=1}^{n} x_i \quad \text{and} \quad \bar{y} = \frac{1}{n}\sum_{i=1}^{n} y_i \tag{7.20}$$

and

$$\sigma_x^2 = \frac{1}{n}\sum_{i=1}^{n}(x_i - \bar{x})^2 \quad \text{and} \quad \sigma_y^2 = \frac{1}{n}\sum_{i=1}^{n}(y_i - \bar{y})^2 \tag{7.21}$$

As pointed out by Embrechts, McNeil and Straumann (1999), the success of correlation is due to its properties for linear analysis, especially for the linear combination of risk factors F, where $\mathrm{var}(\alpha^\top F) = \alpha^\top \mathrm{cov}(F)\alpha$. It provides, however, only a measure of linear association. There are many problems with using correlation to describe multivariate dependence in more general situations, however. In particular;

- σ_x^2 and σ_y^2 have to be finite for ρ to be defined. For example, consider an extreme value type II (Fréchet) distribution with parameter $\tau = -\alpha^{-1}$ so that $\int_0^\infty x^r \, \mathrm{d}F_X(x) = \infty$ for $r > \alpha$. Correlation is then not defined in this quite reasonable and important case for financial applications.
- Independence always implies zero correlation but the converse is true only for an elliptic distribution such as the Gaussian.
- Correlation is not an invariant measure whereas the copula function is invariant to strictly monotone transformations.

The fundamental reason why the Pearson correlation fails as an invariant measure of dependency is that it depends not only on the copula but also on the marginal distributions of the data. Thus the correlation is changed by potentially non-affine transformations in the marginal variables and therefore the units in which we express our data. It is formally not a geometric quantity.

7.4.3 Concordance: scale invariant dependence measures

Despite the impression created by the common usage of correlation to measure dependence it is in fact often far from straightforward to define exactly what form of dependence we are interested in and then to select a statistic that captures exactly what we need to measure. As emphasized above the desire to use a measure that is invariant leads naturally to copula-based measures since the copula captures those properties of the joint distribution which are invariant under almost surely strictly increasing transformations. So invariant measures of dependency will be expressible solely in terms of the copula of the random variables. The most widely used scale invariant measures of association are Kendall's τ and Spearman's ρ both of which measure concordance. Concordance between two random variables arises if large values of one variable tend to occur with large values of the other and small values occur with small values of the other; otherwise they are said to be discordant. So concordance picks up non-linear associations between the performance measures that correlation might miss completely.

Suppose that (X_1, Y_1) and (X_2, Y_2) are independent and identically distributed random vectors with possibly different joint distribution functions H_1 and H_2 with copulae C_1 and C_2 respectively, but with common margins. The population version of Kendall's τ is defined as the probability of concordance minus the probability of discordance,

$$\begin{aligned}\tau &= \tau_{X,Y}\\ &= P[(X_1 - X_2)(Y_1 - Y_2) > 0] - P[(X_1 - X_2)(Y_1 - Y_2) < 0] \end{aligned} \tag{7.22}$$

Nelsen shows that this may be re-expressed simply in terms of the copulae as

$$Q = Q(C_1, C_2) = a \iint_{I^2} C_2(u, v)\, \mathrm{d}C_1(u, v) - 1 \tag{7.23}$$

Spearman's ρ is defined as follows. Let R_i be the rank of x_i among the x's and S_i be the rank of y_i among the y's. The Spearman rank order correlation coefficient is:

$$\rho_S = \frac{\sum_{i=1}^{n}(R_i - \bar{R})(S_i - \bar{S})}{\sqrt{\sum_{i=1}^{n}(R_i - \bar{R})^2}\sqrt{\sum_{i=1}^{n}(S_i - \bar{S})^2}} \tag{7.24}$$

which again may be expressed in terms of copulae as

$$\rho_C = 12 \iint_{[0,1]^2} (C(u, v) - uv)\, \mathrm{d}u\mathrm{d}v \tag{7.25}$$

Spearman's rank correlation coefficient is essentially the ordinary correlation of $\rho(F_1(X_1), F_2(X_2))$ for two random variables $X_1 \sim F_1(.)$ and $X_2 \sim F_2(.)$. Notice the explicit contrast with the product copula in this case. Essentially these two measures of concordance measure the degree of monotonic dependence as opposed to the Pearson correlation which simply measures the degree of linear dependence. They both achieve a value of unity for the bivariate Fréchet upper bound (one variable is an increasing transformation of the other) and minus one for the Fréchet lower bound (one variable is a strictly decreasing transform of the other). These two properties do not hold for the standard correlation coefficient making these two concordance measures more attractive as general measures of dependency or association.

Table 7.4 provides a comparison between the measures of concordance and correlation between the performance measures for the Fleming Calverhouse Trust. What is clear from this comparison is that simple correlation analysis suggests that all the measures are significantly positively related while both concordance measures clearly suggest a lack of concordance between the Sharpe ratio and all the other measures.[11] This implies that we should expect all the performance measures to move in the same direction, either linearly or non-linearly, except the Sharpe ratio. While standard correlation analysis suggests all are linearly related, Kendall's τ and Spearmans's ρ indicate that there is no monotone dependency between the Sharpe ratio and the other

Table 7.4 Comparison between the measures of concordance and correlation between the performance measures for the Fleming Caiverhouse investment trust

	Sharpe ratio	Jensen's alpha	Treynor–Mazuy	HM	PPW
A. Pearson's correlation coefficient					
Sharpe ratio	1.000				
Jensen's alpha	0.199*	1.000			
Treynor–Mazuy	0.191*	0.994*	1.000		
HM	0.147*	0.470*	0.556*	1.000	
PPW	0.230*	0.996*	0.988*	0.470*	1.000
B. Kendal's τ					
Sharpe ratio	1.000				
Jensen's alpha	0.049	1.000			
Treynor–Mazuy	0.050	0.994*	1.000		
HM	0.118*	0.373*	0.397*	1.000	
PPW	0.053	0.955*	0.903*	0.340*	1.000
C. Spearman's ρ					
Sharpe ratio	1.000				
Jensen's alpha	0.060	1.000			
Treynor–Mazuy	0.065	0.993*	1.000		
HM	0.168*	0.506*	0.543*	1.000	
PPW	0.067	0.996*	0.984*	0.458*	1.000

Notes: *represents significance at 5% level.

[11]Similar results were found for the other Investment Trusts.

measures. Superficially these results might appear to be contradictory but really serve to question the value of correlation analysis on data that is non-Gaussian. More importantly for our current objectives it allows us to formally isolate the distinction between the use of relative and absolute risk measures in performance analysis. It is also clear once again that the Treynor, Jensen's alpha and the PPW measures are very tightly related whether we think in terms of correlation or concordance. There is a weaker association between HM and these three but it is still significantly different from zero.

We could from this point consider a range of alternative dependency measures between the performance measures based on copulae such as positive quadrant dependence or positive function dependence (see Joe, 1997) but have instead chosen to examine the relationship between the measures as they take large or small values since we feel this is a case that it is likely to be most important in practice. A manager needing to make a decision based on when one performance measure is taking extreme values might be reassured by the knowledge that the same signal is likely to be provided by some other performance measure.

Tail area dependence

The relationship between the performance measures under extreme market conditions, and hence when the measures themselves are likely to take extreme values, can be captured by examining the potential common behaviour in the tails of their distributions or in other words notions of tail area dependency. If two random variables, in our case performance measures, X and Y follow marginal distribution functions F_X and F_Y respectively then a standard definition of upper tail dependency, λ_U, is given by

$$\lambda_U = \lim_{u \to 1} P(Y > F_Y^{-1}(u) | X > F_X^{-1}(u)) \tag{7.26}$$

and the variables will be asymptotically upper tail dependent if $\lambda_U \in (0, 1]$ and upper tail independent if $\lambda_U = 0$ provided the limit $\lambda_U \in [0, 1]$ exits.[12] In other words we look to see if two measures simultaneously lie in suitably defined tail areas of their marginal distributions. This form of dependence, which again is quite distinct from correlation in the non-Gaussian case, can again be derived directly from the copula function linking the two performance measures (see Joe, 1997) and so will be invariant and independent of the form of the marginal distributions. An equivalent definition is that a copula C shows upper tail dependence where $\lambda_U \in (0, 1]$ and when

$$\lambda_U = \lim_{u \to 1} (1 - 2u + C(u, u))/(1 - u) \tag{7.27}$$

[12] Similar definitions hold for lower tail dependency.

Poon, Rockinger and Tawn (2001) have recently discussed applications of (upper) tail dependence measures in finance and considered χ defined by

$$\chi = \lim_{s\to\infty} P(Y^* > s | X^* > s) \tag{7.28}$$

where $0 \le \chi \le 1$, and the value of s is the extreme event for each variable, and

$$X^* = -\frac{1}{\log F_X(X)} \tag{7.29}$$

$$Y^* = -\frac{1}{\log F_Y(Y)} \tag{7.30}$$

are the original random variables transformed to unit Fréchet marginals so that they are defined on a common scale and events of the form $\{X^* > s\}$ and $\{Y^* > s\}$ correspond to equally extreme events for each variable. In other words

$$P(X^* > s) = P(Y^* > s) \sim s^{-1} \quad \text{as} \quad s \to \infty \tag{7.31}$$

and X^*, Y^* possess the same dependence structure as (X, Y). When $\chi > 0$, the two variables are asymptotically tail area dependent since χ measures dependence that is persistent in the limit. However, when $\chi = 0$, the two variables are asymptotically independent but not necessarily exactly independent and the distinction is important; consider, for instance, a bivariate normal case with any value of the correlation coefficient less than 1 which would imply $\chi = 0$. Exact independence implies

$$P(X^* > s | Y^* > s) = P(X^* > s) \tag{7.32}$$

which clearly goes to zero as $s \to \infty$. When there is exact dependence traditional extreme value methods will impose asymptotic dependence regardless of whether or not the true distribution shows asymptotic independence and hence they will overestimate $P(X^* > s, Y^* > s)$ and other probabilities of joint extreme events and hence a bias emerges. χ describes the degree of asymptotic dependence if the variables are asymptotically dependent and it will be zero for all asymptotically independent variables so χ cannot describe the degree of asymptotic independence.

Coles, Heffernan and Tawn (1999) have therefore developed a different measure, $\bar{\chi}$, which is defined by

$$\bar{\chi} = \lim_{s\to\infty} \frac{2\log \Pr(X^* > s)}{\log \Pr(Y^* > s, X^* > s)} - 1 \tag{7.33}$$

where $-1 < \bar{\chi} \leq 1$ and this provides an accurate measure of asymptotic independence since it describes the rate that $P(X^* > s|Y^* > s)$ goes to zero. When $\bar{\chi} = 0$, the two variables are independent in the tails, and when $\bar{\chi} < 0$ ($\bar{\chi} > 0$), the two variables may be interpreted as being negatively (positively) associated. χ and $\bar{\chi}$ together therefore provide all we need to assess the degree of association between the performance measures in their tails; χ for asymptotic dependence and $\bar{\chi}$ for asymptotic independence.

If we define $Z = \min(X^*, Y^*)$, we can estimate $\bar{\chi}$, following Poon, Rockinger and Tawn (2001), by using the standard Hill estimator as

$$\widehat{\bar{\chi}} = \frac{2}{n_u} \sum_{j=1}^{n_u} \log\left(\frac{z_j}{u}\right) - 1 \tag{7.34}$$

$$\mathrm{var}(\widehat{\bar{\chi}}) = \frac{(\widehat{\bar{\chi}} + 1)^2}{n_u} \tag{7.35}$$

where z_j are those, n_u, observations that exceed u. χ is estimated by

$$\hat{\chi} = \frac{un_u}{n} \tag{7.36}$$

$$\mathrm{var}(\hat{\chi}) = \frac{u^2 n_u (n - n_u)}{n^3} \tag{7.37}$$

If $\widehat{\bar{\chi}}$ is significantly less than 1 (i.e. if $\widehat{\bar{\chi}} + 1.96\sqrt{\mathrm{var}(\widehat{\bar{\chi}})} < 1$) then the inference is that the performance measures are asymptotically independent and χ is taken to be zero. Only if there is no significant evidence to reject $\bar{\chi} = 1$ is χ then estimated (under an assumption that $\bar{\chi} = 1$).

Table 7.5 provides estimates of $\bar{\chi}$ for the five performance measures for the Fleming Claverhouse Trust. We took the upper (lower) 2% of the total observations (given the 195 monthly observations implies four observations) to define the extreme case.[13] The table shows that for the left tail, the Sharpe ratio is negatively associated with Jensen's alpha, TM and PPW, but independent of HM. On the other hand, Jensen's alpha, TM and HM do not show any significant asymptotic left tail dependency. This result would seem to be important and indicates the value of this analysis since it implies all the dependency we have already noted between these performance measures comes about when they take values from within the body of their distributions or from their right tail and not from their left tail behaviour, when they indicate poor performance.

---

[13]We also estimated the independency measure for 4% and found that the results are similar to those in Table 7.5. We recognize that the results in Table 7.5 may be affected by the small number of observations.

Table 7.5 Measures of extreme tail independency for the five performance measures for the case of Fleming Claverhouse

		Sharpe ratio	Jensen's alpha	Treynor–Mazuy	HM
A. Left tail					
Jensen's alpha	Independence measure	−0.7824*			
	Standard error	(0.1088)			
	Correlation	0.1987*			
Treynor–Mazuy	Independence measure	−0.8797*	0.3078		
	Standard error	(0.0601)	(0.6539)		
	Correlation	0.1912*	0.9943*		
HM	Independence measure	−0.4173	−0.1670*	0.4369	
	Standard error	(0.2914)	(0.4165)	(0.7185)	
	Correlation	0.1470*	0.5275*	0.5560*	
PPW	Independence measure	−0.7859*	0.3078	0.3078	−0.2799*
	Standard error	(0.0957)	(0.6539)	(0.6539)	(0.3600)
	Correlation	0.2301*	0.9965*	0.9882*	0.4702*
B. Right tail					
Jensen's alpha	Independence measure	0.8899			
	Standard error	(0.9450)			
	Correlation	0.1987*			
Treynor–Mazuy	Independence measure	0.5805	0.3946		
	Standard error	(0.7903)	(0.6237)		
	Correlation	0.1912*	0.9943*		
HM	Independence measure	−0.3664*	0.0618	0.1277	
	Standard error	(0.3168)	(0.5309)	(0.5043)	
	Correlation	0.1470*	0.5275*	0.5560*	
PPW	Independence measure	1.5945	0.0462	0.1913	−0.2874*
	Standard error	(1.2972)	(0.5231)	(0.5957)	(0.3563)
	Correlation	0.2301*	0.9965*	0.9882*	0.4702*

Notes: The results are obtained with the 195 performance measures reported in Table 7.3. The independence measures are calculated as in Poon, Rockinger and Tawn (2001).
*represents significance from at 5% level.

The results for the right tail, however, are quite different from those of the left tail. None of them are significantly different from zero and thus we conclude that all performance measures are independent in the right tail, in other words when we see large performance values.

Therefore on the basis of these results, when performance measures such as Jensen's alpha, TM and PPW show very large decreases the Sharpe ratio will tend to increase while the HM would not show any particular pattern. On the other hand, when any performance measure indicates that the portfolio performs very well, we will tend not to find any particular pattern between any of the measures despite the fact that correlation analysis indicates a very high association between Jensen's alpha, TM and PPW.

7.4.4 Quantile regressions

Given how these tail area dependency results differ so strongly from the standard correlation results in Table 7.3 we extended this form of analysis in order to investigate how the conditional dependence between the performance measures may vary throughout the entire range of their conditional distributions. Regression methods are one of the most common tools used to capture multivariate dependency. However, given that the performance measures are non-Gaussian it is far from obvious that we should be interested in the conditional mean of the dependent variable rather than some other function of their conditional density. We may instead be interested in the relationship at particular quantiles, say the median, and it is then natural to consider computing quantile regressions and again since the copula captures the entire joint distribution it can be used to make this a relatively easy exercise. Quantile regression thus enables us to explore the conditional dependence of each performance measure given another performance measure's value at any particular range of quantiles and in this way we can extend the tail area dependency analysis into the body of the conditional distribution and explore the dependency structure within the entire conditional density of a performance measure.

If we assume an Archimedean form of the copula[14] so that the conditional distribution of Y given $X_1 \ldots X_k$ is given by

$$F_Y(y|x_1 \ldots x_k) = \frac{\phi^{-k}\{c_k + \phi[F_y(y)]\}}{\phi^{-k}(c_k)} \tag{7.38}$$

where $c_k = \phi[F_1(x_1)] + \ldots + \phi[F_k(x_k)] + \phi[F_Y(y)]$. Elementary statistics show us that the regression function may be rewritten as

$$E(y|x_1 \ldots x_k) = \int_0^{\infty} [1 - F_Y(y|x_1 \ldots x_k)]\,dy + \int_{-\infty}^{0} [F_Y(y|x_1 \ldots x_k)]\,dy \tag{7.39}$$

[14] A general family of copulae is the archimedean form in which $C_\phi(u, v) = \phi^{-1}(\phi(u), \phi(v))$ for $u, v \in (0, 1]^2$ where ϕ is a convex decreasing function with domain $(0, 1]$ and range $[0, \infty)$ such that $\phi(1) = 0$. Several standard copula belong to this family for different choices of generator function ϕ, see Nelsen (1998).

Genest (1987) has shown that using Frank's copula (with an Archimedean generator function $\phi(t) = \ln(\frac{e^{\alpha t}-1}{e^{\alpha}-1})$) we can write the regression function directly as

$$E(Y|X_1 = x) = \frac{(1 - e^{-\alpha})xe^{-\alpha x} + e^{-\alpha}(e^{-\alpha x} - 1)}{(e^{-\alpha x} - 1)(e^{-\alpha} - e^{-\alpha x})} \tag{7.40}$$

Instead of calculating the conditional mean function we can compute the median or any other quantile of the conditional distribution in a similar way. If we define the p'th quantile to be the solution y_p of the equation

$$p = F_Y(y_p|x_1 \ldots x_k) \tag{7.41}$$

or for the bivariate case

$$p = F_Y(y_p|X_1 = x) = C_1[F(x), F_Y(y_p)] \tag{7.42}$$

where C_1 is the partial derivative with respect to the first argument in the copula. So for a specified proportion p and x value we can solve equation (7.42) for the required percentile. In the examples below we have been restricted by software constraints to imposing a linear functional form on these quantile regressions.

So we have examined the conditional dependence between the different performance measures by running bivariate quantile regressions at the 1%, 5%, 10%, 25%, 50%, 75%, 90%, 95% and 99% levels. The results are reported in Table 7.6 for the case of the Fleming Claverhouse Trust. Note that the column heads indicate the explanatory variable in explaining the conditional quantile of the indicated performance measure for the relevant table and the stars indicate significant coefficient values at the 5% level.[15]

From panel A of Table 7.6 we can see that the Sharpe ratio only really provides any explanatory power for Jensen's alpha in the upper half of the distribution and this is most strong in the extreme tail (the 99th quantile). On the other hand, the higher moment measure indicates significant positive dependence throughout the distribution.

Panel B of Table 7.6 indicates virtually no power in explaining the higher moment measure by the Sharpe ratio except at the 75th and 90th quantiles whereas Jensen's alpha would seem to be significantly related to the higher moment measure almost throughout the entire distribution.

Finally panel C of Table 7.6 shows some conditional dependence in explaining the Sharpe ratio by Jensen's alpha above the 90% quantile and the higher moment measure is only significant around the 25th and 50th quantiles. These results reinforce the conclusions drawn earlier from the tail

[15]Notice that these quantile regression results may be regarded as estimates of *exact* rather than *asymptotic* quantile dependency as developed above with the taila rea dependency measure.

Table 7.6 Conditional dependence between the different performance measures for the case of the Fleming Claverhouse trust

	Sharpe ratio		HM	
	Intercept	Slope	Intercept	Slope
A. Quantile regression results for Jensen's α				
1%	−0.409*	1.113	−0.136*	0.437*
5%	−0.121*	0.000	−0.092*	0.381*
10%	−0.158*	0.557*	−0.051*	0.347*
25%	0.028	0.090	0.015	0.366*
50%	0.124*	−0.017*	0.107*	0.478*
75%	0.206*	0.516*	0.198*	0.727*
90%	0.302*	0.514*	0.326*	0.399*
95%	0.323*	0.678*	0.405*	0.280*
99%	0.352*	1.055*	0.497*	0.591*
	Sharpe ratio		**Jensen's α**	
	Intercept	Slope	Intercept	Slope
B. Quantile regression results for HM				
1%	−0.442*	0.418	−0.378*	0.313*
5%	−0.319*	0.139	−0.299*	0.551*
10%	−0.235*	0.256	−0.227*	0.482*
25%	−0.080*	−0.025	−0.151*	0.799*
50%	0.030*	0.235	−0.076*	0.788*
75%	0.102*	0.870*	0.074*	0.614*
90%	0.124*	1.290*	0.268*	0.310*
95%	0.144*	1.480	0.333*	0.291*
99%	0.157	1.672	0.365*	0.357
	HM		**Jensen's α**	
	Intercept	Slope	Intercept	Slope
C. Quantile regression results for Sharpe ratio				
1%	−0.045*	0.386	−0.002	−0.366
5%	−0.012	0.026	0.023	−0.069
10%	0.024*	0.109	0.027*	0.027
25%	0.070*	0.188*	0.069*	−0.042
50%	0.134*	0.108*	0.134*	0.081*
75%	0.195*	0.040	0.194*	0.125
90%	0.265*	−0.117	0.214*	0.358*
95%	0.305*	−0.110	0.229*	0.356*
99%	0.401*	0.312	0.289*	0.269*

Notes: *represents significance at 5% level.

area dependency measure but provide deeper insights as to when we may expect to draw conflicting conclusions regarding performance by adopting one measure rather than another. Again the Sharpe ratio appears as an outlier providing relatively limited explanation for the other two measures and in turn only really showing joint dependence with Jensen's alpha in the upper tail of the bivariate distribution. Jensen's alpha is seen to be related to the HM measure throughout the body of the conditional distribution except in the right-hand tail confirming the previous tail area dependency result.

7.5 AN AGGREGATE PERFORMANCE MEASURE

It has been shown quite widely in the literature (see, for instance, Diebold (1997)) that combining forecasts generated from different models can reduce offsetting biases, and also that the combined forecast can have a lower variance given the interdependence between the forecasts. These advantages clearly seem to be worth pursuing within the context of performance measurement through the proper construction of an aggregate of several potentially competing performance measures. As with forecast combination it may not make sense to combine forecasts that arise from different models that are theoretically inconsistent but when this is not the case the view may be taken that different models simply reflect parts of a more complex data generation process and may legitimately be combined.

From this point of view we would exclude the Sharpe ratio from consideration in the aggregate performance measure below since it differs from the others we have considered in that it is not a relative measure. Moreover given the common information being generated by Jensen's alpha, the Treynor and PPW measures we will just consider the question of how to construct an aggregate performance measure from one of these, Jensen's alpha and the higher moment measure.

Jouini and Clemen (1996) have proposed the use of copula functions to aggregate expert opinions in a decision problem and we shall apply their methodology as an illustration of the method below. There are a range of statistical issues which need to be pursued in following up our suggestion to construct an aggregate performance measure which we do not have space to resolve here but we believe the approach is powerful and worth pursuing. We take Jensen's alpha and the HM measure as representing the evaluations of two 'experts' as to the true underlying performance of a fund and hence describe the methodology for the bivariate case, although the approach can easily be extended to consider the aggregation of a greater number of underlying performance measures if required. Each of the separate performance measures follows a distinct distribution, say $F_1(x)$ and $F_2(x)$ and our problem is then essentially to aggregate these distributions taking into account their interdependence. This sort of question has a long history in statistics (see Genest and Zidek (1986)) and has been applied in many areas. The simplest approach is to construct an aggregate distribution as an average $\bar{F}(x) = [F_1(x) + F_2(x)]/2$ but this ignores the relative accuracy of the two estimates and the fact that they may be dependent, and this is clearly the case in our context from the results given above. It is not straightforward to account for the dependence in any aggregation procedure but given the properties of copulae, outlined above, it is obvious that they capture precisely the information required. Jouini and Clemen adopt a Bayesian approach where the decision maker has access to the historical record and hence empirical distributions of the separate performance measures which he uses to derive the posterior distribution for the aggregate performance measure. The decision maker's problem is essentially one of constructing a likelihood function that brings together the information from the experts and then, by applying Bayes' theorem to the likelihood function and prior, to derive the required posterior distribution from which the aggregate performance measure may be calculated together with any required confidence intervals for a systematic analysis of performance.

Given the observed non-Gaussianity of the performance measures shown in Figure 7.2 above and following Jouini and Clemen we could regard the different observed performance measures as being median-based estimates of the underlying true measure of performance x and there will be some correlation r_x between the errors made by the two different performance estimates and the underlying measure. The posterior distribution for x, the underlying measure of performance, given two expert distributions $F_1(x)$ and $F_2(x)$ with densities $f_1(x)$ and $f_2(x)$, can be written as

$$f_{dm}(x|f_1, f_2) = f_1(x)f_2(x)c[1 - F_1(x), 1 - F_2(x)] \tag{7.43}$$

where $c[\cdot]$ is the copula density function that captures the dependence structure between the two performance measures. One of the outstanding statistical issues that needs to be resolved before implementing this approach is the proper choice of copula in aggregating performance measures. In the demonstration that follows we use a Gaussian copula for simplicity, but notice that this assumption in no way implies that the joint distribution of the separate performance measures is bivariate normal since their marginal distributions are clearly non-Gaussian. Using the Gaussian copula then gives us the following relatively simple formula for the posterior:

$$\begin{aligned} f_{dm}(x|f_1, f_2, r_x) = \frac{f_1(x)f_2(x)}{(1 - r_x^2)^{1/2}} & \exp\{-r_x(r_x(\Phi^{-1}[1 - F_1(x)])^2 \\ & - 2\Phi^{-1}[1 - F_1(x)]\Phi^{-1}[1 - F_2(x)] \\ & + r_x(\Phi^{-1}[1 - F_2(x)])^2)/2(1 - r_x^2)\} \end{aligned} \tag{7.44}$$

where $\Phi^{-1}[\cdot]$ is the inverse of the standard normal cumulative distribution function with correlation coefficient r_x. This posterior distribution then provides all the information needed to construct the aggregated performance measure and to conduct inference on it in any decision framework. The question now turns on how to extract the aggregate performance measure from this distribution and this depends on the specification of the decision maker's utility or loss function. We could simply use the mean or the median of this distribution but as emphasized by Christoffersen and Diebold (1997), what function of the non-Gaussian posterior distribution serves as the optimal estimator of the underlying performance measure will depend critically on the asymmetric loss function the fund manager is almost certainly going to hold. In particular we expect that fund managers would be substantially more loss averse than for an equivalent profit on the up side. This issue is much more complex than can be developed here but see Hwang and Salmon (2002) for an extended discussion of performance measure aggregation.

7.6 CONCLUSIONS

We have carried out a fairly detailed comparison of the statistical properties and the relationships between a set of five performance measures using 14 UK-based investment trusts over a sample period ranging from 1980 to 2001. Our results suggest very clearly that there is almost no difference between Jensen's alpha, the Treynor–Mazuy (TM) measure and the Positive Period Weighting (PPW) measure over our sample period and among our set of 14 investment trusts. This would seem to indicate that there is no timing ability within these fund managers. The Sharpe ratio clearly provides different signals regarding performance than the other measures and is the only absolute measure in the set of measures we have considered. While simple correlation analysis suggests that there is a high degree of dependence between most of the measures, we have shown that there is a lack of significant concordance between the Sharpe ratio and all the other measures. This indicates the inadequacy of correlation analysis with non-Gaussian data. We have also shown that the Sharpe ratio exhibits negative left tail area dependence with respect to Jensen's alpha, TM and PPW but is independent in the left tail from the higher moment measure of Hwang and Satchell, that is when poor performance is indicated. Jensen's alpha, TM and the HM measure do not seem to show any significant asymptotic left tail dependency. All the measures appear to be asymptotically independent in their upper tail when good performance is indicated. These results are further refined by non-asymptotic quantile regression results which indicate finite sample dependency of the HM measure and

Jensen's alpha throughout the body of their conditional distribution and in the left tail but not the upper tail.

Given the question we raised at the outset of this work, we have found that there are important statistically significant differences between the performance measures we have analysed and how they behave in different market conditions. A performance manager would have to take care in justifying which criteria he wanted to use to properly measure performance since the results may differ widely depending on his decision. In particular the standard choice of the Sharpe ratio (cf. the AIMR handbook) seems to be an outlier in many ways when compared to the other relative measures in this study. Moreover, as can be seen from Figures 7.2 and 7.3, the Sharpe ratio provides substantially less discrimination than the other measures we have considered, both over time and hence market conditions and over fund style. We have also discussed how to properly construct an aggregate performance measure taking into account the joint dependence of the individual measures.

REFERENCES

Admati, A., Bhattacharya, S., Pfleiderer, P. and Ross, S. (1986) On timing and selectivity, *Journal of Finance*, **41**, 715–730.

AIMR (1997) *Performance Presentation Standards Handbook*, 2nd edition, Association for Investment Management and Research.

Chen, Z. and Knez, P.J. (1996) Portfolio performance measurement: theory and applications, *Review of Financial Studies*, **9**(2), 507–551.

Christoffersen, P. and Diebold, F.X. (1997) Optimal prediction under asymmetric loss, *Econometric Theory*, **13**, 808–817.

Cochrane, J.H. (1997) Where is the market going? Uncertain facts and novel theories, *Economic Perspectives*, XXI:6 (November/December), Federal Reserve Bank of Chicago.

Coles, S.G., Heffernan, J. and Tawn, J.A. (1999) Dependence measures for extreme value analysis, *Extremes*, **3**, 5–38.

Connor, G. and Korajczyk, R. (1986) Performance measurement with the arbitrage pricing theory: a new framework for analysis, *Journal of Financial Economics*, **15**, 374–394.

Cumby, R. and Glen, J. (1990) Evaluating the performance of international mutual funds, *Journal of Finance*, **45**, 497–521.

Diebold, F. (1997) *Elements of Forecasting*, Cincinnati: South-Western College Publishing.

Embrechts, P., McNeil, A. and Straumann, D. (1999) Correlation: pitfalls and alternatives, *RISK Magazine*, May.

Genest, C. and Zidek, J.V. (1986) Combining probability distributions: A critique and an annotated bibliography (with discussion). *Statistical Science*, **1**, 114–148.

Genest, C., (1987) Frank's family of bivariate distributions, *Biometrika*, **74**, 549–555.

Glosten, L.R. and Jagannathan, R. (1994) A contingent claim approach to performance evaluation, *Journal of Empirical Finance*, **1**, 133–160.

Grinblatt, M. and Titman, S. (1989) Portfolio performance evaluation: old issues and new insights, *Review of Financial Studies*, **2**(3), 393–421.

Grinblatt, M. and Titman, S. (1994) A study of monthly mutual fund returns and performance evaluation techniques, *Journal of Financial and Quantitative Analysis*, **29**(3), 419–444.

Grinblatt, M. and Titman, S. (1995) Performance evaluation, in *Handbooks in operational research and management science*, Vol. 9, R. Jarrow *et al.* (eds), Elsevier Science BV.

Hwang, S. and Satchell, S. (1998) Evaluation of mutual fund performance in emerging markets, *Emerging Markets Quarterly*, **2**(3), 39–50.

Hwang, S. and Satchell, S.E. (1999) Modelling emerging market risk premia using higher moments, *International Journal of Finance and Economics*, **4**(4), 271–296.

Hwang, S. and Salmon, M. (2002) Performance measure aggregation, working paper, Financial Econometrics Research Centre, City University Business School, London.

Jensen, M. (1968) The performance of mutual funds in the period 1945–1964, *Journal of Finance*, **23**, 389–416.

Jensen, M. (1969) Risk, the pricing of capital assets, and the evaluation of investment portfolios, *Journal of Business*, **42**, 167–247.

Jensen, M. (1972) Optimal utilization of market forecasts and the evaluation of investment portfolio performance, in *Mathematical Methods in Investment and Finance*, G. Szego and K. Shell, (eds.), North Holland, Amsterdam.

Joe, H. (1997) Multivariate models and dependence concepts, in *Monographs on Statistics and Applied Probability*, No. 73 Chapman Hall.

Jouini, M.N. and Clemen, R.T. (1996) Copula models for aggregating expert opinions, *Operations Research*, **44**(3), 444–457.

Kraus, A. and Litzenberger, R.H. (1976) Skewness preference and the valuation of risk assets, *Journal of Finance*, **31**(4), 1085–1100.

Lehmann, B. and Modest, D. (1987) Mutual fund performance evaluation: a comparison of benchmarks and benchmark comparisons, *Journal of Finance*, **42**, 233–265.

Nelsen, R. (1998) An introduction to copulas, *Lecture Notes in Statistics*, No. 139 Springer.

Poon Ser-Huang, Rockinger, M. and Tawn, J. (2001) New extreme value dependence measures and financial applications, mimeo (unpublished manuscript).

Roll, R. (1978) Ambiguity when performance is measured by the securities market line, *Journal of Finance*, **33**, 1051–1069.

Sharpe, W. (1966) Mutual fund performance, *Journal of Business*, **39**, 119–138.

Sklar, A. (1959) Functions de répartition à dimensionset leurs marges, Publications de l'Institut de Statistique de l'Université de Paris, **8**, 229–231.

Treynor, J. (1965) How to rate management of investment funds, *Harvard Business Review*, **43**, 63–75.

Treynor, J. and Mazuy, K. (1966) Can mutual funds outguess the market?, *Harvard Business Review*, **44**, 131–136.

Chapter 8

A clinical analysis of a professionally managed portfolio

BOB KORKIE

ABSTRACT

This is a study of a professionally managed Canadian equity and money market portfolio that is available to the public in a wrap account. The study's results indicate that the portfolio had significant abnormal performance in the analysis period. The study employs performance analysis technology that ranges from the various definitions of values and returns as supported by AIMR standards through to martingale pricing methods. Where possible, statistical tests of significance accompany the analyses. The evidence suggests that the Canadian Growth Portfolio's significant abnormal performance came primarily from the management's ability to select superior assets. The estimated long run, value added by management, after fees, was an additional 3% of managed assets per year.

8.1 INTRODUCTION

This chapter presents the results of a long-run, comprehensive study of the trading strategy of a professionally managed portfolio, called the 'Canadian Model Growth Portfolio' by its agent-managers at Nesbitt Burns. Unlike almost all published portfolio studies, this study begins with the buy/sell transactions, which occurred within the study period. Therefore, the study is able to assess the information trades of portfolio managers in a clinical setting. The transactions data allows a much expanded and more precise evaluation of the portfolio's performance than is otherwise possible. Because of the size and stature of Nesbitt Burns, the results should add to our understanding of the efficiency level of the equity market, as well as reflect on the information processing abilities of the Nesbitt Burns analysts and managers.[1]

The study employs performance analysis technology that ranges from the various definitions of values and returns as supported by AIMR standards through to martingale pricing methods.[2] Where possible, we have ensured that statistical tests of significance accompany the analyses. The evidence suggests that the Canadian Growth Portfolio had significant abnormal performance primarily due to the management's ability to select superior assets. The estimated long run, after fees, value added by management, was an additional 3% of managed assets per year.

We begin with a description of the portfolio and its stated investment objectives and policies.

8.2 THE PORTFOLIO

Nesbitt Burns has been one the largest and most prestigious Canadian investment companies and is the result of a 1994 merger between Nesbitt Thompson and Burns Fry, two Canadian investment companies that trace their roots back to 1912 and 1925, respectively. Nesbitt Burns is a subsidiary of the Bank of Montreal but is a separate corporate entity, at the time of writing. The firm manages many classes of investment portfolios, domestic and international. Financial claims to their portfolios are sold in different forms including mutual funds and wrap accounts.

The 'Canadian Model Growth Portfolio', hereafter called simply 'the portfolio', began in May of 1984 and was initially known as the 'Capital Appreciation Portfolio'. According to Nesbitt Burns, the portfolio was designed for investors seeking above average long-term growth with the objective of capital preservation. The portfolio is classified as an equity portfolio; although, it has contained a significant interest bearing component. The portfolio was sold in wrap accounts to clients with a minimum investment of $100,000.

Originally, the portfolio invested in ten top-rated stocks with diversification being an important but not exclusive factor. Cash holdings up to 35% were permitted. The portfolio's investment policies have changed a number of times since May 1984.

- In July 1993, a sector diversification policy was announced stating that 'further diversification will be achieved by targeting seven industry sectors

[1] The Brendan Wood International Survey of Canada's institutional investment community had ranked Nesbitt Thomson research as either first or second in every year from 1980 to 1993 (*NT Alert*, 14 October 1993).

[2] AIMR is the acronym for Association for Investment Management and Research.

for the portfolio'. In September 1993, the policy changed from holding ten stocks to holding up to 15 stocks rated highly by Nesbitt Burns research analysts. The objective of the change was to achieve better diversification via industry sector selection of a larger number of stocks. This policy was implemented in December 1993.
- In July 1994, the maximum number of sectors was increased from seven.
- In June 1995, the maximum number of stocks was increased to 20.
- In February 1996, the investment policy was revised such that the portfolio has full exposure to the TSE300 at all times, investing in 25 selected stocks, with portfolio industry weightings reflecting the weights of all major sectors of the TSE300. Cash holdings were limited to a maximum of 5% of the portfolio's value. An objective was to outperform the TSE300 by 2%/year over a three-year period.

Based upon this policy history, subperiod analyses over the period 5/84 to 2/89, 2/89 to 12/93 and 12/93 to 12/96 were performed. The first two periods are approximately equal partitions of a period when the investment policy was fixed at ten stocks. The third period represents a policy change to a larger stock set beginning to track the sectors of the TSE300 index yet maintaining the bottom-up stock selection in industry sectors. For brevity, only the analysis of the overall period is presented in this chapter.

Management fees were quoted as 2% of portfolio value but were charged as 0.5% quarterly in advance. Fees were not reported or deducted from the quoted portfolio value until the first quarter of 1996. Prior to 1996, our representative investor submits quarterly payments for the fees based upon the closing value at the end of the previous quarter. The post-January 1996 reports are after fees and therefore no cash contributions are required.

8.3 THE DATA

The portfolio's accounts may be broadly classified into the asset (common stocks) account and the cash account. Nesbitt Burns reported the portfolio's account transactions to its claimants and other parties via the monthly report 'Canadian Model Growth Portfolio Update'. The reports included the details of every buy/sell transaction, redistribution, cash account interest payment, dividend receipt, and so on from the portfolio's creation in May 1984 until the study end at the close of December 1996. In total, there were 1,134 transactions, including 459 buy/sell transactions.

Because the asset compositions of the interest bearing portion of the portfolio are not specified in the reports, the asset is called simply the 'cash account' here. Nesbitt Burns names the cash account the 'Freedom Plus' account. The firm provides no documentation as to the source of the interest posted to this account. Here, we simply take the amount of interest stated in the reports as being the amount posted to the cash account.[3]

The portfolio's value is indexed by Nesbitt Burns to approximately $100,000 at the close of 31 May 1984; the reported value using the Nesbitt Burns, May 1984, portfolio report is $101,500. Using DataStream and the CFMRC (Canadian Financial Markets Research Center) database closing prices, the portfolio value is $101,291 at the close of 31 May 1984. We have used this latter number in our analysis in order to maintain the accuracy of the portfolio value and its returns. Book and market values are reported every month providing a means to partially validate our price and return data that was obtained from our secondary data sources.[4]

Index data for performance measurement was obtained from DataStream except for the weights on the TSE35TRI index, which were collected from the Toronto Stock Exchange Monthly Review, and the Scotia McLeod bond index returns, which were obtained from Scotia McLeod publications.

The detailed form of the data permitted us to construct portfolio inventories, trading statistics, and financial sources and uses statements. In addition, we constructed benchmark returns with identical contributions, with and without fees. We performed exhaustive attribution analysis, attributing returns to asset timing and asset selectivity, as well as attributing these partitions to individual stock levels. Measures of arbitrage return, style, market timing, mean-variance performance, and portfolio efficiency and diversification were calculated. Various estimates of management's value added were obtained, including estimates based upon martingale pricing methods. The details and results are presented in the next section.

8.4 THE ANALYSES

8.4.1 Portfolio inventory and trading summary

Table 8.1a contains a summary of the inventory and trading characteristics of the Nesbitt Burns Canadian Growth Portfolio (henceforth 'the portfolio'). Over the entire analysis interval, the portfolio does not hold many assets

---

[3]It is possible that Nesbitt Burns added interest to the account on an *ad hoc* basis. With this type of policy, it is possible to smooth the performance of the portfolio making it appear less volatile or able to avoid declines in value. Regardless, the portfolio claimants would have received the reported amount of 'Freedom Plus' interest. Actual average interest paid per month, as a percentage of the previous month's closing cash balance, was 1.03 times the average of the 1-month T-bill returns, which is suggestive of a policy tied to market short rates.

[4]There were some significant errors in the CFMRC database as well as missing price data for previously listed stocks. In these cases, the data was obtained from DataStream and the Toronto Stock Exchange Review.

Table 8.1a Inventory and trading summary, 5/84–12/96

Total number of traded assets (including cash)	110
Average number of portfolio assets per month (including cash)	13.5
Standard deviation of number of portfolio assets per month	0.55
Average stay in the portfolio (in months)	17.27
Number of buy orders	225
Value of buy orders	$3,235,919.15
Number of sell orders	202
Value of sell orders	$3,115,980.30
Average monthly portfolio value	$326,765.75
Turnover:	
average monthly buys as a fraction of average portfolio value	6.5%
average monthly sales as a fraction of average portfolio value	6.3%
Total fees	$81,146.65

nor does it trade heavily. The average number of assets held is 13.5 per month with each stock staying an average of 17.27 months. This is suggestive of marginal diversification; however, as noted earlier, the portfolio's policy changed in 1993. The evidence from 12/93–12/96 shows that diversification and turnover have increased consistent with the policy change. Turnover is about 6.5% of average portfolio value per month, which is suggestive of a buy-and-hold policy due to a lack of management information signals that would trigger trades.

Table 8.1b summarizes the sources of the portfolio's value increase over the 151-month analysis interval. The value increased from $101,291 to $676,024.25. Interest on the cash account and dividends were about equal and amounted to about $69,000 or 23% of the portfolio's value increase. Consistent with the portfolio's policy, the relative value of the cash account decreased considerably over the analysis interval. Cash infusions were required to pay the portfolio fees. Because of the change in the fee reporting procedure that occurred in 1996, when fees began being subtracted from the cash account, infusions by the representative owner were less than the actual fees of the portfolio.

8.4.2 Comparative returns and portfolio values

Table 8.2a provides the terminal values of an equivalent dollar investment in each of the benchmark alternatives, before and after fees. Benchmark cash contributions were made at the same dates as in the managed portfolio.[5] That

[5] 'With fees' calculations were performed including the representative owner's cash contributions that were required prior to 1996. 'Without fees' calculations excluded the fees deducted by Nesbitt Burns commencing in 1996.

Table 8.1b Sources of the change in portfolio value, 5/84–12/96

	Values	Totals
Initial portfolio value at 5/84 close		
Cash account	\$25,475.00	
Asset account	\$75,816.00	
		\$101,291.00
Change in cash account		
Add: Cash infusions	\$69,063.65	
Dividends	\$68,888.50	
Interest received	\$64,150.00	
Asset sales	\$3,121,044.35	
Subtotal	\$3,323,146.50	
Less: Cash withdrawals	\$0.00	
Fees	\$81,146.65	
Interest paid	\$0.00	
Asset purchases	\$3,243,478.85	
Subtotal	\$3,324,625.50	
Net		−\$1,479.00
		\$576,212.25
Change in asset account		
Terminal portfolio value at 12/96 close		
Cash account	\$23,996.00	
Asset account	\$652,028.25	
		\$676,024.25

is, the before fees value of a benchmark, I, evolved according to the formula

$$V_{It} = V_{It-1}(1 + r_{It}) + C_{pt}$$

where C_{pt} is the cash contribution made to the portfolio in month t and r_{It} is the published monthly return on the benchmark.

Each benchmark has the same initial dollar investment of \$101,291, on 31 May 1984. With fees, the portfolio's investment accumulated to \$676,024 on 31 December 1996. No other Canadian benchmark achieved as large a terminal value, before or after fees. Investment in either of the two US equity indexes (S&P500 or the Wilshire 5000) achieved a larger terminal value; however, US stocks were not permitted in the Canadian Growth Portfolio.

The value's time series are shown in Figure 8.1, for four assets. It is clear from the chart that the portfolio infrequently fell below the TSE300 value during the analysis period, which is suggestive of stochastic dominance of the TSE300 by the portfolio.

Table 8.2a Comparative portfolio values

Asset name	Closing value at 5/84	Closing value at 12/96	
		with fees	without fees
Portfolio	$101,291.00	$676,024.25	$690,263.79
Benchmarks:			
1 month T-bill	$101,291.00	$269,255.42	$281,588.35
TSE300TRI	$101,291.00	$363,787.17	$377,837.74
Smlgovt[a]	$101,291.00	$558,516.31	$571,947.70
Other benchmarks[b]:			
MSCIworld	$101,291.00	$593,213.08	$605,758.72
S&P500TRI	$101,291.00	$736,296.26	$750,056.77
WIL5000TRI	$101,291.00	$681,023.11	$694,643.12

[a]Smlgovt represents the Scotia McLeod long-term government bond benchmark. MSCIworld is the Morgan Stanley World Index. WIL5000TRI is the Wilshire5000 index. All benchmarks include distributions.
[b]These values are approximately hedged against US/CDN exchange rates.

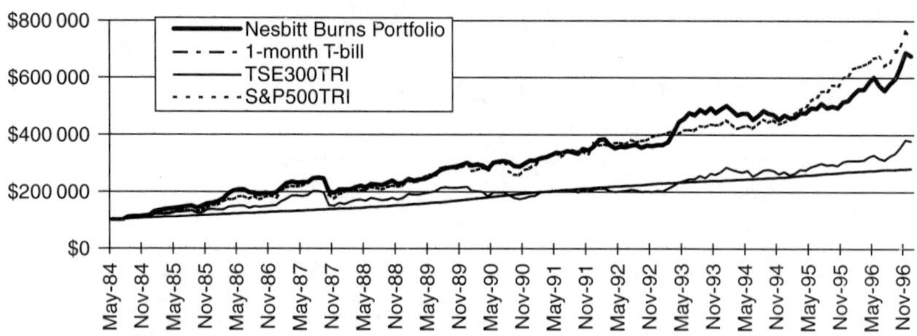

Figure 8.1 Value plots 31/5/84–31/12/96

Table 8.2b contains the return measures for the portfolio and the benchmarks. Holding period returns (also termed 'time weighted' or 'linked' returns) represent the returns received by investors who made no cash contributions or withdrawals in the analysis interval. The 'with fees' return was largest for the portfolio among the Canadian benchmarks. Without charging fees on the benchmarks, the with-fees portfolio return still exceeded all but the Scotia McLeod bond return. With or without benchmark fees, US indices' returns exceeded the portfolio's returns. The *IRR* or 'dollar weighted' return accounts for the cash contributions that were required for the payment of the portfolio's fees. Because of the relatively small size of these cash contributions, the results are similar to the time weighted returns. It is apparent that the portfolio has succeeded in its objective of returning 200 basis points more than the TSE300 benchmark.

Table 8.2b Comparative returns (annual effective), 5/84–12/96

Asset name	Holding period return (time weighted)		IRR (dollar weighted)	
	with fees	without fees	with fees	without fees
Portfolio	13.87%	16.48%	13.91%	16.48%
Benchmarks:				
1-m T-bill	3.96%	8.46%	4.66%	8.46%
TSE300TRI	6.93%	11.03%	7.68%	11.03%
SMIgovt	11.74%	14.75%	11.99%	14.75%
Other benchmarks[a]:				
MSCIworld	13.04%	15.27%	12.59%	15.27%
SP500TRI	14.54%	17.25%	14.78%	17.25%
WIL5000TRI	13.69%	16.53%	13.99%	16.53%

[a]These returns are approximately hedged against US/CDN exchange rates.

Table 8.2c summarizes some statistical properties of the assets that indicate a desirable monthly return distribution. The portfolio has a larger mean return than all benchmarks excepting the two US equity benchmarks. It has smaller unconditional volatility and larger unconditional skewness than the corresponding TSE300 values; however, both the portfolio and the TSE300 have significantly negative skew. The beta of 0.83 and standardized coskewness of 0.83 (both computed with the TSE300) indicate that the portfolio is less responsive to index movements and would contribute to increasing the positive skewness of an index portfolio, respectively. The portfolio's returns are significantly autocorrelated at lag 1 because of the presence of the large interest bearing cash account and the well-known autocorrelation in interest rates. The portfolio's autocorrelation facilitates better forecasting precision than for the uncorrelated TSE300. This is indicative of less total risk than measured by the portfolio's unconditional volatility of 3.71%/month.

Overall, the comparative values and returns indicate that the portfolio performed very well considering its policies. After fees, the portfolio outperformed the relevant benchmarks without fees. However, this analysis does not consider the details of the assets' risks. Figure 8.2 shows the portfolio's location in average return–total risk space. It is apparent that the managed portfolio dominates some benchmarks but not others. The analysis of the portfolio, considering risk, is the subject of the remaining analysis sections.

8.4.3 Market timing and style analyses

In this section, we establish the relationships between the portfolio's returns and a number of other benchmarks. To accomplish this, the Treynor–Mazuy

Table 8.2c Comparative monthly returns moments (without fees), 5/84–12/96

Asset name	Mean	Median	Max.	Min.	Standard deviation	Standard skewness	Beta with		Standardized coskewness with		Returns serial correlation		Squared returns serial correlation	
							TSE300	SMIgovt	TSE300	SMIgovt	lag 1	lag 12	lag 1	lag 12
Portfolio	1.35%	1.37%	10.99%	−18.67%	3.71%	−0.70	0.83	0.31	0.83	5.23	0.12	−0.05	−0.01	−0.03
(p-value)	*(0.00)*				*(0.76)*	*(0.00)*	*(0.00)*	*(0.001)*			*(0.06)*	*(0.25)*	*(0.46)*	*(0.35)*
Benchmarks:														
1-m T-bill	0.68%	0.68%	1.14%	0.23%	0.23%	0.09	0.00	0.01			0.98	0.63	0.98	0.59
(p-value)	*(0.00)*				*(1.00)*	*(0.61)*	*(0.255)*	*(0.13)*			*(0.00)*	*(0.00)*	*(0.00)*	*(0.00)*
TSE300TRI	0.96%	1.03%	11.80%	−22.50%	3.93%	−1.22	1.00	0.37			0.00	−0.10	−0.05	−0.03
(p-value)	*(0.001)*					*(0.00)*	*(0.00)*	*(0.00)*			*(0.50)*	*(0.09)*	*(0.26)*	*(0.34)*
SMIgovt	1.19%	1.36%	8.46%	−6.36%	2.72%	−0.08	0.18	1.00			0.06	0.01	−0.01	0.01
(p-value)	*(0.00)*				*(1.00)*	*(0.69)*	*(0.00)*	*(0.00)*			*(0.23)*	*(0.47)*	*(0.43)*	*(0.47)*
Other benchmarks:														
MSCIworld	1.32%	1.23%	14.67%	−14.50%	5.06%	−0.13	0.65	0.40			0.01	0.05	0.19	0.02
(p-value)	*(0.001)*				*(0.001)*	*(0.52)*	*(0.00)*	*(0.002)*			*(0.46)*	*(0.25)*	*(0.01)*	*(0.38)*
SP500TRI	1.42%	1.59%	13.43%	−21.52%	4.16%	−1.00	0.81	0.46			−0.02	−0.05	0.05	−0.03
(p-value)	*(0.00)*				*(0.25)*	*(0.00)*	*(0.00)*	*(0.00)*			*(0.42)*	*(0.26)*	*(0.29)*	*(0.37)*
WIL5000TRI	1.37%	1.63%	12.80%	−22.78%	4.17%	−1.23	0.83	0.41			0.03	−0.04		
(p-value)	*(0.00)*				*(0.24)*	*(0.00)*	*(0.00)*	*(0.00)*						

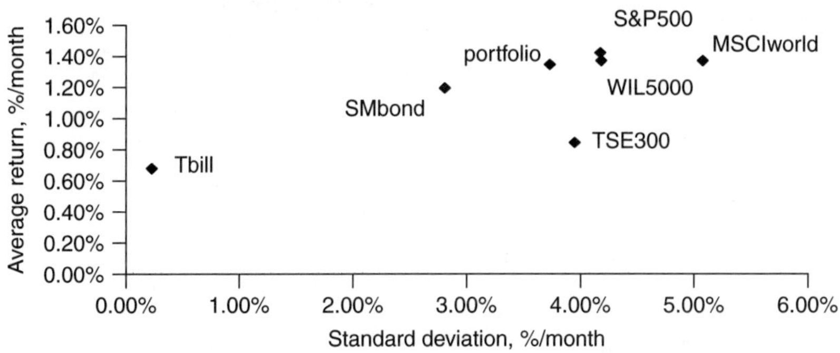

Figure 8.2 Average returns and volatilities (computed over 5/84–12/96)

(1966) timing regression and Sharpe (1988, 1992) style regression were performed, in all cases without fees.

Market timing

Table 8.3a contains the results of the excess return quadratic regression

$$r_{pt} - r_{ft} = \alpha_{pI} + \beta_{pI}(r_{It} - r_{ft}) + \gamma_{pI}(r_{It} - r_{ft})^2 + e_{pt}, \quad t = 1, 2, \ldots, 151$$

which was run separately with the equity and bond indexes as independent variables, and where the subscripts p, I and f indicate the portfolio, a market index, and the 1-month T-bill, respectively. The portfolio's alpha is significantly positive but the portfolio's gamma indicates insignificant equity market timing. The portfolio's gamma computed against the SMIgovt is significantly negative indicating perverse timing with respect to the bond market. The lack of equity market timing is consistent with the portfolio's policy of not attempting to time the market.

Table 8.3a shows that the poor bond market timing is due to the equity market's relation with the bond market rather than poor performance on the part of the portfolio's managers. The TSE300 has a more significantly negative timing gamma with the bond market than does the portfolio.

Style analysis

Style analysis measures a portfolio's exposure to variations in the returns on major asset classes. A style regression forces the intercept to zero and requires that the sum of the coefficient weights adds to one. Although not discussed in the style literature, this is quite similar to the spanning tests of Huberman and Kandel (1987), where one is interested in whether K style benchmarks provide the same mean-variance portfolio opportunities as the K benchmarks

Table 8.3a Traditional measures of market timing and selectivity, 5/84–12/96

Regression in decimals	Indexes	
	TSE300TRI	SMIgovt
Portfolio selectivity alpha	0.004	0.011
(p-value)	*(0.005)*	*(0.003)*
Portfolio market timing gamma	−0.021	−7.905
(p-value)	*(0.951)*	*(0.008)*
Portfolio regression R-squared	0.772	0.095
TSE300 selectivity alpha		0.008
(p-value)		*(0.044)*
TSE300 market timing gamma		−9.579
(p-value)		*(0.002)*
TSE300 regression R-squared		0.127

Table 8.3b Style analysis, 5/84–12/96

	Regression statistics	1-m T-bill	TSE300TRI	SP500TRI	S&P/BARRA 500TRI		MSCIworld
					Growth	Value	
Style weights		0.152	0.749	−2.767	−2.711	5.550	0.027
(p-value)		*(0.000)*	*(0.000)*	*(0.142)*	*(0.136)*	*(0.133)*	
Regression							
R-squared	0.850						
(p-value)	*(0.000)*						
Spanning							
p-value	*(0.006)*						

[a]All non-Canadian benchmarks' returns are approximately hedged against US/Can exchange rates.

and the portfolio. Our set of style benchmarks is shown in Table 8.3b, where the test results of the regression restrictions are also shown.[6]

As one would expect given the portfolio's policies, the T-bill and TSE300 are important descriptors of the portfolio's returns. However, US benchmarks describing the S&P500 equity market and S&P/BARRA growth and value styles are also important.[7] *Ceteris paribus*, the portfolio is negatively related to the S&P500 and the US growth indices and positively related to the T-bill,

[6]Here we allow shorts on the style indexes because they are closely related to the returns on the Nesbitt Burns portfolio. The spanning test permits a one-step approach to estimation and testing that avoids some of the problems of the two-step approach suggested in Sharpe (1988).

[7]The Scotial McLeod long government bond, MSCI world index, gold fix and BZW small cap growth and value bogies were also used but were insignificant.

Canadian market and the US value indices. Because value indexes are defined by stocks that have large book-to-market and low price-earnings ratios, the positive relation with the value index seems consistent with the portfolio's policy of undervalued stock selectivity.

Despite the relatively large R^2 of 0.85, the significant spanning test (*p-value* of 0.006) indicates that there is an insufficient number of style benchmarks to describe all of the portfolio's style. This is probably due to the trading activities of the managers that impart a non-linear structure to the returns. This implies that the standard style regression has misspecification errors that are due to omitted assets and an incorrect functional form. We will adjust for this deficiency in the subsequent section on management value-added.

8.4.4 Attribution analysis

We have selected an attribution technique that has its roots in the relationship between a portfolio's weights and the returns on its constituent assets. This is a different approach from attribution to style factors. The procedure is adapted from Korkie (2001) and is described in the following section, excluding the development of the test statistics. This analysis has some extremely desirable properties in that the attribution does not depend on an asset pricing model, it exhausts 100% of the portfolio's returns, it has well-behaved statistical tests, and it can be performed at any level of asset aggregation within the portfolio. The analysis is particularly useful for the portfolio manager who employs a number of analysts. Stocks may be easily grouped by sector or analyst to determine their respective contributions to the portfolio's return. However, part of the analyses does require a benchmark whose asset weights are observable every month in the analysis interval and which is appropriate in the context of the portfolio's policies.

The attribution technique

In a month t, the continuously compounded portfolio return is

$$r_{pt}^{*} = \ln(1 + r_{pt}) = \ln\left[\sum_{j=1}^{N_t} x_{jpt-1}(1 + r_{jt})\right]$$

where N_t is the number of portfolio assets and x_{jpt-1} is the beginning of month t weight on asset j. Because the month t is short, the continuously compounded portfolio return can be written approximately as the weighted sum of the individual assets' continuously compounded returns[8]

$$r^*_{pt} \approx \sum_{j=1}^{N_t} x_{jpt-1} \ln(1 + r_{jt}) = \sum_{j=1}^{N_t} x_{jpt-1} r^*_{jt}$$

Partitioning the weights into a benchmark component and a self-financing component results in a portfolio return of

$$r^*_{pt} \approx \sum_{j=1}^{N_t} x_{jIt-1} r^*_{jt} + \sum_{j=1}^{N_t} x_{j\Delta t-1} r^*_{jt}$$

where x_{jIt-1} is the index weight and $x_{j\Delta t-1}$ is the asset's weight in the self-financing portfolio, Δ. This latter portfolio is the risky arbitrage portfolio that is the managed portfolio's sidebet against its benchmark, I.

Due to the additivity property of continuously compounded returns, the T-month portfolio return may be written as the sum

$$R^*_{pT} = \sum_{t=1}^{T} r^*_{pt} \approx \sum_{t=1}^{T} \sum_{j=1}^{N_t} x_{jpt-1} r^*_{jpt}$$

and a similar expression may be written for the arbitrage portfolio, $R^*_{\Delta T}$. Henceforth, the superscript * is omitted from the formulae with the understanding that the returns are continuously compounded. By using the definition of covariance, this T-month portfolio return may be written as the sums

$$R_{pT} \approx T \sum_{j=1}^{N} \bar{x}_{jp} \bar{r}_j + T \sum_{j=1}^{N} \mathrm{cov}(x_{jpt-1}, r_{jt})$$

where $\bar{x}_{jp}$ is the average weight on asset j, $\bar{r}_j$ is the average return on asset j, and their product, $\bar{r}_j \bar{x}_{jp}$, is j's 'asset selectivity' component. The covariance between the weights and the returns for an asset j is its 'asset timing' component in portfolio, p.

Over all N assets, this decomposition attributes the portfolio's holding period return to two components,

$$R_{pT} = \mathit{Portfolio\ selectivity} + \mathit{Portfolio\ timing}$$

where the first component is

$$\mathit{Portfolio\ selectivity} = T \sum_{j=1}^{N} \bar{x}_{jp} \bar{r}_j$$

[8]In traditional attribution analysis, such as Brinson and Fachler (1985), this is a common assumption.

and the second component is

$$Portfolio\ timing = T\sum_{j=1}^{N}\mathrm{cov}(x_{jpt-1}, r_{jt})$$

The intuition of these formulae is that the portfolio selectivity is the sum of the individual assets' selectivities. This will be large if large average return assets are held with average weights that are also large. The portfolio timing is the sum of the individual assets' timing. This number will be large if the portfolio allocates large weights to individual assets in advance of periods when their returns are also large. Passive portfolios will have no portfolio timing whereas actively managed portfolios may have significantly negative or positive timing components. Noise traders will have zero timing.

For ease of interpretation in the following application, the components are expressed as the fractions, the sum of which will add to one thereby attributing 100% of the portfolio's return to timing and selectivity. Similarly, the individual asset results may be expressed as fractions for ease of interpretation. The importance of each *asset* in the portfolio's attribution may be determined by computing each asset's fractional contribution

$$Selectivity\ proportion\ of\ asset\,j = \frac{T\bar{x}_{pj}\bar{r}_j}{Portfolio\ selectivity + Portfolio\ timing}$$

$$Timing\ proportion\ of\ asset\,j = \frac{T \times \mathrm{cov}(x_{pjt-1}, r_{jt})}{Portfolio\ selectivity + Portfolio\ timing}$$

$$Return\ proportion\ of\ asset\,j = \frac{T\bar{x}_{pj}\bar{r}_j + T \times \mathrm{cov}(x_{pjt-1}, r_{jt})}{Portfolio\ selectivity + Portfolio\ timing}$$

The advantage of these expressions is that the selectivity and timing fraction of any asset j will add up to the return contribution fraction of the same asset. Additionally, the sum of the return fractions over all of the assets will add up to one.

A similar partitioning of the arbitrage portfolio's T-month return is obtainable resulting in the selectivity and timing components of the arbitrage portfolio.

The attribution results

Table 8.3c contains our attribution analysis, which attributes the portfolio's return to the selection of assets and to the ability to time the purchase of individual assets. The table contains two panels. The first panel attributes the return on the portfolio over the period 5/84 to 12/96; whereas the second

Table 8.3c Attribution of the portfolio's monthly return performance

Asset class	Average weight	Portfolio returns			Portfolio returns proportions		
		Average	Selectivity	Timing	Average	Selectivity	Timing
Portfolio, 05/84 to 12/96							
Cash	0.21	0.16%	0.15%	0.01%	0.12	0.11	0.01
Stocks	0.79	1.19%	1.26%	−0.07%	0.88	0.93	−0.05
Total	1.00	1.35%	1.41%	−0.06%	1.00	1.04	−0.04
(p-value)		*(0.000)*	*(0.000)*	*(1.000)*			
Sidebet portfolio to the TSE35, 05/87 to 12/96 [a]							
Cash	0.19	0.08%	0.08%	0.00%	0.34	0.32	0.02
Stocks	−0.19	0.16%	0.04%	0.12%	0.66	0.16	0.50
Total	0.00	0.24%	0.12%	0.12%	1.00	0.48	0.52
(p-value)		*(0.133)*	*(0.293)*	*(0.000)*			

[a]The monthly return averages on the portfolio and the TSE35TRI are 1.016% and 0.772%, respectively in this period. Therefore, the sidebet portfolio return averages 0.244%/month.

panel attributes the return on the sidebet or risky arbitrage portfolio between the portfolio and the TSE35 benchmark. The portfolio's monthly return average was 1.35% before fees. The selectivity component was significant and contributed 104% (or 1.41% return per month) and the timing component contributed −4% (or −0.06% return per month). This was consistent with the portfolio's policies that were oriented to buying and holding the best stocks from the TSE sectors. On average, cash occupied 21% of the portfolio but contributed 12% of the portfolio's return compared to the stocks' return contribution of 88% with a 79% average weight.

Not shown are specific stock contributions but some highlights are as follows. Power Corp., with an average weight of 2.2%, made the largest return contribution to the portfolio of 7.5% of the portfolio's return (2.9% from selectivity and 4.6% from timing). National Business Systems, with a weight of 0.6%, made the smallest return contribution of −2.9%, which came primarily from trading the stock too often (−3.2% from timing). Bombardier, with an average weight of 2.3%, had the largest selectivity contribution of 5.5% but this was offset by trading the stock too often (−3.8% from timing). Woodwards had the smallest selectivity contribution of −0.3%.

These results suggest that the portfolio's trades in the same stock have a neutral effect on the portfolio's long-run return. They win on some and lose on others such that they would be about as well off by simply holding the stock in its long-run proportions.

The stocks can be aggregated according to the recommending analyst or sector, whose performance can be determined and evaluated. For example, the six bank stocks as a group had an average portfolio weight of 8.4% and in the aggregate contributed 10.5% of the portfolio's return, of which 9.8% was from selectivity and 0.6% from asset timing. The bank recommendations seem sound in that there was a good selectivity contribution and no return was lost from the timing of sales and purchases.

An alternative and related attribution analysis is obtained from the second panel where the sidebet portfolio, that costlessly changes an investment in the TSE35 to an investment in the Nesbitt Burns portfolio, is analysed.[9] In this analysis, we explain the source of the additional 0.24% in average monthly return obtained by the portfolio over the TSE35 index. Because the TSE35 index weights and returns were available only from 5/87, the analysis interval is three years shorter.

The sidebet portfolio has an average monthly return of 0.24% (significant at 0.13) that arises from approximately equal amounts of timing and selectivity, relative to the TSE35. Over the analysis period, the additional holding period return amounts to 3.48%/year. The monthly standard deviation changes from 4.12% on the TSE35 to the portfolio's 3.62% for a marginal decline of 0.50% on the portfolio. The sidebet portfolio is self-financing and yet results in a marginal increase in return and a marginal decrease in volatility, when a change is made from holding the TSE35 to holding the portfolio.[10]

About 34% of the sidebet return comes from the cash account and the remaining 66% from the stock positions. In other words, both the stock and cash accounts contributed to the sidebet return. The timing component arises from the positive relation between a stock's weight in the sidebet portfolio and that stock's return in the analysis interval; whereas, the selectivity component comes from holding the stock's average weight throughout the interval.[11] For example, Renaissance Energy contributed 21% of the sidebet return most of which (17% of the 21%) was due to the changing weights of RES in the sidebet portfolio. (RES was bought three times and sold four times by Nesbitt Burns and entered the TSE35 within the analysis interval.) TD Bank was bought or sold a total of 13 times with a timing contribution of 16% of its 17% return contribution (TD was in the TSE35 throughout the analysis interval). Potash Co. had a contribution of 8% of the sidebet return; but a buy

[9]The sidebet portfolio is also termed the risky arbitrage portfolio, the active portfolio or the self-financing portfolio.

[10]Note that the standard deviation of the sidebet portfolio of 1.8% is not equal to the marginal standard deviation of 0.5%.

[11]The benchmark TSE35 portfolio will have some timing component to it simply because the weights on the components change due to stock issues, deletion from the index, and any momentum effects. Therefore, the sidebet portfolio may not have the same timing and selectivity as the portfolio itself.

and hold would have been better because the timing contribution was −7% and the selectivity contribution was 15%. (POT was bought or sold five times in the portfolio and was not contained in the TSE35.)

It is apparent that the portfolio earned a superior return from its asset selection, which is consistent with its policies. Overall, the portfolio has added an additional return via a combination of asset selectivity and timing and has decreased total risk relative to the TSE35 benchmark. The portfolio's fees seem to have been more than offset by its improved performance; although this issue is addressed in detail in our value added section.

8.4.5 External risk–return performance

In this section, an evaluation of the portfolio's risk–return performance is performed. The intention is to determine whether the portfolio was a good asset to hold either alone or with other benchmarks before fees and considering risk and return at the margin.

Portfolio held alone

If portfolio p is held alone, in the sense that no other assets are in the owner's portfolio, then 'total risk' is the relevant measure of risk for the asset. Typically, we measure total risk using standard deviation, s_p, of p's monthly returns. The average excess return per unit of total risk is

$$Sh_p = \frac{\bar{r}_p - \bar{r}_f}{s_p}$$

which is called the 'Sharpe measure' of performance or the 'reward to volatility ratio'. The statistic for testing the equivalence of the Sharpe performances of the managed portfolio and an index, I, follows a standard normal distribution and is calculated from

$$z = \frac{s_I(\bar{r}_p - \bar{r}_f) - s_p(\bar{r}_I - \bar{r}_f)}{\sqrt{\hat{\theta}}}$$

where:

$$\hat{\theta} = \frac{1}{T}\left[2s_p^2 s_I^2 - 2s_p s_I s_{pI} + \frac{1}{2}\bar{r}_p^2 s_I^2 + \frac{1}{2}\bar{r}_I^2 s_p^2 - \frac{\bar{r}_p \bar{r}_I}{2 s_p s_I}(s_{pI}^2 + s_p^2 s_I^2)\right]$$

and s_{pI}^2 is the square of the covariance between monthly returns on I and p.[12]

Table 8.4a contains the results of the hold alone analysis. The table provides the Sharpe measures of the portfolio and benchmarks together with tests

[12]See Jobson and Korkie (1981) for the details of the test.

Table 8.4a External portfolio analysis, portfolio held alone, 5/84–12/96

Item	Portfolio's and benchmarks' total risk–return properties						
	Portfolio	1-m T-bill	TSE300TRI	SMIgovt	MSCIworld	SP500TRI	WIL5000TRI
Mean return: per month	0.0135	0.0068	0.0096	0.0119	0.0132	0.0142	0.0137
Standard deviation: per month	0.0371	0.0023	0.0393	0.0272	0.0506	0.0416	0.0417
Excess return to volatility (Sharpe ratio):	0.1792	N.A.	0.0697	0.1865	0.1257	0.1779	0.1655
Difference from TSE300 benchmark Sharpe ratio:	0.1095	N.A.	0.0000	0.1168	0.0560	0.1082	0.0957
(p-value)	*(0.004)*	*N.A.*	*N.A.*	*(0.119)*	*(0.244)*	*(0.027)*	*(0.038)*
Difference from SMIgovt benchmark Sharpe ratio:	−0.0073	N.A.	−0.1168	0.0000	−0.0608	−0.0086	−0.0210
(p-value)	*(0.471)*	*N.A.*	*(0.119)*	*N.A.*	*(0.275)*	*(0.465)*	*(0.416)*

All non-Canadian benchmarks' returns are fully and costlessly hedged against US/CDN exchange rates.

of the null hypotheses of equality of the portfolio Sharpe and respectively the TSE300 or the Scotia McLeod Government bond indexes. The portfolio significantly (0.004) outperformed the TSE300, but not the bond index. The US indices also outperformed the TSE300 but the MSCI world index did not.

When evaluating a portfolio manager, hired to manage a dedicated Canadian equity portfolio, the benchmarks should include only Canadian equity benchmarks like the S&P/TSE60, for example. The portfolio's large excess return per unit of total risk of 0.179 is consistent with the results of the previous analyses that point to abnormally good portfolio performance from a portfolio held alone and in competition with competing benchmarks of a similar class. The result is not likely due to chance.

Portfolio held with benchmarks

It is possible that some managed portfolios are not good held alone but they make good additions to an existing portfolio. In this case, the portfolio's total risk is no longer relevant. Rather, the relevant risk is the amount of risk that the portfolio adds to the new portfolio formed from the managed portfolio and the existing portfolio. For example, if the investor already owns a well-diversified domestic portfolio such as the TSE300, then the question is, how much risk does p add to the portfolio resulting from the combination of p and the TSE300?[13] We can determine if there is *any* improvement to be obtained versus simply holding the TSE300 benchmark. Improvement can occur only if the benchmark portfolio is *not* the most efficient portfolio when combined with the managed portfolio. We investigate this by checking whether the Jensen alpha is zero or equivalently whether the Treynor measures of the portfolio and TSE300 are equal. If their associated statistical hypotheses are not rejected, then no improvement to the benchmark is obtained by holding the portfolio with the benchmark.

The Treynor measure of an asset, p, is defined as the reward per unit of non-diversifiable risk given by

$$Tr_{pI} = \frac{\bar{r}_p - \bar{r}_f}{\beta_{pI}}$$

where β_{pI} is the beta of p against I obtained by running the excess return regression

$$(r_{pt} - r_{ft}) = \alpha_{pI} + \beta_{pI}(r_{It} - r_{ft}) + e_{pt}; \quad t = 1, 2, \ldots, T$$

and α_{pI} is the Jensen alpha of p computed against the index I.

The use of alpha to rank portfolios is inappropriately prevalent in the market and in academic literature, in my opinion. For example, Morningstar Inc.'s

[13] Much of the following analysis and discussion is based on Korkie (1983, 2001).

mutual fund ratings (from 5 stars to 1 star) are based upon the size of a measure closely related to alpha. However, neither the alpha nor the Treynor performance measures directly the amount of improvement obtained by adding the evaluated portfolio to the benchmark index. It is quite possible that a rational investor prefers to add a portfolio with a smaller alpha (or Treynor) than a larger alpha (or Treynor).[14]

The magnitude of the improvement, from adding the portfolio to the benchmark, is useful information because we can then compare the magnitudes of improvement with other competitive portfolios. In other words, we can rank the competitors based upon their performance contribution to a benchmark. The improvement measure is called the Treynor–Black 'appraisal ratio', which is defined as the squared value of alpha divided by s_e^2, the unexplained variance (unsystematic risk) from the excess return market model.[15] That is,

$$AR_{pI} = \frac{\alpha_{pI}^2}{s_{e_p}^2}$$

which is also commonly written in its square root form. It can be proven that the appraisal ratio equals the difference in the squared Sharpe performances

$$Sh_m^2 - Sh_I^2 = AR_{pI} = \frac{\alpha_{pI}^2}{s_e^2}$$

Therefore, it indirectly measures the improvement obtained by adding the portfolio to the benchmark index. That is, $Sh_m - Sh_I$ is the amount of this improvement from holding the benchmark, I, to holding the optimal combination, m, of the portfolio and the benchmark. Notice that the improvement is calculable from AR_{pI} and is non-zero only if α_{pI} is non-zero.

The preceding formulae show why you may use appraisal ratios to rank portfolios in terms of their desirability to hold with a given benchmark, I. Suppose that you own the index I. The larger the AR_{pI}, the larger is the resulting optimal Sharpe performance, Sh_m, that is obtainable by optimally combining the portfolio, p, and your index portfolio. If a second portfolio has a larger AR_{pI}, it will be preferred because it adds more performance to your index portfolio, I. Therefore, you would purchase the second portfolio to add to your existing assets. However, one must be cognizant of the significance levels of the alpha and the appraisal ratios.

---

[14]Discussions of these, largely ignored, ranking problems are contained in Larcker, Gordon and Pinches (1980), Jobson and Korkie (1984), Korkie (1986) and Korkie and Laiss (1990).

[15]See Treynor and Black (1973) and Jobson and Korkie (1984).

Table 8.4b shows the results of optimally combining the portfolio with one of the TSE300, the Scotia McLeod bond index, or the currency hedged S&P500. The significant (*p-value* = 0.003) alpha from the TSE300 regression indicates that the TSE300 may be improved by creating a new portfolio from the TSE300 and the Nesbitt Burns portfolio.[16] Similarly, the Scotia McLeod bond portfolio may be improved in combination with the managed portfolio. Identical information is obtained from the test of the equivalence of the portfolio's Treynor measure and the respective benchmarks' Treynor measures. The significant alpha indicates that the Treynor measures are significantly different, indicating that the benchmarks may be improved with the addition of the portfolio.

The maximum amounts of improvement, measured by the difference in the maximum Sharpe performance and a benchmark's Sharpe, are 0.187 and

Table 8.4b External portfolio analysis, portfolio held with an index and before fees, 5/84–12/96

	Index	
	TSE300TRI	SMIgovt
Indicators of index inefficiency in a two asset set with the portfolio:		
Jensen alpha:	0.0044	0.0051
(p-value)	*(0.003)*	*(0.091)*
Portfolio's excess return to beta ratio (Treynor measure):	0.0081	0.0218
Index excess return to beta ratio (Treynor measure):	0.0028	0.0051
Differences:	0.0054	0.0167
Measures of index improvement from adding the portfolio to the index:		
Maximum Sharpe measure from the portfolio held with the respective index:	0.2573	0.2345
Index Sharpe measure:	0.0701	0.1874
Difference:	0.1872	0.0470
Appraisal ratio (Treynor–Black measure):	0.0613	0.0110
(p-value)	*(0.003)*	*(0.091)*
Other properties of the two asset IOS		
Portfolio's weight required for the portfolio/index optimum:	3.2229	0.4074
vertex mean: per month	0.0124	0.0124
vertex standard deviation: per month	0.0369	0.0242
T-bill average return	0.0068	0.0068
tangent mean: per month	0.0222	0.0125
tangent standard deviation: per month	0.0612	0.0246

All non-Canadian benchmarks' returns are fully and costlessly hedged against US/CDN exchange rates.

[16]Equivalently, the benchmark is not efficient in the two asset set formed from the portfolio and the benchmark.

0.047 in the respective cases of the TSE300 and the SMIbond. The maximums were computed from the appraisal ratio shown in the table. The other properties panel shows that the portfolio would be held in a long position with both benchmarks, indicative of good performance. However, in the case of the TSE300, maximum improvement is obtained by shorting the TSE300.

Overall, the portfolio has been a good portfolio for investors to hold alone. For those investors already owning a portfolio similar to the bond or equity market indexes of Canada, the addition of the managed portfolio would have enhanced an index's performance. None of these results appears due to chance.

8.4.6 Internal performance analyses

Here, some reasons for the portfolio's external performance are investigated. From Table 8.5a, we determine whether the portfolio had effective asset weights that were efficient relative to optimal weightings and relative to naïve equal weights. From Table 8.5b, we determine whether the portfolio had sufficient assets in the portfolio by comparison with a customized benchmark and by testing for the change in the investment opportunity set arising from additional assets.

The statistical test for unconditional efficiency measures the distance from the Markowitz (1952) efficient set as the difference in the Sharpe measures of the tangency portfolio, Sh_m, and the managed portfolio, Sh_p, and is given by

$$F_{N-1,T-N} = \left(\frac{T-N}{N-1}\right)\left(\frac{Sh_m^2 - Sh_p^2}{1 + Sh_p^2}\right)$$

which follows an F-distribution with $N-1$ and $T-N$ degrees of freedom. The tangency is on the investment opportunity set formed from $N-1$ assets and T return observations.[17]

Table 8.5a indicates that the portfolio dominates the equal weight portfolio constructed from the portfolio's stocks: it has a larger mean and a smaller volatility. Additionally, the portfolio is not significantly (0.993) different from the efficient tangency portfolio even though the tangency portfolio implicitly allows for short sales in this particular test. The portfolio would be located even closer to an efficient portfolio that did not permit shorts.

The expression $\sqrt{ac-b^2}$ is called the 'performance of an N-asset set', because the larger its value the greater is the size of the investment opportunity

[17]See Campbell, Lo and MacKinlay (1997) for a summary of the tests.

Table 8.5a Mean-variance efficiency of the portfolio, 5/84–12/96

Portfolio mean return: per month	1.35%
Portfolio standard deviation: per month	3.71%
Equal weight portfolio mean return: per month	1.29%
Equal weight portfolio standard deviation: per month	4.30%
Maximum tangent portfolio Sharpe ratio created from the portfolio's assets:	0.56
Portfolio Sharpe ratio:	0.18
Distance from efficient set, $Sh_m - Sh_p$:	0.38
(p-value)	*(0.993)*
Number of assets used in the opportunity set	50
Number of monthly returns used in the calculation	150

set. A measure of the improvement obtained from adding the extra $(N - N_1)$ assets to the investment opportunity set of N_1 assets is therefore

$$\Delta P = \sqrt{ac - b^2} - \sqrt{a_1 c_1 - b_1^2}$$

where a, b and c are the Lintner (1965), Merton (1972) and Roll (1977) efficient set constants calculated from two asset sets of size N and $N_1 < N$, respectively. The statistical test for spanning utilizes

$$F_{2(N-N_1),2(T-N))} = \left(\frac{T - N}{N - N_1}\right)\left(\frac{\sqrt{c + ac - b^2} - \sqrt{c_1 + a_1 c_1 - b_1^2}}{\sqrt{c_1 + a_1 c_1 - b_1^2}}\right)$$

which follows an F-distribution with $2(N - N_1)$ and $2(T - N)$ degrees of freedom. A summary of efficiency tests, spanning tests and related literature is available in Jobson and Korkie (1989).[18]

Table 8.5b has mixed results regarding the number of portfolio assets. On average the portfolio held 12.5 stocks, which theoretically would be considered a marginally sufficient number. However, the policy change in 1993 increased that number such that 33 stocks were held at the close of 12/96. A portfolio formed from the T-bill and the TSE300, with the same average return, provided a much larger volatility resulting in a lower Sharpe measure of 0.07 compared to 0.18. This specialized benchmark requires borrowing at the T-bill and investing the proceeds into the TSE300 to give a weight of 2.39 in the TSE300. Therefore, the portfolio seems sufficiently well diversified.

To examine if there was a sufficient number of assets considered for the portfolio, the entire asset set contained in the portfolio at any time in the 5/84 to 12/96 interval was obtained. Its opportunity set was measured against the same opportunity set augmented by the TSE300 index. There is a significant

[18] A detailed treatment of spanning is in Kan and Zhou (2000).

Table 8.5b Portfolio diversification and opportunity set spanning, 5/84–12/96

Portfolio	
Average number of portfolio assets (including cash)	13.5
Portfolio average return: per month	1.35%
Portfolio standard deviation: per month	3.71%
Portfolio Sharpe ratio	0.18
Specialized benchmark created from TSE300 and T-bill	
Benchmark standard deviation (with same average return as the portfolio)	9.40%
Benchmark Sharpe ratio	0.070
Benchmark weight in the TSE300	2.39
Spanning	
Performance measure of the portfolio's asset set plus the TSE300 benchmark	173181.66
Performance measure of the portfolio's asset set	89498.51
Spanning difference in the asset sets, ΔP:	83683.14
(p-value)	*(0.00)*

increase in the investment opportunity set obtained by adding the TSE300 benchmark to the set as indicted by the spanning test *p-value* of 0.00. However, our previous external analysis indicated that an optimal combination of the portfolio and the TSE300 would have required a short position on the TSE300. Because the managed portfolio does not permit shorts, we may tentatively conclude that the portfolio selected from a sufficient number of assets.

8.4.7 Management value-added

Arguably, the most important measure of a managed portfolio's performance is the value added by its management. If the value added by management does not exceed the portfolio's fees and expenses on a present value basis, then the portfolio does not represent a positive *NPV* investment. In general, a manager is creating an asset whose payoffs are contingent upon the payoffs from assets that are traded and priced in the market. Because of the active trading, the payoffs are likely to be a non-linear function of the traded assets' payoffs. The value added by management is non-zero when this non-linear contingent claim has a theoretical value that exceeds the present value of the fees. The task is to identify the functional form of the contingent claim and to price it.

Here, I adopt two procedures for this valuation. The first is based on the expected utility derived from the distribution of monthly portfolio payoffs. It uses the certainty equivalent valuation obtained from an exponential utility function with a risk aversion parameter derived from the equity market. Building on the work of Henrikkson and Merton (1981), Glosten and Jagannathan (1988, 1994), Korkie, Nakamura and Turtle (2001) and Korkie and Turtle (2002), the second method estimates and prices the portfolio's replicating contingent claim.

Certainty equivalent valuation

Consider a portfolio with a random monthly payoff from a \$1 investment of $(1 + r_{pt})$, where r_{pt} is the monthly return in decimal form. If the portfolio returns are normally distributed, the possible dollar payoffs and returns are completely described by the mean and standard deviation of return $(\bar{r}_p, s_p)$. A rational investor choosing this portfolio is paying for a gamble that must have a positive expected return exceeding the known riskless return, r_{ft}; otherwise, the investor will choose the riskless Treasury bill. To value the return moments, $(\bar{r}_p, s_p)$, a utility function is required that incorporates an investor's risk aversion and converts a monetary payoff to a utility value.

The 'exponential utility' function is given by

$$U(1 + r_{pt}) = 1 - \mathrm{e}^{-(1+r_{pt})/a}$$

where $e = 2.718\ldots$ is Euler's number and a is the 'risk tolerance' of the investor. Because there are many possible monthly returns and therefore utility values, one requires the payoffs' *expected* utility value that is calculable from the moment generating function and is given by

$$E[U(1 + r_{pt})] = E[1 - \mathrm{e}^{-(1+r_{pt})/a}] = 1 - \mathrm{e}^{-\frac{(1+\bar{r}_p - s_p^2/2a)}{a}}$$

By the definition of certainty equivalent, this expected utility must be equal to the utility value of a riskless dollar payoff represented by θ, where

$$E[U(1 + r_{pt})] = U(\theta) = 1 - \mathrm{e}^{-\theta/a}$$

Equating the two expected utility equations shows that the certainty equivalent value of the portfolio is

$$\theta = 1 + \bar{r}_p - \frac{s_p^2}{2a}$$

indicating that value is reduced with larger volatility and smaller risk tolerance. The value added from the portfolio is therefore the present value of θ, calculated at the riskless return, less the initial dollar invested. Here, I use the average monthly Treasury bill return, $\bar{r}_f$, resulting in the certainty equivalent

$$\textit{Certainty equivalent value added}_p = \frac{1 + \bar{r}_p - \dfrac{s_p^2}{2a}}{1 + \bar{r}_f} - 1 = \frac{\bar{r}_p - \dfrac{s_p^2}{2a} - \bar{r}_f}{1 + \bar{r}_f}$$

The remaining implementation problem is the determination of the investor's risk tolerance a. This may be obtained from the implied risk tolerance of a market index that is appropriate for benchmarking the portfolio's performance. Because a market index is not managed, its certainty equivalent value added is zero. By calculating the mean and volatility of the index, $(\bar{r}_I, s_I)$, the market's risk tolerance can be calculated from the preceding equation set to equal zero. That is, risk tolerance based on index I is

$$a_I = \frac{s_I^2}{2(\bar{r}_I - \bar{r}_f)}$$

The portfolio's value added is then obtained by substituting a_I for a resulting in

$$\textit{Certainty equivalent value added}_p$$

$$= \frac{\bar{r}_p - \dfrac{s_p^2}{2a_I} - \bar{r}_f}{1 + \bar{r}_f} = \frac{\bar{r}_p - \dfrac{s_p^2(\bar{r}_I - \bar{r}_f)}{s_I^2} - \bar{r}_f}{1 + \bar{r}_f}$$

From 5/84 to 12/96, the TSE300 average return and volatility were 0.96% and 3.93% per month, respectively and the T-bill average return was 0.68%. The market's implied risk tolerance was therefore

$$a_I = \frac{s_I^2}{2(\bar{r}_I - \bar{r}_f)} = \frac{0.0393^2}{2(0.0096 - 0.0068)} = 0.281$$

In the same interval, the Canadian Growth Portfolio average return and volatility were 1.35% and 3.71% per month, respectively. After substitution, the monthly value added by management before fees was

$$\textit{Certainty equivalent value added}_p = \frac{\bar{r}_p - \dfrac{s_p^2}{2a_I} - \bar{r}_f}{1 + \bar{r}_f}$$

$$= \frac{0.0135 - \dfrac{0.0371^2}{2 \times 0.281} - 0.0068}{1 + 0.0068} = 0.0042/\text{month per dollar invested}$$

This is equivalent to 0.42% of assets under management per month or on an annual basis about 5.2%/year.

Replicating contingent claim pricing[19]

An active portfolio manager actively buys and sells assets creating a potentially complex description of a function that relates the portfolio's monthly

[19]The specifics of this approach are developed in Korkie and Turtle (2002) and the managed portfolio's price is also shown in Korkie (2001). See Kon and Jen (1978) and Fabozzi, Francis and Lee (1980) for an early look at functional form as well as Fung and Hsieh (1997).

payoffs to the contingent and traded assets. In most cases, there is no plan by the manager to provide a specific type of payoff; rather, the resulting payoff is simply the result of active and dynamic trading on the part of the manager. The implication is that the Henrikkson and Merton (1981) timing call option is quite restrictive and not universally applicable to all portfolios. A variation on the approach uses derivative or 'Martingale methods' to value any type of payoffs that portfolio management has provided.

If the portfolio's monthly returns can be defined by a function of style portfolios' returns, then we will be able to price the portfolio's management value added. The most difficult aspect of the process is identifying a good functional relationship between the portfolio's monthly returns and the style portfolios' monthly returns. The monthly returns may be arbitrarily closely fit using higher order polynomials of the style portfolios' returns. For the Canadian Growth Portfolio, a quadratic regression is estimated with three style indexes, I_1, I_2, I_3, as in

$$r_{pt} = \alpha_p + \beta_{p1} r_{I1t} + \lambda_{p1} r_{I1t}^2 + \beta_{p2} r_{I2t} + \lambda_{p2} r_{I2t}^2 + \beta_{p3} r_{I3t} + \lambda_{p3} r_{I3t}^2 + e_{pt}$$

With this return in decimal form, the portfolio's dollar payoff in one month's time, ignoring the error term, is

$$\begin{aligned} 1 + r_{pt} &= 1 + \alpha_p + \sum_{k=1}^{3} \beta_{kp} r_{Ikt} + \sum_{k=1}^{3} \lambda_{pk} r_{Ikt}^2 \\ &= 1 + \alpha_p + \sum_{k=1}^{3} (\lambda_{pk} - \beta_{pk}) + \sum_{k=1}^{3} (\beta_{pk} - 2\lambda_{pk})(1 + r_{Ikt}) \\ &\quad + \sum_{k=1}^{3} (\lambda_{pk}(1 + r_{Ikt})^2) \end{aligned}$$

where $(1 + r_{Ikt})$ is the dollar payoff on index I_k. Assuming that the portfolio and index prices follow lognormal diffusions in the month, one can price the preceding payoffs using Martingale methods. That is, one can price the payoffs by taking the expectation under the risk-neutral probability measure. The discounted, at r_f, claim prices are a Martingale and the discounted value of the payoff can be shown to be

$$V = \frac{1 + \alpha_p + \sum_{j=1}^{3} (\lambda_{pk} - \beta_{pk})}{(1 + r_f)} + \sum_{k=1}^{3} (\beta_{pk} - 2\lambda_{pk}) + (1 + r_f) \sum_{k=1}^{3} \lambda_{pk} \{e^{\sigma_{Ik}^2}\}$$

The intuition of this valuation is that the first term is the present value of fixed payments one month hence. The second term is the values sum of $\beta_{pk} - 2\lambda_{pk}$ units of each of the three marketed indexes, each with a unit price of \$1. The third term is the sum of the values of λ_{pk} units of each index's squared payoff, where σ^2_{Ik} is the variance of index k's continuously compounded monthly return. Similar to options, the value increases with the underlying indexes' volatilities, which are assumed constant here.

A portfolio manager delivering the payoffs has a value added for a \$1 investment equal to the net present value

$$\begin{aligned} \textit{Management value added} &= NPV = V - 1 \\ &= \frac{1 + \alpha_p + \sum_{j=1}^{3} (\lambda_{pk} - \beta_{pk})}{(1 + r_f)} \\ &\quad + \sum_{k=1}^{3} (\beta_{pk} - 2\lambda_{pk}) \\ &\quad + (1 + r_f) \sum_{k=1}^{3} \lambda_{pk} \{e^{\sigma^2_{Ik}}\} - 1 \end{aligned}$$

A three index style regression was fit to the 5/84–12/96 monthly returns on the Canadian Growth Portfolio with the following results

$$\begin{aligned} r_{pt} &= 0.003 - 1.31 r_{TBt} + 216.36 r^2_{TBt} + 0.836 r_{TSEt} \\ &\quad - 0.025 r^2_{TSE} - 0.013 r_{Bt} + 0.139 r^2_{Bt} + e_{pt} \\ R^2 &= 0.78 \end{aligned}$$

where *TB* is the 1-month T-bill, *TSE* is the TSE300TRI and *B* is the Scotia MacLeod long Government bond index. Applying the valuation formula and utilizing the average T-bill return of 0.0068 for discounting, the management value added per dollar invested is

$$\begin{aligned} &= \frac{1 + \alpha_p + \sum_{j=1}^{K} (\lambda_{pj} - \beta_{pj})}{(1 + \bar{r}_f)} + \sum_{j=1}^{K} (\beta_{pj} - 2\lambda_{pj}) + (1 + \bar{r}_f) \sum_{j=1}^{K} \lambda_{pj} \{e^{\sigma^2_{Ij}}\} - 1 \\ &= \frac{1 + 0.003 + 216.36 + 1.31 - 0.025 - 0.836 + 0.139 + 0.013}{1 + 0.0068} \\ &\quad + (-1.31 - 2 \times 216.36 + 0.836 + 2 \times 0.025 - 0.013 - 2 \times 0.139) \\ &\quad + (1 + 0.0068)(216.36 e^{0.0000005} - 0.025 e^{0.001616} + 0.139 e^{0.000726}) - 1 \end{aligned}$$

Table 8.6 Value added by portfolio management in the Canadian Growth Equity Portfolio (values are estimated from data over the analysis interval, 5/84–12/96)

Valuation method	Valuations
Fees: annualized compounded per cent of asset value	2.1%
Expected utility method	
Estimated value added using exponential utility with the equity market benchmark's risk tolerances:	
Before fees value added: per dollar of asset value per month	\$0.0042
Before fees value added: per cent of asset value per year	5.2%
Derivative valuation method	
Estimated value added using a quadratic three index model	
Before fees value added: per dollar of asset value per month	\$0.0044
Before fees value added: per cent of asset value per year	5.4%

$$= 216.499 - 433.444 + 217.949 - 1$$

$$= \$0.004406/\text{month}$$

That is, the value-added is about 0.44% of the value of assets under management each month or about 5.4% per year.

The Table 8.6 summarizes the results of the two pricing methods that produced very similar annual values added of close to 5%. After annual fees of 2%, it is apparent that the managers of the Canadian Growth Portfolio were able to add value to the managed portfolio in the amount of about 3%/year of the assets under management.

8.5 CONCLUSIONS

The foregoing analysis provides evidence that the Nesbitt Burns Canadian Growth Portfolio significantly outperformed the market, for the analysis period of more than 12 years. Value added by management was worth about an additional 3% of assets under management. The value added came primarily from management's ability to select stocks. Because this is a clinical study, there is a clear selection bias that might prevent us from extrapolating our conclusions to other time periods of the same portfolio or other managed portfolios.

ACKNOWLEDGEMENT

My thanks to Sami Ylaoutinen who assisted in the transaction records entry and researched missing data records. The opinions and research in this paper are those of the author. This research was conducted while the author was at the University of Alberta.

REFERENCES AND FURTHER READING

Admati, A., Bhattacharya, S., Pfleiderer, P. and Ross, S. (1985) On timing and selectivity, *Journal of Finance*, **41**, 715–730.

Brinson, G.P. and Fachler, H. (1985) Measuring non-US equity performance, *Journal of Portfolio Management*, Spring, 73–76.

Brinson, G.P., Hood, L.R. and Beebower, G.L. (1986) Determinants of portfolio performance, *Financial Analysts Journal*, July–August, 39–44.

Campbell, J.Y., Lo, A.W. and MacKinlay, A.C. (1997) *The Econometrics of Financial Markets*, Princeton University Press, Princeton, New Jersey.

Chen, Z. and Knez, P. (1996) Portfolio performance measurement, *Review of Financial Studies*, **9**, 551–556.

Coggin, T.D. and Fabozzi, F.J. eds. (1995) *The Handbook of Equity Style Management*, New Hope PA: Frank J. Fabozzi Associates.

Daniel, K., Grinblatt, M., Titman, S. and Wermers, R. (1997) Measuring mutual fund performance with characteristic based benchmarks, *Journal of Finance*, **52**, 1035–1058.

Fabozzi, F., Francis, J. and Lee, C. (1980) Generalized functional form for mutual fund returns, *Journal of Financial and Quantitative Analysis*, **15**, 1107–1120.

Fung, W. and Hsieh, D. (1997) Empirical characteristics of dynamic trading strategies: the case of hedge funds, *Review of Financial Studies*, **10**, 275–302.

Glosten, L.R. and Jagannathan, R. (1988) A contingent claim approach to performance evaluation, Northwestern University working paper, No. 54.

Glosten, L.R. and Jagannathan, R. (1994) A contingent claim approach to performance evaluation, *Journal of Empirical Finance*, **1**, 133–160.

Grant, D. (1978) Market timing and portfolio management, *Journal of Finance*, **33**, 1119–1131.

Henrikkson, R.D. and Merton, R.C. (1981) On market timing and investment performance II: statistical procedures for evaluating forecasting skills, *Journal of Business*, **54**, 513–533.

Huberman, G. and Kandel, S. (1987) Mean-variance spanning, *Journal of Finance*, **42**, 873–888.

Jensen, M. (1969) Risk, the pricing of capital assets, and the evaluation of investment performance, *Journal of Business*, **42**, 167–247.

Jobson, J.D. and Korkie, B. (1981) Performance hypothesis testing with the Sharpe and Treynor measures, *Journal of Finance*, **36**, 889–908.

Jobson, J.D. and Korkie, B. (1982) Potential performance and tests of portfolio efficiency, *Journal of Financial Economics*, **10**, 433–456.

Jobson, J.D. and Korkie, B. (1984) A note on the Jensen measure and marginal improvements in portfolio performance, *Journal of Finance*, **39**, 245–251.

Jobson, J.D. and Korkie, B. (1985) Some tests of linear asset pricing with multivariate normality, *Canadian Journal of Administrative Studies*, **2**, 114–138.

Jobson, J.D. and Korkie, B. (1989) A performance interpretation of multivariate tests of asset set intersection, spanning, and mean-variance efficiency, *Journal of Financial and Quantitative Analysis*, **24**, 185–204.

Kan, R. and Zhou, G. (2000) Tests of mean-variance spanning, unpublished University of Toronto and Washington University.

Kon, S.J. and Jen, F.C. (1978) Estimation of time-varying systematic risk and performance for mutual fund portfolios: an application of switching regression, *Journal of Finance*, **33**, 457–475.

Korkie, B. (1983) External vs. internal performance evaluation, *Journal of Portfolio Management*, **9**, 36–42.

Korkie, B. (1986) Market line deviations and market anomalies with reference to small and large firms, *Journal of Financial and Quantitative Analysis*, **21**, 161–180.

Korkie, B. (2001) *Portfolio Management: Tools and Applications*, unpublished book manuscript.

Korkie, B. and Laiss, B. (1990) Optimal portfolio rules and maximum gains from economic events, *Journal of Accounting, Auditing, and Finance*, **5**, 593–618.

Korkie, B., Nakamura, M. and Turtle, H. (2001) A contingent claim analysis of closed-end fund premia, *International Review of Financial Analysis*, **10**, 365–394.

Korkie, B. and Turtle, H. (2002) What's a portfolio manager worth?, *Journal of Portfolio Management*, **28**, Winter, 65–73.

Larcker, D.F., Gordon, L.A. and Pinches, G.E. (1980) Testing for market efficiency: a comparison of the cumulative average residual methodology and intervention analysis, *Journal of Financial and Quantitative Analysis*, **15**, 267–288.

Lehmann, B. and Modest, D. (1987) Mutual fund performance evaluation: a comparison of benchmarks and benchmark comparisons, *Journal of Finance*, **42**, 233–265.

Lintner, J. (1965) The valuation of risk assets and the selection of risky investments in stock portfolios and capital budgets, *Review of Economics and Statistics*, **47**, 13–37.

Markowitz, H. (1952) Portfolio selection, *Journal of Finance*, **7**, 77–91.

Merton, R.C. (1972) An analytic derivation of the efficient portfolio frontier, *Journal of Financial and Quantitative Analysis*, **7**, 1851–1872.

Merton, R.C. (1981) On market timing and investment performance I: an equilibrium theory of value for market forecasts, *Journal of Business*, **54**, 363–406.

Roll, R. (1977) A critique of the assets pricing theory's tests: on past and potential testability of the theory, *Journal of Financial Economics*, **4**, 129–176.

Treynor, J.L. (1965) How to rate management of investment funds, *Harvard Business Review*, **48**, 63–75.

Treynor, J.L. and Mazuy, F. (1966) Can mutual funds outguess the market? *Harvard Business Review*, **44**, 131–136.

Treynor, J.L. and Black, F. (1973) How to use security analysis to improve portfolio selection, *Journal of Business*, **46**, 66–86.

Sharpe, W.F. (1988) Determining a fund's effective asset mix, *Investment Management Review*, December, 59–69.

Sharpe, W.F. (1992) Asset allocation: management style and performance measurement, *Journal of Portfolio Management*, Winter, 7–19.

Chapter 9

The intertemporal performance of investment opportunity sets

BOB KORKIE AND HARRY TURTLE

ABSTRACT

Investment opportunity sets (IOS) are the feasible set of expected returns and risks available from a set of risky assets, unrestricted by an asset pricing model. We consider the development, estimation and stochastic evolution of IOS conditional on time and instrument variables. We model conditional means and volatilities as functions of economic and time series information instruments satisfying prescribed rationality conditions. Our IOS contain both small and large risk assets, the performance of which we measure with an unbiased estimator of the limiting IOS slope and a new spanning test for a continuous risk IOS. Non-rejection of the spanning test may be viewed as a necessary condition for a subset representation of the performance of the asset universe. An iterated generalized method of moments (GMM) is employed to estimate the sequence of conditional IOS. Substantial predictable intertemporal variation in the IOS is present. Spanning tests are sensitive to the instrument set chosen and the imposition of conditional moment rationality restrictions.

9.1 INTRODUCTION

The fundamental investment-consumption decisions of economic agents are dependent on available investment opportunities. A great deal of financial research has been devoted to the asset pricing problem of describing the conditional mean relation among financial assets over time and to the performance measurement of managed portfolios. Little research has been devoted to describing and estimating the conditional investment opportunity set (IOS), unencumbered by any asset pricing model, or to measuring the performance of a portfolio's assets, as opposed to the portfolio itself. We focus on the estimation, evolution and performance of assets with a large range of volatilities, especially small risk assets that produce a continuous risk structure. The procedure can be applied to a specific set of assets under portfolio management or to broader set definitions. In Chapter 8, we examined the performance of a managed Canadian portfolio; in this chapter, we address sets of US fixed income and equity assets.[1]

Examples of assets with small risks include: a cash account, rollovers of short-term bills and bonds within an IOS time interval, bills and bonds with maturity close to the interval, and any asset portfolio with a large weight on a near-default-free asset with maturity arbitrarily close to the interval.[2] Conditionally, any asset (including common stock) with highly predictable returns and small prediction error variance has small risk. Thus, richer information, which is a rationale for active trading, provides assets with relatively smaller conditional risk. Inclusion of any of these nearly riskless assets imparts a substantial change in the representation of the investment opportunity set and its performance.

Our development departs from the usual definition of the conditional IOS as a hyperbola in mean-standard deviation space. Consideration of a continuous risk structure in a rational economy results in an IOS that can be described by a single ray emanating from the riskless rate. This ray is not the usual capital allocation line that occurs as a result of a tangency in the CAPM. Rather the ray arises solely from the existence of small, non-zero risk assets in the IOS. The continuous risk structure IOS represents a considerable simplification because it is fully described using a bivariate stochastic process of the riskless rate and the IOS slope. The slope is a measure of the performance of the entire asset set in the sense that an IOS with a larger slope spans the return and risk possibilities of an IOS with a smaller slope.

The conditional IOS depends on well-known efficient set constants that are functions of conditional means and covariances for the assets. We empirically describe conditional means and volatilities as linear functions of predetermined information instruments with unknown coefficients. Information instruments include both time series and economic regressors. To facilitate estimation of the coefficients and the conditional moments that define the opportunity set, Muth's rationality conditions are extended to all equations

[1] See Korkie and Turtle (1998).

[2] A typical time interval $(t, t_1]$ is one month; although, the small risk argument holds for any finite interval providing the assets are available.

that describe moment dynamics. These conditions are restrictions on the relations between the information instruments and the forecast errors that result from the conditional mean and volatility specifications. These rationality conditions are essential in order to avoid return error predictability using known information.

Rationality requires that conditional mean and conditional volatility errors display no own or cross lag relationships. For example, predictability of mean disturbances with prior volatility disturbances implies an omitted mean regressor. Because our estimation approach does not impose any asset pricing restrictions, conditional moments are estimated only under the restrictions of rational forecasts of the underlying investment opportunity set.[3] Given estimates of the parameters for conditional moments, conditional efficient set constants and the conditional IOS are then computed from an asset set encompassing a large range of volatilities.

Goodness of fit performance tests for one IOS relative to another are measured by unconditional and conditional spanning tests, adapted specifically to the continuous risk structure IOS. We differentiate existing tests in the literature based on the information set employed in the inference procedure. The spanning restriction is a zero intercept in the multivariate regression of the asset superset raw returns on the asset subset raw returns. This result is a special case of traditional spanning tests, which have a zero intercept in an excess return regression and the sum of coefficients equal to one.

A well-specified IOS is a necessary condition for any asset pricing investigation: the spanning and rationality conditions are part of the specification. We observe that the spanning performance of an asset set is sensitive to the asset universe considered, the instruments included and the rationality restrictions employed. We contend that omission of the rationality conditions would seriously misspecify the spanning performance test.

Much of our development considers the existence of assets with total risks that are arbitrarily near zero for the data interval considered. These assets impart a special shape to the opportunity set that we present in section 9.2. The conditional regression restrictions for one investment opportunity set to span another are developed in section 9.3. Rationality conditions, conditional moment specifications and test statistics are developed in section 9.4. Results

---

[3]Previous work has provided mixed results regarding the sign, significance and stability of the intertemporal relationship between conditional means and conditional variances. These prior results seem to depend quite strongly on the asset universe, the estimation procedure and the possible restrictions. Representative research includes Fama and Schwert (1977), French, Schwert and Stambaugh (1987), Chan, Karolyi and Stulz (1992), Gallant, Rossi and Tauchen (1992) and Whitelaw (1994).

of the GMM estimation and testing of the overidentifying restrictions are presented in section 9.5. Finally, in section 9.6, we offer concluding comments.

9.2 INVESTMENT OPPORTUNITY SETS WITH CONTINUOUS RISK STRUCTURES

This section presents the conditional investment opportunity set that reflects the continuum of volatilities available on traded financial assets. We begin by presenting the familiar conditional IOS hyperbola as described in Merton (1972). Next we discuss the conditional IOS in the context of a continuous risk structure. The resultant IOS represents a considerable simplification because it can be described by a bivariate process governing the IOS vertex and slope.

An investment opportunity set represents the risk and return possibilities from a set of risky financial assets held over a fixed time interval, $(t, t_1]$, such as one month. For convenience, the time subscript t is omitted in all notation and it is implicit that an opportunity set is conditional on information at a given point in time, and for a given interval length.

Following Merton (1972), the conditional investment opportunity set is described by a hyperbola in mean-standard deviation space,

$$f(\sigma_p) = \mu_p = \frac{b}{c} \pm \left[\left(a - \frac{b^2}{c}\right)\left(\sigma_p^2 - \frac{1}{c}\right)\right]^{1/2} \tag{9.1a}$$

where $\mu_p = X_p'\mu$ is the conditional mean of the portfolio determined by the $(n \times 1)$ vector of portfolio weights, X_p, and the $(n \times 1)$ vector of asset means, μ; $\sigma_p = \sqrt{X_p'\Sigma X_p}$ is the conditional standard deviation of the portfolio determined by the portfolio weight vector, X_p, and the $(n \times n)$ covariance matrix of asset returns, Σ; and $a = \mu'\Sigma^{-1}\mu$, $b = e'\Sigma^{-1}\mu$ and $c = e'\Sigma^{-1}e$ are the efficient set constants determined by the mean vector, μ, covariance matrix inverse, Σ and the $(n \times 1)$ vector of ones, e.[4]

The hyperbola's asymptote equations are described by,

$$g(\sigma_p) = \frac{b}{c} \pm \left[a - \frac{b^2}{c}\right]^{1/2} \sigma_p \tag{9.1b}$$

and the mean and standard deviation of the least risky or vertex portfolio are $\mu_o = b/c$ and $\sigma_o = 1/\sqrt{c}$, respectively.

[4]For tractability in our empirical work, we assume a non-singular covariance matrix of asset returns. More general results can be shown using generalized inverses when the covariance matrix is of less than full rank (c.f. Graybill (1969), Buser (1977) and Ross (1977)).

A restricted set of risky assets, such as common stocks, is a coarse approximation to the actual investment opportunity set faced by economic agents. As demonstrated by Stambaugh (1982) and Kandel (1984), asset omissions almost surely cause a misspecification of the opportunity set. Here, we are interested in the omission of risky assets with risks arbitrarily close to zero.[5] To proceed, we define a *continuous risk structure opportunity set* in terms of the volatilities on available traded assets. The development and proof of the continuous risk structure investment opportunity set, described by equation (9.2), is available in Korkie and Turtle (1997).

Definition: *A* **continuous risk structure investment opportunity set** *is a feasible set of expected returns and risks from financial assets with a sequence of volatilities arbitrarily close to zero, for all bounded time intervals. The continuous risk structure IOS can then be described by the mean equation,*

$$\mu_p = r_f \pm sl\sigma_p \tag{9.2}$$

where r_f represents the known riskless rate for the interval $(t, t_1]$, and sl denotes the finite IOS slope.

Because the vertex mean, b/c, has converged to the known riskless rate, r_f determines the minimum or zero risk portfolio's return and the IOS slope, sl, can be estimated using $\sqrt{a - b^2/c}$ or $\sqrt{a - br_f}$.

The investment opportunity set depends mathematically upon the current level of interest rates through both the IOS vertex and the IOS slope. This is not surprising given an abundance of early empirical research on the subject. For example, Fama and Schwert (1977) find that the spread between stock and bond returns is related to the interest rate level. In addition, they find that stock returns are negatively related to anticipated inflation rates, which may be proxied by the Treasury bill rate (Fama and Gibbons, 1984). Geske and Roll (1983) explain the causality in the linkage between interest rates and stock returns, which is supported in Solnik (1984) and James, Koreisha and Partch (1985). In Fama (1984), term premia predict future spot rates of interest. In Chen, Roll and Ross (1986), the Treasury bill rate is in the term structure shift factor. In Keim and Stambaugh (1986), term structure spreads are important determinants of conditional expected returns. Ferson (1989) found that the information contained in one month Treasury bill rates implies time variation

[5] Stambaugh (1982) and Kandel (1984) describe the robustness of mean-variance parameters used in asset pricing tests to omitted assets. Although they were not concerned specifically with the omission of nearly riskless assets, in general they find that the omission of assets causes potentially severe measurement error in the parameters of the investment opportunity set.

in the risks of individual assets. In the modern theory of the term structure, the level of interest rates depends upon the uncertainty in future rates.

The continuous risk structure opportunity set is considerably easier to estimate than the usual conditional hyperbola. At any time, the riskless rate, r_f, is known and only the slope parameter requires estimation. Therefore, the stochastic evolution of the opportunity set can be parsimoniously described by a bivariate process describing the evolution of the interest rate and the IOS slope. Much research, such as Chan *et al.* (1992) has addressed the interest rate process; however, little research has addressed the slope process. In the following section, we empirically investigate the discrete time process generating the IOS slopes. Because the r_f is common to all, one IOS outperforms another IOS if its slope is larger. Over time, we determine if one conditional IOS sequence outperforms another via a conditional spanning test.

9.3 MEASURING THE PERFORMANCE OF INVESTMENT OPPORTUNITY SETS

A well-defined investment opportunity set is one that is sufficiently similar to the investment opportunities provided by the market's population of investment opportunities. Because the latter is unobservable, financial economists have measured the 'goodness of fit' of one set to another by tests of set intersection and spanning, usually accompanied by an asset pricing hypothesis. These tests have been conducted by MacKinlay and Richardson (1991), using Hansen's (1982) generalized methods of moments (GMM), and the tests have been extended to examine richer information sets and conditional asset pricing in Ferson, Foerster and Keim (1993), for example.

Our primary interest is in the 'goodness of fit' of an investment opportunity set rather than asset pricing; hence, a spanning test is of prime importance. The spanning hypotheses and the accompanying test statistic are expressible in terms of regression coefficient restrictions or equivalently in terms of restrictions on the opportunity set constants.[6] We begin first with the point estimate of the slope that can be interpreted as the performance of the asset set.

9.3.1 Point estimates of the IOS slope

In a random sampling with τ return observations from a multivariate normal population of n assets with parameters (μ, Σ), an unbiased estimator of the

[6] Roll (1977) shows the regression restrictions, and Huberman and Kandel (1987) develops the spanning test statistic for the restrictions. An application is in Lehmann and Modest (1988). Jobson and Korkie (1989) express the Roll, and Huberman and Kandel results in terms of restrictions on the efficient set constants. Kan and Zhou (2000) have a detailed analysis of spanning and stochastic discount factor tests.

squared slope is shown in Korkie and Turtle (1997) to be

$$\left(\hat{a} - \frac{\hat{b}^2}{\hat{c}}\right) \frac{(\tau - n - 1)}{(\tau - 1)} - \frac{(n - 1)}{\tau}$$

For the continuous risk structure IOS, the unbiased squared slope estimator is obtained by substituting the limiting value of the vertex mean resulting in

$$(\hat{a} - \hat{b} r_f) \frac{(\tau - n - 1)}{(\tau - 1)} - \frac{(n - 1)}{\tau}$$

This unbiased estimator indicates that the maximum likelihood estimator of the slope is positively biased. If the slope is interpreted as a market price of risk, the ML estimate of the risk price is expected to be too large. The bias worsens as the number of assets increases.[7]

These expressions are estimators of the set's performance in any specific period, from which the efficient set constants are derived.

9.3.2 Spanning conditions for a continuous risk structure IOS

In this section, the linear spanning restrictions are developed for the case of an opportunity set with a continuous risk structure. The results apply to either conditional or unconditional opportunity sets.

Define a partition of the return vector

$$r = \begin{pmatrix} r_{n_1} \\ r_{n_2} \end{pmatrix}$$

with partitioned mean vector and covariance matrix given by

$$\mu = \begin{pmatrix} \mu_{n_1} \\ \mu_{n_2} \end{pmatrix}$$

[7] The investment opportunity set formed from the moments of asset returns has been used for estimating the risk aversion of a representative market agent (Mehra and Prescott, 1985) as well as establishing volatility bounds on the intertemporal marginal rate of substitution (Gallant, Hansen and Tauchen, 1990). An advantage of the continuous risk structure IOS considered here is that the IOS slope, or total risk price, is constant for all standard deviations. An unbiased estimator of this continuous risk structure IOS slope may prove useful in future investigations of market risk preferences and the equity premium puzzle. This has considerable implications for studies that infer intertemporal marginal rates of substitution from the location of the investment opportunity set.

and

$$\Sigma = \begin{pmatrix} \Sigma_{n_1n_1} & \Sigma_{n_1n_2} \\ \Sigma_{n_2n_1} & \Sigma_{n_2n_2} \end{pmatrix}$$

respectively. Now consider two locally continuous risk structure opportunity sets with n_1 and n assets, respectively as

$$\mu_p = r_f \pm \sqrt{a_{n1} - b_{n1}r_f}\sigma_p \tag{9.3a}$$

and

$$\mu_p = r_f \pm \sqrt{a_n - b_n r_f}\sigma_p \tag{9.3b}$$

respectively. The n_1 assets are a subset of the larger set of $n = n_1 + n_2$ assets and all efficient set constants are defined relative to the underlying set of n_1 or n assets. Both opportunity sets are defined to have assets of sufficiently small risks such that the global minimum variance portfolio is of negligible risk in both cases.

The spanning question may then be posited as a test of the equality of IOS slopes, shown in equation (9.3). Equal IOS slopes are equivalent to the subset in (9.3a) spanning the superset in (9.3b), in which case,

$$\sqrt{a_n - b_n r_f} = \sqrt{a_{n1} - b_{n1} r_f} \Leftrightarrow \Delta a = \Delta b r_f$$

where the marginal efficient set constants are

$$\begin{aligned} \Delta a = a_n - a_{n1} &= \left(\mu_{n_2} - \Sigma_{n_2n_1}\Sigma_{n_1n_1}^{-1}\mu_{n_1}\right)' \\ &\quad \times \Sigma_{n_2n_2n_1}^{-1}\left(\mu_{n_2} - \Sigma_{n_2n_1}\Sigma_{n_1n_1}^{-1}\mu_{n_1}\right) \\ \Delta b = b_n - b_{n1} &= \left(e_{n_2} - \Sigma_{n_2n_1}\Sigma_{n_1n_1}^{-1}e_{n_1}\right)' \\ &\quad \times \Sigma_{n_2n_2n_1}^{-1}\left(\mu_{n_2} - \Sigma_{n_2n_1}\Sigma_{n_1n_1}^{-1}\mu_{n_1}\right) \end{aligned}$$

and where

$$\Sigma_{n_2n_2n_1} = \Sigma_{n_2n_2} - \Sigma_{n_2n_1}\Sigma_{n_1n_1}^{-1}\Sigma_{n_1n_2}.$$ [8]

The constants Δa and Δb are expressible in terms of the coefficients in the multivariate regression of the raw returns from the n_2 assets on the *raw*

---

[8] Partition expressions can be found in Morrison (1967). Marginal efficient set constants are defined in Jobson and Korkie (1989).

returns from the n_1 assets. Let α_{n_2} be the $(n_2 \times 1)$ vector of intercepts and $\beta_{n_2 n_1}$ be the $(n_2 \times n_1)$ matrix of slope coefficients in[9]

$$r_{n_2} = \alpha_{n_2} + \beta_{n_2 n_1} r_{n_1} + \varepsilon_{n_2} \tag{9.4}$$

where $E(\varepsilon_{n_2}) = E(\varepsilon_{n_2} r_{n_1}) = \mathbf{0}$ and $\mathbf{0}$ is the $(n_2 \times 1)$ null vector.

Then from the definitions of the regression estimators, one can express

$$\Delta a = \alpha'_{n_2} \Sigma_\varepsilon^{-1} \alpha_{n_2} \tag{9.5a}$$

$$\Delta b = (e_{n_2} - \beta_{n_2 n_1} e_{n_1})' \Sigma_\varepsilon^{-1} \alpha_{n_2} \tag{9.5b}$$

$$\Delta c = (e_{n_2} - \beta_{n_2 n_1} e_{n_1})' \Sigma_\varepsilon^{-1} (e_{n_2} - \beta_{n_2 n_1} e_{n_1}) = 0 \tag{9.5c}$$

where Σ_ε is the $(n_2 \times n_2)$ covariance matrix of the errors, and e_{n_1} and e_{n_2} are conformable vectors of ones, $\beta_{n_2 n_1} = \Sigma_{n_2 n_1} \Sigma_{n_1 n_1}^{-1}$, $\Sigma_{n_1 n_1}$ is the $(n_1 \times n_1)$ covariance matrix of the n_1 assets, and $\Sigma_{n_2 n_1}$ is the $(n_2 \times n_1)$ matrix of covariances between the n_2 and the n_1 assets.

From (9.3) and (9.5), the necessary and sufficient condition for spanning in a continuous risk structure is,

$$\Delta a - \Delta b r_f = [\alpha_{n_2} - r_f(e_{n_2} - \beta_{n_2 n_1} e_{n_1})]' \Sigma_\varepsilon^{-1} \alpha_{n_2} = 0$$

For two asset sets of equivalently small minimum risk, $\Delta c = 0$, which occurs if and only if $e_{n_2} - \beta_{n_2 n_1} e_{n_1} = 0$. Imposing this condition on the previous equation produces the simple spanning restriction,

$$\alpha_{2j} = 0, \quad \forall j = n_1 + 1, n_1 + 2, \ldots, n \tag{9.6}$$

Condition (9.6) is the restriction of a zero intercept in the multivariate regression of the n_2 asset *raw* returns on the *raw* returns of the n_1 assets, when the opportunity set has a locally continuous risk structure. Therefore, a test of whether the n_1 asset opportunity set spans the n asset set is a test of the restriction (9.6).[10]

---

[9]Because the opportunity set is conditional on t and an information set, the regression is a relation on the conditional return space at time t, rather than on unconditional returns. This will affect the possible tests of the restrictions; for example, Ferson, Foerster and Keim (1993) require that ratios of the conditional betas are fixed in their spanning tests, which may be unrealistic.

[10]Similarly, a test of (μ, σ) efficiency of a single portfolio p is equivalent to a test of whether

$$\frac{\mu_p - r_f}{\sigma_p} = \sqrt{a_n - b_n r_f}$$

or whether $\alpha_{2j} = 0$, $\forall j = 2, 3, \ldots, n$, in the multivariate regression of the $n_2 = n - 1$ asset raw returns on the raw returns of the portfolio, p.

The spanning test in the case of continuous maturity opportunity sets differs from the traditional spanning test of Huberman and Kandel (1987). The traditional spanning test examines the joint restriction of a zero multivariate intercept and the unit sum of the slope coefficients in a raw return regression. The simplified test statistic in this chapter follows from the small risk assets in a continuous risk structure opportunity set and requires only a zero intercept.

A well-specified conditional opportunity set is one that has sufficiently many assets to statistically span all relevant asset supersets. This is a different approach from asset pricing tests that seek a small set of n_1 assets that intersects a larger set of n assets. The advocated approach here is first to find a proxy to the population opportunity set; asset pricing investigations would follow thereafter.[11]

9.4 RATIONALITY RESTRICTIONS ON CONDITIONAL RETURN MOMENTS AND GMM ESTIMATION

Section 9.3 has developed the restrictions necessary for one asset set to span another set, given the assets' conditional moments and the existence of a continuous risk structure opportunity set. These spanning restrictions are independent of the conditions that must accompany rational forecasts of the moments of the assets' multivariate return distribution. We now consider the implications of rational forecasts on the general specification of conditional moments and the estimation of the conditional IOS.

9.4.1 A general specification of the conditional return moments

Let r_t be the $(n \times 1)$ vector of returns on the n assets in the investment opportunity set,

$$r_t = \mu_t + e_t, \quad e_t \sim D(0, \sigma_t^2) \tag{9.7a}$$

where the $(n \times 1)$ conditional return means are $\mu_t = E[r_t|\phi_{t-1}^{\mu}]$, e_t is the $(n \times 1)$ vector of errors for the conditional mean return forecasts, and ϕ_{t-1}^{μ} is

[11] Given an approximately continuous risk structure opportunity set, the mean return on any asset, j, may be written in terms of the conditional moments of *any* asset, m, located on the upper boundary of the set as $\mu_j = r_f + (\mu_m - r_f)\frac{\sigma_{jm}}{\sigma_m^2} = r_f + \sqrt{a - br_f}\sigma_j\rho_j, \forall j$, where $\rho_j = \rho_{jm}$ is the conditional correlation between the returns on j and m. Any efficient portfolio m is sufficient to describe the cross-section of expected asset returns. In the case where m is the market portfolio, then the equation describes the myopic, conditional CAPM in an IOS that approximates the locally continuous risk structure IOS.

the information set for returns at $t-1$. An element of the $(n \times 1)$ vector of conditional standard deviations or volatility is defined in terms of the error as

$$\sigma_{jt} = \{E[e_{jt}^2|\phi_{t-1}^\sigma]\}^{1/2} = (\psi_{jt}^2 + \sigma_{\eta j}^2)^{1/2} \tag{9.7b}$$

where the return error magnitude and its expectation, respectively, are

$$|e_{jt}| = \psi_{jt} + \eta_{jt} \tag{9.7c}$$

and $\eta_{jt} \sim D(0, \sigma_{\eta j}^2)$ is the homoskedastic error for the conditional error magnitude equation, ϕ_{t-1}^σ is the information set for standard deviations at $t-1$, and $\phi_{t-1}^\sigma \cup \phi_{t-1}^\mu = \phi_{t-1}$ is the complete information set. To obtain (9.7b), the conditional mean must be orthogonal to the instruments contained in ϕ_{t-1}^σ and ϕ_{t-1}^μ.

Let $\{Z_{t-1}\} = \{Z_{t-1}^\mu; Z_{t-1}^\sigma\}$ be the $(L \times 1)$ instrument set for the information, ϕ_{t-1}, thereby making μ_t and σ_t unknown functionals of $\{Z_{t-1}\}$, where $\{Z_{t-1}^\mu\}$ denotes the mean instruments and $\{Z_{t-1}^\sigma\}$ denotes the volatility instruments. The elements of $\{Z_{t-1}^\mu\}$ may include lagged values of r_t and errors (e.g. ARCH and VAR terms) as well as economic variables affecting means. Similarly, the elements of $\{Z_{t-1}^\sigma\}$ may include lagged values of $|e_t|$ and ψ_t (e.g. AGARCH terms), as well as economic variables affecting conditional volatilities.

We model absolute errors and standard deviation rather than variance; because, empirical univariate evidence supports models of magnitude or standard deviation, rather than variance models. For example, work by Taylor (1986), Davidian and Carroll (1987), Pagan and Schwert (1990), Schwert (1989), Nelson and Foster (1994), Hentschel (1995) and Korkie, Sivakumar and Turtle (2002) support the use of standard deviation and AGARCH models. Glosten, Jagannathan and Runkle (1993) estimate variance-based systems using a variety of linear and non-linear functional forms. They find that the GARCH-M model is misspecified without the inclusion of other instruments including asymmetric responses of conditional variance to unexpected return shocks. This asymmetry is supported by Engle and Ng (1993).

Although alternative specifications are available (e.g. Gallant Rossi and Tauchen (1992)), modelling conditional error magnitude allows us to specify a simple model with the ability to capture important changes in both first and second moments. Our approach results in conditional volatility equation disturbances, η_{jt}, of the same units as conditional return mean equation disturbances, e_{jt}, and requires only one equation per variate in the system; whereas, a full covariance system requires $n(n+1)/2$ equations. We also developed and tested a model based on a Cholesky decomposition of the second moment matrix of mean equation disturbances. Preliminary evidence suggests that a simpler model with direct emphasis on the evolution of conditional volatilities has better ability to capture system dynamics.

9.4.2 Rationality restrictions on conditional return moments

To this point, no explicit assumptions were made about the construction of the expectations, $E[r_t \mid \phi_{t-1}^{\mu}]$ and $E[|e_t| \mid \phi_{t-1}^{\sigma}]$. We require that these expectations satisfy the rationality conditions associated with conditional expectations. The basic premise underlying our specification of the conditional moments, which define the opportunity set, is rational expectations after Muth (1960, 1961).[12] Rationality conditions are applied to both conditional first and second moments to ensure that forecasts do not contain systematic errors. This avoids problems induced by temporal relationships between conditional moments that may cause irrational forecasts, as well as potential instability in relationships among the contemporaneous conditional moments (Whitelaw, 1994).

There are a number of alternatives available for implementing rationality. The strongest requirement is that the errors from equations (9.7a) and (9.7b) are mutually independent of the instrument set $\{Z_{t-1}\}$. A weak requirement is that the errors and the instruments are pairwise uncorrelated. The presence of correlation violates rational expectations in the sense that errors are predictable with the mean or volatility instruments. This causes systematic misspecification of the investment opportunity set. The most common implementation of rationality requires that the mean and volatility instruments are uncorrelated with the mean and volatility errors. Applying this restriction to mean and volatility disturbances we have the conditions,

$$E[e_{jt}Z_{lt-1}] = 0 \quad \text{and} \quad E[\eta_{jt}Z_{lt-1}] = 0, \quad i, j = 1, 2, \ldots, n; \quad l = 1, 2, \ldots, L \tag{9.8}$$

9.4.3 Conditional mean and volatility specifications and derived conditional covariances

We adopt a linear specification for means and volatilities conditioned upon selected information instruments that include both time series regressors and economic factors.[13] All instruments are in the information set at time $t-1$. An

[12] An early integration of estimation and means rationality is in Cumby, Huizinga and Obstfeld (1983).

[13] Assuming that expectations and covariances are constant linear functions of the instruments is a common practice. See Harvey (1989) and Shanken (1990), for example.

asset's volatility equation models the correlation between the volatility instruments and the mean error magnitude, $|e_t|$, resulting in significant coefficients on the instruments. However, if functional correlation also exists between the mean instruments and the $|e_t|$, then the mean instruments may also be significant in the volatility equation.[14] Thus, instruments with significant coefficients in both the mean and the volatility equations are correlated with the return and functionally correlated with the return error. Significant coefficients on mean equation instruments alone imply that instruments are correlated with the return; significant coefficients on the volatility equation instruments imply that the instruments are functionally correlated with the mean error.

Following (9.7), we estimate equations of the following form to define conditional expected excess returns, μ_t, in

$$\begin{aligned} R_t &= \mu_t + e_t \\ &= \alpha_0 + \alpha_K F_{Kt} + \phi_1 R_{t-1} + \phi_2 |R_{t-1}| + e_t \end{aligned} \tag{9.9a}$$

where R_t is the $(n \times 1)$ excess return vector in period t, F_{Kt} is a $(K \times 1)$ vector of predetermined economic information variables, ϕ_1 and ϕ_2 are $(n \times n)$ coefficient matrices for VAR and absolute VAR terms, and e_t is the disturbance vector.

In a similar manner, we write conditional error magnitudes as mixed AGARCH models, which include asymmetric response coefficients as proposed by Glosten, Jagannathan and Runkle (1993),

$$\begin{aligned} |e_t| &= \psi_t + \eta_t \\ &= \beta_0 + \beta_K F_{Kt} + \varphi_1 \operatorname{pos}(e_{t-1}) + \varphi_2 |e_{t-1}| + \eta_t \end{aligned} \tag{9.9b}$$

where $|e_t|$ is the $(n \times 1)$ vector of absolute values of the excess return conditional mean error in period t, β_K is the $(n \times K)$ coefficient matrix for F_{Kt} a $(K \times 1)$ vector of predetermined economic information variables, φ_1 and φ_2 are $(n \times n)$ coefficient matrices for the vector of lags of positive mean disturbances,

$$\operatorname{pos}(e_{jt-1}) = \begin{cases} e_{jt-1} & \text{for } e_{jt-1} > 0 \\ 0 & \text{otherwise} \end{cases} \qquad \text{for } j = \{1, 2, \ldots, n\}$$

[14]Functional correlation means that functions of the basic variables are correlated implying that the basic variables are dependent. In this case, the basic variables are the instruments and the errors. For example, e_{jt} is uncorrelated with Z_{lt-1} but they are functionally correlated because $|e_{jt}|$ is correlated with Z_{lt-1}.

and absolute values of lagged mean disturbances, $|e_{t-1}|$, respectively. The volatility disturbance vector is given by η_t with homoskedastic variance vector, σ_η^2. An asset's conditional volatility is obtained by substituting the estimated ψ_{jt}^2 and $\sigma_{\eta j}^2$ into equation (9.7b) to obtain the estimated volatilities, $\hat{\sigma}_{jt}$, $j = 1, 2, \ldots, n$.

Our subsequent implementation of the IOS estimation requires the covariances as well as the preceding means and volatilities. We do not directly estimate conditional covariances between assets' returns; rather, we assume constant conditional correlations, ρ_{ij}, calculated from pairs of the assets' standardized return residuals,

$$\omega_{jt} = \frac{e_{jt}}{\sigma_{jt}}, \quad j = 1, 2, \ldots, n, \quad t = 1, 2, \ldots, T$$

Then, the conditional covariance matrix is

$$\Sigma_t = \mathrm{diag}(\sigma_t)\rho\ \mathrm{diag}(\sigma_t)$$

where diag (σ_t) is the diagonal matrix of the vector of conditional volatilities, σ_t, and ρ is the $(n \times n)$ correlation matrix constructed from standardized return residuals. If correlations are truly time varying, our econometric model is underspecified in equations (9.7).

9.4.4 Iterated GMM estimation of the conditional means and volatilities

In this section, we discuss the GMM estimation of the IOS over time, which simultaneously imposes rationality restrictions through moment restrictions. We begin by specifying a linear model in various economic and time-series-motivated instruments. We allow instruments to vary by equation to avoid finite-sample bias problems associated with using too many instruments and to allow us to choose enough useful instruments per equation to improve the asymptotic efficiency of our estimates.

Equations (9.9a) and (9.9b) determine the $(n \times 1)$ mean equation disturbance vector $e_t = \{e_{jt}\}$ and the $(n \times 1)$ vector of volatility disturbances $\eta_t = \{\eta_{jt}\}$. The conditional moments disturbance vector is therefore

$$u_t(\theta) = \begin{bmatrix} e_t \\ \eta_t \end{bmatrix} \tag{9.10}$$

where θ represents the true vector of model parameters contained in equations (9.9). Other models for spanning tests will have a model specific disturbance vector, discussed in section 9.4.5.

Following Hansen (1982), we define the model moment conditions based on a set of information instruments, Z_{t-1}, and a selected parameter vector, θ, as the Kronecker product

$$g_t(\theta) = u_t(\theta) \otimes Z_t \tag{9.11}$$

To impose the rationality restrictions, $E[g_t(\theta)] = \mathbf{0}$ from (9.8), the following quadratic form is minimized,

$$C(\theta) = \bar{g}(\theta)' W \bar{g}(\theta)$$

by choice of a parameter vector, $\hat{\theta}$, for a given symmetric non-singular weighting matrix, W, where

$$\bar{g}(\theta) = \frac{1}{T} \sum_{t=1}^{T} g_t(\theta) = \mathbf{0}$$

is the empirical moment equivalent of $E[g_t(\theta)] = \mathbf{0}$.

For a given set of mean and volatility regressors in (9.9), we begin with an initial weighting matrix, W_1, equal to the identity matrix. $C(\theta_1)$ is then minimized to produce an initial parameter vector, say $\hat{\theta}_1$. A new weighting matrix, W_2, is then calculated according to

$$W_{j+1} = T \left[\sum_{t=1}^{T} g_t(\hat{\theta}_j) g_t(\hat{\theta}_j)' \right]^{-1} \tag{9.12}$$

$C(\theta_2)$ is then minimized to produce $\hat{\theta}_2$, and the weighting matrix is updated for the next iteration. This process continues until the gradient vector is numerically zero. In general, updates to the W matrix for the $j+1$st iteration are constructed from the jth iteration parameter vector using (9.12).[15]

The sample statistic,

$$\Phi = TC(\hat{\theta}) \tag{9.13}$$

is asymptotically distributed as a χ^2 random variable with $m - p$ degrees of freedom, where m is the number of orthogonality conditions and p is the number of parameters.

The variance–covariance matrix for the final resultant parameter vector, $\hat{\theta}$, is computed as

$$\text{VCOV}(\hat{\theta}) = \left[T \left(\frac{\partial \bar{g}(\hat{\theta})'}{\partial \theta} \right) W \left(\frac{\partial \bar{g}(\hat{\theta})}{\partial \theta'} \right) \right]^{-1} \tag{9.14}$$

[15]Further discussion of the iterative GMM approach can be found in Ferson and Foerster (1994).

where W denotes the value of the weighting matrix based on the final and convergent iteration of the estimation.

Under the null hypothesis, the system (9.9) is overidentified because we choose only a limited number of regressors from the information set to model conditional means and volatilities. If the chi-square statistic of overidentifying restrictions from Φ is significant, then the orthogonality conditions are violated. This occurs if the instrument set regressors do not adequately specify the conditional means and volatilities. In the following section, we establish the instruments and orthogonality conditions for various combinations of rationality and spanning performance of the asset sets.

9.4.5 GMM spanning and rationality tests

An objective of the analysis is to obtain an investment opportunity set from a small set of assets with performance that is representative of a larger population IOS. We test this objective by considering the spanning restriction given by (9.6) and at the same time we determine the importance of the rationality restrictions. We follow previous studies in using the instrument set only as overidentifying restrictions on (9.4). These tests, as in previous literature, are actually 'quasi-conditional' because mean equations only contain the spanning assets as regressors, volatility equations are not modelled, and the implementation of an intercept restriction in this context requires an assumption on the constancy of betas or their ratios, the latter described in Ferson, Foerster and Keim (1993). Depending upon the test, listed below, the instrument set consists of spanning assets, economic instruments, or both.

Unconditional spanning tests

We use the term 'unconditional spanning' to refer to IOS spanning tests in unconditional moments in which only spanning assets are included as GMM test instruments and no additional conditioning information is employed.

To implement the test, we follow Newey and West (1987), MacKinlay and Richardson (1991) and Ferson, Foerster and Keim (1993).[16] Define the $(n \times 1)$ disturbance vector constructed from equation (9.4),

$$\varepsilon_{n_2t} = r_{n_2t} - (\alpha_{n_2} \vdots \beta_{n_2n_1}) \begin{pmatrix} 1 \\ \cdots \\ r_{n_1t} \end{pmatrix}, \quad t = 1, 2, \ldots, T \tag{9.15}$$

[16]MacKinlay and Richardson (1991) find that the GMM statistic is more robust to normality departures and more powerful than the Wald statistic.

where the n_1 spanning assets are a proper subset of the total number of n assets, r_{n_2t} is the $(n_2 \times 1)$ vector of raw returns on the $n_2 = n - n_1$ assets, r_{n_1t} is the $(n_1 \times 1)$ vector of raw returns on the n_1 assets, α_{n_2} is the $(n_2 \times 1)$ vector of estimated intercepts, and $\beta_{n_2n_1}$ is the $(n_2 \times n_1)$ matrix of coefficients on the spanning assets. The sample moment restrictions are then constructed from

$$g_t(\beta_{n_2}) = \{\varepsilon_{n_2t} \otimes [r_{n_1t}, Z_{t-1}]\} \tag{9.16}$$

and the $\beta_{n_2} = (\alpha_{n_2} \vdots \beta_{n_2n_1})$ parameters are estimated by minimizing the GMM χ^2 statistic.

To perform the unconditional spanning test, we estimate $\beta_{n_2n_1}$ under the zero-intercept restriction $\alpha_{n_2} = 0$ and we consider an instrument set, $\{Z_{t-1}\}$, given only by a constant and the $(n_2 \times 1)$ vector of spanning assets. The GMM 'goodness-of-fit' χ^2 statistic, similar to (9.13) with n_2 degrees of freedom and denoted Φ_1, is used to test the multivariate zero-intercept restriction for unconditional spanning.

Conditional tests of rationality

Conditional tests of rationality examine rationality restrictions on disturbances from (9.4). To implement the conditional test of rationality, we estimate the unrestricted intercept model (9.4) subject to rationality conditions that disturbances are uncorrelated with the overidentifying instruments. The instrument set, $\{Z_{t-1}\}$, is expanded to include the $(n_2 \times 1)$ vector of spanning assets and the additional economic instruments. The GMM χ^2 statistic, denoted Φ_2, with degrees of freedom given by the number of overidentifying restrictions, is used to test the restriction. The orthogonality instruments are defined in the subsequent tables. This test does not appear in Ferson, Foerster and Keim (1993).

Conditional tests of rationality and spanning restrictions

Finally, joint tests of rationality and spanning are implemented using the GMM test statistic, Φ_3, for the restricted zero intercept and overidentified model from (9.4). This test is similar to the test for rationality using Φ_2 except that the estimation is with a zero intercept and the instrument set, $\{Z_{t-1}\}$, is expanded to include a constant, the $(n_2 \times 1)$ vector of spanning assets, and the additional economic instruments. Therefore, it is the same test as used in Ferson, Foerster and Keim (1993).

These tests allow the researcher to disentangle the effects of spanning and rationality restrictions. We wish to determine if previous studies' rejections in spanning tests may be rejections of both spanning and rationality, thereby implying misspecified models. Our testing framework demonstrates the dependence of spanning tests on joint rationality restrictions and makes the importance of rationality restrictions clear. It is entirely possible for neither spanning restrictions nor rationality restrictions to hold, for both to hold, or for either set of restrictions to hold. A well-specified system should span the asset universe and meet prescribed rationality conditions.

9.5 EMPIRICAL ANALYSES

9.5.1 The asset and instrument data

The data consists of 14 monthly excess return series that are used as assets in the multivariate analysis, along with nine series that are used as information instruments. Data is from January 1965 to December 1999; because of the use of up to 12 lags of return variables, the analysis period is 1/1966 to 12/1999, inclusive. As in Fama and French (1989), we choose assets to develop a continuous maturity structure IOS that occurs in an integrated financial market of short- and long-term debt and equity markets. The 14 assets include excess returns of one month holding period returns on the following assets; US Treasury bills with three months to maturity, five year Treasury bonds, 30 year Treasury bonds, the CRSP value weighted index and ten equal weighted size-based decile portfolios.[17]

Table 9.1 reports summary statistics of sample means, standard deviations, skewness and kurtosis for each of the assets. The first two columns show the unconditional sample means and standard deviations for all excess return series. As expected, the Treasury bill series displays a relatively small unconditional sample mean and standard deviation. The value weighted equity

Table 9.1 Summary excess return statistics for the sample period from January 1966 through December 1999

Asset series	Mean*10^2	Std. dev.*10^2	Standard skewness	Kurtosis	Normality test
R_{TB3t}	0.0513	0.1081	40.698	374.99	0.00
R_{5Bt}	0.1229	1.6910	0.0251	−2.985	0.00
R_{30Bt}	0.0944	3.1178	0.0031	−2.999	0.00
R_{Et}	0.5335	4.5091	0.0042	−2.999	0.00

Sample means, standard deviations, skewness, and kurtosis are presented for one month holding period, excess returns on three month Treasury bills, R_{TB3t}, five year Treasury bonds, R_{5Bt}, thirty year Treasury bonds, R_{30Bt}, and the CRSP value weighted index, R_{Et}, respectively. The final column reports *p-values* from Bowman and Shenton (1975) tests for normality.

[17] The asset set is similar to the set in Evans (1994), who studies the ICAPM.

portfolio shows a substantially larger portfolio mean and standard deviation. This sample period produced smaller 30 year bond portfolio performance than the five year bonds. This smaller sample mean comes without a substantial reduction in the unconditional standard deviation. Short maturity Treasury bills tend to be the most right skewed relative to the small skewness in the remaining assets. All excess return series display marked leptokurtism relative to the normal distribution. The final column of the table reports the Bowman and Shenton (1975) test for normality, which is distributed as a χ^2 random variable. In general, we conclude that the excess return series have significant departures from normality.

We choose a large set of information instruments to proxy for the information set facing investors at the beginning of any investment period. Our conditional moment estimates are directly influenced by the instrument set used. We seek information instruments that are economically meaningful as found in previous research. In addition, we include time series instruments to proxy for missing economic variables and to mitigate possible microstructure effects. All information instruments used as conditioning information in a month t conditional moment equation, are known at the beginning of month t.

Economic information instruments for conditional mean and volatility equations include a constant, the first difference in one month Treasury bill returns, the excess junk yield on corporate bonds rated Baa by Moodys, one lag of Standard and Poors 500 dividend yield, the first difference of the lag of the natural logarithm of total volume on the NYSE and a January dummy variable.

Existing literature using variants on these economic regressors is well established. Previous research examining changes in the riskless rate include Campbell (1987) and Schwert (1989). In our context, this variable measures changes in the continuous risk structure vertex location from one period to the next. Yields on long-term bonds and spreads between high-yield debt and comparable Government debt have been included in various forms in many studies requiring economic motivations for conditional asset means (c.f. Chen, Roll and Ross (1986), or Fama and French (1989)). Lamoureux and Lastrapes (1990) find contemporaneous volume may be used as a regressor in conditional volatility equations to eliminate ARCH effects. We include first differences of lagged volume as information instruments in both mean and volatility equations to accommodate both information arrival and microstructure explanations for volume. Lagged volume is also motivated by the findings of Gallant, Rossi and Tauchen (1992) and Conrad, Hameed and Niden (1994). Further discussion of important predictor variables can be found in Keim and Stambaugh (1986), Breen, Glosten and Jagannathan (1989) Kandel and Stambaugh (1989) and Jegadeesh (1991).

The inclusion of lags of own excess returns and absolute values of own excess returns in the conditional mean equations allows us to capture asymmetric responses to lags of own excess returns. In a similar manner, own lags of both positive conditional mean disturbances and absolute values of conditional mean disturbances, in volatility specifications, admit general moment relationships as suggested by Bodurtha and Mark (1991) and Glosten, Jagannathan and Runkle (1993).

9.5.2 Estimates of the conditional return moments under rationality

In this section, we present the empirical results of our model of conditional means and volatilities for returns on three month US Treasury bills, the five and thirty year bond indexes, and the equity index. Conditional means, μ_t, and volatilities, σ_t, are modelled using equation (9.9a) and equation (9.9b) combined with (9.7b), respectively. For parsimony, we restrict our attention to the special case of only own time series effects, in which case ϕ_1, ϕ_2, φ_1, and φ_2 are diagonal.

Table 9.2 reports estimation results for the conditional expected returns and volatilities, given by (9.9). Panel A reports mean equation parameter estimates and asymptotic t-statistics, followed by conditional volatility equation results in panel B. We first selected a subset of our information instruments as regressors to model conditional means and conditional volatilities. Information instruments not included as regressors are reported as blank spaces in the table. Heteroskedastic t-statistics are reported in parentheses below all parameter estimates. In panel C, we report the GMM goodness of fit test of the rationality restrictions.

Interpreting the conditional mean specification in panel A shows that the three month Treasury bill series displays a significant coefficient on prior one month Treasury bill changes, lagged dividend yields, January, as well as lagged absolute own excess returns. The strong significance and positive coefficients for absolute own excess return lags suggest an intuitively appealing positive relationship between excess return shocks of either sign and conditional means for both short-term Treasury bills and five year bonds. We find little evidence of a January seasonal in conditional means, with the exception of a significant positive coefficient for three month Treasury bills. Positive changes in NYSE volume appear to be weakly negatively related to conditional means on debt instruments. This may suggest an interesting timing effect related to asset allocation choices between equity and debt instruments. Equity returns are significantly related to one month Treasury bill changes and increase insignificantly with default premia, as measured by the excess yield on junk bonds. The former indicates that increases in the short-term

Table 9.2 GMM estimation results for the sample period from January 1966 through December 1999

Asset Regressand	Information instruments							
	Const.*10^2	$r_{TB1_t} - r_{TB1_{t-1}}$	Excess Baa yield	S&P500 div yield$_{t-1}$	$\ln(vol_{t-1})-\ln(vol_{t-2})$	Jan	R_{jt-1}	$\|R_{jt-1}\|$
Panel A. Mean equations								
R_{TB3t}	−3.1400	−0.2580		0.0062	−0.0990	0.0372		0.2737
	(−1.68)	(−3.67)		(2.81)	(−2.91)	(3.42)		(3.70)
R_{5Bt}	−0.0785	−1.3932			−0.6516		0.0600	0.1698
	(−0.76)	(−1.29)			(−1.31)		(1.25)	(2.53)
R_{30Bt}	−0.0589	−1.9196			−1.5016		0.0492	0.0778
	(−0.28)	(−1.12)			(−1.72)		(0.98)	(1.06)
R_{Et}	0.0591	−5.9053	1.4059			0.7918	0.0554	
	(0.14)	(−2.32)	(1.32)			(0.95)	(1.17)	
Asset Regressand	Const.*10^2	$r_{TB1_t} - r_{TB1_{t-1}}$	Excess Baa yield	S&P500 div yield$_{t-1}$	$\ln(vol_{t-1})-\ln(vol_{t-2})$	Jan	pos(e_{jt-1})	$\|e_{jt-1}\|$
Panel B. Error magnitude equations								
$\|e_{TB3t}\|$	−0.0470			0.0090				0.2681
	(−3.07)			(4.92)				(4.29)
$\|e_{5Bt}\|$	−0.1692			0.1408			−0.0348	−0.01
	(−0.72)			(5.34)			(−0.52)	(−0.14)

(*continued overleaf*)

Table 9.2 *(continued)*

Asset Regressand	Information instruments							
	Const.*10^2	$r_{TB1t} - r_{TB1t-1}$	Excess Baa yield	S&P500 div yield$_{t-1}$	$\ln(vol_{t-1})-\ln(vol_{t-2})$	Jan	$\text{pos}(e_{jt-1})$	$\lvert e_{jt-1}\rvert$
$\lvert e_{30Bt}\rvert$	0.4345			0.1832			0.0510	0.0147
	(1.19)			(4.74)			(0.77)	(0.24)
$\lvert e_{Et}\rvert$	2.4829		−2.3285	0.1330		0.8939	−0.2500	0.1791
	(4.78)		(−3.86)	(2.48)		(1.88)	(−4.73)	(3.95)

Panel C. GMM Goodness of Fit Test, Φ	χ^2 value	*p-value*
	21.50	0.716

Excess returns are computed for one month holding periods on three month Treasury bills, R_{TB3t}, five year Treasury bonds, R_{5Bt}, thirty year Treasury bonds, R_{30Bt}, and the CRSP value weighted index, R_{Et}, respectively. Mean equation information instruments include a constant, the first difference of one month Treasury bill returns $(r_{TB1t} - r_{TB1t-1})$, excess yields on Corporate bonds rated Baa by Moody's (excess junk yield), one lag of Standard and Poors 500 dividend yield, one lag of the first difference of the natural logarithm of total volume on the NYSE $(\ln(vol_{t-1}) - \ln(vol_{t-2}))$, a January dummy, one own lag for each regressand (R_{jt-1} for $j \in \{TB3, 5B, 30B, E\}$), and one own lag of the absolute value of each regressand ($\lvert R_{jt-1}\rvert$ for $j \in \{TB3, 5B, 30B, E\}$). Error magnitude equations model the absolute value of mean equation disturbances, $\lvert e_{jt}\rvert$ for $j \in \{TB3, 5B, 30B, E\}$, as linear functions of information instruments that include a constant, the first difference of one-month Treasury bill returns, excess yields on Corporate bonds rated Baa by Moodys, one lag of Standard and Poors 500 dividend yield, a January dummy, one own lag of each regressand's positive residual, $\text{pos}(e_{jt-1}) = \begin{cases} e_{jt-1} & \text{for } e_{jt-1} > 0 \\ 0 & \text{otherwise} \end{cases}$ for $j \in \{TB3, 5B, 30B, E\}$, and one own lag of the absolute value of each regressand's residual. Mean and absolute error equation regressors are chosen from the information instrument set to ensure a parsimonious fit as determined by the GMM test statistic. Rationality restrictions are imposed. Heteroskedastic-consistent t-statistics are reported in parentheses for the included regressors.

interest rate result in changes in expected returns. The latter is consistent with a positive relation between the default and equity premium over the business cycle.

In Panel B, we find that conditional volatilities of all assets are significantly dependent upon known instruments, especially dividend yields. Conditional equity volatility appears nonlinearly related to prior equity disturbances as indicated by the significant coefficients on both $\text{pos}(e_{jt-1})$ and $|e_{jt-1}|$. Equity volatility is negatively related to the excess Baa yield. Equity volatility also appears positively related to January and dividend yields. The latter may suggest that an increase in dividend yields increases leverage, and hence volatility. Alternatively, dividend increases may imply an increase in earnings potential.

The reported χ^2 goodness of fit test statistic of 21.50 in panel C shows that the model is not rejected based upon the chosen information instrument set. Thus, given the information instruments selected, we do not reject the rationality restrictions. Therefore, we conclude that we have a well-specified set of conditional moment equations estimated under our rationality restrictions.

9.5.3 Estimates of the conditional IOS

In this section, we empirically demonstrate the behaviour of the continuous risk structure IOS using excess returns on three month US Treasury bills, the five and thirty year bond indexes, and the equity index. Given the GMM coefficients' estimates from equations (9.9a) and (9.9b) and the residual variance from (9.9b), conditional mean and volatility vectors are constructed.

The estimated conditional mean vector, $\hat{\mu}_t$, is computed as the sum of the one month Treasury bill rate plus the conditional excess mean return, constructed using Table 9.2 parameter estimates. The estimated conditional covariance matrix, $\hat{\Sigma}_t$, is then constructed as described in section 9.4.3 using

$$\hat{\Sigma}_t = \text{Diag}(\hat{\sigma}_t)\hat{\rho}\ \text{Diag}(\hat{\sigma}_t) \tag{9.17}$$

where $\text{Diag}(\hat{\sigma}_t)$ is the diagonal matrix of the conditional vector of estimated volatilities, $\hat{\sigma}_t$, and $\hat{\rho}$ is the $(n \times n)$ estimated correlation matrix constructed subsequent to estimation from estimated standardized model residuals,

$$\hat{\omega}_{jt} = \frac{\hat{e}_{jt}}{\hat{\sigma}_{jt}}, \quad j = 1, 2, \ldots, n, t = 1, 2, \ldots, T \tag{9.18}$$

From the estimates of $\hat{\mu}_t$ and $\hat{\Sigma}_t$, the efficient set constants, $\hat{a}_{nt} = \hat{\mu}_t' \hat{\Sigma}_t^{-1} \hat{\mu}_t$, $\hat{b}_{nt} = e' \hat{\Sigma}_t^{-1} \hat{\mu}_t$, and $\hat{c}_{nt} = e' \hat{\Sigma}_t^{-1} e$, are constructed. These constants enable us to specify the ML estimate of the intertemporal IOS slope $\sqrt{\hat{a}_t - \frac{\hat{b}_{nt}^2}{\hat{c}_{nt}}}$ and vertex $\frac{\hat{b}_{nt}}{\hat{c}_{nt}}$, for each month t.

The figure consolidates the estimation results in a 3-dimensional graph of the estimated intertemporal IOS. The date is presented on the foremost axis, with conditional volatility and conditional mean represented as depth and height, respectively, in the figure. Variability in the riskless rate is visible in the '$\sigma = 0$' plane along the date axis. The upper asymptote for the traditional hyperbola can be seen for any particular 'date plane'. The graph shows markedly different trade-offs between conditional mean and volatility over time. In particular, variability in low volatility assets appears more important than previous research has recognized.

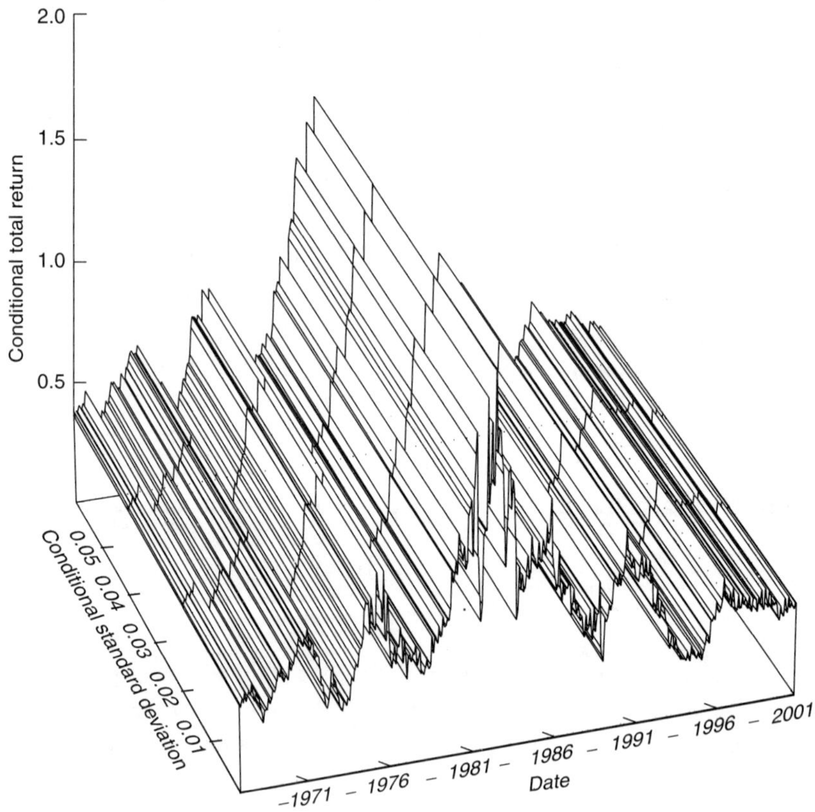

Figure 9.1 Conditional means and the efficient set over time

9.5.4 Tests of rationality and spanning

Table 9.3 reports the unconditional and conditional tests of spanning and rationality developed in Section 9.4.5. For comparability with earlier research, we expand our analysis to include an additional ten equally weighted, size-based, decile portfolios as well as the equity index, the five and thirty year bond indexes, and the three month US Treasury bill return series.

Unconditional spanning results

Panel A of the table reports the unconditional spanning tests for a variety of asset sets and spanning asset subsets. In all cases, we consider an asset universe comprised of ten decile portfolios and a subset of the three month Treasury bill, five year bond, thirty year bond and equity index as spanning assets. We begin with an asset universe consisting of the ten decile portfolios and then add spanning assets from largest to smallest variability to test the spanning hypothesis. The final column of the table reports Φ_1, the computed χ^2 statistic with n_2 degrees of freedom. For example, the first row considers an asset universe consisting of the equity portfolio in addition to the ten decile portfolios. The spanning test statistic of 183.53 with an associated *p-value* of 0.0001 shows that the equity index is insufficient to span this asset set at the 5% level.

The spanning tests reported in the final column of panel A are subject to the assumption of a continuous risk structure opportunity set. For example, the unconditional spanning test, examining whether only the equity portfolio spans the space of the ten decile portfolios and the equity portfolio, is poorly specified. In this case, the smallest risk asset does not satisfy the continuous risk structure assumption. Notice that this test is also uninteresting for a more important reason – the opportunity set of possible investment alternatives omits important assets. When the opportunity set of assets is corrected to include readily available low risk investment alternatives, the test will again be well specified. Using the continuous risk structure spanning test implicitly assumes that the global minimum portfolios have equivalent and small standard deviations.

The remaining rows of panel A suggest that unconditional spanning is difficult to obtain. In particular, even when the spanning asset set includes the equity index, the bond index, and both the five month and two month US Treasury bill return series, the asset universe is not spanned.[18]

[18]Additional tests that consider the smallest and fifth decile portfolios as spanning assets lead to smaller test statistics, but do not alter the unconditional spanning inferences.

Table 9.3 Unconditional and conditional tests of rationality and spanning for the sample period from January 1966 through December 1999

Panel A. Unconditional χ^2 tests

Asset set	Spanning assets	Spanning test statistic, Φ_1
$r_{D1t}, r_{D2t}, r_{D3t}, \ldots, r_{D10t}, r_{Et}$	r_{Et}	183.53 (0.0001)
$r_{D1t}, r_{D2t}, r_{D3t}, \ldots, r_{D10t}, r_{Et}, r_{30Bt}$	r_{Et}, r_{30Bt}	145.37 (0.0001)
$r_{D1t}, r_{D2t}, r_{D3t}, \ldots, r_{D10t}, r_{Et}, r_{30Bt}, r_{5Bt}$	$r_{Et}, r_{30Bt}, r_{5Bt}$	139.65 (0.0001)
$r_{D1t}, r_{D2t}, r_{D3t}, \ldots, r_{D10t}, r_{Et}, r_{30Bt}, r_{5Bt}, r_{TB3t}$	r_{Et}	191.54 (0.0001)
	r_{Et}, r_{30Bt}	167.49 (0.0001)
	$r_{Et}, r_{30Bt}, r_{5Bt}$	153.37 (0.0001)
	$r_{Et}, r_{30Bt}, r_{5Bt}, r_{TB3t}$	77.57 (0.0001)

Panel B. Conditional χ^2 tests

Additional information instruments	Test statistics	
	Rationality Φ_2	Spanning and rationality Φ_3
r_{Djt-1}	54.062 (0.0001)	121.97 (0.0001)
r_{Djt-1}, r_{Djt-2}	88.049 (0.0001)	139.14 (0.0001)
$r_{Et-1}, r_{30Bt-1}, r_{5Bt-1}, r_{TB3t-1}$	90.450 (0.0001)	154.51 (0.0001)
$r_{Et-1}, r_{30Bt-1}, r_{5Bt-1}, r_{TB3t-1}, r_{Et-2}, r_{30Bt-2}, r_{5Bt-2}, r_{TB3t-2}$	124.52 (0.0011)	174.97 (0.0001)
$r_{Djt-1}, r_{Et-1}, r_{30Bt-1}, r_{5Bt-1}, r_{TB3t-1}$	129.55 (0.0001)	171.08 (0.0001)
$r_{Djt-1}, r_{Et-1}, r_{30Bt-1}, r_{5Bt-1}, r_{TB3t-1}$, $r_{Djt-2}, r_{Et-2}, r_{30Bt-2}, r_{5Bt-2}, r_{TB32t-2}$	163.38 (0.0001)	190.93 (0.0001)
$r_{Djt-1}, j = 1, 2, \ldots 10$	163.21 (0.0001)	221.21 (0.0001)
$r_{Djt-1}, r_{Djt-2}, j = 1, 2, \ldots 10$	246.26 (0.0143)	277.40 (0.0013)
$r_{Djt-1}, j = 1, 2, \ldots 10, r_{Et-1}, r_{30Bt-1}, r_{5Bt-1}, r_{TB3t-1}$	239.56 (0.0001)	258.16 (0.0001)
$r_{Djt-1}, r_{Djt-2}, j = 1, 2, \ldots 10, r_{Et-1}, r_{30Bt-1}$, $r_{5Bt-1}, r_{TB3t-1}, r_{Et-2}, r_{30Bt-2}, r_{5Bt-2}, r_{TB3t-2}$	328.23 (0.0250)	342.99 (0.0176)

Asset sets are constructed from one month holding period total returns on three month Treasury bills, r_{TB3t}, five year Treasury bonds, r_{5Bt}, thirty year Treasury bonds, r_{30Bt}, the CRSP value weighted index, r_{Et}, and ten equally weighted CRSP size portfolios, $r_{D1t}, r_{D2t}, r_{D3t}, \ldots, r_{D10t}$, respectively. GMM χ^2 test statistics are reported with associated *p-values* in parentheses. Unconditional tests are based upon the GMM system estimated under the no-intercept restriction with no additional instruments. The notation, r_{Djt-1} or r_{Djt-2}, is used to refer to the inclusion of one or two own lags of decile size portfolio returns, respectively, as additional information testing instruments. Conditional tests examine rationality restrictions in isolation, and joint tests of spanning and rationality for a variety of instrument sets.

Conditional spanning and/or rationality results

Panel B of the table considers conditional tests of rationality, and joint tests of rationality and spanning. Following the development of Section 9.4.5, conditional tests of rationality are reported first, (Φ_2), followed by joint tests of spanning and rationality, (Φ_3). Our joint tests of spanning and rationality are comparable with Ferson, Foerster and Keim's (1993) tests. However, our analysis makes clear the dependence of rationality restrictions on the information instruments. In general, rejection of joint spanning and rationality tests may be due to a rejection of either rationality or spanning.

All rows of panel B are based on the largest asset set considered in panel A, including ten decile portfolios, the equity index, the thirty year bond index, the five year Treasury bond, and the three month Treasury bill. The spanning assets again include the equity index, both bond indices, and the three month Treasury bill. We consider a variety of additional information instruments to provide overidentification of the system and to examine the sensitivity of tests to different rationality constraints. In the first and second rows of panel B, we consider the inclusion of one or two own lags of the total returns on each of the ten decile portfolios, r_{Djt-1} or r_{Djt-1} and r_{Djt-2}, respectively. In the third and fourth rows, we consider the inclusion of one or two lags of all spanning portfolio returns, r_{Et-1}, r_{30Bt-1}, r_{5Bt-1}, r_{TB3t-1}, or r_{Et-1}, r_{30Bt-1}, r_{5Bt-1}, r_{TB3t-1} and r_{Et-2}, r_{30Bt-2}, r_{5Bt-2}, r_{TB3t-2}, respectively. The next two rows consider one or two own lags of the total returns on each of the ten decile portfolios and the spanning portfolios, r_{Djt-1}, r_{Et-1}, r_{30Bt-1}, r_{5Bt-1}, r_{TB3t-1}, or r_{Djt-1}, r_{Et-1}, r_{30Bt-1}, r_{5Bt-1}, r_{TB3t-1} and r_{Et-2}, r_{30Bt-2}, r_{5Bt-2}, r_{TB3t-2}, respectively. The final four rows of the table examine the importance of extending the instrument set. In particular, rather than include only own lags of decile portfolio returns as instruments, we now include lags of *all* decile portfolios as instruments for each test asset. The difference between Φ_3 and Φ_2 is itself a χ^2 test statistic with degrees of freedom given by the differences in degrees of freedom for Φ_3 and Φ_2. In our example, the degrees of freedom for this marginal test is always ten (the number of intercept restrictions). The difference may be interpreted as the significance of the spanning restriction alone (marginal to the imposed rationality restrictions). For example, the final two statistics in Table 9.3 differ by 14.76 and the associated *p-value* is 0.15. The rejection of rationality by Φ_2 and the lack of significance in the difference $\Phi_3 - \Phi_2$ suggests that the spanning rejection is due primarily to the rationality restrictions.

9.6 CONCLUDING REMARKS

The performance of managed portfolios is a function of both the asset sets as well as the selected weights. The analysis presented here allows one to analyse the performance of the sets, distinct from the performance of the asset allocation and security selection weights.

In this chapter, we develop, estimate, and examine the intertemporal performance of continuous risk structure investment opportunity sets (IOS). We empirically estimate conditional IOS evolution using GMM. The continuous risk structure IOS is estimated without asset pricing restrictions; however, rationality restrictions on conditional means and volatilities are imposed.

Conditional moments are constructed from a large set of information instruments. Conditional mean information instruments include changes in the riskless rate, excess yields on low grade bonds, dividend yields, changes in equity market volume, a January dummy, own excess return lags, and absolute own excess return lags. Conditional volatility information instruments replace own lags of excess returns with positive realizations of own lags of mean equation residuals and replace absolute values of own lags of excess returns with absolute values of own lags of mean residuals. We find only a small set of information instruments is required to capture conditional mean and volatility dynamics.

We extend previous spanning tests and integrate tests of spanning and rationality in a conditional setting. In general, we observe that rejections of spanning restrictions in the extant literature may be caused by a rationality failure, a spanning failure, or a failure of both sets of restrictions. In general, we find that rationality conditions are rejected suggesting previous tests may be misspecified. It seems that a large and diverse instrument set is required to prevent rationality rejections.

ACKNOWLEDGEMENTS

The research assistance of Kevin Buhr is gratefully acknowledged. This research was sponsored in part by the SSHRC and the Brinson Summer Fellowship programme. We thank Steve Beveridge, Mark Huson, Marie Racine and Chu Zhang for their comments.

REFERENCES AND FURTHER READING

Bodurtha, J.N. and Mark, N.C. (1991) Testing the CAPM with time-varying risks and returns, *Journal of Finance*, **46**, 1485–1505.

Bollerslev, T., Engle, R.F. and Wooldridge, J.M. (1988) A capital asset pricing model with time-varying covariances, *Journal of Political Economy*, **96**, 116–131.

Bowman, K.O. and Shenton, L.R. (1975) Omnibus test contours for departures from normality based on $\sqrt{b_1}$ and b_2, *Biometrika*, **62**, 243–250.

Breen, W., Glosten, L.R. and Jagannathan, R. (1989) Economic significance of predictable variations in stock index returns, *Journal of Finance*, **44**, 1177–1189.

Buser, S. (1977) Mean-variance portfolio selection with either a singular or non-singular covariance matrix, *Journal of Financial and Quantitative Analysis*, **12**(3), 347–361.

Campbell, J. (1987) Stock returns and the term structure, *Journal of Financial Economics*, **18**, 373–399.

Cecchetti, S.G., Lam, P-S. and Mark, N.C. (1994) Testing volatility restrictions on intertemporal marginal rates of substitution implied by Euler equations and asset returns, *Journal of Finance*, **49**, 123–152.

Chan, K.C., Karolyi, G.A. and Stulz, R. (1992) Global financial markets and the risk premium on US equity, *Journal of Financial Economics*, **32**, 137–167.

Chan, K.C., Karolyi, G.A., Longstaff, F.A. and Sanders, A.B. (1992) An empirical comparison of alternative models of the short-term interest rate, *Journal of Finance*, **47**, 1209–1227.

Chen, N-F., Roll, R. and Ross, S.A. (1986) Economic forces and the stock market, *Journal of Business*, **59**, 383–404.

Conrad, J.S., Hameed, A. and Niden, C. (1994) Volume and autocovariances in short-horizon individual security returns, *Journal of Finance*, **49**, 1305–1330.

Cumby, R.E., Huizinga, J. and Obstfeld, M. (1983) Two-step two-stage least squares estimation in models with rational expectations, *Journal of Econometrics*, **21**, 333–355.

Davidian, M. and Carroll, R.J. (1987) Variance function estimation, *Journal of the American Statistical Association*, **82**, 1079–1091.

Dybvig, P.H. and Ingersoll, J.E., Jr. (1982) Mean-variance theory in complete markets, *Journal of Business*, **55**, 233–251.

Engel, C. and Rodrigues, A.P. (1989) Tests of international CAPM with time-varying covariances, *Journal of Applied Econometrics*, **4**, 119–138.

Engle, R.F. and Ng, V.K. (1993) Measuring and testing the impact of news on volatility, *Journal of Finance*, **48**, 1749–1778.

Evans, M.D. (1994) Expected returns, time-varying risk, and risk premia, *Journal of Finance*, **49**, 655–680.

Fama, E.F. (1984) The information in the term structure, *Journal of Financial Economics*, **13**, 509–528.

Fama, E.F. (1993) Common risk factors in the returns on stocks and bonds, *Journal of Financial Economics*, **33**, 3–56.

Fama, E.F. and Schwert, G.W. (1977) Asset returns and inflation, *Journal of Financial Economics*, **5**, 115–146.

Fama, E.F. and Gibbons, M. (1984) A comparison of inflation forecasts, *Journal of Monetary Economics*, **13**, 327–348.

Fama, E.F. and French, K.R. (1989) Business conditions and expected returns on stocks and bonds, *Journal of Financial Economics*, **25**, 23–49.

Ferson, W. (1989) Changes in expected security returns, risk, and the level of interest rates, *Journal of Finance*, **44**, 1191–1217.

Ferson, W.E. and Foerster, S.R. (1994) Finite sample properties of the generalized method of moments in tests of conditional asset pricing models, *Journal of Financial Economics*, **36**(1), 29–55.

Ferson, W.E., Foerster, S.R. and Keim, D.B. (1993) General tests of latent variable models and mean-variance spanning, *Journal of Finance*, **48**, 131–156.

French, K.R., Schwert, G.W. and Stambaugh, R.F. (1987) Expected stock returns and volatility, *Journal of Financial Economics*, **14**, 217–236.

Gallant, R.A., Larsen, L.P. and Tauchen, G.E. (1990) Using conditional moments of asset payoffs to infer the volatility of intertemporal marginal rates of substitution, *Journal of Econometrics*, **45**, 141–180.

Gallant, R.A., Rossi, P.E. and Tauchen, G.E. (1992) Stock prices and volume, *Review of Financial Studies*, **5**, 199–242.

Geske, R. and Roll, R. (1983) The fiscal and monetary linkage between stock returns and inflation, *Journal of Finance*, **28**, 7–33.

Giovannini, A. and Jorion, P. (1989) The time variation of risk and return in the foreign exchange and stock markets, *Journal of Finance*, **44**, 307–325.

Glosten, L.R., Jagannathan, R. and Runkle, D.E. (1993) On the relation between the expected value and the volatility of the nominal excess return on stocks, *Journal of Finance*, **48**, 1779–1801.

Graybill, F.A. (1969) *Introduction to Matrices with Applications in Statistics*, Wadsworth, Belmont.

Hansen, L.P. (1982) Large sample properties of general methods of moments estimators, *Econometrica*, **50**, 1024–1054.

Hansen, L.P. and Richard, S.F. (1987) The role of conditioning information in deducing testable restrictions implied by dynamic asset pricing models, *Econometrica*, **55**, 587–613.

Hansen, L.P. and Jaganathan, R. (1991) Implications of security market data for models of dynamic economies, *Journal of Political Economy*, **99**, 225–262.

Harvey, C.R. (1989) Time-varying conditional covariances in tests of asset pricing models, *Journal of Financial Economics*, **24**, 289–318.

Hintschel, L. (1995) All in the family: nesting symmetric and asymmetric GARCH models, *Journal of Financial Economics*, **39**, 71–104.

Huberman, G. and Kandel, S. (1987) Mean-variance spanning, *Journal of Finance*, **42**, 873–888.

James, C., Koreisha, S. and Partch, M. (1985) A VARMA analysis of the causal relations among stock returns, real output, and nominal interest rates, *Journal of Finance*, **40**, 1375–1384.

Jegadeesh, N. (1991) Seasonality in stock price mean reversion: evidence from the US and the UK, *Journal of Finance*, **46**, 1427–1444.

Jobson, J.D. and Korkie, B. (1980) Estimation for Markowitz efficient portfolios, *Journal of the American Statistical Association*, **75**, 544–554.

Jobson, J.D. and Korkie, B. (1989) A performance interpretation of multivariate tests of asset set intersection, spanning, and mean-variance efficiency, *Journal of Financial and Quantitative Analysis*, **24**, 185–204.

Kan, R. and Zhou, G. (2000) Tests of mean-variance spanning, working paper, University of Toronto and Washington University.

Kandel, S. (1984) On the exclusion of assets from tests of the mean variance efficiency of the market portfolio, *Journal of Finance*, **39**, 63–75.

Kandel, S. and Stambaugh, R.F. (1990) Expectations and volatility of consumption and asset returns, *Review of Financial Studies*, **3**, 307–232.

Keim, D.B. and Stambaugh, R.F. (1986) Predicting returns in the stock and bond markets, *Journal of Finance*, **487**, 357–390.

Korkie, R. (1983) External vs. internal performance evaluation, *Journal of Portfolio Management*, **9**, Spring, 36–42.

Korkie, R. and Turtle, H. (1997) A note on the analytics and geometry of limiting mean-variance investment opportunity sets, *Review of Quantitative Finance and Accounting*, **9**.

Korkie, R. and Turtle, H. (1998) The Canadian investment opportunity set: 1967–1993, *Canadian Journal of Administrative Sciences*, **15**, 213–229.

Lamoureux, C.G. and Lastrapes, W.D. (1990) Persistence in variance, structural change, and the GARCH model, *Journal of Business and Economic Statistics*, **8**(2), 225–234.

Lehmann, B.N. and Modest, D.M. (1988) The empirical foundations of the arbitrage pricing theory, *Journal of Financial Economics*, **21**, 213–254.

MacKinlay, A.C. and Richardson, M. (1991) Using the generalized method of moments to test mean-variance efficiency, *Journal of Finance*, **46**, 511–528.

Mehra, R. and Prescott, E. (1985) The equity premium: a puzzle, *Journal of Monetary Economics*, **15**, 145–162.

Merton, R.C. (1972) An analytical derivation of the efficient portfolio frontier, *Journal of Financial and Quantitative Analysis*, **7**, 1851–1872.

Morrison, D.F. (1967) *Multivariate Statistical Methods*, McGraw Hill, New York.

Muth, J.F. (1960) Optimal properties of exponentially weighted forecasts, *Journal of the American Statistical Association*, **55**, 299–306.

Muth, J.F. (1961) Rational expectations and the theory of price movements, *Econometrica*, **29**, 315–335.

Nelson, D. and Foster, D. (1994) Asymptotic filtering theory for univariate ARCH models, *Econometrica*, **62**, 1–41.

Newey, W.K. and West, K.D. (1987) Hypothesis testing with efficient method of moments estimation, *International Economic Review*, **28**, 777–787.

Ng, L. (1991) Tests of the CAPM with time-varying covariances: a multivariate GARCH approach, *Journal of Finance*, **46**, 1507–1521.

Pagan, A.R. and Schwert, G.W. (1990) Alternative models for conditional stock volatility, *Journal of Econometrics*, **45**, 267–290.

Pesaran, M.H. and Timmermann, A. (1995) Predictability of stock returns: robustness and economic significance, *Journal of Finance*, **50**, 1201–1228.

Roll, R. (1977) A critique of the asset pricing theory's tests: part I, *Journal of Financial Economics*, **4**, 129–176.

Ross, S.A. (1977) The capital asset pricing model (CAPM), short-sale restrictions and related issues, *Journal of Finance*, **32**, 177–183.

Sargent, T. (1987) *Macroeconomic Theory*, Academic Press, New York.

Schwert, G.W. (1989) Why does stock market volatility change over time?, *Journal of Finance*, **44**, 1115–1153.

Shanken, J. (1985) Multivariate tests of the zero-beta CAPM, *Journal of Financial Economics*, **14**, 327–348.

Shanken, J. (1990) The intertemporal asset pricing model: an empirical investigation, *Journal of Econometrics*, **45**, 99–120.

Solnik, B. (1984) The relation between stock prices and inflationary expectations, *Journal of Finance*, **38**, 35–48.

Stambaugh, R.F. (1982) On the exclusion of assets from tests of the two-parameter model: a sensitivity analysis, *Journal of Financial Economics*, **10**, 237–268.

Tauchen, G. (1986) Statistical properties of generalized method-of-moments estimators of structural parameters obtained from financial market data, *Journal of Business and Economic Statistics*, **4**, 397–425.

Taylor, S.J. (1986) *Modelling Financial Time Series*, Chichester: John Wiley.

Turtle, H., Buse, A. and Korkie, B. (1994) Tests of conditional asset pricing with time-varying moments and risk prices, *Journal of Financial and Quantitative Analysis*, **29**, 15–29.

Whitelaw, R.F. (1994) Time variations and covariations in the expectation and volatility of stock market returns, *Journal of Finance*, **49**, 515–542.

Zhou, G. (1994) Analytical GMM tests: asset pricing with time-varying risk premiums, *Review of Financial Studies*, **7**, 687–709.

Chapter 10

Performance measurement of portfolio risk based on orthant probabilities

MARK LUNDIN AND STEPHEN SATCHELL

ABSTRACT

Portfolio risk estimation and risk budgeting play central roles in performance measurement and the development of future performance expectations. The risk aspect of investing provides the standardization necessary for the comparison of strategies and the measurement of success on equal scales. In this discussion, the volatility characteristics of investment portfolios are re-examined from the perspective of long/short investment strategies and long-only investment strategies which are underweight or overweight assets with respect to a benchmark. An alternative formulation for the description of portfolio risk proposed by Acar and Satchell (1998) is expanded upon. The standard and commonly accepted variance/covariance framework accounts for correlation between assets. However, a new formulation, based on orthant probabilities, extends standard portfolio risk estimation in order also to account for potential correlation between the asset selection decisions which periodically occur in the investment process. The differences between the two approaches suggest that conventional estimates may not apply to the absolute risk estimation of long/short strategies or to the benchmark relative risk of long-only strategies. The orthant probability-based estimate of portfolio volatility is found to be systematically greater than that provided by commonly employed methods and may help explain both the underforecasted absolute risk of some alternative investment strategies as well as the underforecasted tracking error of more conventional investment strategies.

10.1 INTRODUCTION

The past 20 years have been witness to a healthy expansion of the alternative investment industry, which caters largely to the sophisticated investor. Hedge funds and managed futures funds account for a large subsection of this field. Although the number and size of such investment funds remain small compared to conventional mutual funds, their growth has risen by more than 25% per year since the late 1980s (Ackermann, McEnally and Ravenscraft, 1999). These vehicles often offer enhanced diversification through the possibility to participate in a wide variety of financial instruments, many of which are not available in traditional investment products. A primary motivation for this is the provision of enhanced portfolio returns in market environments in which traditional equity and fixed income strategies offer limited opportunities. One path towards this end is to hold short positions in addition to long. In practice this can be achieved by the selling of assets which are not actually held, but rather which have been borrowed for this express purpose, or by the selling of derivative securities. Losses by some of these hedge funds have prompted questions of the reliability of the implemented risk hedges, especially during periods of higher volatility.

For any investment portfolio, risk can primarily be controlled by holding a reasonably large number of different assets whose returns are as uncorrelated as possible. Some alternative investment strategies aim for what is perhaps the natural extrapolation of risk diversification by being simultaneously long and short on different securities. In such a strategy, investors seek to profit by exploiting pricing inefficiencies between related securities, while neutralizing some or all of their exposure to global, or local, market risk. However, previous authors have theorized that this may be difficult to achieve in practice, since an investor may inevitably use similar techniques in performing asset selection and obtaining relative asset portfolio weightings (Richards, 1999). Even if returns on different trades are uncorrelated, results suggest that the variances of returns can be correlated. This can lead to the distribution of returns for a given investment strategy being more fat-tailed, or the realization of larger gains or losses with greater frequency than would normally be expected. Risk in and of itself is not a bad thing and risk tolerance is required if exceptional returns are desired. However, accurate estimates of potential losses are crucial to preservation of assets and investment strategies should be systematically moderated in view of positions taken.

Researchers and investors alike have also identified a related risk estimation problem with respect to more conventional long-only investment strategies. In such a strategy, portfolio managers are typically assigned a benchmark portfolio which corresponds to a client's risk appetite. Active managers are expected to deviate from this benchmark, becoming overweight or underweight in individual assets according to their current market views. In this benchmark relative context, a long-only strategy in absolute terms can be viewed as a long/short strategy in benchmark relative terms. One method for controlling the extent to which these benchmark deviations are allowed is the allocation of an acceptable window of risk measured, not in absolute terms, but with respect to the benchmark itself (Litterman *et al.*, 2000). A common measure of this relative risk is the standard deviation of portfolio returns minus benchmark returns, or tracking error (Roll, 1992). In constructing the portfolio, the investment manager is expected to make some estimate, or forecast, of the tracking error that will result. There are various methods for producing such a risk forecast and these vary in terms of sophistication and success. However, one common thread to most, if not all, methods is that they tend to systematically underforecast tracking error which is subsequently realized afterwards. This can lead to serious, long-term difficulties as performance measurement monitoring is typically set in place to ensure that risk budget windows are not systematically violated.

In this discussion, the volatility characteristics of investment portfolios are re-examined from the perspective of long/short investment strategies. The conclusions drawn from these investigations also facilitate discussion of the implications for long-only investment strategies. An alternative formulation for the description of portfolio risk proposed by Acar and Satchell (1998) is outlined in section 10.2. The standard and commonly accepted variance/covariance framework accounts for correlation between assets. However, the new formulation, based on development of orthant probabilities, extends standard portfolio risk estimation in order also to account for potential correlation between the relative asset weighting decisions that periodically occur in actively managed long/short investment strategies. The difference between the two approaches suggests that conventional risk estimation may not apply to long/short strategies in absolute terms or to long-only strategies in benchmark relative terms. Within this framework, an instantaneous estimation of association is introduced as a stochastically varying gauge of similarity between asset weighting decisions at the time of portfolio construction or adjustment. For a given investment subperiod, this approach is viewed as more accurate than historical measures of association which estimate an average correlation over a previous, often arbitrarily selected, time period. A generalized, multivariate orthant probability structure is then developed for variance estimation involving investment portfolios containing any number of assets. The implications of the new risk formulation for long-only and long/short investment strategies are discussed in section 10.3.

The orthant probability risk framework is then applied to the description of the value added by one particular style of long/short asset management, the market neutral investment strategy, which is described in section 10.4. Monte Carlo simulations are performed in order to compare conventional long/short portfolio volatility estimates with the orthant probability based formulation, the latter also accounting for the correlation between asset weighting decisions. Taken as a step-ahead investment subperiod risk forecast, the orthant probability-based estimate of portfolio volatility is systematically greater than that provided by the standard and commonly accepted method of estimation. The source of this additional risk component is the result of a 'peso problem' related phenomenon (Krasker, 1980); the consideration of events which have small probabilities of occurrence, but with important consequences when they do occur. Neglect of similarities within asset selection processes is potentially a major source of both long/short portfolio absolute risk underestimation and long-only portfolio, benchmark relative risk underestimation, and is discussed in the conclusions of section 10.5.

10.2 ORTHANT PROBABILITY DESCRIPTION OF PORTFOLIO DISTRIBUTIONS

It has been recognized for some time that, while portfolio returns have a conditional linearity property in individual asset returns, unconditionally the situation is more complex. In this case, one would expect a bilinear pattern or something much more involved. The analysis which follows represents a worked example whereby the distribution of portfolio returns with stochastic weights is revealed.

Investment portfolio gains and losses, or returns, are realized by changes in individual asset prices over an investment subperiod ranging from some given time $t-1$ to time t. For a portfolio of N assets, this return on investment (R_t) is commonly described by a linear combination of the products of asset weights applied at the beginning of the investment subperiod ($w_{i,t-1}$) and individual asset returns which are realized over the subperiod duration ($r_{i,t}$):

$$R_t = \sum_{i=1}^{N} w_{i,t-1} r_{i,t} \tag{10.1}$$

Acar and Satchell (1998) have proposed separation of the magnitude and sign of weights on portfolio assets in order to formulate the probabilities for long/short combinations. Investment return at time t can then be alternatively described as the linear combination of equation (10.2):

$$R_t = \sum_{i=1}^{N} w_{i,t-1} r_{i,t} = \sum_{i=1}^{N} \delta_{i,t-1} \omega_{i,t-1} r_{i,t} \tag{10.2}$$

where $\omega_{i,t-1}$ represents the absolute magnitude of the weight applied to asset i at time $t-1$. $\delta_{i,t-1}$ refers to the sign of the weight applied to asset i at time $t-1$. For a long-only investment portfolio $\delta_{i,t} = 1$ for all i and all t. The product of the two, $\delta_{i,t-1}\omega_{i,t-1}$, can be considered as a 'trading model' decision which supplies an investment weight to the ith asset in a portfolio and for a given investment subperiod. For a long/short portfolio strategy there exist *a priori* no restrictions on assets' weights and $\delta_{i,t} \in \{-1, +1\}$, though constraints which specify leveraging limits can easily be applied.

One can expand the latter part of equation (10.2) for the case of a simple two asset portfolio:

$$R_{p,t} = \delta_{1,t-1}\omega_{1,t-1}r_{1,t} + \delta_{2,t-1}\omega_{2,t-1}r_{2,t} \tag{10.3}$$

whose characteristic function can be derived in the usual manner via the bivariate normal probability distribution function (pdf). The characteristic function is important because, when expanded in powers, it can be used to yield the moments of the distribution and in this case is therefore also a moment generating function (mgf). However, if desired, one can also express the global mgf as a linear combination of orthantized mgfs which contain the probabilities for being long or short on both assets in all possible combinations or quadrants:

$$\begin{aligned} E[e^{izR_{p,t}}] = {} & \Pr[\delta_{1,t-1} > 0, \delta_{2,t-1} > 0]E[\exp(iz(\omega_{1,t-1}r_{1,t} + \omega_{2,t-1}r_{2,t}))] \\ & + \Pr[\delta_{1,t-1} > 0, \delta_{2,t-1} \leq 0]E[\exp(iz(\omega_{1,t-1}r_{1,t} - \omega_{2,t-1}r_{2,t}))] \\ & + \Pr[\delta_{1,t-1} \leq 0, \delta_{2,t-1} > 0]E[\exp(iz(-\omega_{1,t-1}r_{1,t} + \omega_{2,t-1}r_{2,t}))] \\ & + \Pr[\delta_{1,t-1} \leq 0, \delta_{2,t-1} \leq 0]E[\exp(-iz(\omega_{1,t-1}r_{1,t} + \omega_{2,t-1}r_{2,t}))] \end{aligned} \tag{10.4}$$

The individual probabilities of equation (10.4) can be solved under normal distribution assumptions by considering that the standard form of the Cauchy distribution[1] is the distribution of the central Student-t with one degree of freedom and is thus the distribution of the ratio U/V where U and V are independent, centred, unit normal distributions with correlation ρ_{UV}. This result can be used to derive the quadrant bivariate normal orthant probabilities,

[1] The standard form here refers to location of the distribution at zero and scale equal to one. These quantities are analogous to mean and standard deviation, respectively.

e.g. $\Pr[\delta_1 > 0, \delta_2 > 0]$, where $(\delta_1\omega_1, \delta_2\omega_2)$ has a standard bivariate normal distribution with mean equal to zero:

$$\Pr[\delta_{1,t-1} > 0, \delta_{2,t-1} > 0] = \frac{1}{4} + \frac{1}{2\pi}\arcsin(\rho_{12,t-1}(\delta_{1,t-1}\omega_{1,t-1}, \delta_{2,t-1}\omega_{2,t-1})) \tag{10.5}$$

$$\Pr[\delta_{1,t-1} > 0, \delta_{2,t-1} \leq 0] = \frac{1}{4} - \frac{1}{2\pi}\arcsin(\rho_{12,t-1}(\delta_{1,t-1}\omega_{1,t-1}, \delta_{2,t-1}\omega_{2,t-1})) \tag{10.6}$$

$$\Pr[\delta_{1,t-1} \leq 0, \delta_{2,t-1} > 0] = \frac{1}{4} - \frac{1}{2\pi}\arcsin(\rho_{12,t-1}(\delta_{1,t-1}\omega_{1,t-1}, \delta_{2,t-1}\omega_{2,t-1})) \tag{10.7}$$

$$\Pr[\delta_{1,t-1} \leq 0, \delta_{2,t-1} \leq 0] = \frac{1}{4} + \frac{1}{2\pi}\arcsin(\rho_{12,t-1}(\delta_{1,t-1}\omega_{1,t-1}, \delta_{2,t-1}\omega_{2,t-1})) \tag{10.8}$$

where $\rho(\delta_{1,t-1}\omega_{1,t-1}, \delta_{2,t-1}\omega_{2,t-1})$ is the correlation between asset positioning decisions (or trading models), and should not be confused with the correlation between assets themselves. Equation (10.5) is most commonly known as Sheppard's theorem on median dichotomy and holds only for the particular case of the multivariate mean being equal to zero (for various proofs of equations (10.5)–(10.8), see Sheppard (1898), Kepner, Harper and Keith (1989), Stigler (1989), Farebrother (1989), Johnson, Kotz and Balakrishnan (1994) and Acar and Satchell (1998)). In practical terms, equation (10.5) is an expression of the probability of holding, or being long on, both assets in a two asset investment portfolio. Equations (10.6) and (10.7) then refer to similar probabilities for being long the first asset and selling (or being short) the second asset or being short the first asset and long the second, respectively. The remaining equation (10.8) expresses the probability for being short of both assets.

One should note that, although the correlations between asset positioning decisions have been written as time varying quantities, this is not pertinent to the validity of equations (10.5)–(10.8). In theory, these could also be written as non-stochastic quantities. We have chosen here to do so out of practical considerations regarding the precision of the description of portfolio returns in view of the fact that establishing the theoretical correlation between trading rules has been demonstrated to be an extremely difficult task (Brock, Lakonishok and LeBaron (1992)). In practical time series analysis, correlation between variables is usually estimated over a sample period which is long enough to guarantee sufficient statistical significance for the application at hand. Very often, however, the analyst neglects the fact that this estimated correlation may actually be an average of a time varying correlation. As is often done in the case of asset returns themselves, this type of historical estimate can also be performed in order to gauge the correlation between asset positioning decisions. However, a difference between the two exists; for a given investment subperiod, the weights applied to portfolio assets is known exactly, at least at the fixed point in time that positions are taken.[2]

This difference is especially important where an investment subperiod step-ahead forecast is concerned. In this context, there is little or no uncertainty about the similarity between asset positioning decisions as the weights applied to assets deliver a more precise estimate of association than the covariation of these decisions over time. Therefore we propose an 'instantaneous' measure of association between asset positioning decisions; one whose definition is dependent only on asset weights for an investment holding period running from time $t-1$ to time t. This definition is described concisely as the following:

At the beginning of a given investment subperiod, the similarity between two asset weighting decisions is equal to the cosine of the angle between the two-dimensional Cartesian space vector formed by the weights and the isometric reflection of this vector against the mirror line $x = y$ (corresponding to perfect correlation). The transformation from the original vector to this particular reflection defines a Jacobi transformation matrix which is diagonal with zeros on the main diagonal and with ones in non-main diagonal matrix elements.

This geometrical definition is invoked in view of the Cartesian-vector interpretation of product–moment correlation. The positions taken on two assets at time $t-1$ can be considered as forming a vector, $\vec{a}$, in two-dimensional Cartesian space (abscissa component $= \delta_1\omega_1$, ordinate component $= \delta_2\omega_2$) which originates at the origin and ends at the point $(\delta_{1,t-1}\omega_{1,t-1}, \delta_{2,t-1}\omega_{2,t-1})$. Correlation between the two asset weighting decisions (ρ_{12}) presumably exists, but in the absence of further information (for example, weights on the two assets during another investment subperiod) there is no observable variance or covariance and therefore product–moment correlation is not defined. Now define another vector, $\vec{b} = \vec{a}_r$, as the isometric reflection of $\vec{a}$ against the mirror line $\delta_1\omega_1 = \delta_2\omega_2$ (a 45° line representing perfect correlation between trading models). Given $\vec{a}_{12,t-1} = (\delta_{1,t-1}\omega_{1,t-1}, \delta_{2,t-1}\omega_{2,t-1})$, the reflection vector is then defined as $\vec{b}_{12,t-1} = (\delta_{2,t-1}\omega_{2,t-1}, \delta_{1,t-1}\omega_{1,t-1})$. If $\delta_{1,t-1}\omega_{1,t-1} \neq$

[2]Currency denominated asset weights change during an investment subperiod due to fluctuations in unrealized assets' values. Deviations from starting values can only be controlled by reducing the duration of the investment subperiod (or points at which risk estimation occurs).

$\delta_{2,t-1}\omega_{2,t-1}$, then $\vec{a}$ and $\vec{b}$ are linearly independent and, by symmetry, the weights on the two assets in each vector have equal correlation, ρ_{12}. Vector correlation is related to sample correlation and, for two independent vectors, each containing equally correlated asset weights, can be defined via the law of cosines (see, for example, Rencher (1995)) which is given in vector form in equation (10.9):

$$\rho_{12,t-1}(\delta_{1,t-1}\omega_{1,t-1}, \delta_{2,t-1}\omega_{2,t-1}) \equiv \cos\theta_{\vec{a},\vec{b}} = \cos\theta_{\vec{a}',\vec{a}_r} = \frac{\vec{a}', \vec{a}_r}{\sqrt{(\vec{a}'\vec{a})(\vec{a}_r'\vec{a}_r)}} \tag{10.9}$$

If $\delta_{1,t-1}\omega_{1,t-1} = \delta_{2,t-1}\omega_{2,t-1}$, then $\vec{a}$ and $\vec{b}$ are linearly dependent (since one can be written as a linear combination of the other) and the correlation between them (and the set of asset weights) is one, by definition.

There exist various alternative measures of association and the one preferred may depend on the application at hand. For a given investment subperiod, the instantaneous measure of association defined in equation (10.9) may differ greatly from the overall average correlation of asset allocation (trading model) decisions. However, a historically estimated, sample dependent average of what is very likely to be a time varying quantity is viewed as less precise for the application of a step-ahead forecast than that conditional only on current assets' weights.

Returning from our digression on estimation of the correlation between asset positioning decisions, we insert the results of equations (10.5)–(10.8) into the characteristic function of equation (10.4), yielding equation (10.10):

$$\begin{aligned}
E[e^{izR_{p,t}}] = {} & \left(\frac{1}{2} + \frac{1}{\pi}\arcsin(\rho_{12,t-1}(\delta_{1,t-1}\omega_{1,t-1}, \delta_{2,t-1}\omega_{2,t-1}))\right) \\
& \times \exp\left(-\frac{z^2}{2}(\omega_{1,t-1}^2\sigma_{r1}^2 + \omega_{2,t-1}^2\sigma_{r2}^2\right. \\
& \left. + 2\omega_{1,t-1}\omega_{2,t-1}\sigma_{r1}\sigma_{r2}\rho(r_1, r_2))\right) \\
& + \left(\frac{1}{2} - \frac{1}{\pi}\arcsin(\rho_{12,t-1}(\delta_{1,t-1}\omega_{1,t-1}, \delta_{2,t-1}\omega_{2,t-1}))\right) \\
& \times \exp\left(-\frac{z^2}{2}(\omega_{1,t-1}^2\sigma_{r1}^2 + \omega_{2,t-1}^2\sigma_{r2}^2\right. \\
& \left. - 2\omega_{1,t-1}\omega_{2,t-1}\sigma_{r1}\sigma_{r2}\rho(r_1, r_2))\right)
\end{aligned} \tag{10.10}$$

It should be recalled that this derivation refers to a bivariate normal distribution whose financial interpretation is that of two trading models whose positions are distributed equally around zero. The second moment of this portfolio description can then be obtained as the second derivative of the moment generating function[3] (mgf) with $z = 0$:

$$\mu_2 = \omega_{1,t-1}^2\sigma_{r1}^2 + \omega_{2,t-1}^2\sigma_{r2}^2 + 2\omega_{1,t-1}\omega_{2,t-1}\sigma_{r1}\sigma_{r2}\rho(r_1, r_2) \times \frac{2}{\pi}\arcsin(\rho_{12,t-1}(\delta_{1,t-1}\omega_{1,t-1}, \delta_{2,t-1}\omega_{2,t-1})) \tag{10.11}$$

This result differs from the conventional description of bivariate variance of a linear combination of assets. There are various methods for derivation of this commonly accepted quantity, all of which are formulated in terms of asset weights as they were written previously in equation (10.1). For purposes of comparison, we remind the reader of this form in equation (10.12):

$$\mu_2 = w_{1,t-1}^2\sigma_{r1}^2 + w_{2,t-1}^2\sigma_{r2}^2 + 2w_{1,t-1}w_{2,t-1}\sigma_{r1}\sigma_{r2}\rho(r_1, r_2) \tag{10.12}$$

whose multivariate generalization is the product of the vector of asset weights, the asset set covariance matrix and the transpose of the vector of asset weights. Equation (10.11) does not necessarily refute the familiar result described by equation (10.12). Rather, it makes the additional consideration of also accounting for the correlation which exists between asset positioning decisions. However, one can ascertain the conditions under which equation (10.12) is valid by setting equations (10.11) and (10.12) equal to each other and eliminating like quantities in order to obtain:

$$\frac{2}{\pi}\arcsin(\rho_{12,t-1}(\delta_{1,t-1}\omega_{1,t-1}, \delta_{2,t-1}\omega_{2,t-1})) = \frac{\omega_{1,t-1}\omega_{2,t-1}}{w_{1,t-1}w_{2,t-1}} \in \{1, -1\} \tag{10.13}$$

The ratio of the product of the absolute magnitudes of asset weightings to the weighting themselves is equal to +1 if weightings are like-signed ($w_{1,t-1}w_{2,t-1} > 0$), and equal to -1 if unlike signed ($w_{1,t-1}w_{2,t-1} < 0$). Equation (10.12) then appears fully valid under the assumption that the correlation between asset positioning decisions is unity in absolute magnitude and whose sign is determined as follows:

$$\begin{aligned} \rho_{12,t-1}(\delta_{1,t-1}\omega_{1,t-1}, \delta_{2,t-1}\omega_{2,t-1}) &= 1 \quad \text{if} \quad \frac{\omega_{1,t-1}\omega_{2,t-1}}{w_{1,t-1}w_{2,t-1}} = 1 \\ &= -1 \quad \text{if} \quad \frac{\omega_{1,t-1}\omega_{2,t-1}}{w_{1,t-1}w_{2,t-1}} = -1 \end{aligned} \tag{10.14}$$

[3]Note that the first moment obtained through the mgf is equal to zero, and therefore $\mu_2 = \mu_2' - \mu_1' = \mu_2'$. In addition, Stuart and Ord (1994) point out that for many formal purposes it is sufficient to write $\theta = iz$, and treat it as real in order to avoid negative even moments.

This result is equivalent to defining the covariance matrix of assets' decisions to be singular. Under conditions in which the correlation between asset positioning decisions is less than unity in absolute magnitude, equation (10.11) can therefore be viewed as producing a more accurate estimate than the conventional description of portfolio variance as it does not require the simplifying assumptions of relation (10.14).

In the absence of full correlation (or anti-correlation) between asset positioning decisions, equation (10.11) also implies the rather startling conclusion that the portfolio covariance matrix should account for the covariance in the asset weighting process, in addition to the covariance between asset returns themselves. Examination of the terms of equation (10.11) dictates that the combination of the two should be written as:

$$\begin{aligned}\mathrm{cov}(w_{1,t-1}r_1, w_{2,t-1}r_2) &= \omega_{1,t-1}\omega_{2,t-1}\sigma_{r1}\sigma_{r2}\rho(r_1, r_2)\\ &\quad\times \frac{2}{\pi}\arcsin(\rho_{12,t-1}(\delta_{1,t-1}\omega_{1,t-1}, \delta_{2,t-1}\omega_{2,t-1}))\end{aligned} \tag{10.15}$$

Equation (10.15) reduces to the conventional formulation of asset variance for the case where both assets are one and the same.

Recapitulating, equation (10.11) uses the bivariate normal orthant, long/short quadrant framework in order to formulate the variance of a two asset portfolio by considering that correlation between asset positioning decisions may also play a role. For a portfolio of N assets, a generalized normal orthant formulation of portfolio variance would involve 2^N sections. Although the bivariate linear combination may be used in order to derive useful insights, it is of little or no use in financial practice unless it can be expanded to include larger numbers of assets. As with the bivariate normal orthant probabilities of equations (10.5)–(10.8), solutions to trivariate octant probabilities are also known exactly. However, an exact multivariate solution (or even one involving a fixed number of variates greater than three) has thus far eluded statistical science.

Our inability to arrive at a generalized 2^N sections framework can be circumvented in the portfolio context by considering the investment portfolio from the $O(N^2)$, N-variate perspective in which orthant probabilities are exactly known. This is precisely what is used in the conventional formulation of portfolio variance; a combination of the pairwise covariances of assets' marginal distributions.[4] Equation (10.15) can then be used to arrive at

[4]For a portfolio of any number of assets, this is usually written as $\sigma^2 = x\Sigma x'$, where x is a vector of asset weights, Σ is the asset covariance matrix and x' is the transpose of x.

a generalized multivariate formulation of equation (10.11) for a portfolio of N assets:

$$\mu_2 = \sum_{i=1}^{N}\sum_{j=1}^{N} \omega_{i,t-1}\omega_{j,t-1}\sigma_{ri}\sigma_{rj}\rho(r_i, r_j) \times \frac{2}{\pi}\arcsin(\rho_{ij,t-1}(\delta_{i,t-1}\omega_{i,t-1}, \delta_{j,t-1}\omega_{j,t-1})) \qquad (10.16)$$

Given equation (10.15), the proof for this multivariate generalization can trivially be derived from the bivariate case via induction, or by any of the other methods used to derive the conventional multivariate variance formulation (e.g. the delta-method or by integrating over assets' moments).

The nature of equation (10.16) differs from the description of portfolio variance which we are most familiar with and deserves further elucidation. The implications of this distributional characterization for several investment strategies are discussed in section 10.3. For reasons of tractability, illustrations are made using the most basic application of a portfolio of two assets.

10.3 IMPLICATIONS FOR ABSOLUTE AND RELATIVE RISK

Investment strategies can broadly be classified as either passive or active and as either long only (conventional investment style), long/short (typical hedge fund style) or short only. The discussion which follows is applicable for active as well as passive investment strategies; the only difference between the two is the duration (or number) of holding periods. The implications of the orthant-normal distributional characterization of equation (10.16) are discussed for a simple two asset long/short investment strategy in section 10.3.1. For such a portfolio, a benchmark of zero cumulative return is most appropriate. As a consequence of this absolute performance benchmark, absolute risk is the pertinent measure of portfolio volatility.

Section 10.3.2 outlines the consequences of the orthant-normal framework for estimation of the relative risk of long-only investment strategies. The more commonly employed long-only investment strategy involves being fully, or close to fully, invested by buying and holding assets which are in line with a predetermined asset subset. This subset is commonly defined according to a benchmark portfolio. Asset managers, primarily active ones, attempt to provide returns in excess of the benchmark by becoming underweight or overweight in assets with respect to the same benchmark. As a direct consequence of this relative performance measurement, portfolio volatility is also estimated with respect to the benchmark. In modern investment analysis this is commonly referred to as tracking error. At least in theory, conclusions drawn regarding long-only strategies should be equally valid for short-only strategies. Both involve truncations of the asset weighting distributions which are equal in magnitude (at least in our particular examples), though one restriction is implemented from below and the other from above.

10.3.1 Absolute risk of long/short investment strategies

Assuming positive correlation between assets, the commonly accepted portfolio risk formulation(equation (10.12)) implies that a two asset portfolio consisting of a long position in one asset plus a short position in another asset reduces global portfolio volatility. This occurs as the last term of the equation becomes negative and risk is effectively subtracted. At the same time, however, equation (10.11) reduces fully only to equation (10.12) for the case where $\omega_{1,t-1} = \omega_{2,t-1}$; in this case the instantaneous measure of association between long and short investment decisions is -1 and the orthant probability-based description of portfolio volatility reduces fully to the conventional definition.

However, for the more likely situation in which long and short passive investment decisions are not exactly matched in size ($\omega_{1,t-1} \neq \omega_{2,t-1}$), equation (10.11) relates that the rate at which risk is reduced, increases only geometrically according to the correlation between trading model signals, rather than linearly according to the comparative size of the long and short positions as related by equation (10.12).

The standard formulation of risk makes no attempt to account for correlation between trading model decisions applied to assets. In the case of the long/short investment strategy, equation (10.12) tends to underestimate volatility compared to the alternative formulation related in bivariate form by equation (10.11). For a simple two asset portfolio with equal asset risks ($\sigma_{r1} = \sigma_{r2}$) the distribution of portfolio variance as a function of asset correlation and asset selection correlation can be seen graphically in Figure 10.1.

The conclusions already drawn by thoughtful examination of the bivariate version of the orthant probability variance framework call for verification. This is obtained empirically in section 10.4, where comparisons are made between the conventional multivariate estimation of portfolio variance and equation (10.16), the mutivariate form of the orthant probability-based formulation.

10.3.2 Relative risk (tracking error) of long-only investment strategies

Relative portfolio risk, or that with respect to a benchmark, has been collectively termed ‘tracking error’, even if there exists more than one acknowledged

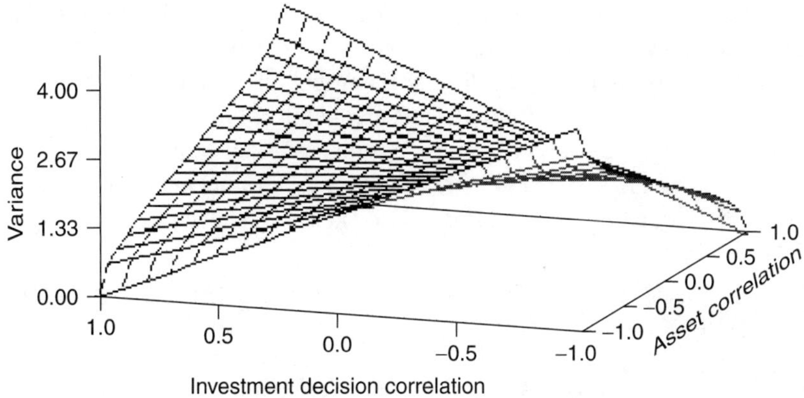

Figure 10.1 Portfolio variance for a simple two asset investment as a function of correlation of assets and trading rules correlation. Risk of both assets were taken to be equal

method for estimating it. *Ex post*, or backward looking, tracking error is typically defined as the annualized standard deviation of portfolio returns minus returns of a relevant benchmark (Roll, 1992). *Ex ante*, or forward looking, tracking error estimates often involve assumptions on the characteristics of assets' distributions, such as is the case for equations (10.11) or (10.12). The currently available *ex ante* tracking error estimation methods vary in terms of their sophistication and forecasting power.

The difference between forecasted and realized tracking error is a very relevant issue for investors today, as such risk budgeting estimations are increasingly used to control and measure performance. To date, little has appeared on the subject in the academic literature. Quantitative financial analysts, however, have empirically identified tracking error forecasting methods which provide good forecasts on shorter time horizons, for example one month (Scowcroft, 1999). Disappointingly, these same methods tend to underforecast realized tracking error by typically 25% on a six month time horizon, degrading further to as much as a 40% under estimation on a one year time horizon and a 50% under estimation on a two year time horizon. The problem is not consistent with the expected increasing random noise typical to forecasting errors as time horizon increases. Rather, realized estimations tend to be consistently greater than forecasts as opposed to both under and over. More discussion on the challenges and recent developments in tracking error estimation and forecasting, along with other references can be found in Brown (2001).

We note that the absolute risk of an investment portfolio which has equal probability to be long or short on assets is no different from the relative risk of a portfolio which has equal probabilities to be overweight or underweight assets with respect to benchmark weights. The previously described orthant-normal framework should hold for both; only the benchmark with respect to which the portfolio is tilted differs. Empirical results on absolute portfolio risk follow in section 10.4; these results are therefore equally valid for relative risk, or tracking error of a symmetric, benchmark tilted strategy. One possible explanation for the systematic increase over time of tracking errors, based on the orthant-normal framework, is discussed in the conclusions of section 10.5.

10.4 EMPIRICAL COMPARISONS USING SIMULATED LONG/SHORT INVESTMENT STRATEGIES

The distributional form of asset positioning decisions has been assumed to be mean $= 0$, multivariate normal. This is a requirement of the normal-orthant framework derivation obtained in section 10.2, but also tends to lead to more generalizable results which are independent of any particular trading strategy or set of trading rules. However, in order to derive realistic conclusions, empirical testing should, presumably, most realistically be performed via trading simulations using actual returns of financial assets whose return distributions exhibit non-normal behaviour. For such tests to be performed, however, it is first required that an actual long/short investment strategy be selected. This is the case even if one assumes that stochastically varying, individual asset positioning decisions exist. Section 10.4.1 attempts to clearly define one potential strategy, that which has become known as market neutral investing. Such a strategy is then used in order to perform Monte Carlo simulations, the results of which are discussed subsequently in section 10.4.2.

10.4.1 Market neutral investment portfolios

The description of portfolio returns given in equation (10.2) can be further separated between market or benchmark related returns, $R_{m,t}$, and residual returns ($\alpha_{i,t}$) derived from individual assets which deviate from the market, as in equation (10.17):

$$R_{p,t} = \sum_{i=1}^{N} \delta_{i,t-1}\omega_{i,t-1}(\beta_{i,t} R_{m,t} + \alpha_{i,t}) \tag{10.17}$$

where $\beta_{i,t}$ links each asset to the market portfolio and is proportional to the covariance between an individual asset's returns and market returns:

$$\beta_{i,t} = \frac{\text{cov}_{t-1}[r_i, R_m]}{\text{var}_{t-1}[R_m]} \tag{10.18}$$

Long/short portfolios are said to be neutral if long positions are offset by equal amounts of short positions. The power of such a constraint in terms of risk reduction during all market conditions is the underlying reason that a hedge fund earns its title (see, for example, Liang (1999), Ackermann, McEnally and Ravenscraft (1999) and references therein). A currency neutral strategy implies the following constraint:

$$\sum_{i=1}^{N} \delta_{i,t-1}\omega_{i,t-1} = 0 \tag{10.19}$$

However, a more generalizable market neutral investment strategy, beta neutral, specifies global neutrality with respect to the market or portfolio of available assets:

$$\sum_{i=1}^{N} \delta_{i,t-1}\omega_{i,t-1}\beta_{i,t} = 0 \tag{10.20}$$

There are a number of methods of varying sophistication for enforcing portfolio beta neutrality. Section 10.4.1 contains a description of Monte Carlo simulations which obtain beta neutrality by simple normalization of positive or negative weights for a given investment subperiod. An enforced constraint of beta neutrality then provides a portfolio independent of market returns and equation (10.17) can be reduced to equation (10.21):

$$R_{\alpha,t} = \sum_{i=1}^{N} \delta_{i,t-1}\omega_{i,t-1}\alpha_{i,t} \tag{10.21}$$

Similarly, portfolio risk can be expressed for a beta neutral portfolio in terms of residual risk by adapting equation (10.16) to account for the beta neutral constraint of equation (10.20):

$$\begin{aligned}\mu_{2\alpha} &= \sum_{i=1}^{N}\sum_{j=1}^{N} \omega_{i,t-1}\omega_{j,t-1}\sigma_{\alpha i}\sigma_{\alpha j}\rho(\alpha_i, \alpha_j) \\ &\quad \times \frac{2}{\pi}\arcsin(\rho_{ij,t-1}(\delta_{i,t-1}\omega_{i,t-1}, \delta_{j,t-1}\omega_{j,t-1}))\end{aligned} \tag{10.22}$$

The value added by a beta neutral investment strategy can be estimated through the information ratio, which measures achievement *ex post*, and forecasts opportunity *ex ante* (looking forward). The information ratio defines a mean-variance point on the residual feasible set of investment opportunities:

$$IR_t = \frac{R_{\alpha,t}}{\mu_{2\alpha}} = \frac{\sum_{i=1}^{N} \delta_{i,t-1}\omega_{i,t-1}\alpha_{i,t}}{\sum_{i=1}^{N}\sum_{j=1}^{N} \omega_{i,t-1}\omega_{j,t-1}\sigma_{\alpha i}\sigma_{\alpha j}\rho(\alpha_i, \alpha_j) \times \frac{2}{\pi}\arcsin(\rho_{ij,t-1}(\delta_{i,t-1}\omega_{i,t-1}, \delta_{j,t-1}\omega_{j,t-1}))} \quad (10.23)$$

10.4.2 Monte Carlo simulations of active, beta neutral risk

Monte Carlo simulations involving a diversified portfolio of financial instruments were performed in order to gauge the application of equation (10.16) versus the more commonly recognized (multivariate version of) equation (10.12). Four years of daily returns (26/10/95 to 26/10/99) were generated from the 45 assets reported in Table 10.1. The group of assets consisted of 30 stock indices, 11 bond indices and four foreign exchange rates. Distributional characteristics of individual asset returns are also reported along with characteristics of a benchmark static portfolio consisting of equal weights on all 45 assets. Also reported in Table 10.1 are estimations of the product–moment correlations between assets and the benchmark market portfolio over the entire study period.

Monte Carlo simulations involved an active (daily adjusted) long/short investment strategy based on randomly distributed trading signals for all assets. Trading signals were derived from normal (0,0.37) random number generators. A normal distribution was selected in order to conform to the normal-orthant derivations derived in section 10.2. In addition, however, it is worth noting that this common distributional type relatively well approximates a typical distribution of indicator-based trading model signals. These typically have a much greater probability to be neutral than fully short or fully long a particular asset. Random trading signals less than zero were interpreted as weights applied to short a particular asset while those greater than zero were interpreted as weights indicating asset purchase. An absolute value of a trading signal equal to one was defined as being fully long or short to the credit limit allowed for each asset. Credit limits for all assets were equal. Regardless of how small the standard deviation which defines a normal distribution is, there still remains some finite possibility for values greater in magnitude than unity, indicating an exposure greater than the assigned credit limits. Therefore, any random trading signals generated with a magnitude greater than unity were reset to 1 or −1. A standard deviation which was a

Table 10.1 Distributional characteristics (estimated *ex post*) of daily returns of individual assets contained in the Monte Carlo market portfolio. Also reported are the individual correlations between individual asset daily returns and market returns over the five year historical sample

Instrument	Mean (%)	Std. dev. (%)	Sum (%)	Min. (%)	Max. (%)	Corr.
S&P 500	0.08	1.07	78.88	−7.11	4.99	0.58
Nikkei 225	0.00	1.43	−1.68	−5.96	7.66	0.47
CAC 40	0.09	1.28	98.13	−5.63	6.10	0.81
DJ Euro STOXX 50	0.10	1.23	100.21	−5.65	6.22	0.88
All Ordinaries	0.03	0.85	30.30	−7.45	6.07	0.52
FTSE 100	0.05	1.01	54.35	−3.66	4.35	0.78
DAX performance	0.09	1.40	91.88	−8.38	6.11	0.79
SMI	0.08	1.24	80.56	−5.23	7.46	0.79
TOPIX	0.01	1.17	7.36	−5.25	6.60	0.48
Nikkei 300	0.01	1.24	10.79	−4.98	7.10	0.49
ATX	0.02	1.18	21.53	−8.70	5.26	0.67
OMX	0.09	1.38	95.80	−6.88	11.02	0.75
AEX	0.09	1.34	98.34	−6.12	5.73	0.81
KOSPI 200	−0.02	2.40	−22.48	−11.60	10.02	0.31
Hang Seng	0.03	2.05	26.27	−14.73	17.25	0.55
IBEX 35	0.10	1.39	106.48	−7.34	6.32	0.75
Budapest BUX	0.14	2.30	150.85	−18.03	13.62	0.58
ALSI	0.02	1.19	18.50	−11.85	6.70	0.65
DJ STOXX 50	0.09	1.19	97.23	−5.09	6.51	0.88
TSE 35	0.06	1.08	59.10	−7.69	5.19	0.60
Dow Jones IA	0.07	1.04	77.34	−7.45	4.86	0.59
MIB 30	0.08	1.54	87.79	−6.43	6.97	0.71
Nasdaq 100	0.14	1.80	144.00	−10.38	6.72	0.43
MSCI Taiwan Index	0.05	1.62	49.05	−7.09	9.17	0.21
Bel20	0.08	1.01	84.57	−4.48	4.48	0.74
S&P 400 Midcap	0.06	0.99	58.91	−6.62	4.54	0.64
Russell 2000	0.03	0.92	33.36	−6.32	4.19	0.64
Bovespa	0.09	2.80	97.09	−17.23	28.82	0.50
PSI	0.09	1.34	93.75	−15.29	9.49	0.62
FTSE mid 250	0.03	0.59	35.23	−5.15	3.04	0.70
JPM GBI US	0.00	0.27	−3.76	−1.56	0.85	0.04
JPM GBI Japan	0.00	0.26	2.55	−1.31	1.11	−0.08
JPM GBI Europe	0.03	0.20	33.52	−1.06	0.84	0.15
JMP GBI Australia	0.00	0.33	1.93	−2.08	1.21	0.04
JPM GBI UK	0.01	0.33	10.90	−2.18	1.83	0.07
JPM GBI Germany	0.00	0.20	0.40	−0.92	0.83	0.10
JPM GBI Switzerland	0.04	0.45	46.34	−2.49	1.99	0.46
JPM GBI Sweden	0.01	0.26	6.37	−1.29	1.17	0.17
JPM GBI Spain	0.02	0.24	15.73	−1.37	0.89	0.17
JPM GBI Canada	0.00	0.29	4.62	−1.79	1.25	0.14
JPM GBI Italy	0.02	0.25	20.32	−1.11	1.06	0.22
USD/JPY	0.00	0.80	3.54	−6.58	3.57	0.10
USD/CHF	0.03	0.61	28.65	−3.36	2.49	0.46
GBP/USD	0.00	0.44	4.61	−1.96	2.01	−0.27
EUR/USD	−0.03	0.52	-26.31	−1.70	2.29	−0.31
MARKET	**0.05**	**0.57**	**46.95**	**−2.94**	**2.72**	**1.00**

factor of 2.7 times smaller than one was used in order to avoid excessive tail peaks in the random distributions at +1 or −1. This distributional censoring introduces a bias on the order of 0.7% of events, but is implemented in an attempt to keep simulations financially realistic.

For all results which follow, simulated trading signals were generated for ten successive times and applied to the four year sample period of actual historic returns in order to boost statistics (resulting in 10,440, events). Individual trading signals were then further constrained to ensure Beta market neutrality of the active portfolio, as defined by equation (10.20). This was achieved by comparison of the sum of long and short positions and reductive normalization of the greater of the two in order to ensure perfect beta neutrality. All asset weights were then multiplied by a common factor which ensured 100% market exposure as measured by the sum of the absolute values of trading weights. As a first step, all randomly distributed trading signals were ensured to be uncorrelated.

Although the trading signals were uncorrelated as estimated on average over the entire sample period, on a daily basis discrete instantaneous measures of association between trading signals can exist according to equation (10.9). Daily, step-ahead portfolio risk was then forecasted using equation (10.16), which takes into account the daily similarity of trading model signals as defined by equation (10.9). In addition, time varying daily risk was forecasted using the commonly accepted definition of portfolio standard deviation (multivariate generalization of equation (10.12)). Each method requires as input a daily forecast of the standard deviations and betas of individual assets, along with a forecast of the correlation matrix of assets. These quantities were estimated historically for each new investment subperiod (the subsequent day) via the previous year of daily returns in a moving window fashion. Presumably, a better forecast can be obtained for these quantities, but this should not effect our goal of gauging the relative merits of the step-ahead risk forecast provided by equation (10.16).

Table 10.2, column 2 provides the standard deviation of daily returns provided by an active, beta neutral, investment strategy driven by daily varying, randomly distributed and uncorrelated trading signals. This quantity is estimated at the end of the total data period and therefore is not available on a daily basis as a forecast. However, it can be considered as an estimation of the average risk over the entire active investment period and serves as a benchmark for comparison of the accuracy of the two measures of stochastically varying risk forecasts. Column 3 reports the average of daily portfolio standard deviation forecasts as calculated by the orthant probability-based formulation of standard deviation which includes daily, instantaneous measures of association between trading signals. Column 4 of Table 10.2 reports the average

Table 10.2 Comparison of estimated standard deviation of daily returns for: (a) A static investment strategy composed of an equally weighted combination of the assets listed in Table 10.1. (b) An active, beta neutral, investment strategy driven by daily varying randomly distributed and uncorrelated trading signals. (c) The average of daily portfolio standard deviations as calculated by the orthant probability-based formulation of standard deviation which includes daily similarity between trading signals. (d) The average of daily portfolio standard deviations as calculated by the standard formulation of standard deviation. Standard errors are also reported

(a) σ Equal market	(b) σ Time varying portfolio	(c) $\bar{\sigma}$ Equation (10.16)	(d) $\bar{\sigma}$ Equation (10.12)
0.567 %	$(0.178 \pm 0.008)\%$	$(0.188 \pm 0.001)\%$	$(0.168 \pm 0.001)\%$

of daily forecasts of portfolio standard deviations as calculated by the standard formulation (multivariate generalization of equation (10.12)). Finally, for purposes of comparison only, Table 10.2, column 1 reports a daily standard deviation of returns derived from a static investment strategy composed of an equally weighted combination of the assets listed in Table 10.1. Standard errors are also reported.

Table 10.2 confirms the assertion of section 10.3.2; on average, daily varying risk forecasts as estimated by the orthant probability-based definition of equation (10.16) exceeds daily varying risk forecasted according to the standard definition (multivariate generalization of equation (10.12)). It is also interesting to note that Table 10.2 reflects the fact that a static long investment strategy with the portfolio net asset value divided equally among the 45 assets and which is always 100% invested, delivers a daily risk of 0.57%. The time varying, beta neutral, fully invested portfolio with trading models defining asset weights on a daily basis delivers a daily risk of only 0.18%, or roughly a factor of three times lower risk with equal market exposure.

These results apply only to the case of trading signals which are, on average, uncorrelated, even though strong correlations can exist for a particular investment subperiod. Given the persistent correlation between individual assets and even among different asset classes, this assumption may not be fully valid and two vital questions immediately present themselves. First, does the standard estimation taken as a naïve forecast systematically underestimate *ex post* estimated risk? Second, does the orthant probability-based estimation method which accounts for correlation between trading signals produce results which, on average, overestimate realized risk to roughly the same extent?

In order to address these questions, further Monte Carlo simulations were generated using appropriate mixtures of random signal generators in order to produce trading signals for individual assets which are equally correlated one to another. This was achieved by linear combination of each of the 45 daily asset trading signals derived from independent, normally distributed random number generators with a separate, 46th random normal distribution. This mixing produced 45 new asset trading signals which were, on average, correlated equally one to another. The magnitude of these correlations is then in relation to the fraction taken from the 46th random normal distribution. Following this process, the 45 distributions were corrected to ensure their width remained constant and finally to ensure 100% investment for the entire, final portfolio.

Results are shown in Figure 10.2, where the *ex post* (estimated) standard deviation of active (beta neutral) investment strategy returns is reported (triangles) as a function of the product–moment correlation induced between randomly distributed trading model signals. Also reported are the average of daily varying risk estimations for both the standard estimation method (multivariate generalization of equation (10.12)) and the orthant probability-based estimation method which accounts for daily varying correlation between trading signals (equation (10.16)). Standard errors for these estimations were also calculated and in all cases lie within the data markers.

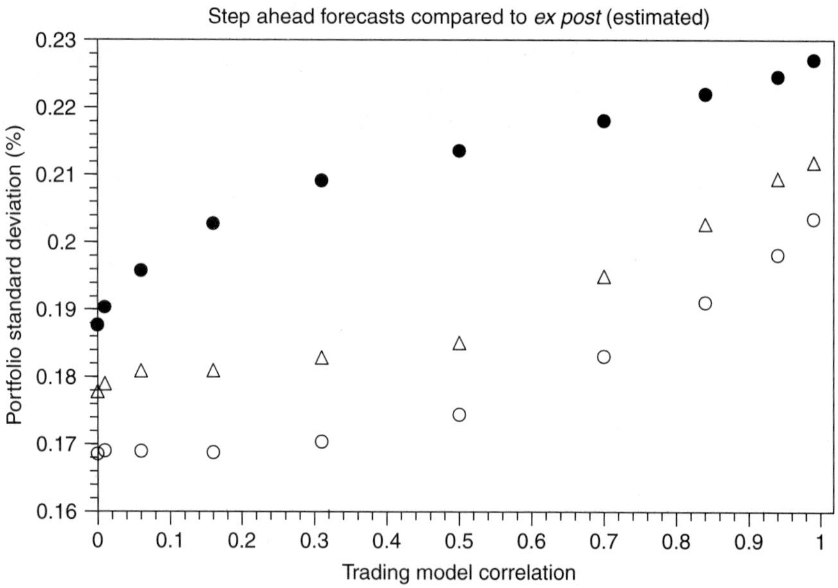

Figure 10.2 Monte Carlo estimated standard deviations of daily returns derived from an active, beta neutral, investment strategy as a function of induced correlation between randomly distributed long/short trading signals. Reported are the *ex post* estimations of portfolio standard deviations (triangles), the average of time varying standard deviations according to the orthant probability-based definition of risk described by equation (10.16) (darkened circles) and the average of time varying standard deviations estimated according to the commonly accepted multivariate form of equation (10.12) (empty circles)

Figure 10.2 provides evidence to support useful conclusions. The standard forecast estimation of active investment strategy risk (empty circles, representing equation (10.12) taken as a step-ahead forecast) systematically underestimates actual portfolio risk measured *ex ante* as the standard deviation of portfolio returns (triangles). The underestimation is on average a factor of 0.94 and does not appear to depend on the correlation induced between trading models. This is an expected consequence of the orthogonality of security returns, an important result of which is the variance inequality derived by LeRoy and Porter (1981) and Shiller (1981) (see also Campbell, Lo and MacKinlay (1997) and Lo and MacKinlay (1999) for in-depth discussion of the implications for variance ratios):

$$\mathrm{var}[r_t^*] = \mathrm{var}[r_t] + \mathrm{var}[r_t^* - r_t] \geq \mathrm{var}[r_t] \tag{10.24}$$

where r_t is the asset return at time t, and r_t^* is the realized return. The variance inequality describes the fact that a forecast conditional on historical estimates cannot be more variable than the quantity it is forecasting. In our portfolio context, a naïve portfolio risk forecast based on a finite sample of past asset returns will not be greater than that estimated in-sample, while the realized volatility does have the potential to be greater.

On the contrary, the orthant probability-based forecast estimation method, which accounts for time varying measures of association between trading signals (darkened circles representing equation (10.16) taken as a step-ahead forecast), systematically overestimates realized portfolio risk (triangles representing the standard deviations of portfolio returns over the entire study period). This overestimation is (on average) a factor of 1.06 for the case of uncorrelated trading model delivered weightings and increases as correlation approaches 0.50. Beyond this level, the overestimation again decreases as the realized estimation of risk accelerates more quickly. Empirical comparison of the normal-orthant probability-based formulation of volatility with *ex post* estimated volatility provides evidence of a 'peso problem' related phenomenon (Krasker, 1980). The risk forecast based on the normal orthant volatility formulation is on average greater than *ex post* estimated volatility due to the potential occurrence of events which have small probability but important potential consequences. When these events are not realized in a particular sample period, the normal-orthant forecast appears overly conservative.

At all correlation levels the orthant probability-based definition provides a step-ahead forecast which is consistently more conservative than the forecast arrived at through the conventional method (empty circles). The enhanced forecast magnitudes are a result of the fact that the orthant probability-based methodology includes information which is independent of the previous finite sample periods used to estimate individual asset volatilities. This information is the potential danger of correlation between the processes of making decisions about individual asset weights.

One also notes an asymptotic structure in the orthant probability-based forecast estimation which is not present in the *ex post* estimation. This structure is a direct result of the arcsine of trading model correlation present in equation (10.16). First, the risk forecast tends to be reduced at low correlation between trading models. When combining the risk of two assets, their individual risk is added in quadrature in the conventional way. However, a third term in the summation which involves correlation between assets is also dependent on correlation between asset weighting decisions. This latter term tends to be reduced at lower trading model decision correlation, a possibility that doesn't exist in the standard formulation (equation (10.12)). Second, at higher levels of correlation between trading model decisions, risk forecasts tend to be boosted as the non-linear effect of the arcsine again becomes apparent.

10.5 CONCLUSIONS

The volatility characteristics of investment portfolios have been re-examined from the perspective of long/short investment strategies. An orthant probability-based formulation for the description of portfolio risk proposed by Acar and Satchell (1998) was discussed. The standard and commonly accepted variance/covariance framework accounts for correlation between assets. However, the new formulation extends standard portfolio risk estimation in order also to account for potential correlation between the asset selection and weighting decisions which may periodically occur. The differences between the two approaches suggest that conventional estimation methods may not apply fully to the absolute risk of long/short strategies or the benchmark relative risk of long-only strategies, even under normal distribution assumptions.

Within this framework, an instantaneous estimation of association is introduced as a gauge of the similarity between asset weighting decisions at the time of portfolio construction or adjustment. For a given investment subperiod, this approach is viewed as more accurate than historical measures of association which estimate an average correlation over a previous, often arbitrarily selected, time period. In addition, a generalized, multivariate-orthant probability structure has been developed for variance estimation of portfolios containing any number of assets. This was achieved by circumventing the 2^N orthant sections framework and reducing the problem to a pairwise asset consideration of order N^2. This is similar to the treatment prescribed by the conventional variance estimate of multivariate linear combinations. To date, statistical science has provided an exact solution only for bivariate and trivariate orthant probabilities and the multivariate step is viewed as a critical necessity in view of the investment portfolio application.

This framework was then applied to the description of the value added by market neutral investment strategies. It is interesting to note that Monte Carlo results indicate that beta neutral investment strategies can be less risky than standard passive long investment strategies by a factor of 3 (as measured by the square root of the second moment of distributions with normal assumptions).

Monte Carlo results indicate that the commonly accepted method of estimating portfolio risk, when taken as a naïve step-ahead forecast, slightly but systematically underestimates active investment risk. This is the result of a variance inequality, previously observed in the literature, which dictates that a naïve portfolio risk forecast based on a finite sample of past asset returns cannot be greater than that estimated in-sample, while the realized volatility can be.

Simulations also indicate that the orthant probability-based method, taken as a step-ahead risk forecast, appears to overestimate volatility on average, when compared to *ex post* estimated volatility. The source of this additional risk is information which is independent of historical sample estimates of asset volatilities and correlations. Specifically, it is the correlation which exists between asset selection/weighting decisions. Empirical comparison of the orthant probability-based formulation of volatility with *ex post* estimated volatility provides evidence of a 'peso problem' related phenomenon. The risk forecast using the normal-orthant formulated volatility is on average greater than *ex post* estimated volatility due to the additional consideration of events which have small probabilities of occurrence, but important potential consequences when they do occur. When these events are not realized in a particular sample period, the normal-orthant-based forecast appears to have been overly conservative in its estimate. This additional risk component may explain both the underforecasted absolute risk of some alternative investment strategies as well as the underforecasted tracking error of more conventional investment strategies.

ACKNOWLEDGEMENTS

This work benefited greatly from discussions with Alan Scowcroft and Stephen Wright of UBS Warburg and Rudolph J. Rummel, Professor Emeritus of Political Science, University of Hawaii (http://www.mega.nu:8080/ampp/rummel/welcome.html).

REFERENCES

Acar, E. and Satchell, S. (1998) The portfolio distribution of directional strategies, in *Advanced Trading Rules*, E. Acar and S. Satchell (eds), pp. 103–111, Butterworth-Heinemann, Oxford, UK.

Ackermann, C., McEnally, R. and Ravenscraft, D. (1999) The performance of hedge funds: risk, return and incentives, *Journal of Finance*, **54**(3), June.

Brock, W., Lakonishock, J. and LeBaron, B. (1992) Simple technical rules and the stochastic properties of stock returns, *Journal of Finance*, **47**, 1731–1764.

Brown, L. (2001) An alternative calculation of tracking error, forthcoming in the *Journal of Asset Management*.

Campbell, J.Y., Lo, A.W. and MacKinlay, A.C. (1997) *The Econometrics of the Financial Markets*, Princeton University Press, Princeton, USA.

Farebrother, R.W. (1989) Letter to the editor: bivariate normal orthant probabilities, *The American Statistician*, **43**(4), 291.

Johnson, N., Kotz, S. and Balakrishnan, N. (1994) *Continuous Univariate Distributions*, Vol. 1, 2nd edition, p. 318, John Wiley & Sons, Inc. NY, USA.

Kepner, J.L., Harper, J.D. and Keith, S.Z. (1989) A note on evaluating a certain orthant probability, *The American Statistician*, **43**, 48–49.

Krasker, W.S. (1980) The peso problem in testing the efficiency of the forward exchange markets, *Journal of Monetary Economics*, **6**, 269–276.

LeRoy, S. and Porter, R. (1981) The present value relation: tests based on variance bounds, *Econometrica*, **49**, 555–577.

Liang, B. (1999) On the performance of hedge funds, *Financial Analysts Journal*, July/August 1999.

Litterman, R., Longerstaey, J., Rosengarten, J. and Windelmann, K. (2000) Risk budgeting for active investment managers, in *Risk Budgeting*, edited Leslie Rahl (ed.), pp. 131–158, Risk Waters Group Ltd, London, UK.

Lo, A.W. and MacKinlay, A.C. (1999) *A Non-Random Walk Down Wall Street*, Princeton University Press, Princeton, USA.

Rencher, A.C. (1995) *Methods of Multivariate Analysis*, pp. 55–57, John Wiley & Sons, Inc., NY, USA.

Richards, A.J. (1999) Idiosyncratic risk: an empirical analysis, with implications for the risk of relative-value trading strategies, International Monetary Fund Working Paper 99/148, November, 1999.

Roll, R. (1992) A mean-variance analysis of tracking error, *Journal of Portfolio Management*, **18**, 13–22.

Scowcroft, A. (1999) Tracking errors, Equities Quantitative Research Group Report, Warbug Dillon Read.

Sheppard, W.F. (1898) On the application of the theory of error to cases of normal distributions and normal correlations, *Phil. Trans., A*, **192**, 101f and *Proc. Roy. Soc.*, **62**, 170f.

Shiller, R. (1981) Do stock prices move too much to be justified by subsequent changes in dividends, *American Economic Review*, **71**, 421–436.

Stigler, S.M. (1989) Letter to the editor: normal orthant probabilities, *The American Statistician*, **43**(4), 291.

Stuart, A. and Ord, K. (1994) *Kendall's Advanced Theory of Statistics*, 6th edition, Vol. 1, p. 81, Edward Arnold, London.

Chapter 11

Relative performance and herding in financial markets

EMANUELA SCIUBBA

ABSTRACT

We consider a stylized model of a financial market where assets are traded over two periods by three agents: two fund managers and a third large trader who represents the rest of the market. Fund managers are rewarded at the end of the second period by a bonus that is awarded to the manager who obtains the best cumulative performance. We show that, even when information is symmetric, inefficient herding may be observed as an equilibrium outcome. Herding among fund managers occurs when the size of the rest of the market is large, but finite, so that the impact of the herd on equilibrium prices is not negligible and indeed destabilizing for asset prices.

11.1 INTRODUCTION

11.1.1 Motivation

The aim of this chapter is to assess the influence of relative performance incentives on portfolio choices and on asset price dynamics. We ask whether, to what extent and with which consequences on asset prices, portfolio choices can be affected by the fact that professional money managers aim at maximizing their relative, rather than absolute, performance.

Institutions hold an increasing portion of the value of equities. US institutional investors, who owned only 6.1% of all equities in 1950, now hold a total of $6.3 trillion, equivalent to 49.6% of total outstanding equities.[1] Private and public pension funds alone hold together $3.1 trillion, or 24% of equities. In Europe, the presence of institutional investors has not reached the same magnitude as in the US, but becomes increasingly conspicuous. In 1997, managed funds as a percentage of GDP were 70% in Italy, 59% in Germany, 93% in France, 58% in Spain, 197% in the Netherlands and 174% in the UK.[2]

Not only do institutional investors hold the largest share of equities, but they also account for most of the trading volume with their trading activity; most institutional investors follow strategies of actively picking and trading stocks. As a result, large institutions have become increasingly important in determining market prices. Understanding the behaviour of stock prices therefore requires an understanding of the investment strategies of institutional investors.

The common belief is that institutional investors move in and out of stocks in a herd-like manner. The idea that investors in general are influenced by the decisions of other investors dates back at least to Keynes' well-known metaphor of the beauty contest.[3] In particular, when it comes to institutional investors, both casual empiricism and empirical evidence[4] suggest that their portfolio decisions display herding behaviour. Fund managers are aware of this and often bluntly admit to following the crowd. Lakonishock, Shleifer and Vishny (1992) report from an interview to a pension fund manager: 'Institutions are herding animals. We watch the same indicators and listen to the same prognostications. Like lemmings, we tend to move in the same direction and at the same time. And that, naturally, exacerbates price movements' (p. 25). This latter observation is a major concern for practitioners and a challenge for financial economists: is herding behaviour destabilizing for stock prices?

The issue does not have an obvious answer. In general terms, one could be tempted to define herding as behaviour patterns that are correlated across individuals. However, if many investors are purchasing promising 'hot' stocks, correlated action might be due to the fact that they have all received positive relevant information on the same stocks. If so, investors are indeed making the market more efficient and speeding up the process of adjustment of prices to fundamentals. On the contrary, the notion of herding that one tends to

---

[1] American data are from the New York Stock Exchange *Fact Book*, 1998. For a better comparison with European data that follow, note that in the US the capital held by institutions in 1998 was 72% of GDP.

[2] European data are from the Bank of Italy (1998).

[3] Keynes (1936) claimed that professional investors behave like judges in a beauty contest who vote on the basis of contestants' expected popularity with other judges rather than on the basis of their absolute beauty.

[4] See for example Lakonishock, Shleifer and Vishny (1992) and Grinblatt, Titman and Wermers (1995).

associate with institutional investors is instead a negative one that leads to systematic suboptimal decision making.[5]

Recent empirical studies[6] have provided extensive evidence of inefficient herding behaviour by fund managers and have showed that the impact of institutional trading on stock prices has often been destabilizing.[7] Most of these studies have been motivated by the stock market crash of October 1987 and by the analysis of the crash itself made by the Brady Commission (Brady *et al.*, 1988), that mainly blamed institutional investors who followed formal and informal dynamic hedging strategies, or 'portfolio insurance' policies. As Lakonishock, Schleifer and Vishny (1992) point out, hedging strategies can clearly prove destabilizing if they lead institutions to 'jump on the bandwagon' and buy overpriced stocks and sell underpriced stocks, causing further divergence of prices from fundamentals.

Why do money managers herd? Grinblatt, Titman and Wermers (1995) study the correlation between the tendency of individual funds to herd and the fund performance and observe that the relation is indeed controversial. It is not at all clear that herding behaviour pays off in terms of absolute performance.

Two recent empirical studies have investigated the relation between performance and tendency to herd, but in the opposite direction: successful money managers will display a higher tendency to herd. Brown, Harlow and Starks (1996) and Chevalier and Ellison (1997) test the hypothesis that managers with either extremely good or bad relative returns at mid-year have incentives to alter the characteristics of their portfolios and change their risk profiles. Worst performing funds will take more risks, while better performing funds will tend to lock in their gains and 'index' the market. They examine portfolio changes in the last quarter of the year and attribute this striking result to the strong relationship between the inflow of new investment in the fund and the fund's past relative performance. In order to maximize investment inflow, money managers have to maximize the ranking of their funds. The flow–performance relationship works as an implicit incentive contract for the fund manager. Finally, the current system of assessing and reporting fund performance on an annual basis causes the 'end of the year' effect. Calendar year data appears to be the most generally available to consumers: listings

[5]See for example Banerjee (1992) and Bikhchandani, Hirshleifer and Welch (1992).

[6]See, for example, Cutler, Poterba and Summers (1990), De Long *et al.* (1990), Grinblatt, Titman and Wermers (1995) and Lakonishock, Shleifer and Vishny (1992), on the 1987 crash. Frankel and Froot (1990) study herding behaviour in the foreign exchange market.

[7]The empirical literature on 'excess price volatility' is too vast to try and attempt a review here. Seminal contributions are, for example, Shiller (1981a, 1981b, 1984) and Summers (1986). For an extended review of the empirical literature on the topic, see Shiller (1990).

of mutual funds, accompanied by calendar year returns, are published on an annual basis in many news, business and financial publications.

Ashton, Crossland and Moizer (1990) report some interesting interviews with money managers. They admit a tendency to herd: 'Fund managers as a group are complete wimps basically. There is fund manager risk aversion which I am sure you are becoming aware of, which is the desire to be in with the crowds, so that if everybody gets it wrong, then it doesn't matter' (p. 8). They confirm that relative performance is what matters: 'The fact of the matter is, if you are in the top decile. . ., you get patted on the head by the client. If you are in the bottom decile, you'll probably be fired. So the temptation is to be in the 3rd to the 7th and that means not deviating usually from the [index]. And because the [index] is what everybody else is doing, we're all chasing our own tail' (p. 8). 'It does not matter what your absolute performance is. It doesn't matter if you're plus 200%, if the market's plus 210%. What I have to do is to ensure that this fund can act as a window for our sales force. It's got to be median or above, otherwise we can't sell it' (p. 9).

In this chapter we do not question relative performance evaluation. We take such incentive schemes as given and we aim at providing a theoretical framework to study the relation between relative performance evaluation of fund managers, herding behaviour and destabilization of asset prices.

We consider a stylized dynamic model of a financial market where two assets, a risk-free and a risky asset, are traded over two periods by three agents: two fund managers and a third large trader who represents the rest of the market. Fund managers are rewarded at the end of the second period by means of a bonus that is awarded to the manager who obtains the best cumulative performance. The information on fundamentals is symmetric: all agents know the correct probability distribution over the return of the risky asset. Portfolio decisions are taken simultaneously by all agents at the beginning of each time period, and markets clear. We assume that rewards to fund managers are purely based on rank. In section 11.4.1 we discuss to what extent our results may extend to a model with mixed compensation schemes, based both on rank and absolute performance.

Our main result is that, even though information is symmetric, relative performance incentives serve as a coordination device for fund managers to herd. Herding can be observed as an equilibrium outcome under interesting economic circumstances. After a good realization of the risky asset and if the risky asset is still likely to yield a high payoff in the future, fund managers may herd on the safe asset. After a bad realization of the risky asset and if the risky asset is still likely to yield a low payoff in the future, fund managers may herd on the risky asset. Clearly the herding behaviour we obtain in equilibrium is inefficient. Relative performance evaluation may fail to provide the right incentives, and, as a result, fund managers might not pursue expected wealth maximization. This happens because of the dynamic framework that we are adopting. After one of the two fund managers has acquired a leadership position, in the last stage of the game his opponent might have no better alternative than to force him into an inefficient equilibrium.

More in detail, fund managers play a two-stage game, where they both prefer to play different strategies in at least one of the two stages, so that each of them has a positive chance of ending the first stage of the game in a leadership position. Suppose that, when they reach the beginning of the second period, one of the two fund managers displays superior interim performance. In the second stage, the game between fund managers becomes asymmetric and optimal strategies differ across the two players. In order to have a chance to catch up, the laggard wants to differentiate himself as much as possible from the leading manager; on the contrary, the leading manager wants to imitate the follower, to ensure that he stays ahead. However, if the wealth gap between the two funds is large enough, then the laggard may not have any possibility of catching up and will find it optimal to herd with the leader. It might happen, in fact, that by the end of the first period, the performance gap between the two funds is so large that only the riskiest strategy (the one that pays the highest payoff with the smallest probability) allows the laggard fund to catch up with the leader. The leading fund manager recognizes that the follower has a dominant investment strategy and, to ensure that he stays ahead, optimally chooses exactly the same portfolio as his opponent. Herding constitutes an equilibrium since the laggard has clearly no better alternative than his dominant strategy.

We characterize the conditions that may lead to herding as an equilibrium outcome. If the risky asset paid a high payoff in the first stage, herding in the safe asset may occur in the second stage if the probability of a good realization of the risky asset in the next stage is high enough. If the risky asset paid a low payoff in the first stage, herding in the risky asset may occur in the second stage if the probability of a high realization of the risky asset in the next stage is sufficiently low. The herding outcome we obtain is, therefore, inefficient. Moreover, interestingly enough, inefficient herding occurs when the size of the rest of the market is large, but finite, so that the impact of herding on equilibrium prices is not negligible and we can conclude that the presence of institutional investors is indeed destabilizing for asset prices.

This result proves particularly surprising in the light of the fact that we obtain herding behaviour and price destabilization, without assuming any degree of asymmetric information. It would seem reasonable to expect that the presence of information asymmetries, as in Gennotte and Leland (1990), should reinforce our results.

11.1.2 Related literature

There are at least three strands of literature that are related to this chapter: the literature on the economic rationale for relative performance evaluation and its effects; the vast literature on herding in financial markets; and finally the literature on excess volatility and price crashes.

It is well known that relative performance evaluation can enhance efficiency in a single-principal multi-agent setting. Mookherjee (1984) considers the situation where the agent's output depends not only on effort and idiosyncratic noise, but also on a common shock experienced by other agents. In these circumstances the optimal contract is based on relative performance evaluation. Nalebuff and Stiglitz (1983) consider a rank order tournament, i.e. a compensation scheme in which contestants' rewards are based on their ordinal positions alone and not on the size of their output, and show that such a structure is preferable to individualistic reward structures when environmental uncertainty is large. They prove that, in the limit, as the number of contestants becomes large, the outcome of a rank order tournament approximates first best. Gibbons and Murphy (1989) find similar properties for a relative performance evaluation scheme for chief executive officers. They also suggest that relative performance evaluation distorts workers' incentives whenever agents can take actions that affect the average output of their reference group; for example, when they get to choose their co-workers, or when they can collude.

Most of these contributions, however, analyse the agency problem in a static setting. Meyer and Vickers (1997) show that, in a dynamic setting, comparative performance evaluation has an ambiguous impact, and that it is not guaranteed that it enhances efficiency. Indeed, some recent work[8] proves that relative performance evaluation might be undesirable in specific dynamic settings; for example, when agents not only choose the level of effort (expected return) but also the riskiness of their actions (variance). This is particularly relevant for money managers, who clearly control both the expected return and the risk of their portfolios. Hvide (2002) studies a situation where agents also get to decide on the riskiness of their actions. He proves that a contract that ranks agents according to the relative closeness of their output to a benchmark (rather than ranking them against each other) can be beneficial to limit the risk that the agent might be willing to take. He argues that this could serve as a rationale for the fact that sometimes modest outcomes are more highly rewarded than very high performances.

Hvide and Kristiansen (1999) also look at the efficiency of relative performance evaluation when agents can decide on risks to be taken. Differently from Hvide (2002), they analyse how well contests select talented

[8] See, for example, Hvide (2002), Hvide and Kristiansen (1999) and Palomino and Prat (1999).

agents, rather than how well contests provide the right incentives to elicit effort. Their main result is rather counterintuitive: a better quality of the pool of contestants might reduce the efficiency of the contest. This happens because a more competitive tournament (a tournament with participants of higher quality) induces agents to adopt riskier strategies, which might harm the selection of high quality individuals. Riskier projects create more noise in the selection contest, thereby reducing the informativeness of the rank.

Finally, Palomino and Prat (1999) develop a general model of delegated portfolio management with the feature that the agent can control the riskiness of the portfolio. In the static case, the optimal contract is a bonus contract, based on relative performance. In the multi-period case, the bonus contract is no longer first-best. The intuition for their result lies in the fact that in a dynamic setting the agent can revise his portfolio choice after observing his performance at intermediate stages. This is particularly true if we believe that investors can evaluate the agent's performance less often that he can revise his portfolio decisions. The same idea is in the empirical work by Chevalier and Ellison (1997): mutual fund managers control investment volatility continuously, while investors receive performance information at discrete time intervals.

In the setting that we investigate, the results by Palomino and Prat are put to work in a market setting. We show that a bonus contract may indeed prove inefficient and we characterize the type of distortion that it may cause both on portfolios and on asset prices.

Within the literature on relative performance evaluation, some contributions have also looked at the problem of information acquisition. Eichberger, Grant and King (1997) look at a model where fund managers are rewarded on the basis of relative performance and have to decide whether to gather information and how to allocate their portfolios. They find that there are multiple equilibria, so that relative performance evaluation might or might not provide the right incentives. Gümbel (1998) considers a similar model in a market setting. Interestingly enough, he obtains efficient herding as an equilibrium outcome. Herding in information acquisition is induced by the principal (agents want to acquire the same piece of information as their competitors) and it increases the informational efficiency of prices.[9]

[9]Herding in information acquisition due to relative performance incentives is also one of the results of Maug and Naik (1996) and Palomino (1999). Palomino (1999) considers an oligopolistic market model à la Kyle (1985) where fund managers that aim at maximizing relative performance, decide on both information acquisition and portfolio composition. He finds that, in portfolio decisions, relative performance evaluation leads to overly-risky strategies. Moreover, a risk neutral (or weakly risk averse) fund manager will invest too little in information acquisition; a strongly risk averse fund manager, on the contrary, invests too much in information. Maug and Naik (1996) find conditions such that better informed fund managers ignore their own superior information to reduce deviations from the benchmark.

There is a clear similarity and several important differences between Gümbel (1998) and this chapter. In Gümbel, the author obtains herding in equilibrium as an effect of relative performance evaluation. However, in Gümbel herding is in the information acquisition policy, while we obtain herding in portfolios. Moreover, in Gümbel herding is efficient and makes asset prices more informative, while in this chapter herding can also be inefficient and drive asset prices further away from fundamentals. Finally, the market structure in Gümbel is an oligopoly à la Kyle (1985), while we look at a competitive market.

This chapter is close in spirit to some recent work by Cabral (1999) and Palomino and Prat (1999). Cabral considers an infinite-period race where players choose between alternative growth technologies. He provides sufficient conditions under which, in equilibrium, the leader chooses a safe technology and the laggard a risky one; and conditions under which the laggard prefers to differentiate from the leader whereas the leader prefers to imitate the follower. Palomino and Prat analyse competition over two investment periods between two money managers that have ranking-based objectives. They derive conditions on intermediate performances under which managers play conservative and overly risky strategies and find that, if the difference in performances in the first period is large, the interim winner has incentives to minimize the level of risk undertaken in the second period to lock in his gain of the first period.

This chapter shares some of the intuition for its results with Cabral (1999) and Palomino and Prat (1999). However, we adapt their analysis to a financial market setting, with the main difference that Cabral and Palomino and Prat only analyse the game between contestants, while we also look at the market equilibrium and at the effects of contestants' behaviour on endogenous asset prices.[10]

The second strand of literature that is related to this chapter is the literature on herding behaviour. Within the research on herding we can distinguish two different views: a non-rational view, that attributes inefficient herding behaviour to imitation and mimicry instincts and to investors' psychology; and a rational view, that shows that inefficient herding may obtain as an equilibrium outcome of a game played by fully rational investors. The rational

[10]General equilibrium implications of fund managers' compensation fees are also studied by Cuoco and Kaniel (1999). They develop a continuous-time market model and analyse the implications on portfolios and asset pricing of different types of fund managers' compensation fees. They find that symmetric (fulcrum type) performance fees, that also penalize funds' underperformance with respect to the benchmark, tilt fund managers' portfolios towards stocks that are represented in the benckmark. On the contrary, asymmetric compensation fees that reward performance without penalizing underperformance to the same extent, may tilt funds' portfolios towards stocks that have a very low correlation with the benchmark.

view (which this chapter adopts) has centred on three different approaches, that can be summarized as follows: presence of payoff externalities, informational cascades and principal–agent models. An example within the first approach is given by models of information acquisition. Agents might herd on information acquisition as they find it worthwhile to acquire further information only if other agents also do.[11] In the model we propose there is neither information acquisition externalities nor other payoff externalities, but herding is still obtainable as an equilibrium outcome.

The second approach provides the most common explanation of herding. It builds on the idea that agents gain useful information from observing previous agents' decisions, to the point that they optimally and rationally completely ignore their own private information, and herd. Informational cascades have been introduced[12] by Bikhchandani, Hirshleifer and Welch (1992), Banerjee (1992) and Welch (1992). In this chapter decision making is simultaneous and information is symmetric, so that social learning and informational cascades have no role.

Here, herding occurs because of relative performance incentives, so that our framework is closer to the third approach, where herding is obtained as an outcome of agency problems. A similar perspective is adopted by Scharfstein and Stein (1990). They develop a model where managers are concerned about their reputation and therefore simply mimic the investment decisions of other managers, ignoring substantial private information. A 'sharing the blame' effect drives them to herd. A crucial feature of their model is that they assume that a manager does not know his quality; however, he knows that if he is smart he will observe the same signal as other smart managers in the market.

A similar setting is developed by Zwiebel (1995). He obtains the same result as Scharfstein and Stein (1990), but with a different information structure. He assumes that managers know their own ability; however, because of reputational concerns, they still refrain from undertaking innovations that stochastically dominate the industry standard and get locked in inferior equilibria. Zwiebel calls this type of behaviour 'corporate conservatism'.

The main differences between Scharfstein and Stein (1990) and Zwiebel (1995) and this chapter are the following: first of all, herding behaviour in our setting does not stem from reputational concerns, but from relative performance evaluation. We assume that fund managers have the same ability and the same quality of information. Second, and most importantly, we analyse a market setting, where the effect of herding on asset prices is also studied.

[11] See, for example, Gümbel (1998).

[12] See also Gale (1996) that argues on the robustness of some of the results obtained by the literature on social learning and informational cascades.

Finally, this chapter is also related to the literature on price crashes and in particular to the literature that studies the role of the behaviour of institutional investors in price crashes.[13] Gennotte and Leland (1990) develop a financial market model where a relatively small amount of dynamic hedging strategies can cause asset prices to fall significantly. The driving force of their result lies in the fact that, even if there are only a few hedgers, there are traders who infer information from market prices. As a result, the effects of hedging activity on asset prices are magnified. A similar setting is in Jacklin, Kleidon and Pfleiderer (1992). They examine the role played by formal and informal dynamic hedging strategies in the market crash of October 1987. They provide a theoretical underpinning for the stylized fact that, in the period prior to the crash, prices are higher than fundamentals would imply. The intuition for their result is that information on the extent of portfolio insurance is revealed only slowly through time, so that, prior to a crash, the market is indeed underestimating the size of hedgers that are active in the market. When the amount of portfolio insurance is fully revealed, the price falls.

In this chapter we obtain excess volatility. The driving force in our case is not the presence of hedgers, but the custom of rewarding money managers according to their relative performance.

11.1.3 Overview

The outline of the rest of this chapter is as follows. In section 11.2 we present the basic structure of our model in a simplified setting: we look at a two-period investment model where investors choose between alternative assets whose returns are assumed to be exogenous. In sections 11.2.1 and 11.2.2 we respectively solve for the equilibria of the game played by investors in the last and interim stages. In section 11.2.3 we summarize and characterize all the different equilibrium paths that we can obtain in the two-stage game. Section 11.2.4 shows that one important simplifying assumption that we use in the analysis is without loss of generality in our setting. Finally section 11.2.5 highlights some of the features of this simple model and suggests how to extend it to a financial market model, where asset prices are indeed endogenous.

In section 11.3 we extend our analysis to a financial market model and we present our main results. In particular, in section 11.3.1 we look at the game played by fund managers in the interim stage; in section 11.3.2 we prove

[13] Another approach to price crashes is, for example, in Bulow and Klemperer (1994). They argue that when buyers can also decide on the timing of their purchases, then 'willingness to pay' is much more elastic than demand to price. They show how this feature may lead to 'frenzies' (all agents buying at once) and 'crashes' in a simple auction setting.

existence and uniqueness of a market clearing equilibrium for each stage of the game; finally, in section 11.3.3 we present the main results of our analysis: we characterize sufficient conditions for inefficient herding to be obtained as an equilibrium outcome in the second stage of the game and we show that the herding behaviour thus obtained is indeed destabilizing for asset prices.

In section 11.4 we examine the robustness of our analysis in less simplified environments and we suggest directions for future research.

Section 11.5 concludes the chapter.

For ease of exposition, all proofs are in the appendix.

11.2 A MODEL WITH LINEAR TECHNOLOGIES

Consider a simple two-period investment model where investors, at the beginning of each time period, choose between two alternative technologies to store wealth: a safe technology A and a risky technology B. Both technologies are linear, so that, if wealth available for investment at the beginning of period t (end of period $t-1$), w_{t-1}, is invested in the safe technology A, the total return at the end of period t is:

$$w_t = Aw_{t-1}$$

If the risky technology B is chosen for investment in period t, then the investment income at t is:

$$w_t = \tilde{B}_t w_{t-1}$$

where $\tilde{B}_t$ is equal to B^H with probability $p > 0$ and to B^L with probability $(1-p) > 0$. We assume that $B^L < A < B^H$.

There are two professional investors that manage identical wealth endowments at $t = 0$, both normalized to be equal to 1. Investors choose technologies twice (at $t = 0$ and at $t = 1$) and cash investment incomes twice (at $t = 1$ and $t = 2$). Technology choices last for one period only, so that investors may or may not adopt the same technology twice. Investors have no other way to store wealth, so that the initial endowment is entirely invested in the technology chosen for the first period. Similarly, the investment income from the first period is entirely invested in the technology chosen for the second period. We also assume that investors cannot hold 'portfolios' of technologies, but only invest in one technology at a time. In what follows (see section 11.2.4), we show that this assumption is without loss of generality in our setting: if investors care only about their ranking, they prefer to hold 'extreme portfolios', where only one technology is represented.[14]

[14]When investors also care about their absolute performance, they have an incentive to diversify. However, in section 11.4 we argue that how our main results should prove robust to such changes in the model, provided that the reward component based on ranking is large compared to the reward component based on absolute performance.

The economic agents that get to choose which technology to adopt are indeed professional investors managing clients' money, rather than their own. Hence we assume that they do not derive utility directly from the investment incomes that they obtain on behalf of their clients. Investors in our model only care about their compensation. The investor that ends up with the largest wealth at $t = 2$ obtains a strictly positive bonus; in case of tie, nobody gets the bonus.[15] This latter feature implies that investors will never want to adopt the same sequence of technologies, with the result that a tie will never be observed in equilibrium.

11.2.1 The bonus stage

In the simple world we are describing, fund managers play a two-stage game, where payoffs (the bonus) are distributed only at the end of the second stage. Players aim at reaching the leadership position in order to win the bonus. We can solve the game backwards: call the two stages of play interim and bonus stage respectively, and focus on the bonus stage first.

We need to fix a history for the interim stage. Suppose that investors choose different assets in the first stage of play, so to reach the bonus stage with 'leader' and 'follower' roles. Moreover, consider the case $\tilde{B}_1 = B^H$ first. After a 'good' realization of the risky technology in the interim stage, at $t = 1$, the player who invested in technology B is the leader and the player who invested in the safe technology A is the follower. Call asymmetric bonus subgame the game that leader and follower play against each other in the bonus stage, after having played asymmetrically in the first stage. Let us call player i and player j the leader and the follower at date $t = 1$, respectively. Also let us follow the convention of having the interim follower as first (row) player and the interim leader as second (column) player.

In the asymmetric bonus subgame, if both managers invest in the same technology (strategy profiles AA and BB), then clearly the interim leader (player i) will win the bonus with probability 1. If they invest in different technologies then the interim follower might (or might not) catch up with the interim leader. In particular, if, in the bonus stage, follower and leader invest in the risky and safe technologies respectively (strategy profile BA), player i's wealth is equal to $B^H A$ and player j's wealth is equal to $A\tilde{B}_2$. As a result, if in the second stage $\tilde{B}_2 = B^H$, we have a tie (and nobody gets the bonus), if $\tilde{B}_2 = B^L$ then player i wins the bonus. If we normalize the size of the bonus

[15] This assumption simplifies our analysis. It also finds support by the empirical evidence: Brown, Harlow and Starks (1996) and Chevalier and Ellison (1997) show that the fund's new money flow-performance relationship, that acts as an implicit incentive contract for the fund manager, is convex. 'Real' leaders are more generously compensated.

to 1, expected payoffs to the interim follower and leader, with the strategy profile BA, are 0 and $(1 - p)$, respectively. One last case to consider is the strategy profile AB; when the interim follower invests in the safe technology and the interim leader in the risky one, then the follower might indeed have the chance to outperform the leader. The outcome will depend on our parametric assumptions. If $A^2 > B^H B^L$ then the follower will outperform the leader and win the bonus. If, on the contrary, $A^2 < B^H B^L$, then the interim leader will stay leader and get the bonus. Finally, if $A^2 = B^H B^L$, we have a tie and none of the investors wins the bonus.

The asymmetric bonus subgame that interim leader and follower play, under these three different parametric assumptions, can be summarized by the following payoff matrices, where bold payoffs identify equilibria:

1. If $A^2 > B^H B^L$:

Follower/Leader	A	B
A	**0; 1**	$1 - p$; p
B	0; $1 - p$	0; 1

2. If $A^2 < B^H B^L$:

Follower/Leader	A	B
A	**0; 1**	**0; 1**
B	0; $1 - p$	**0; 1**

3. If $A^2 = B^H B^L$:

Follower/Leader	A	B
A	**0; 1**	0; p
B	0; $1 - p$	**0; 1**

In case (1), the asymmetric bonus subgame has a unique Nash equilibrium, AA. When players reach the second stage of the game with non-identical wealth, after a good realization of the risky technology in the first stage, both players will play safe in the bonus stage and invest their whole endowment in the safe technology. In case (2), Nash equilibria for the asymmetric bonus subgame (in pure strategies) are: AA, AB, BB. Players will either both invest in the safe technology, or both in the risky technology, or, finally, both adopt the same technologies they had chosen in the interim stage (i.e. leader and follower will respectively invest in the risky and the safe technology). In case (3), Nash equilibria for the asymmetric bonus subgame (in pure strategies) are: AA, BB.

Similarly, we can examine what is the play in the bonus stage, after the history $\tilde{B}_1 = B^L$ for the interim stage. Once again, suppose that investors choose different assets in the first stage of play, so to reach the bonus stage with 'leader' and 'follower' roles. In this case, we call player i the player who invested his endowment in the safe technology in the interim stage, so that i is the interim leader at $t = 1$. We call j the player who invested his wealth in the risky technology in the interim stage, so that j is the interim follower at $t = 1$. In the bonus stage, if both players invest in the same technology, clearly player i (the interim leader) will stay leader and win the bonus with probability 1. If they invest in different technologies, then the interim follower, under some conditions, outperforms the interim leader. Like above, different parametric assumptions imply different sets of equilibria for the asymmetric bonus subgame (equilibrium payoffs are in bold):

1. If $A^2 < B^H B^L$:

Follower/Leader	A	B
A	0; 1	0; p
B	p; $1-p$	**0; 1**

2. If $A^2 > B^H B^L$:

Follower/Leader	A	B
A	**0; 1**	0; p
B	**0; 1**	**0; 1**

3. If $A^2 = B^H B^L$:

Follower/Leader	A	B
A	**0; 1**	0; p
B	0; $1-p$	**0; 1**

As one might have expected, the results we obtain are symmetric to what we found in the previous case above. In case (1), the asymmetric bonus subgame has a unique Nash equilibrium, BB. In the last stage of game, if players have non-identical wealth and after a bad realization of the risky asset in the interim stage, both players play risky and invest their whole endowment in the risky technology. In case (2), Nash equilibria for the asymmetric bonus subgame (in pure strategies) are: AA, BA, BB. Players will either both invest in the safe technology, or both in the risky technology, or, finally, both adopt the same technologies they had chosen in the interim stage (i.e. leader and follower will respectively invest in the risky and the safe technology). In case (3), Nash equilibria for the asymmetric bonus subgame (in pure strategies) are: AA,

BB. Once again, in the second stage of play, investors will adopt the same technology in equilibrium.

Let us now consider a different history for the interim stage. Suppose that investors choose the same technology to store wealth in the first period. The two fund managers (identical at $t = 0$) will reach the bonus stage with identical wealth endowments. Since there is no 'interim leader', investors play a symmetric subgame in the bonus stage, where they both try to reach for the leadership.

Recall that we are assuming that in the case of a tie nobody gets the bonus; fund managers have to outperform their opponents in order to qualify for the reward.[16] As a result, in the symmetric bonus subgame investors will choose to store wealth in different technologies. Payoffs can be summarized by the following matrix, where equilibrium payoffs are denoted in bold.

First player/Second player	*A*	*B*
A	0; 0	$\mathbf{1-p}$; $\boldsymbol{p}$
B	$\boldsymbol{p}$; $\mathbf{1-p}$	0; 0

In this case the (pure strategies) Nash equilibria of the symmetric bonus subgame are *AB* and *BA*.

Summarizing, depending on parametric assumptions, the bonus subgame that follows an asymmetric play in the interim stage may display one, two or three Nash equilibria. All equilibria are payoff equivalent. In particular it is always possible for the interim leader to keep his leadership in equilibrium and win the bonus with probability one at the end of the second stage. Whenever investors play asymmetrically in the interim stage, the actual bonus winner is in fact determined by the end of the first period.

On the contrary, when investors play symmetrically in the first period, the bonus winner is to be determined in the second stage of the game. In this case, the bonus subgame always has two Nash equilibria. Both equilibria are asymmetric and they are not payoff equivalent. Depending on how likely the risky asset is to yield a high payoff (the value of the probability p), each fund manager will be better off in one equilibrium rather than in the other.

11.2.2 The interim stage

Solving the game backwards, we can now ask which strategies will fund managers optimally choose in the interim stage, given the equilibrium outcomes of the following subgames.

[16] Recall footnote 15 above.

The payoffs to fund managers who invest asymmetrically in the first stage (strategy profiles AB and BA) are easy to compute. When investors play different strategies in the first stage of the game, the asymmetric bonus subgame displays payoff equivalent Nash equilibria. Hence, solving the game backwards, one does not need to distinguish between different equilibrium outcomes in the bonus stage. In fact, along any equilibrium path which starts with investors following asymmetric play, the interim leader is guaranteed to be bonus winner, so that expected payoffs to each of the players are indeed equal to the probabilities of becoming interim leaders. As a result, the expected payoff to a fund manager that invests in the risky technology, while his opponent is investing in the safe technology, is equal to p; his opponent's expected payoff is $(1 - p)$.

When investors choose the same technology in the first stage of play (strategy profiles AA and BB), the bonus subgame displays two Nash equilibria which are not payoff equivalent. Hence, expected payoffs in the interim stage are conditional on the specific equilibrium that prevails in the second stage of the game. We can therefore distinguish between four different cases.

1. Suppose, first, that after symmetric play in the first stage (strategy profiles AA and BB), the equilibrium AB prevails in the second stage of the game, so that the first player wins the bonus with probability $(1 - p)$ and the second player wins the bonus with probability p. In the interim stage the payoff matrix would look as follows:

First player/Second player	A	B
A	$1 - p;\quad p$	$1 - p;\quad p$
B	$p;\quad 1 - p$	$1 - p;\quad p$

   The (pure strategies) Nash equilibria of the game played in the interim stage depend on the value of p. If p is small (in particular, if $p < 1/2$), then AA and AB are equilibria. If p is large (in particular, if $p > 1/2$), then BB and AB are equilibria.

2. Suppose, on the opposite, that after both AA and BB in the first stage, the equilibrium BA prevails in the second stage of the game, so that the first player wins the bonus with probability p and the second player wins the bonus with probability $(1 - p)$. In the interim stage the payoff matrix would look as follows:

First player/Second player	A	B
A	$p;\quad 1 - p$	$1 - p;\quad p$
B	$p;\quad 1 - p$	$p;\quad 1 - p$

The (pure strategies) Nash equilibria of the game played in the interim stage depend on the value of p. If p is small (in particular, if $p < 1/2$), then AA and BA are equilibria. If p is large (in particular, if $p > 1/2$), then BB and BA are equilibria.

3. Suppose, now, that after AA in the first stage, the equilibrium that prevails in the second stage is AB and that, after BB in the first stage, the equilibrium that prevails in the second stage is BA. In the interim stage the payoff matrix would look as follows:

First player/Second player	A	B
A	$1-p$; p	$1-p$; p
B	p; $1-p$	p; $1-p$

The (pure strategies) Nash equilibria of the game played in the interim stage depend on the value of p. If p is small (in particular, if $p < 1/2$), then AA and AB are equilibria. If p is large (in particular, if $p > 1/2$), then BB and BA are equilibria.

4. Finally, suppose that after AA in the first stage, the equilibrium that prevails in the second stage is BA and that, after BB in the first stage, the equilibrium that prevails in the second stage is AB. In the interim stage the payoff matrix would look as follows:

First player/Second player	A	B
A	p; $1-p$	$1-p$, p
B	p; $1-p$	$1-p$; p

The (pure strategies) Nash equilibria of the game played in the interim stage depend on the value of p. If p is small (in particular, if $p < 1/2$), then AA and BA are equilibria. If p is large (in particular, if $p > 1/2$), then BB and AB are equilibria.

11.2.3 Equilibrium paths

In the previous two sections we have solved the two-stage game between fund managers by backward induction. We can now finally summarize and characterize the whole equilibrium paths.

The game between fund managers clearly displays a multiplicity of equilibria. However, we can conveniently distinguish between two types of equilibrium paths, according to players' behaviour in the first stage of the game.

Symmetric play in the first stage

If the two players invest in the same technology in the interim stage (strategy profiles AA and BB), then they will invest in different technologies in the bonus stage. In particular, if the risky technology has a higher probability than the safe technology of paying the highest return (i.e. $p > \frac{1}{2}$), then both players will invest in the risky technology in the first stage. Hence we will observe BB in the first period, followed by either AB or BA in the bonus stage. On the contrary, if the safe technology has a higher probability than the risky technology of paying the highest return (i.e. $p < \frac{1}{2}$), then both players will invest in the safe technology in the first stage. Hence we will observe AA in the first period, followed by either AB or BA in the bonus stage.

Along these equilibrium paths fund managers 'herd' in the first stage of play. They both invest in the risky asset if it pays a high payoff with a sufficiently large probability; they herd on the safe asset if its risky alternative has a small probability of yielding a high payoff. Herding in this case cannot be asserted to be necessarily 'inefficient'. In fact the behaviour of fund managers is consistent with the maximization of the expected value of some increasing and concave function of wealth.

Throughout the rest of this chapter we call 'efficient' a herding behaviour that is consistent with expected utility maximization, while we call inefficient the behaviour which is not consistent with the maximization of the expected value of an increasing and concave function of wealth.

Asymmetric play in the first stage

If the two players invest in different technologies in the interim stage (strategy profiles AB and BA), then in the bonus stage we might have either one or two or even three payoff equivalent Nash equilibria, depending on parameter values and on the realization of the risky technology in the interim stage. Interestingly enough one notices that the only equilibrium outcome which all parametric specifications have in common is such that in the second period investors herd in the technology which has been the least successful in the first period. In particular, fund managers herd in the safe technology in the bonus stage, if the risky technology has paid a high payoff in the interim stage. On the contrary, they herd in the risky technology in the bonus stage, if the risky technology has paid a low payoff in the interim stage. Moreover, the expected return of the risky technology plays no role in such an equilibrium outcome and indeed both players might find themselves optimally investing in the risky technology even when it yields a lower expected return than the safe technology.

For the insights that they provide, and namely for the fact that they might lead to inefficient herding, these equilibrium paths are more interesting than the first ones. For this reason in what follows we will mainly focus on the behaviour of fund managers after asymmetric play (i.e. we will concentrate on the behaviour of fund managers in the asymmetric bonus subgame).

11.2.4 Do fund managers hold 'Extreme' portfolios?

In the model described in this section, we have assumed that fund managers can either invest in the safe technology or in the risky technology: they cannot invest their endowments in a diversified portfolio of technologies. We can show that, so long as investors are rewarded on the basis of their relative performance, this assumption is without loss of generality. Namely, even if allowed to hold portfolios of technologies, they would optimally choose 'extreme' portfolio compositions and invest their entire endowments in only one of the available technologies.

For example, let us consider the asymmetric bonus subgame after a good realization of the risky technology in the interim stage. We know from our previous analysis that, when fund managers cannot diversify, under the parametric condition $A^2 > B^H B^L$, the unique Nash equilibrium of the asymmetric bonus subgame is AA, i.e. both players will choose the safe technology. We can easily prove that, even when we assume that money managers can diversify their portfolios (and hence consider a larger strategy space for the two players), under the same parametric conditions, 'all the money in safe' is still a Nash equilibrium of the extended subgame.

Suppose, in fact, that the interim follower is having all his endowment invested in the safe technology. It is clearly a best reply for the interim leader to mimic his opponent's portfolio. Hence 'all the money in safe' is what the leader will rationally choose to do. Suppose, now, that the interim leader is having all his endowment invested in the safe technology; does the interim follower have an incentive to deviate from 'all the money in safe'? If he diverts part of his resources to the risky technology, he cannot do any better, as our parametric conditions guarantee that catching up with the interim leader is excluded anyway. If we assume that there is a small (even lexicographic) cost in investing in two technologies (or assets) rather than one, then clearly the follower will strictly prefer to herd with the leader, rather than holding a diversified portfolio that costs him more and yields the same expected bonus.

Moreover, the assumption of a small (even lexicographic) cost for diversification implies that (for example, in the same parametric case we have considered above) 'all the money in safe' for both fund managers is the unique Nash equilibrium, also in the subgame where the strategy space is given by portfolios of technologies.

In fact, any strategy profile such that one fund manager is investing in an 'extreme' portfolio and the other fund manager is investing in a mix of technologies cannot be an equilibrium. The player who is holding a diversified portfolio, can optimally respond with a single technology (the same as his opponent's if he is the interim leader; the one that his opponent is not adopting, if he is the interim follower). If he deviates from the candidate equilibrium, his expected bonus will be the same and he will save on lexicographic costs.

Similarly we can show that we cannot have an equilibrium where both fund managers hold diversified portfolios. Suppose in fact that a fund manager is facing an opponent that is holding a diversified portfolio, then he can optimally respond to his opponent by using a single technology. Once again, his expected bonus will be the same and he will save on lexicographic costs.

Following similar arguments we can show that fund managers optimally choose to hold 'extreme' portfolios in the symmetric bonus subgame and in the interim stage.

Clearly, if we consider a framework where fund managers are not compensated on the basis of their relative performance only, but also on account of their absolute performance, fund managers will retain some incentives to diversify. In section 11.4.1, however, we show how and to what extent our analysis might hold in a more general setting.

11.2.5 Towards a market model

The model we have described in this section is extremely simple. Yet it seems to provide a plausible explanation of how relative performance incentives lead to herding behaviour. It allows us to characterize the resulting herding behaviour as (possibly) efficient, when it occurs in the first stage of the game, and as (possibly) inefficient when it occurs in the second stage. Within this simple model we can also show how this latter type of herding outcome (herding in the bonus stage) is path dependent in a rather counterintuitive fashion. In particular, we showed that, after a good realization of the risky technology, investors might in fact abandon it and move in a herd like manner towards the available alternative, the safe technology. Symmetrically, after a bad realization of the risky technology, all fund managers might abandon its safer alternative. Both effects are well known in the empirical literature in finance respectively as the 'lock-in effect' and the 'gambling effect'.[17]

However, we would encounter serious difficulties in stretching the validity of this simple model's implications to the functioning of a financial market. This is primarily because of the fact that in the technologies' adoption model that we have described, rates of return (A and $\tilde{B}_t$) are exogenously given as parameters of the model. In a financial market, on the contrary, one would expect rates of return to depend on asset prices and hence to be a market outcome. In section 11.3 we try to overcome this problem, modelling a similar relative incentive structure within a competitive market, so that rates of return are endogenous. We will show that a market model retains all the interesting

[17]See, for example, Chevalier and Ellison (1997) and Brown, Harlow and Starks (1996).

features of the simple model with linear technologies. In particular, we prove that inefficient herding can be observed as an equilibrium outcome. Moreover, we show that the same counterintuitive path dependency as in the model with linear technologies obtains in the market model: provided that they reach the second stage of the game with non-identical wealth and under some simple parametric conditions, fund managers herd on the safe asset, if the risky asset just paid a high return; on the contrary, they herd on the risky asset, if it just paid a low return in the interim stage.

Moreover, in the next section we show that a market model displays a clear advantage with respect to the simple model with linear technologies. The fact that the values of A, B^H and B^L are not exogenous in a market model, besides from being more realistic, helps our results. In fact we are able to identify simple parametric conditions on the probability distribution of the returns of the risky asset and on the market size, such that in the second stage of the game (and after asymmetric play in the interim stage) conditions equivalent to $A^2 > B^H B^L$ when $\tilde{B}_1 = B^H$ in the interim stage, and $A^2 < B^H B^L$ when $\tilde{B}_1 = B^L$ in the interim stage, are endogenously obtained. The parametric conditions needed to obtain our herding result clearly suggest that herding behaviour in the bonus stage is inefficient. Namely the fund managers' demand for the risky asset is decreasing in the probability of the risky asset paying a high payoff, which is inconsistent with the maximization of any increasing and concave utility function of wealth. Moreover, we show that inefficient herding among fund managers occurs when the size of the rest of the market is large, but finite, so that the impact of the herd on equilibrium prices is not negligible and indeed destabilizing for asset prices.

11.3 A MARKET MODEL

We consider a market where two assets are traded: a safe asset A and a risky asset B. In each period there is one unit of each asset available: one unit of asset A pays a known payoff w_A at the end of each period, irrespective of the state of nature; one unit of asset B pays w_B^H with probability p and w_B^L with probability $(1 - p)$. We assume that $w_B^L < w_A < w_B^H$. Denote the market prices of the two assets, in period t, by ρ_{At} and ρ_{Bt}. (*Ex post*) rates of return are:

$$A_t = \frac{w_A}{\rho_{At}} \tag{11.1}$$

$$B_t^H = \frac{w_B^H}{\rho_{Bt}} \tag{11.2}$$

$$B_t^L = \frac{w_B^L}{\rho_{Bt}} \tag{11.3}$$

There are three different investors in this market: investors i and j, fund managers who are motivated by relative performance incentives identical to what we described for the model with linear technologies, and a trader endowed with a logarithmic utility function which is representative of the rest of the market.[18] At $t = 0$, the two fund managers have identical wealth endowments, which we normalize to be equal to 1; the rest of the market has wealth equal to M. Investing in the two available assets is the only way to store wealth, so that the entire endowment is invested in the first stage and the entire investment income obtained in the first stage is reinvested in the second stage. The objective of the two fund managers is to win the bonus at the end of the second stage; the objective of the rest of the market, in each stage, is to maximize the expected log of end of period wealth.[19]

All traders are price takers. However, the two fund managers take their portfolio decisions strategically to outperform each other and win the bonus.

11.3.1 The interim stage

In the interim stage, the two fund managers behave exactly as we have described in section 11.2.2 for the model with linear technologies. Since in the case of a tie nobody wins the bonus, fund managers who are initially endowed with identical wealth will try and differentiate their investment strategies in at least one of the two stages. If they invest in the same asset in the interim stage, then only asymmetric equilibria are possible in the bonus subgame. In equilibrium, the asset on which both money managers herd in the first period is the one with higher probability of paying the highest return. As we argued in the previous section, this behaviour can be consistent with some type of expected utility maximization. Hence when fund managers herd in the first stage of play their behaviour is not inefficient in the sense used in this chapter.

Matters get more interesting if we focus, instead, on asymmetric play in the interim stage. Suppose that, in the first period of trade, each fund manager entrusts his unitary wealth endowment to a different asset. Recall from section 11.2.4 that, if investors only care about their ranking, they will

[18]Our choice to model the trader that is representative of the rest of the market as a logarithmic utility maximizer, finds support in the literature on survival of traders in financial markets. Logarithmic utility maximization is the 'fittest' behaviour in a risky environment like the one modelled here: in a financial market with heterogeneous traders, logarithmic utility maximizers will dominate, determine asset prices asymptotically and drive to extinction any other trader who does not behave as a logarithmic utility maximizer, at least in the long run. See, for example, the seminal paper by Blume and Easley (1992) and some recent work by Sciubba (1999a) and (1999b).

[19]Another clear advantage of logarithmic utility is that the 'myopic' optimization problem that we are solving period by period (maximizing expected log of end of period wealth) yields the same results as a dynamic optimization problem, over both periods and with any discount rate.

optimally choose not to diversify and will instead hold 'extreme' portfolios. Hence, one of the two money managers will demand $1/\rho_{A,1}$ of asset A; his opponent will demand $1/\rho_{B,1}$ of asset B.

The rest of the market will choose a portfolio so as to maximize the expected log of end of period wealth. At the end of the interim stage, at $t = 1$, the wealth of the logarithmic trader that has chosen a portfolio with weights α_1 and $(1 - \alpha_1)$ in assets A and B respectively, is as follows:

$$\tilde{w}_1^{\log} = \alpha_1 A_1 + (1 - \alpha_1)\tilde{B}_1$$

where $\tilde{B}_1 = B_1^H$ with probability p and $\tilde{B}_1 = B_1^L$ with probability $(1 - p)$. The subscript denotes time. In this market model rates of return are time dependent as they are endogenously determined by market prices. In particular, in the interim stage:

$$A_1 = \frac{w_A}{\rho_{A,1}} \tag{11.4}$$

$$B_1^H = \frac{w_B^H}{\rho_{B,1}} \tag{11.5}$$

$$B_1^L = \frac{w_B^L}{\rho_{B,1}} \tag{11.6}$$

The logarithmic trader chooses α_1 so as to maximize $E[\log \tilde{w}_1^{\log}]$. The first order condition yields:

$$\alpha_1 = (1 - p)\frac{B_1^H}{B_1^H - A_1} + p\frac{B_1^L}{B_1^L - A_1}$$

Therefore, the portfolio weight invested in the risky asset can be written as:

$$\beta_1 \equiv (1 - \alpha_1) = \frac{A_1}{(B_1^H - A_1)(A_1 - B_1^L)}[E(\tilde{B}_1) - A_1]$$

where $E(\tilde{B}_1) = pB_1^H + (1 - p)B_1^L$.

11.3.2 Equilibrium

In order to solve for equilibrium prices we have to consider market demands for each asset. Asset prices (hence rates of return) will be different in the three different strategic scenarios for the two fund managers (both invest in A; one invests in A and the other invests in B; both invest in B).

In what follows, we will concentrate on those equilibrium paths that start with the two fund managers playing asymmetrically.[20] The reason for doing so is that, when fund managers herd in the first stage, the market model adds no further insight to the analysis that we have already conducted in the previous sections for the simple model with linear technologies. Hence, let us assume that in the interim stage one of the two fund managers is investing in asset A and his opponent is investing in asset B.

Since both fund managers are endowed with identical wealth, we do not need to distinguish whether it is i rather than j who invests in the safe as opposed to the risky asset, and vice versa: asset prices will be the same in both cases. One of the two fund managers will invest his unitary wealth in the safe asset and the other fund manager will invest his unitary wealth in the risky asset. Since they have identical wealth, the two strategic scenarios that we will observe in equilibrium display the same relative prices. Market clearing requires

$$ak_1 \equiv \frac{\rho_{A,1}}{\rho_{B,1}} = \frac{\alpha_1 M + 1}{(1 - \alpha_1)M + 1} \tag{11.7}$$

where α_1 is clearly a function of the relative price of the safe asset k_1. Equilibrium in this economy requires the relative price to satisfy equation (11.7) and no arbitrage. No arbitrage requires that $\forall t = 1, 2$:

$$B_t^L < A_t < B_t^H$$

Simple manipulation allows us to state the following:

Remark 1. No arbitrage in this economy is satisfied when

$$\frac{w_A}{w_{B^H}} < k_t < \frac{w_A}{w_{B^L}}$$

From equation (11.7) we can also claim the following:

Proposition 1 (Equilibrium in the interim stage). In the interim stage there is always one and only one market clearing equilibrium.

Proof. See appendix.

11.3.3 The bonus stage

As before, it is convenient to fix a history for the interim stage. First, consider the case $\tilde{B}_1 = B_1^H$, so that the fund manager who invested in the risky asset

[20] However one could follow similar arguments to those suggested here to prove existence and uniqueness of market clearing equilibrium in each of the two stages along the equilibrium paths that start with both fund managers playing symmetrically.

is the interim leader (call him player i) and the fund manager who invested in the safe asset is the interim follower (call him player j).[21]

If $\tilde{B}_1 = B_1^H$, at $t = 1$ the wealth of the logarithmic trader available for investment in the bonus stage is:

$$w_1^{\log} = \alpha_1 A_1 + (1 - \alpha_1) B_1^H$$

We can easily show that the portfolio weights chosen for the bonus stage are the same as the ones chosen for the interim stage. In fact, for a logarithmic trader portfolio weights do not depend on wealth available for investment.

At the end of the second stage, at $t = 2$, the logarithmic trader has wealth equal to:

$$\tilde{w}_2^{\log} = [\alpha_2 A_2 + (1 - \alpha_2)\tilde{B}_2] w_1^{\log}$$

The log trader chooses α_2 so as to maximize

$$E[\log \tilde{w}_2^{\log}] = E[\log\{\alpha_2 A_2 + (1 - \alpha_2)\tilde{B}_2\}] + \log w_1^{\log}$$

and as a result the level of wealth available for investment has no role in the maximization problem (it does not appear in the first order condition).

Therefore portfolio weights as a function of asset prices are as in the interim stage:

$$\alpha_2 = (1 - p)\frac{B_2^H}{B_2^H - A_2} + p\frac{B_2^L}{B_2^L - A_2}$$

$$\beta_2 \equiv (1 - \alpha_2) = \frac{A_2}{(B_2^H - A_2)(A_2 - B_2^L)}[E(\tilde{B}_2) - A_2]$$

As a result, existence and uniqueness of market clearing equilibrium in the bonus stage and for each of the strategic scenarios for fund managers, can be proved in the same way as for the interim stage, using the no arbitrage condition.

Proposition 2 (Equilibrium in the bonus stage). In the bonus stage there is always one and only one market clearing equilibrium.

Proof. See appendix.

We consider now the strategic interaction between the two fund managers in the bonus stage. Consider the asymmetric bonus subgame that follows the history B_1^H in the interim stage. To find out how the asymmetric bonus

---

[21] Recall that we are concentrating on those equilibrium paths that start with fund managers playing asymmetrically.

subgame will be played by the two fund managers we need to ask who wins the bonus under the four different strategic scenarios. No arbitrage guarantees:

$$B_2^L < A_2 < B_2^H$$

1. If AA, then the leader ends up with wealth equal to $B_1^H A_2$ and the follower with wealth $A_1 A_2$. Clearly the leader stays leader and wins the bonus.
2. If BB, then the leader ends up with wealth equal to $B_1^H \tilde{B}_2$ and the follower with wealth $A_1 \tilde{B}_2$. Irrespective of the realization of the random return, the leader stays leader and wins the bonus.
3. If AB (follower in the safe, leader in the risky), then the leader ends up with wealth equal to $B_1^H \tilde{B}_2$ and the follower with wealth $A_1 A_2$. If $\tilde{B}_2 = B_2^H$, then clearly the leader gets the bonus. If $\tilde{B}_2 = B_2^L$, then the follower might be able to outperform the leader.
4. If BA (follower in the risky, leader in the safe), then the leader ends up with wealth equal to $B_1^H A_2$ and the follower with wealth $A_1 \tilde{B}_2$. If $\tilde{B}_2 = B_2^L$, then the leader stays leader and wins the bonus. If $\tilde{B}_2 = B_2^H$, then the follower might be able to outperform the leader.

We want to characterize sufficient conditions so that AA is a Nash equilibrium of the asymmetric bonus subgame. For the interim leader, imitating the follower is always a best reply. On the contrary, the interim follower will in general have an incentive to differentiate his portfolio choice from the leader's, in order to still enjoy some positive chance of catching up. However, if the wealth gap between the two fund managers is large enough, then the interim follower has no positive chance of outperforming the leader and as a result, he will not have any incentive to deviate from our candidate equilibrium, where both fund managers invest in the safe asset. More in detail: if both fund managers invest in the safe asset, then the leader wins the bonus with probability 1, so that the expected payoff to the follower is equal to zero. Clearly the leader has no incentive to deviate. We can show that if the risky asset pays a high payoff with a sufficiently high probability and the rest of the market is large enough, the price of the risky asset is so high that the return that the follower might get, even if he invests his whole portfolio in the risky asset and the risky asset pays a high payoff, would not be sufficient for the follower to catch up with the leader, so that in fact he has no incentive to deviate from AA.

An intuitive explanation of why this happens is as follows. When the risky asset is very likely to pay a high payoff (i.e. p is large), the demand for the risky asset by the logarithmic utility maximizer that represents the rest of the market is also very high. When the size M of the market is sufficiently large, the impact of the logarithmic utility maximizer on asset prices is substantial. As a result, a high demand for the risky asset will rise its price and lower its return in both states of nature (B_2^L and B_2^H). In order to catch up with the leader the follower needs to outperform his opponent in the second stage by an amount large enough, that would also cover for the initial wealth gap. His only chance to do so is investing in the safe asset A. In fact, if he plays safe and his opponents play risky, then he might make it if the interim leader gets a low return, as B_2^L is particularly low. If the follower invests in the risky asset instead, then, even if the risky asset pays a high payoff, he has no chance to outperform the leader since B_2^H is quite low.

A simple diagram can be useful to understand what is the role of the parametric conditions that we pose. Consider the diagram in Figure 11.1. The situation depicted in the figure corresponds to a large value of p. The risky asset is very likely to pay a high payoff; as a result, market demand for the risky asset is quite high; hence its price is also high and its return relatively low, in both states of nature. Clearly a large market size M reinforces the effect on rates of return. Now, suppose that in the first trading period the risky asset paid a high payoff. The initial disadvantage of the follower with respect to the interim leader can be represented by the distance between A and B^H. Since B^H is not very high with respect to A, the follower might still succeed in catching up with the leader. However, his only chance to do so is investing in the safe asset hoping that his opponent will invest in the risky asset and get a low return. In this case his initial (small) disadvantage will be more than compensated by his (large) overperformance, that can be represented by the distance between B^L and A. Clearly rates of return are endogenous and vary from period to period. However, the parametric conditions we pose on p and M guarantee that something very similar to what we have depicted in the diagram in Figure 11.1 is at work. As a result, playing safe becomes a dominant strategy for the follower. The good outcome of the risky strategy is not 'distant' enough from the outcome of the safe strategy and would not allow catching up, not even if the follower got lucky. The leader's best reply is to imitate his opponent, so that he also plays safe.

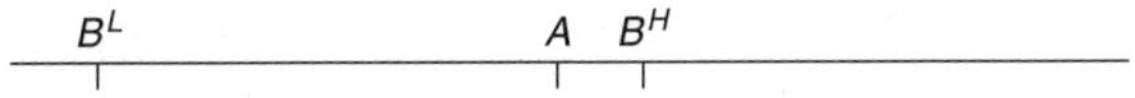

Figure 11.1 Rates of return for large p and large M

We can therefore state the following:

Proposition 3 (Herding in the safe asset: lock-in). After a good realization of the risky asset in the interim stage, if the market is large enough with respect to each of the two funds, and the probability of a good payoff from the risky asset is high enough, we obtain equilibrium herding in the safe asset. Formally, if $\tilde{B}_1 = B_1^H$, $\exists \overline{M} < \infty$ and $\exists \bar{p} < 1$ such that, $\forall p \geq \bar{p}$ and $\forall M \geq \overline{M}$, AA is a Nash equilibrium of the asymmetric bonus subgame.

Proof. See appendix.

We therefore get herding in the safe asset as an equilibrium outcome of the game played by fund managers. Interestingly enough, herding in the safe asset takes place when it is inefficient: it occurs when the risky asset pays a good payoff with a sufficiently high probability. The fund managers' portfolio weight in the safe asset is increasing in the probability of the risky asset paying a high payoff, which is inconsistent with the maximization of the expected value of an increasing and concave function of wealth. Whatever the utility function of the actual investors, we can assert that fund managers take actions that are inconsistent with its maximization. The herding that occurs in these circumstances is therefore inefficient as defined above.

Remark 2. After a good realization of the risky asset in the interim stage, if the market is large enough with respect to each of the two funds, and the probability of a good payoff from the risky asset is high enough, we obtain inefficient equilibrium herding in the safe asset.

Consider now a different history for the interim stage. Suppose that in the interim stage the risky asset paid a low payoff, so that $\tilde{B}_1 = B_1^L$. As in the previous case, in order to find out how the asymmetric bonus subgame will be played we need to ask who wins the bonus under the four different strategic scenarios. No arbitrage guarantees:

$$B_2^L < A_2 < B_2^H$$

1. If AA, then the leader ends up with wealth equal to $A_1 A_2$ and the follower with wealth $B_1^L A_2$. Clearly the leader stays leader and wins the bonus.
2. If BB, then the leader ends up with wealth equal to $A_1 \tilde{B}_2$ and the follower with wealth $B_1^L \tilde{B}_2$. Irrespective of the realization of the random return, the leader stays leader and wins the bonus.
3. If AB (follower in the safe, leader in the risky), then the leader ends up with wealth equal to $A_1 \tilde{B}_2$ and the follower with wealth $B_1^L A_2$. If $\tilde{B}_2 = B_2^H$, then clearly the leader gets the bonus. If $\tilde{B}_2 = B_2^L$, then the follower might be able to outperform the leader.
4. If BA (follower in the risky, leader in the safe), then the leader ends up with wealth equal to $A_1 A_2$ and the follower with wealth $B_1^L \tilde{B}_2$. If $\tilde{B}_2 = B_2^L$, then the leader stays leader and wins the bonus. If $\tilde{B}_2 = B_2^H$, then the follower might be able to outperform the leader.

We want to characterize sufficient conditions such that BB is a Nash equilibrium of the bonus subgame following asymmetric play in the interim stage.

The reasoning is the same as above. For the interim leader, imitating the follower is always a best reply. On the contrary, the interim follower will in general have an incentive to differentiate his portfolio choice from the leader's, in order to still enjoy some positive chance of catching up. However, if the wealth gap between the two fund managers is large enough, then the interim follower will see forgone any positive chance of outperforming the leader and as a result, he will not have any incentive to deviate from our candidate equilibrium, where both fund managers invest in the risky asset. More in detail: if both fund managers invest in the risky asset, then the leader wins the bonus with probability 1, so that the expected payoff to the follower is equal to zero. Clearly the leader has no incentive to deviate. We show that if the risky asset pays a low payoff with a sufficiently high probability and the rest of the market is large enough, the price of the safe asset gets so high that the return that the follower might get, investing even a small portion of his wealth in the safe asset, would not be sufficient for the follower to catch up with the leader, not even if the leader invested his whole wealth in the risky asset and got a low return, so that in fact the follower has no incentive to deviate from BB.

An intuitive explanation of why this happens is as follows. When the risky asset is not very likely to pay a high payoff (i.e. p is small), the demand for the risky asset by the logarithmic utility maximizer that represents the rest of the market is also very small. When the size M of the market is sufficiently large, the impact of the logarithmic utility maximizer on asset prices is substantial. As a result, a low demand for the risky asset will lower its price and raise its return in both states of nature (B_2^L and B_2^H). In order to catch up with the leader the follower needs to outperform his opponent in the second stage by a large amount, that would also cover for the initial wealth gap. His only chance to do so is investing in the risky asset B. In fact, if his opponent plays safe and he plays risky, then he might make it if he gets lucky, as B_2^H is particularly high. If the follower invests in the safe asset instead, then, even if his opponent plays risky and gets a low return, the follower has no chance to outperform the leader since B_2^L is still quite high.

As above, we can help our intuitive understanding of this result with the aid of a diagram. Consider the diagram in Figure 11.2. The situation depicted in Figure 11.2 corresponds to a small value of p. The risky asset is very unlikely to pay a high payoff; as a result, market demand for the risky asset is quite low; hence its price is also low and its return relatively high, in both states of

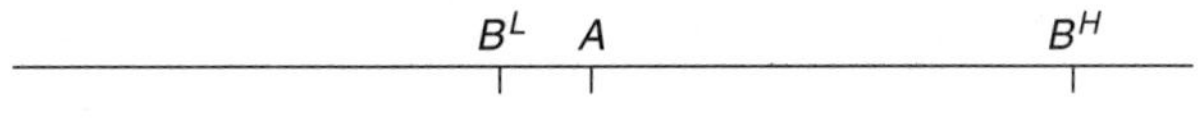

Figure 11.2 Rates of return for small p and large M

nature. Clearly a large market size M reinforces the effect on rates of return. Now, suppose that in the first trading period the risky asset paid a low payoff. The initial disadvantage of the follower with respect to the interim leader can be represented by the distance between B^L and A. Since A is not very high with respect to B^L, the follower might still succeed in catching up with the leader. However, his only chance to do so is investing in the risky asset hoping that his opponent will invest in the safe asset and that his own risky investment will pay a high payoff. In this case his initial (small) disadvantage will be more than compensated by his (large) overperformance, that can be represented by the distance between A and B^H. Clearly rates of return are endogenous and vary from period to period. However, the parametric conditions we pose on p and M guarantee that something very similar to what we have depicted in the diagram in Figure 11.2 is at work. As a result, playing risky becomes a dominant strategy for the follower. The outcome of the safe strategy is not 'distant' enough from the bad outcome of the risky strategy and would not allow catching up, not even if his opponent got a low return. The leader's best reply is to imitate his opponent, so that he also plays risky.

We can therefore state the following:

Proposition 4 (Herding in the risky asset). After a bad realization of the risky asset in the interim stage, if the market is large enough with respect to each of the two funds, and the probability of a bad payoff for the risky asset is high enough, we obtain equilibrium herding in the risky asset. Formally, if $\tilde{B}_1 = B_1^L$, $\exists \widehat{M} < \infty$ and $\exists \widehat{p} > 0$ such that, $\forall M \geq \widehat{M}$ and $\forall p \leq \widehat{p}$, BB is a Nash equilibrium of the asymmetric bonus subgame.

Proof. See appendix.

We therefore get herding in the risky asset as an equilibrium outcome of the game played by the two fund managers. Interestingly enough, herding in the risky asset occurs whenever it is most inefficient, i.e. when the risky asset pays a bad payoff with a sufficiently high probability. As above, we find that the fund managers' portfolio weight in the safe asset is increasing in the probability of the risky asset paying a high payoff, which is inconsistent with the maximization of the expected value of an increasing and concave function of wealth. Whatever the utility function of the actual investors, we can assert that fund managers take actions that are inconsistent with its maximization. The herding that occurs in these circumstances is therefore inefficient as defined above.

Remark 3. After a bad realization of the risky asset in the interim stage, if the market is large enough with respect to each of the two funds, and the probability of a bad payoff for the risky asset is high enough, we obtain inefficient equilibrium herding in the risky asset.

In summary, given some parametric conditions, inefficient herding can be observed as an equilibrium outcome, whenever fund managers are motivated by relative performance incentives. Herding occurs when the rest of the market is large enough with respect to the fund managers, but it is not necessarily infinite. As a result, the two fund managers are not negligible with respect to (the rest of) the market and their demands will significantly affect equilibrium prices. A clear consequence of inefficient herding is therefore the presence of price movements that cannot be fully reconciled with the maximization of the expected value of any increasing and concave function of investors' wealth. Figure 11.3 illustrates the impact of herding behaviour on asset prices. We can plot[22] the market clearing conditions and identify equilibrium price ratios (ρ_A/ρ_B), under three different scenarios:

1. fund managers maximize, along with the rest of the market, a logarithmic function of wealth (equilibrium price ratio E^L);
2. fund managers, motivated by relative performance incentives, herd on the safe asset (equilibrium price ratio E^S);
3. fund managers, motivated by relative performance incentives, herd on the risky asset (equilibrium price ratio E^R).

One can notice how equilibrium asset prices are significantly different in the three cases considered, so that herding has a non-negligible impact on asset prices.

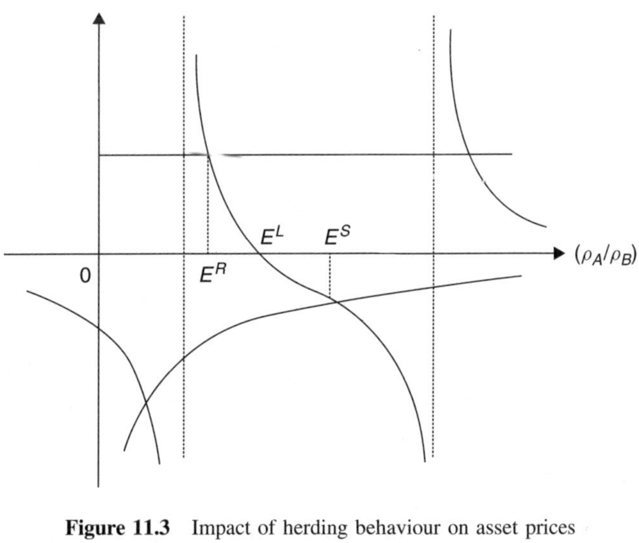

Figure 11.3 Impact of herding behaviour on asset prices

[22]For a more detailed explanation of the diagrams in Figure 11.3, see the Proof of Propositions 1 and 2 in the appendix.

11.4 EXTENSIONS

11.4.1 Mixed compensation scheme

One might ask what are the effects on portfolio choice and asset prices of a compensation scheme for fund managers that rewards both absolute and relative performance. We believe that our results are robust, at least to a certain extent, to such changes in the model.

As we argued in section 11.2.4, one main consequence of partially rewarding fund managers according to their absolute performance is the fact that they would no longer choose to hold extreme portfolios, but instead diversify across the two different available assets. Provided that they are at least partially rewarded on the basis of their relative performance, they would still be after a leadership position, so that they would choose to hold different portfolios in at least one of the two stages. Suppose the symmetry between the two fund managers is broken by the time they get to the end of the first stage, so that each of them reaches the bonus stage either in a leader or follower position. The wealth gap between them implies that there will still exist a set of portfolios such that the leader wins the bonus with probability one and a herding equilibrium will be possible on one of such portfolios. Clearly the smaller the portion of their compensation that is based on relative, rather than absolute, performance, the closer to optimality their portfolio choice will be. So that the herding outcome will get less and less inefficient, the closer to zero the portion of their compensation linked to relative performance. However, we believe that our findings on inefficient equilibrium herding would be robust, so long as fund managers receive a small, but positive, compensation for their relative performance.

11.4.2 A multi-period model with endogenous expectations

The present setting could be extended to an n-period model and the inefficient herding results would prove robust. In fact, in the last period (or possibly before) the fund managers would find themselves in a bonus stage game, that they would play in a similar fashion as in the last stage of a two-period model.

The possibility of obtaining robustness of our results in an n-period setting leads us to what we believe is a valuable and interesting extension of our simple framework. In the present model we have assumed that everyone in the market knows the probability distribution over the payoffs of the risky asset. Suppose that the actual value for p, the probability that the risky asset will pay a high payoff, is not initially known. Traders start from a common prior and revise their beliefs in a Bayesian fashion, after each realization of the risky asset.[23] If a sufficiently long sequence of good realizations for the risky asset occurs, the belief that traders attach to a good realization of the risky asset increases monotonically until it reaches the threshold level that triggers the lock-in effect: fund managers will suddenly leave the risky asset. As a result, the price of that same asset that yielded high payoffs and looked very promising for the future suddenly falls. We believe that this consideration could shed some light on price crashes. In particular, it would provide an alternative explanation to Jacklin, Kleidon and Pfleiderer (1992) of the fact that in the period prior to the crash, prices are higher than would be implied by fundamentals. Here, as in Jacklin, Kleidon and Pfleiderer, in the period prior to the crash, asset prices are overpriced; when herding occurs, prices suddenly fall.

11.5 CONCLUDING REMARKS

We build a model of dynamic competition between money managers who are motivated by relative performance incentives. We consider a stylized financial market where two assets are traded over two periods by three agents: two fund managers and a third large trader who represents the rest of the market. Unlike the third trader, that makes his portfolio choices maximizing expected utility from investment income, the two fund managers only care about their ranking, as they want to maximize the probability of obtaining a strictly positive bonus that is awarded at the end of the second period to the fund manager who displays the best cumulative performance over the two periods.

We show that inefficient herding between fund managers can be observed as an equilibrium outcome in the second trading period. Our main result is to characterize sufficient conditions such that herding obtains. We show that such an herd occurs when the size of the rest of the market is large, but not necessarily infinite. Hence the impact of the herd on equilibrium prices is not negligible and fund managers' behaviour is indeed destabilizing for asset prices. We also prove that the direction of the herd crucially depends on funds' past performances and, in particular, on the realization of the risky asset in the period prior to the herd. If, prior to the herd, the risky asset yields a high payoff and it is very likely to keep on yielding high payoffs in the future, then fund managers might herd on the safe asset; on the contrary, if the risky asset yields a low payoff and it is very likely to keep on yielding

[23] The main difference between this approach to herding and the traditional 'Bayesian' herding approach (as in, for example, Banerjee (1992), Bikhchandani, Hirshleifer and Welch (1992), and Welch (1992) is that here information does not need to be asymmetric. Everyone in the market observes the same signals and updates his beliefs identically. Information asymmetries would of course reinforce the results.

low payoffs in the future, then a herd might develop in the risky asset. Hence we characterize the resulting herding behaviour as inefficient: ranking-based competition between fund managers makes them take portfolio decisions that cannot be reconciled with the maximization of the expected value of any increasing and concave function of wealth.

Our results are consistent with the empirical observations of Brown, Harlow and Starks (1996) and Chevalier and Ellison (1997). From a theoretical perspective, our findings should be compared to Cabral (1999) and Palomino and Prat (1998): our main contribution with respect to their papers is that we consider a similar incentive structure to theirs in a market setting, where asset prices are endogenous and therefore the effects of herding on market prices can be ascertained.

11.6 APPENDIX

Proof of Proposition 1 (Equilibrium in the interim stage). In the interim stage market clearing requires:

$$k_1 \equiv \frac{\rho_{A,1}}{\rho_{B,1}} = \frac{\alpha_1 M + 1}{(1-\alpha_1)M + 1}$$

where α_1 and $(1-\alpha_1)$ are portfolio weights of the logarithmic trader in the safe and risky assets respectively. Recall that:

$$\alpha_1 = (1-p)\frac{B_1^H}{B_1^H - A_1} + p\frac{B_1^L}{B_1^L - A_1}$$

which can be rewritten as follows:

$$\alpha_1 = (1-p)\frac{w_B^H/\rho_{B,1}}{w_B^H/\rho_{B,1} - w_A/\rho_{A,1}} + p\frac{w_B^L/\rho_{B,1}}{w_B^L/\rho_{B,1} - w_A/\rho_{A,1}}$$

And finally:

$$\alpha_1 = (1-p)\frac{(w_B^H/w_A)k_1}{(w_B^H/w_A)k_1 - 1} + p\frac{(w_B^L/w_A)k_1}{(w_B^L/w_A)k_1 - 1}$$

Similarly one obtains:

$$(1-\alpha_1) = -(1-p)\frac{1}{(w_B^H/w_A)k_1 - 1} - p\frac{1}{(w_B^L/w_A)k_1 - 1}$$

Hence market clearing requires:

$$k_1 = \frac{(1-p)\dfrac{(w_B^H/w_A)k_1}{(w_B^H/w_A)k_1 - 1}M + p\dfrac{(w_B^L/w_A)k_1}{(w_B^L/w_A)k_1 - 1}M + 1}{-(1-p)\dfrac{1}{(w_B^H/w_A)k_1 - 1}M - p\dfrac{1}{(w_B^L/w_A)k_1 - 1}M + 1} \tag{11.8}$$

We can solve for equilibrium by computing the solutions of (11.8), which is a third order equation in k_1. Equation (11.8) generally admits three solutions, but only one also satisfies no arbitrage conditions. In fact, with simple manipulation, (11.8) can be rewritten as:

$$F(k_1) = G(k_1)$$

where:

$$F(k_1) \equiv (1-p)\frac{1 + (w_B^H/w_A)}{(w_B^H/w_A)k_1 + 1} + p\frac{1 + (w_B^L/w_A)}{(w_B^L/w_A)k_1 + 1} \tag{11.9}$$

$$G(k_1) \equiv \frac{1}{M} \cdot \frac{k_1 - 1}{k_1} \tag{11.10}$$

We can plot $F(k_1)$ and $G(k_1)$ on a diagram (Figure 11.4), to obtain a geometrical proof of our claim. The solid line is $F(k_1)$ and the dotted line is $G(k_1)$. They intersect three times; however, only one intersection corresponds to a price ratio such that no arbitrage is guaranteed: $F(k_1)$ has two vertical asymptotes in w_A/w_B^H and in w_A/w_B^L. From remark 1, we know that a price ratio satisfying no arbitrage has to be such that: $w_A/w_B^H < k_t < w_A/w_B^L$, so that the only price ratio that at the same time clears the markets and satisfies no arbitrage in the interim stage is k_1^* (as denoted on the diagram in Figure 11.4).

Proof of Proposition 2 (Equilibrium in the bonus stage). In the bonus stage, when the two fund managers operate in different markets (i.e. each of them invests in a different asset), the proof is identical to the proof of proposition 1. When both fund managers invest in the risky asset, market clearing requires:

$$k_2 = \frac{(1-p)\dfrac{(w_B^H/w_A)k_2}{(w_B^H/w_A)k_2 - 1}w_1^{\log} + p\dfrac{(w_B^L/w_A)k_2}{(w_B^L/w_A)k_2 - 1}w_1^{\log}}{-(1-p)\dfrac{1}{(w_B^H/w_A)k_2 - 1}w_1^{\log} - p\dfrac{1}{(w_B^L/w_A)k_2 - 1}w_1^{\log} + (w_1^L + w_1^F)} \tag{11.11}$$

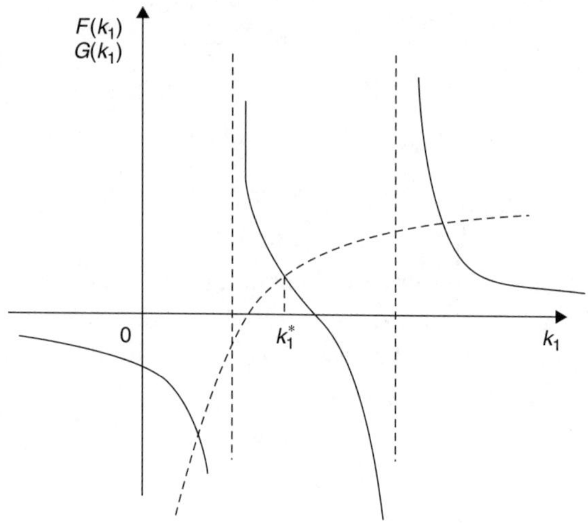

Figure 11.4 Market clearing in the interim stage

where $w_1^{\log}$, w_1^L and w_1^F are respectively the investment incomes of the rest of the market, the leader and the follower at the end of the interim stage. Equation 11.11 admits only one solution that also satisfies no arbitrage. In fact, with simple manipulation, (11.11) can be rewritten as:

$$F(k_2) = G \equiv \frac{w_1^L + w_1^F}{w_1^{\log}}$$

where:

$$F(k_2) \equiv (1-p)\frac{1 + (w_B^H/w_A)}{(w_B^H/w_A)k_2 + 1} + p\frac{1 + (w_B^L/w_A)}{(w_B^L/w_A)k_2 + 1}$$

We can plot $F(k_2)$ on a diagram (see Figure 11.5), to obtain a geometrical proof of our claim. The solid line is $F(k_2)$, which equals G twice; $F(k_2)$ has two vertical asymptotes in w_A/w_B^H and in w_A/w_B^L. From remark 1, we know that a price ratio satisfying no arbitrage has to be such that: $w_A/w_B^H < k_t < w_A/w_B^L$, so that the only price ratio that at the same satisfies equation (11.11) and no arbitrage in the bonus stage is k_2^* (as denoted on the diagram in Figure 11.5). Similarly one can show that one and only one equilibrium exists when both fund managers invest in the safe asset. Market clearing requires:

$$k_2 = \frac{(1-p)\dfrac{(w_B^H/w_A)k_2}{(w_B^H/w_A)k_2 - 1}w_1^{\log} + p\dfrac{(w_B^L/w_A)k_2}{(w_B^L/w_A)k_2 - 1}w_1^{\log} + (w_1^L + w_1^F)}{-(1-p)\dfrac{1}{(w_B^H/w_A)k_2 - 1}w_1^{\log} - p\dfrac{1}{(w_B^L/w_A)k_2 - 1}w_1^{\log}} \qquad (11.12)$$

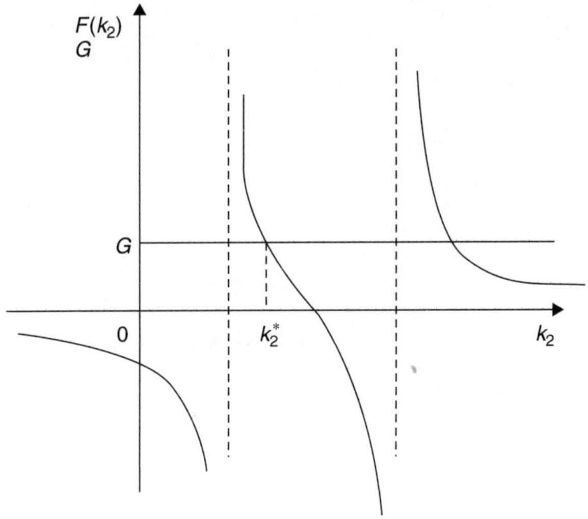

Figure 11.5 Herd in the risky asset: market clearing

Equation (11.12) admits only one solution that also satisfies no arbitrage. In fact, with simple manipulation, (11.12) can be rewritten as:

$$F(k_2) = Q(k_2)$$

where:

$$F(k_2) \equiv (1-p)\frac{1+(w_B^H/w_A)}{(w_B^H/w_A)k_2+1} + p\frac{1+(w_B^L/w_A)}{(w_B^L/w_A)k_2+1} \tag{11.13}$$

$$Q(k_2) = -\frac{w_1^L + w_1^F}{w_1^{\log} k_2} \tag{11.14}$$

We can plot $F(k_2)$ and $Q(k_2)$ on a diagram (see Figure 11.6), to obtain a geometrical proof of our claim. The solid line in the diagram is $F(k_2)$, while the dotted line is $Q(k_2)$. They intersect twice; $F(k_2)$ has two vertical asymptotes in w_A/w_B^H and in w_A/w_B^L. From remark 1, we know that a price ratio satisfying no arbitrage has to be such that: $w_A/w_B^H < k_t < w_A/w_B^L$, so that the only price ratio that satisfies equation (11.12) and no arbitrage in the bonus stage is k_2^* (as denoted on the diagram in Figure 11.6).

Proof of Proposition 3 (Herding in the safe asset: lock-in). We want to characterize conditions such that AA is a Nash equilibrium of the asymmetric bonus subgame, after $\tilde{B}_1 = B_1^H$ in the interim stage. Consider the interim leader first: if he does not deviate, his expected payoff is 1, since he is guaranteed to keep his leadership and win the bonus; clearly he has no incentive

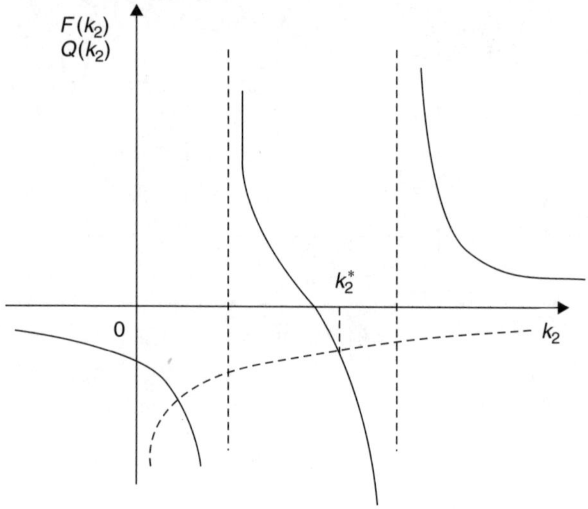

Figure 11.6 Herd in the safe asset: market clearing

to deviate. Consider now the follower: if he does not deviate, his expected payoff is zero; he will deviate if he can do better than zero. If the follower deviates from AA, then the strategy profile becomes BA: the performance of the interim follower is $A_1\tilde{B}_2$, while the performance of the interim leader is $B_1^H A_2$; in fact, if $\tilde{B}_1 = B_1^H$, then it must be the case that, in the interim stage, interim leader and follower invested respectively in the risky and safe asset. If $\tilde{B}_2 = B_2^L$, then clearly:

$$A_1\tilde{B}_2 = A_1 B_2^L < B_1^H A_2$$

so that the leader stays leader and wins the bonus. Hence, when $\tilde{B}_2 = B_2^L$, the interim follower has no incentive to deviate from our candidate equilibrium. As a result, the only situation in which the interim follower might indeed obtain a strictly positive payoff is the case $\tilde{B}_2 = B_2^H$. It is sufficient to have:

$$A_1 B_2^H \leq B_1^H A_2 \tag{11.15}$$

to guarantee that the interim follower has no incentive to deviate from the candidate equilibrium. Simple manipulation shows that (11.15) is equivalent to:

$$k_2 \leq k_1 \tag{11.16}$$

where $k_t \equiv \rho_{A,t}/\rho_{B,t}$, for $t = 1, 2$. Recall that, when in the interim stage $\tilde{B}_1 = B_1^H$ and in the bonus stage the strategy profile is BA (follower in the risky, leader in the safe), by simple market clearing:

$$k_2 = \frac{\alpha_2 M' + B_1^H}{(1-\alpha_2)M' + A_1} \tag{11.17}$$

where:

$$M' = \alpha_1 A_1 M + (1-\alpha_1) B_1^H M \tag{11.18}$$

Substituting (11.18) into (11.17), we find that condition (11.16) requires:

$$\frac{\alpha_1\alpha_2 M + (1-\alpha_1)\alpha_2 (w_B^H/w_A)k_1 M + (w_B^H/w_A)k_1}{\alpha_1(1-\alpha_2)M + (1-\alpha_1)(1-\alpha_2)(w_B^H/w_A)k_1 M + 1} \le k_1 \tag{11.19}$$

We can express (11.19) as an inequality for M as:

$$[(1-\alpha_1)(w_B^H/w_A)k_1 + \alpha_1][(1-\alpha_2)k_1 - \alpha_2]M \ge [(w_B^H/w_A) - 1]k_1 \tag{11.20}$$

Inequality (11.20) is satisfied when both:

$$(1-\alpha_2)k_1 - \alpha_2 > 0 \tag{11.21}$$

and:

$$M \ge \overline{M} \equiv \frac{[(w_B^H/w_A) - 1]k_1}{[(1-\alpha_1)(w_B^H/w_A)k_1 + \alpha_1][(1-\alpha_2)k_1 - \alpha_2]} \tag{11.22}$$

The last step in our proof is to find conditions such that (11.21) is satisfied. Recall that by no arbitrage k_1 is bounded below by w_A/w_B^H. Hence:

$$(1-\alpha_2)k_1 - \alpha_2 > (1-\alpha_2)\frac{w_A}{w_B^H} - \alpha_2 = \frac{w_A}{w_B^H} - \alpha_2\left(\frac{w_A}{w_B^H} + 1\right)$$

It follows that (11.21) is necessarily satisfied when:

$$\frac{w_A}{w_B^H} - \alpha_2\left(\frac{w_A}{w_B^H} + 1\right) \ge 0$$

which can be reformulated as:

$$\alpha_2 \le \frac{w_A}{w_A + w_B^H} \tag{11.23}$$

We can finally show that a sufficiently large value for p implies α_2, and *a fortiori* (11.21). Recall that:

$$\alpha_2 = (1-p)\frac{w_B^H k_2}{w_B^H k_2 - w_A} - p\frac{w_B^L k_2}{w_B^L k_2 - w_A}$$

so that (11.23) can be rewritten as:

$$(1-p)\frac{w_B^H k_2}{w_B^H k_2 - w_A} - p\frac{w_B^L k_2}{w_B^L k_2 - w_A} \leq \frac{w_A}{w_A + w_B^H}$$

which implies:

$$p \geq \bar{p} \equiv \frac{(w_B^H k_2)/(w_B^H k_2 - w_A) - w_A/(w_A + w_B^H)}{(w_B^H k_2)/(w_B^H k_2 - w_A) + (w_B^L k_2)/(w_B^L k_2 - w_A)} \tag{11.24}$$

Summarizing: $p \geq \bar{p}$ and $M \geq \overline{M}$ guarantee that (11.16), and hence (11.15) are satisfied, so that the interim follower has no incentive to deviate from the candidate equilibrium. Notice that $\bar{p} < 1$ and $\overline{M} < \infty$, so that parameter values such that the conditions we pose are satisfied indeed exist.

Proof of Proposition 4 (Herding in the risky asset). We want to characterize conditions such that BB is a Nash equilibrium of the asymmetric bonus subgame, after $\tilde{B}_1 = B_1^L$ in the interim stage. Consider the interim leader first: if he does not deviate, his expected payoff is 1, since he is guaranteed to keep his leadership and win the bonus; clearly he has no incentive to deviate. Consider now the follower: if he does not deviate, his expected payoff is zero; he will deviate if he can do better than zero. If the follower deviates from BB, then the strategy profile becomes AB: the performance of the interim follower is $B_1^L A_2$, while the performance of the interim leader is $A_1 \tilde{B}_2$; in fact, if $\tilde{B}_1 = B_1^L$, then it must be the case that, in the interim stage, interim leader and follower invested respectively in the safe and risky asset. If $\tilde{B}_2 = B_2^H$, then clearly:

$$A_1 \tilde{B}_2 = A_1 B_2^H > B_1^L A_2$$

so that the leader stays leader and wins the bonus. Hence, when $\tilde{B}_2 = B_2^H$, the interim follower has no incentive to deviate from the candidate equilibrium. As a result, the only situation in which the interim follower might outperform the leader and gain a strictly positive payoff is the case $\tilde{B}_2 = B_2^L$. It is sufficient to have:

$$A_1 B_2^L \geq B_1^L A_2 \tag{11.25}$$

to guarantee that the interim follower has no incentive to deviate from the candidate equilibrium. Simple manipulation shows that (11.25) is equivalent to:

$$k_1 \leq k_2 \tag{11.26}$$

where $k_t \equiv \rho_{A,t}/\rho_{B,t}$, for $t = 1, 2$. Recall that, when in the interim stage $\tilde{B}_1 = B_1^L$ and in the bonus stage the strategy profile is AB (follower in the safe, leader in the risky), by simple market clearing:

$$k_2 = \frac{\alpha_2 M' + B_1^L}{(1 - \alpha_2)M' + A_1} \tag{11.27}$$

where:

$$M' = \alpha_1 A_1 M + (1 - \alpha_1) B_1^L M \tag{11.28}$$

Substituting (11.28) into (11.27), we find that condition (11.26) requires:

$$\frac{\alpha_1\alpha_2 M + (1 - \alpha_1)\alpha_2(w_B^L/w_A)k_1 M + (w_B^L/w_A)k_1}{\alpha_1(1 - \alpha_2)M + (1 - \alpha_1)(1 - \alpha_2)(w_B^L/w_A)k_1 M + 1} \geq k_1 \tag{11.29}$$

We can express (11.29) as an inequality for M as:

$$[(1 - \alpha_1)(w_B^L/w_A)k_1 + \alpha_1][\alpha_2 - (1 - \alpha_2)k_1]M \geq [1 - (w_B^L/w_A)]k_1 \tag{11.30}$$

Inequality (11.30) is satisfied when both:

$$\alpha_2 - (1 - \alpha_2)k_1 > 0 \tag{11.31}$$

and:

$$M \geq \widehat{M} \equiv \frac{[1 - (w_B^L/w_A)]k_1}{[(1 - \alpha_1)(w_B^L/w_A)k_1 + \alpha_1][\alpha_2 - (1 - \alpha_2)k_1]} \tag{11.32}$$

The last step in our proof is to find conditions such that (11.31) is satisfied. Recall that by no arbitrage k_1 is bounded above by w_A/w_{B^L}. Hence:

$$\alpha_2 - (1 - \alpha_2)k_1 > \alpha_2 - (1 - \alpha_2)\frac{w_A}{w_B^L} = \alpha_2\left(\frac{w_A}{w_B^L} + 1\right) - \frac{w_A}{w_B^L}$$

It follows that (11.31) is necessarily satisfied when:

$$\alpha_2\left(\frac{w_A}{w_B^L}+1\right)-\frac{w_A}{w_B^L}\geq 0$$

which can be reformulated as:

$$\alpha_2 \geq \frac{w_A}{w_A+w_B^L} \tag{11.33}$$

We can finally show that a sufficiently small value for p implies (11.33), and *a fortiori* (11.31). Recall that:

$$\alpha_2=(1-p)\frac{w_B^H k_2}{w_B^H k_2-w_A}-p\frac{w_B^L k_2}{w_B^L k_2-w_A}$$

so that (11.33) can be rewritten as:

$$(1-p)\frac{w_B^H k_2}{w_B^H k_2-w_A}-p\frac{w_B^L k_2}{w_B^L k_2-w_A}\geq\frac{w_A}{w_A+w_B^L}$$

which implies:

$$p\leq\widehat{p}\equiv\frac{(w_B^H k_2)/(w_B^H k_2-w_A)-w_A/(w_A+w_B^L)}{(w_B^H k_2)/(w_B^H k_2-w_A)+(w_B^L k_2)/(w_B^L k_2-w_A)} \tag{11.34}$$

Summarizing: $p\leq\widehat{p}$ and $M\geq\widehat{M}$ guarantee that (11.26), and hence (11.25) are satisfied, so that the interim follower has no incentive to deviate from our candidate equilibrium. Notice that $\widehat{p}>0$ and $\widehat{M}<\infty$, so that parameter values such that the conditions we pose are satisfied indeed exist.

REFERENCES

Ashton, D., Crossland, M. and Moizer, P. (1990) The performance evaluation of fund managers, mimeo, School of Business and Economic Studies, University of Leeds.

Banca d'Italia (1998) *Relazione Annuale del Governatore.*

Banerjee, A.V. (1992) A simple model of herd behaviour, *Quarterly Journal of Economics*, **107**, 797–817.

Bikhchandani, S., Hirshleifer, D. and Welch, I. (1992) A theory of fads, fashion, custom and cultural change as informational cascades, *Journal of Political Economy*, **100**, 992–1026.

Blume, L. and Easley, D. (1992) Evolution and market behaviour, *Journal of Economic Theory*, **26**, 318–339.

Brady, N. *et al.* (1988) *Report of the Presidential Task Force on Market Mechanisms*, US Government Printing Office, Washington.

Brown, K.C., Harlow, W.V. and Starks, L.T. (1996) Of tournaments and temptations: an analysis of managerial incentives in the mutual fund industry, *Journal of Finance*, **51**, 85–110.

Bulow, J. and Klemperer, P. (1994) Rational frenzies and crashes, *Journal of Political Economy*, **102**, 1–23.

Cabral, L.M.B. (1999) Football, sailing, and R&D: dynamic competition with strategic choice of variance and covariance, mimeo, London Business School.

Chevalier, J. and Ellison, G. (1997) Risk taking by mutual funds as a response to incentives, *Journal of Political Economy*, **105**, 1167–1200.

Cuoco, D. and Kaniel, R. (1999) General equilibrium implications of fund managers' compensation fees, mimeo, The Warthon School, University of Pennsylvania.

Cutler, D.M., Poterba, J.M. and Summers, L.H. (1990) Speculative dynamics and the role of feedback traders, *American Economic Review*, **80**, 63–68.

De Long, J.B., Shleifer, A., Summers, L.H. and Waldman, R.J. (1990) Positive feedback investment strategies and destabilising rational speculation, *Journal of Finance*, **45**, 379–395.

Eichberger, J., Grant, S. and King, S.P. (1997) On relative performance and fund manager's Incentives, working paper n. 327, The Australian National University.

Frankel, J.A. and Froot, K.A. (1990) Chartists, fundamentalists, and trading in the foreign exchange market, *American Economic Review*, **80**, 181–185.

Gale, D. (1996) What have we learned from social learning?, *European Economic Review*, **40**, 617–628.

Gennotte, G. and Leland, H. (1990) Market liquidity, hedging and crashes, *American Economic Review*, **80**, 999–1021.

Gibbons, R. and Murphy, K.J. (1989) Relative performance evaluation for chief executive officers, NBER working paper n. 2944.

Grinblatt, M., Titman, S. and Wermers, R. (1995) Momentum investment strategies, portfolio performance, and hedging: a study of mutual fund behaviour, *American Economic Review*, **85**, 1088–1105.

Gümbel, A. (1998) Herding in delegated portfolio management. When is comparative performance information desirable?, working paper n. 98/22, European University Institute.

Hvide, H.K. (2002) Tournament rewards and risk taking, *Journal of Labor Economics*, forthcoming.

Hvide, H.K. and Kristiansen, E.G. (1999) Risk taking in selection contests, mimeo, Norwegian School of Economics.

Jacklin, C.J., Kleidon, A.W. and Pfleiderer, P. (1992) Underestimation of portfolio insurance and the crash of October 1987, *Review of Financial Studies*, **5**, 35–63.

Keynes, J.M. (1936) *The General Theory of Employment, Interest and Money*, MacMillan, London.

Kyle, A.S. (1985) Continuous auctions and insider trading, *Econometrica*, **53**, 1315–1335.

Lakonishock, J., Schleifer, A. and Vishny, R.W. (1992) The impact of institutional trading on stock prices, *Journal of Finance*, **32**, 23–43.

Maug, E. and Naik, N. (1996) Herding and delegated portfolio management: the impact of relative performance evaluation on asset allocation, LBS working paper n. 223.

Meyer, M.A. and Vickers, J. (1997) Performance comparisons and dynamic incentives, *Journal of Political Economy*, **105**, 547–581.

Mookherjee, D. (1984) Optimal incentive schemes with many agents, *Review of Economic Studies*, **51**, 433–446.

Nalebuff, B.J. and Stiglitz, J.E. (1983) Prizes and incentives: towards a general theory of compensation and competition, *Bell Journal of Economics*, **14**, 21–43.

New York Stock Exchange (1998) *Fact Book.* NYSE Publications Department, New York.

Palomino, F. (1999) Relative performance objectives in financial markets, mimeo, Tilburg University.

Palomino, F. and Prat, A. (1998) Dynamic incentives in the money management tournament, mimeo, Tilburg University.

Palomino, F. and Prat, A. (1999) Risk taking and optimal contracts for money managers, mimeo, Tilburg University.

Scharfstein, D.S. and Stein, J.C. (1990) Herd behaviour and investment, *American Economic Review*, **80**, 465–479.

Sciubba, E. (1999a) The evolution of portfolio rules and the Capital Asset Pricing Model, DAE working paper n. 9909, University of Cambridge.

Sciubba, E. (1999b) Asymmetric information and survival in financial markets, DAE working paper n. 9908, University of Cambridge.

Shiller, R.J. (1981a) Do stock prices move too much to be justified by subsequent changes in dividends?, *American Economic Review*, **71**, 421–436.

Shiller, R.J. (1981b) The use of volatility measures in assessing market efficiency, *Journal of Finance*, **36**, 291–304.

Shiller, R.J. (1984) Stock prices and social dynamics, *Brookings Papers on Economic Activity*, **2**, 457–498.

Shiller, R.J. (1990) *Market Volatility*, MIT Press, London.

Summers, L.H. (1986) Does the stock market rationally reflects fundamental values?, *Journal of Finance*, **41**, 591–601.

Welch, I. (1992) Sequential sales, learning and cascades, *Journal of Finance* **47**, 695–732.

Zwiebel, J. (1995) Corporate conservatism and relative compensation, *Journal of Political Economy*, **103**, 1–25.

Chapter 12

The rate-of-return formula can make a difference

DAVID SPAULDING

ABSTRACT

The purpose of this chapter is to present a discussion concerning the strengths and weaknesses of different ways of calculating rates of return. Difficulties associated with cash flows and daily volatilities are identified. Some calculations demonstrate that the different methods can give surprisingly different answers.

12.1 INTRODUCTION

Since the mid-1980s, we've identified numerous ways to calculate rates of return. The simplest approach:

$$ROR = \frac{EMV - BMV}{BMV} \tag{12.1}$$

where:
EMV = ending period market value
BMV = beginning period market value
ROR = rate of return

works perfectly. Unless, of course, there are cash flows. And since we first started to measure rates of return, we've realized that cash flows cause us the greatest challenge. And strive as we may, they still can be problematic.

Some of the formulae can be grouped into a category called 'approximation methods', because we *know* they have some inaccuracies, usually because of irregular pricing of the portfolio. Until the 1980s, it was common for the securities within portfolios to be priced on a weekly or monthly basis. This was especially true of fixed income securities. Even today, we find firms that don't do daily pricing because of the costs for pricing services.

The formula proposed by the Investment Council Association of America (ICAA)[1] and the early formula offered by Peter Dietz[2] assumed that cash flows occurred at the middle of the measurement period. While this assumption didn't usually cause much of a problem, we quickly learned that when large cash flows (usually considered flows greater than or equal to 10% of the portfolio's market value) took place early or late in the period, the accuracy could suffer greatly.

Consequently, we saw the introduction of day-weighting factors that assured that the flow would be included in the formula for only the number of days the money was available to the manager. Dietz's day-weighting formula,[3] later referred to as the 'modified Dietz by the Association for Investment Management and Research (AIMR)',[4] was such a formula. We'll demonstrate the use of this factor below.

Day-weighting methodologies still only produce approximate rates of return. Inaccuracies arise because of market volatility, and the more volatility, the greater the inaccuracy. The industry has therefore continued to try to improve the accuracy of these numbers. There's also been pressure (from portfolio managers and clients) to have returns measured more frequently to enhance both internal and client reporting. Consequently, we're moving to daily rates of return.

There is another reason we're seeing a shift to daily: both the Global Investment Performance Standards (GIPS®) and the Association for Investment Management and Research's Performance Presentation Standards® (AIMR-PPS®) call for revaluing the portfolio whenever a cash flow occurs, by January 2010.[5]

There's a common belief that by moving from mid-point to day-weighting, and then to daily rates of return, that our returns are more accurate. But are they?

This chapter contrasts some of the more popular methods of deriving returns and demonstrates that the differences can be significant. And that cash flows can create some huge problems for us, if they're not properly handled.

---

[1] ICAA (1971), page 7.
[2] Dietz and Kirschman (1983), page 622.
[3] Dietz and Kirschman (1983), page 623.
[4] AIMR (1993), page 21.
[5] AIMR (1999), page 7; AIMR (2001), page 15.

12.2 ALTERNATIVE METHODOLOGIES TO MEASURE PERFORMANCE

The mid-point Dietz formula has been a very simple approach to deriving rates of return. It enhances the basic equation shown above by introducing a treatment for cash flows (C):

$$ROR = \frac{EMV - BMV - C}{BMV + 0.5 \times C} \tag{12.2}$$

The numerator ($EMV - BMV - C$) provides us with the net amount of money realized during the period. By multiplying the cash flows by one-half (0.5) in the denominator, we're saying that the flow was only available to the manager for half the time.

The appeal of this formula is its simplicity. Problems arise when flows, especially large ones, take place early or late in the period – the mid-point or '0.5' assumption no longer works.

To improve the treatment of flows and eliminate this distortion, we can day-weight the flows. To do this, we introduce the W_i term, or the 'weighting factor'. It's derived as follows[6]:

$$W_i = \frac{CD - D_i}{CD} \tag{12.3}$$

where:
CD = the number of calendar days in the period
D_i = the day of the flow.

For example, an in-flow that occurred on the 10th day of a 30 day month would yield:

$$W = \frac{30 - 10}{30} = \frac{20}{30} = 0.67 \tag{12.4}$$

meaning that the money was available to the manager for 67% of the month.

With the day-weighting factor, we can progress to the day-weighting or modified Dietz formula:

$$ROR = \frac{EMV - BMV - \sum_{i=1}^{n} C_i}{BMV + \sum_{i=1}^{n} W_i C_i} \tag{12.5}$$

[6]This formula presumes that the flow occurred at the end of the day. To have the flow take place at the start of the day, simply add 1 to the numerator.

The numerator still yields the net amount of money realized while the denominator gives us the amount of money that was available to the manager for the period.

This approach only prices the portfolio at the start and end of the period. To enhance the return's accuracy, we should revalue whenever a flow occurs. The true daily rate of return formula

$$ROR = \frac{EMV_1}{BMV_1} + \frac{EMV_2}{BMV_2} + \cdots + \frac{EMV_n}{BMV_n} \tag{12.6}$$

is intended to produce an accurate rate of return, devoid of the affects of flows or market volatility.

Each individual fraction demarcates the periods from one flow to the next, starting with the beginning period market value and ending with the period's ending value. The tricky part is determining whether or not the flow occurred at the *start* or *end* of the day. But we'll discuss this further below.

There are other methods available, such as the modified BAI, ICAA and unit value formulae. Space does not permit going into these in detail. However, the ones described above are the most commonly used ones and will be discussed further below.

12.3 CONTRASTING THE METHODS

12.3.1 The scenario we'll use

We'll use the following example to contrast the various approaches and to demonstrate the importance of properly handling cash flows:

31 May:	End-of-month market value = \$100,000
4 June:	End-of-day market value = \$100,500
5 June:	Cash flow of \$500,000
	End-of-day market value (without cash flow) = \$130,500
	End-of-day market value (with cash flow included) = \$630,500
30 June:	End-of-month market value = \$640,000

The portfolio ended the month of May with a market value of \$100,000. During the month of June, a single (but very large) cash flow of \$500,000 occurred; this happened on 5 June. The market value from the preceding day was \$100,500 (i.e. the portfolio had increased by \$500 from the start of month). At the end of 5 June, there was an appreciation of \$30,000. If we add this amount to the start-of-day value, we get \$130,500; if we add it to the start-of-day plus the cash flow, we get \$630,500. The market value at the end of June was \$640,000.

12.3.2 Mid-point Dietz

We'll begin by using the 'mid-point Dietz' method. It assumes that all cash flows occur at the middle of the period. As noted earlier, the formula is pretty straightforward:

$$ROR_{MPD} = \frac{EMV - BMV - C}{BMV + 0.5 \times C} \tag{12.7}$$

where:

ROR_{MPD} = the rate of return, using the mid-point Dietz method
EMV = the ending period market value
BMV = the beginning period market value
C = the sum of the cash flows for the period.

The '0.5' in the denominator is what causes the cash flows to be treated as if they occurred at the middle of the period.

If we substitute the values from above, we get:

$$ROR_{MPD} = \frac{640{,}000 - 100{,}000 - 500{,}000}{100{,}000 + 0.5 \times 500{,}000} = \frac{40{,}000}{350{,}000} = 11.43\% \tag{12.8}$$

The advantage of this method is its simplicity. It requires you to calculate only two market values: the starting and ending. And you simply sum all the cash flows and treat them as if they occurred in the middle.

While some people have used this method in the past for periods as long as a calendar quarter or even a full year, it's been more appropriate of late to use it for calculating monthly returns. It is, however, also suitable for shorter periods.

The main problem with this approach is that it treats flows as if they occurred in the middle of the period. This is obviously not always the case. The accuracy of this approach diminishes when (1) the actual flow date moves farther away from the middle of the month and (2) when the size of the flow, relative to the starting market value, is large.

Traditionally, the industry has accepted 'large' to mean 10% or more of the market value.[7] In our case, a cash flow of $10,000 (10% of $100,000) would qualify as large. Therefore, a flow of $500,000 would have to be described as *very* large. And, given that the actual flow date was 5 June, a whole 10 days earlier than the mid-point of 15 June, we'd expect the accuracy to be questionable.

---

[7]This is one of those 'unwritten' rules that has become a *de facto* standard.

12.3.3 Day-weighted (or modified) Dietz

Dietz recognized the problem with the mid-point method and suggested that 'Recognizing that cash flows do not all occur at the mid-point of a time interval, and in an attempt to minimize the distortion that might result from such an assumption, some performance measurement algorithms day-weight cash flows'.[8]

Dietz simply referred to this as 'day-weighting'. AIMR uses the moniker 'modified' to signify day-weighting.[9]

To accomplish this, we need a *day-weighting* factor:

$$W_i = \frac{CD - D_i}{CD} \tag{12.9}$$

where:

W_i = the weighting factor for the ith cash flow
CD = the number of calendar days in the period
D_i = the day of the ith cash flow.

The result is the per cent the money was in (or out, in the case of outflows) the portfolio for the period.

In our case, there is a single cash flow of \$500,000 which took place on the 5th of the month. So, we have:

$$W_i = \frac{30 - 5}{30} = \frac{25}{30} = 0.8333 = 83.33\% \tag{12.10}$$

The additional \$500,000 is therefore present for 83.33% of the month, as opposed to 50% of the month that is assumed in the mid-point method. We would expect to see increased accuracy in the return by increasing the weight of the cash flow in the denominator by the additional 33.33%.

The actual rate of return formula for this method is identical to the mid-point formula, except that the weighting factor is substituted for the '0.5' in the denominator:

$$ROR_{MD} = \frac{EMV - BMV - \sum_{i=1}^{n} C_i}{BMV + \sum_{i=1}^{n} W_i \times C_i} \tag{12.11}$$

[8]Dietz (1983), page 623.
[9]AIMR (1997), page 45.

While the presence of the capital Greek letter sigma (Σ) tends to make this equation appear more onerous, it really isn't.

What we've introduced is the mathematical expression known as the Riemann sum. The expression

$$\sum_{i=1}^{n} W_i \times C_i \qquad (12.12)$$

means to sum the weights (W) times their respective cash flows (C). (The i represents the starting value (1) and the n signifies the last value.)

If, for example, we had three flows ($10,000 on the 5th of the month, $20,000 on the 15th of the month, and $30,000 on the 20th of the month), in a 30 day month, we'd have weights of 0.8333 for the first, 0.5000 for the second and 0.1667 for the third.[10]

Employing the above equation, we have:

$$\sum_{i=1}^{3} W_i \times C_i = W_1 \times C_1 + W_2 \times C_2 + W_3 \times C_3 = 0.8333 \times 10{,}000 + 0.5 \times 20{,}000 + 0.1667 \times 30{,}000 = 23{,}334 \qquad (12.13)$$

Now, back to calculating the rate of return. If we employ the Modified Dietz approach to our portfolio, we get:

$$ROR_{MD} = \frac{640{,}000 - 100{,}000 - 500{,}000}{100{,}000 + 0.8333 \times 500{,}000} = \frac{40{,}000}{516{,}666.67} = 0.0774 = 7.74\% \qquad (12.14)$$

This is quite a difference from our mid-point result (11.43%), isn't it? The difference of 3.69% would be considered significant. And yet, the use of day-weighting is merely a suggestion – not a requirement. Portfolio managers who have such large flows, which occur on days far from the mid-point, should recognize a distortion (using Dietz's term) when the mid-point method

[10]For the flow that occurred on the 15th, we have:

$$\frac{CD - D}{D} = \frac{30 - 15}{30} = \frac{15}{30} = 0.5000$$

This means the money was available for half the month.

For the final flow on the 20th, we have

$$\frac{30 - 25}{30} = \frac{5}{30} = 0.1667$$

meaning the money was in the portfolio for only 16.67% of the month.

is relied upon. So, we should consider the 7.74% to be a more accurate assessment of the return.

Why such a lower return? Because this approach recognizes that the additional $500,000 wasn't present for only 50% of the month, but for 83.33%! Therefore, the net appreciation in value for the month of $40,000 has now been more attributed to the flow than the mid-point method would.

12.3.4 Achieving greater accuracy – the true daily rate of return

The modified approach is still considered an *approximation* method because we are not capturing the market value of the portfolio at the time of the flow. The real purpose of time weighting is to measure the return of the manager, for the amount he/she had under his/her control, for the various times in the period. As noted at the start of this chapter, both the AIMR and Global performance presentation standards call for revaluing portfolios each time a cash flow occurs. This will result in a *daily* rate of return.[11]

At first glance, one might presume that there's not much too deal with other than revaluing the portfolio. But, with this method, we need once again to think about the timing of the cash flow: did it occur at the start, end, or middle of the day?[12] In other words, did the manager have use of the funds for the entire day, not at all, or for half the day?

The basic formula

The true time-weighted rate of return is arrived at by calculating the market values whenever a flow occurs, and dividing the ending daily value by the

[11]At first glance, one might presume that we must revalue for *every* day in the period to achieve a daily return, but this isn't true. For example, let's just calculate the return for the first five days of a month, revaluing for each day, with no cash flows. If the daily values are $100, $101, $102, $103, $104, we'd have:

$$\frac{101}{100} \cdot \frac{102}{101} \cdot \frac{103}{102} \cdot \frac{104}{103}$$

From your elementary school arithmetic, you should recall that you can cancel out 'like terms'. That is to say when there's a number in the denominator that's the same as the numerator, you cancel them. Doing this, we have the 101, 102 and 103 cancel out, ending up with

$$\frac{104}{100}$$

which is our ending value divided by the beginning. So, we need only to revalue when flows take place.

[12]There may be some who would argue that we want to be even more precise, and use a weighting factor, similar to the day-weighting factor, to calculate the precise amount of hours (or minutes?) the manager had use of the money. But I'd suggest that this type of treatment has little, if any, value, and won't address it at this time.

preceding starting value, and multiplying these numbers together:

$$\prod_{i=1}^{n} \frac{EMV_i}{BMV_i} - 1 \tag{12.15}$$

Like the Riemann sum, the $\prod$ symbol means to take the *product* of the expression which immediately follows.

1. Start-of-day

Let's begin by assuming the manager had full use of this $500,000 for the full day. Any appreciation in market value on that date would therefore be attributed to the starting value (i.e. the value from the prior day's close) *and* the inclusion of the cash flow amount.

We need to calculate the return from the beginning of the month through the 4th, for the 5th of the month, and then from the 5th through the end of month.[13]

The first period goes from 31 May through 4 June. The starting value is $100,000 and the ending is $100,500. For the 5th, we have use of the $500,000 cash flow, so the starting value is the prior day's closing market value ($100,500) plus the cash flow ($500,000), or $600,500. The ending day's market value includes the day's appreciation of $30,000, resulting in a value of $630,500. This amount also serves as the beginning value for the third part of the month, terminating with the ending month value of $640,000. Mathematically, we have:

$$ROR_{SOD} = \frac{100{,}500}{100{,}000} \times \frac{630{,}500}{600{,}500} \times \frac{640{,}000}{630{,}500} - 1 = 0.0711 = 7.11\% \tag{12.16}$$

This is close to our modified Dietz result of 7.74%. Assuming this is the proper treatment of cash flows (that is, that the flow *did* occur at the start of day), then the 63 basis point[14] improvement can be important. But, there's a cost associated with this improvement. In addition to pricing the portfolio for every cash flow, we must ensure that the contents of our portfolio are accurate (i.e. that our holdings, corporate actions and trades have been properly accounted for and agree with the 'official books and records' (i.e. custodian records) of the portfolio. This 'cost' can be significant and must be weighed with the increased accuracy.

[13] In actuality, we need only calculate the return from the beginning to the 4th, and then from the 5th through month-end, since there will be the calculation of the ending day market value from the 5th and the starting market value for the last period of the month. But to make it very clear as to what is occurring, we'll add the intervening day's return.

[14] A basis point is 0.01 or 1/100 of a per cent (i.e. there are 100 basis points in a percentage point).

2. End-of-day

What if the flow took place at the end of 5 June? This would mean the manager did *not* have use of the money on that day and that any appreciation that occurred should be solely attributed to the start-of-day (i.e. prior day's closing value) market value of \$100,500.

The first period again goes from 31 May through 4 June. The starting value is \$100,000 and the ending is \$100,500. For the 5th, we have the \$100,500 as the starting value, ending with the inclusion of the \$30,000 appreciation (\$130,500). We now add the cash flow (\$500,000), to come up with the starting value for the remaining period of the month (\$630,500), terminating with the ending month value of \$640,000. Mathematically, we have:

$$ROR_{EOD} = \frac{100{,}500}{100{,}000} \times \frac{130{,}500}{100{,}500} \times \frac{640{,}000}{630{,}500} - 1 = 0.3247 = 32.47\% \quad (12.17)$$

Wow, where did that come from? Can this be right? 32.47%?

By assuming that the contribution of \$500,000 wasn't available on the 5th, we're attributing the entire day's appreciation (\$30,000) to the starting day's value (\$100,500). For that day alone, we have a 29.85% (130,500/100,500 – 1) return. Is it possible that the portfolio jumped this much in a single day? Of course it is. But probably unlikely.

If this approach were to have been used and this result derived, we'd suggest that the manager check the overall market. In the start-of-day approach, the return for this day was 5% (630,500/600,500 – 1). If the market moved approximately 5% that day, then one might properly conclude that the money was there for the full day.

3. Middle-of-day

What if we're not sure whether the money was present for the full day or not? Then we might want to use a mid-day approach. Here, we interject the mid-point Dietz expression into our return for the 5th of the month:

$$ROR_{MOD} = \frac{100{,}500}{100{,}000} \times \left(\frac{630{,}500 - 100{,}500 - 500{,}000}{100{,}500 + 0.5 \times 500{,}000} - 1\right) \times \frac{640{,}000}{630{,}500} = 0.1075 = 10.75\% \quad (12.18)$$

The return for the 5th is 8.56%. We're attributing the appreciation that occurred on 5 June to the beginning of day market value (\$100,500) plus half of the cash flow (\$250,000).

The monthly return (10.75%) seems to be better than the mid-point Dietz return but actually less precise than the modified Dietz result. While there

Table 12.1

Mid-point Dietz	11.43%
Modified Dietz	7.74%
Start-of-day daily	7.11%
End-of-day daily	32.47%
Mid-point daily	10.75%

may be times when this approach is appropriate, this time doesn't seem to be one of them.

12.4 CONCLUSION – SUMMARIZING THE FINDINGS

We've now tried five different methods and obtained five different results:

There are some considerable differences here, aren't there? With a low of 7.11% and a high of 32.47%, one must be confused as to which is right. And to think that this large range doesn't include either of the approximation method returns!

So, which is correct?

Technically either of the approximation methods would be acceptable. Again, the idea of day-weighting is an option (although it will become a requirement for the AIMR and GIPS standards in 2005[15]). Hopefully, the firm has adopted the notion that large flows will cause the day-weighting of cash flows, which will result in a more accurate result.

This example demonstrates the problem that can occur when one *thinks* the daily method will yield a more accurate return, regardless of how cash is treated. While we can see that cash treatment is important for monthly approximation methods, it can be even *more* important for daily.

12.4.1 But really, can this happen?

One might think that this fabricated example was created to make a point but wouldn't occur in reality. Well, think again.

Here's an example that was given to me by a client:

> Beginning of month market value = \$30,635,060
> Withdrawal on first business day of month = \$20,000,000
> Depreciation in market value on first of month = \$2,948,532
> End of month market value = \$7,071,916.

Again, we have, what everyone would agree is, a large cash flow (close to two-thirds of the starting value is going away). And it's occurring on the first day of the month.

[15] AIMR (1999), page 7; AIMR (2001), page 15.

Using the five methods, we get the following results:

Mid-point Dietz

$$ROR_{MPD} = \frac{7{,}071{,}916 - 30{,}635{,}060 - (-20{,}000{,}000)}{30{,}635{,}060 + 0.5 \times (-20{,}000{,}000)}$$
$$= \frac{-3{,}563{,}144}{20{,}635{,}060} = -17.27\% \qquad (12.19)$$

Modified Dietz

$$ROR_{MD} = \frac{7{,}071{,}916 - 30{,}635{,}060 - (-20{,}000{,}000)}{30{,}635{,}060 + 0.9667 \times (-20{,}000{,}000)}$$
$$= \frac{-3{,}563{,}144}{11{,}301{,}060} = -0.3153 = -31.53\% \qquad (12.20)$$

Start-of-day daily

$$ROR_{SOD} = \frac{30{,}635{,}060}{30{,}635{,}060} \times \frac{7{,}686{,}528}{10{,}635{,}060} \times \frac{7{,}071{,}916}{7{,}686{,}528} - 1$$
$$= -0.3350 = -33.50\% \qquad (12.21)$$

End-of-day daily

$$ROR_{EOD} = \frac{30{,}635{,}060}{30{,}635{,}060} \times \frac{27{,}686{,}528}{30{,}635{,}060} \times \frac{7{,}071{,}916}{7{,}686{,}528} - 1$$
$$= -0.1685 = -16.85\% \qquad (12.22)$$

Middle-of-day daily

$$ROR_{MOD} = \frac{30{,}635{,}060}{30{,}635{,}060}$$
$$\times \left(\frac{7{,}686{,}528 - 30{,}635{,}060 - (-20{,}000{,}000)}{30{,}635{,}060 + 0.5 \times (-20{,}000{,}000)} - 1\right)$$
$$\times \frac{7{,}071{,}916}{7{,}686{,}528} = -0.2114 = -21.14\% \qquad (12.23)$$

Here we have a situation where a very large outflow took place. But did it occur at the start or end of day? If at the start, we will have a return of −33.50%. If at the end, it's −16.85%. Either are possible, but the difference is huge.

What we know is that there was a drop in the market value (ignoring the cash flow) of $2,948,532 on the first of the month. Do we compare this with the start of day with or without the flow? It would probably make sense that sales took place to generate the funds for the withdrawal, so it's probable that the end-of-day treatment is appropriate.

Again, we find that the mid-day treatment for the daily return doesn't appear to provide any increased accuracy, so its use seems questionable.

12.4.2 The method does matter

Hopefully, what you've concluded from this brief chapter is that you can get some very different results, using perfectly accepted methods of calculating returns. Cash flow treatment has always been an issue when measuring performance. It's even more important when we're trying to generate daily results.

One key is consistency. Whatever approach you select, you should stick with it, unless specific circumstances suggest otherwise. What you cannot do is *game it*. That is, try all the methods and take the one that provides you with the highest result. This would be unethical.

The second example was given to me to analyse because the client's software vendor used the start-of-day approach and calculated the −33.50% return. Because the vendor's software wouldn't allow an end-of-day treatment, what appears to be a significantly flawed result took place. So, another key is that your software vendor has to be flexible, allowing both start- and end-of-day treatment.

The industry *is* moving to daily returns. But for them to be accurate, the data has to be correct (to avoid the old GIGO – garbage in/garbage out – phenomenon) and cash flows have to be properly handled.

REFERENCES

AIMR (1993) *Performance Presentation Standards*, Association for Investment Management and Research, Charlottesville, VA.

AIMR (1997) *Performance Presentation Standards*, Association for Investment Management and Research, Charlottesville, VA.

AIMR (1999) *Global Investment Performance Standards*, Association for Investment Management and Research, Charlottesville, VA.

AIMR (2001) *AIMR Performance Presentation Standards*, Association for Investment Management and Research, Charlottesville, VA.

Dietz, P.O. and Kirschman, J.R. (1983) Evaluating portfolio performance, in J.L. Maginn and D.L. Tuttle (eds), *Managing Investment Portfolios*, Warren, Gorham & Lamont, Boston, MA.

ICAA (1971) *The Standards of Measurement and use for Investment Performance Data*, Investment Council Association of America, New York, NY.

Chapter 13

Measurement of pension fund performance in the UK

IAN TONKS

ABSTRACT

We investigate the performance of the UK equity portfolios of 2,175 segregated UK pension funds over the period 1983–1997. We find that there is a similar pattern in the returns on most of the pension funds and the FT All Share index, leading us to conclude that most funds in the sample are 'closet-trackers'. Any measures of outperformance were therefore bound to be small. Over the whole period and across all funds average outperformance was insignificantly different from zero. We investigated the sensitivity of the fund returns to the addition of a size premium, which we found to be significant, and important for the smaller funds in our sample. During three subperiods we found that there was significant average underperformance during the strong bull market of the mid-1980s, but significant outperformance since 1987. In particular in the period 1987–1992 the average outperformance across pension funds was one-half of a percentage point per year. Decomposing this abnormal performance we found that most of it could be explained by the ability of both large and small funds to time the size premium. On the whole there were negative returns to both selectivity and to market timing. There was little evidence of any differences in the performance between mature and immature funds.

13.1 INTRODUCTION

This chapter examines the performance of a sample of UK pension funds' equity investments over the period 1983–1997. Assessing the investment performance of pension funds is important since a number of recent UK policy documents have argued that pension contributions in particular should be investing in tracker funds, on the basis that 'there is little evidence that active fund management can deliver superior investment returns for the consumer'.[1] The objectives of this project are thus twofold: first, we examine the performance of UK pension funds over a 14 year period relative to alternative specifications of single factor and multifactor benchmarks. Second, we examine whether the characteristics of the pension fund affect its performance. The characteristic that we focus on is fund size, to examine whether large funds outperform small funds or vice versa.[2]

The pension funds in our sample are funded occupational pension schemes. Occupational pension schemes are usually funded and require contributions throughout the employee's working life. In a funded scheme an employee pays into a fund which accumulates over time, and then is allowed to draw on this fund in retirement. These schemes are provided by an employer and may pay on a defined benefit or a defined contribution basis. The fund is administered by trustees, usually nominated by the employer. Defined benefit (or final salary) schemes offer a pension, guaranteed by the employer, usually defined in terms of some proportion of final year earnings, and are related to the number of years of employment. Defined contribution (or money purchase) schemes are always funded and convert the value of the pension fund at retirement into an annuity.

In part the size of the pension fund will depend on the size of the employer, but some large employers may have a number of separate schemes operating for subgroups of employers. We will examine whether there is an optimal fund size in terms of performance. For market liquidity reasons large funds may be constrained in the portfolio of assets in which they invest, whereas smaller funds may be able to take advantage of investing in a wider range of securities.

The significance of this work for trustees and plan advisers is compelling. At the most fundamental asset allocation level, the conclusions of the analysis of the distribution of returns will aid trustees in their decision as to whether to invest their pension fund monies in an active or in a passive vehicle.

13.2 PREVIOUS EVIDENCE ON PERFORMANCE OF MANAGED FUNDS

Empirical evidence suggests that the performance of the average portfolio manager relative to external benchmarks has been disappointing. The early

[1]Paragraph 420, page 71, Office of Fair Trading (1997). See also Consumers' Association (1997); Department of Social Security (1998); Financial Services Agency (1999).

[2]Another characteristic of a fund is its maturity. Thomas and Tonks (2001) show that the maturity of the fund does not affect its performance.

literature of the performance of mutual funds in the US (Jensen, 1968) found that simple tests of abnormal performance did not yield significant returns.[3] Although on average fund managers do not outperform, in any sample there is a distribution to the performance, and more recently research has investigated whether the outperformers in the sample continue to outperform in the future. Grinblatt and Titman (1992) find that differences in mutual fund performance between funds persist over five year time horizons and this persistence is consistent with the ability of fund managers to earn abnormal returns. Hendricks, Patel and Zeckhauser (1993) analysed the short-term relative performance of no-load, growth-oriented mutual funds, and found the strongest evidence for persistence in a one year evaluation horizon. Malkiel (1995), however, argues that survivorship bias is more critical than previous studies have suggested.[4] When an allowance is made for survivorship bias in aggregate, funds have underperformed benchmark portfolios both after management expenses and even gross of expenses. Further he finds that while considerable performance persistence existed in the 1970s, there was no consistency in fund returns in the 1980s. Brown and Goetzmann (1995) examine the performance persistence of US mutual funds and claim that the persistence is mostly due to funds that lag the S&P. They demonstrate that a relative performance pattern depends on the period observed and is correlated across managers, suggesting that persistence is probably not due to individual managers – it is a group phenomenon, due to a common strategy that is not captured by standard stylistic categories or risk adjustment procedures. This is consistent with herding theories of behaviour (Grinblatt, Titman and Wermers, 1994). They suggest that the market fails to discipline underperformers, and their presence in the sample contributes to the documented persistence. Carhart (1997) demonstrates that common factors in stock returns and investment expenses explain persistence in equity mutual funds' mean and risk-adjusted returns. Only significant persistence not explained is concentrated in strong underperformance by the worst return mutual funds. Carhart's results do not support the existence of skilled or informed mutual fund portfolio managers. Daniel *et al.* (1997) using normal portfolio analysis show that mutual fund managers – in particular aggressive-growth funds – exhibit some selectivity ability but that funds exhibit no timing ability. They introduce a measure

[3]The early work of Jensen (1968) and others all established that during bull markets fund managers cannot outperform a market index. However, in bear markets, active managers are more likely to outshine passive alternatives.

[4]Malkiel points out that only the more successful mutual funds survive. Higher risk funds that fail tend to be merged into other products to hide their poor performance. Also bias from tendency to run incubator funds – run ten different products – see which are best and market those, ignoring the poor record of the rest.

that identifies if a manager can time the market, size, book to market, or momentum strategies. Gruber (1996) poses the question: why do people buy mutual funds when their performance is so poor? He postulated that it might be because unitized products are bought and sold at NAV so management ability is not priced into the product. If management ability exists then performance should be predictable. Some investors will be aware of this and will invest accordingly. In the UK Blake and Timmermann (1998) examine 2,300 UK open-ended mutuals over 23 year period (1972–1995), using bid prices and net income gross of fees. Over the period the data includes 973 dead and 1,402 surviving funds, and by studying the termination of funds, they are able to shed light on the extent of survivorship bias. They find economically and statistically very significant underperformance that intensifies as the termination date approaches, and they conclude that survivorship does not alter the results significantly.

Turning to pension funds specifically Ippolito and Turner (1987) examine returns on 1,526 US pension funds and find underperformance relative to the S&P500 Index. Lakonishok, Shleifer and Vishny (1992) provide evidence on the structure and performance of the money management industry in the US in general but focus on the role of pension funds, examining 769 pension funds, with total assets of $129 billion at the end of 1989. They find the equity performance of funds underperformed the S&P500 by 1.3% per year throughout the 1980s. Lakonishok, Shleifer and Vishny emphasize that although there is a long literature on the underperformance of mutual funds, pension funds also underperform relative to mutual funds on average.

Coggin, Fabozzi and Rahman (1993) investigate the investment performance of a random sample of 71 US equity pension fund managers for the period January 1983 through December 1990, and find average selectivity measure is positive and average timing ability is negative; though both selectivity and timing are sensitive to the choice of benchmark when management style is taken into consideration. For example, they find that funds that target value strategies yielded outperformance of 2.1% per annum, but funds that adopted growth strategies underperformed by −0.96%.

In the UK Brown, Draper and McKenzie (1997) examine the consistency of UK pension fund performance, and find limited evidence of persistency of performance for a small number of fund managers. Their sample consists of 232 funds 1981–1990 and 409 funds 1986–1992; all funds retained a single fund manager. Consistency holds over different time horizons, samples and classification schemes. Blake, Lehmann and Timmermann (1999) examine a sample of 364 UK pension funds that retained the same fund manager over the period 1986–1994. They find that the total return is dominated by asset allocation. Average return from stock selection is negative, and average return to market timing is very negative. Although UK equity managers are comparatively good at selecting equities – only 16% of the sample beat peer group average. Thomas and Tonks (2001) using the same dataset as the one in this chapter find that average pension fund performance is insignificantly different from zero using a two factor benchmark.

13.3 MEASURING FUND PERFORMANCE

Jensen's technique is to regress the excess returns on the individual fund above the risk-free rate $R_{pt} - R_{ft}$ against the excess return on the market $R_{mt} - R_{ft}$. In the case of a single factor, this is equivalent to specifying the CAPM as the benchmark. We also specify a three factor model, where the additional two factors are the returns on a size factor and a default risk factor, which includes the single factor CAPM as a special case when $\gamma_p = \lambda_p = 0$. We estimate

$$R_{pt} - r_{ft} = \alpha_p + \beta_p(R_{mt} - r_{ft}) + \gamma_p(R_{mt} - R_{HGt}) + \lambda_p(R_{dt} - r_{ft}) + \varepsilon_{pt} \tag{13.1}$$

for each fund p over the t data periods, and save the coefficients α_p, β_p, γ_p and λ_p. This three factor model is a version of the Fama and French (1993) three factor model, where their SML factor is replaced with the difference between the returns on the market minus the returns on the Hoare–Govett Small Firm Index. The book-to-market HML factor is replaced with a default risk premia defined as the quarterly return on UK long-term corporate bonds (from DataStream) minus the risk-free rate. Fama and French (1996) suggest that their HML factor is related to the default risk in the economy. Carhart (1997) suggests that a fourth factor representing momentum should also be included in tests of portfolio performance, but such a factor is not readily available for UK data.

Under the null hypothesis of no-abnormal performance the α_p coefficient should be equal to zero. For each fund we may test the significance of α_p as a measure of that fund's abnormal performance. We may test for overall fund performance, by testing the significance of the mean α when there are N funds in the sample

$$\bar{\alpha} = \frac{1}{N}\sum_{p=1}^{N}\alpha_p \tag{13.2}$$

The appropriate t-statistic is

$$t = \frac{1}{\sqrt{N}}\sum_{p=1}^{N}\frac{\alpha_p}{SE(\alpha_p)} \tag{13.3}$$

The original Jensen technique made no allowance for market timing abilities of fund managers when fund managers take an aggressive position in a bull market, but a defensive position in a bear market. When portfolio managers expect the market portfolio to rise in value, they may switch from bonds into equities and/or they may invest in more high beta stocks. When they expect the market to fall they will undertake the reverse strategy: sell high beta stocks and move into 'defensive' stocks.

If managers successfully engage in market timing then returns to the fund will be high when the market is high, and also relatively high when the market is low. More generally fund managers may time with respect to any factor. If managers successfully market time, then a quadratic plot will produce better fit (Treynor–Mazuy test). For the single factor model

$$R_{pt} - r_f = \alpha_p + \beta_p(R_{mt} - r_f) + \delta_p(R_{mt} - r_f)^2 + \varepsilon_{pt} \tag{13.4}$$

The significance of market timing is measured by δ_p. An alternative test of market timing for the single factor model suggested by Merton–Henriksson is

$$R_{pt} - r_f = \alpha_p + \beta_p(R_{mt} - r_f) + \delta_p(R_{mt} - r_f)^+ + \eta_{pt} \tag{13.5}$$

where $(R_{mt} - r_f)^+ = \max(0, R_{mt} - r_f)$.

Recently Ferson and Schadt (1996) advocate allowing for the benchmark parameters to be conditioned on economic conditions – called conditional performance evaluation – on the basis that some market timing skills may be incorrectly credited to fund managers, when in fact they are using publicly available information to determine future market movements. In which case Ferson and Schadt argue that the predictable component of market movements should be removed in order to assess fund managers' private market timing skills. Under a conditional version of the CAPM, the Jensen regression becomes

$$R_{it} - r_{ft} = \alpha_i + \beta_i(Z_{t-1})(R_{mt} - r_{ft}) + \varepsilon_{it} \tag{13.6}$$

where Z_{t-1} is a vector of instruments for the information available at time t (and is therefore specified as $t - 1$) and $\beta_i(Z_t)$ are time conditional betas, and their functional form is specified as linear

$$\beta_i(Z_t) = b_0 + B'z_{t-1} \tag{13.7}$$

where $z_{t-1} = Z_{t-1} - E(Z)$ is a vector of deviations of the Zs from their unconditional means. Implementing this approach involves creating interaction terms between the market returns and the instruments. Instruments used are: lagged Treasury bill rate, dividend yield, default premium (difference between low and high quality corporate bonds), and the slope of the term structure (difference between long- and short-run Government bond yields).

The test for market timing now isolates the effect of public information. The amended Treynor–Mazuy test for the single factor model is

$$R_{pt} - r_f = \alpha_p + b_p(R_{mt} - r_f) + B'z_{t-1}(R_{mt} - r_f) + \delta_p(R_{mt} - r_f)^2 + \varepsilon_{pt} \quad (13.8)$$

where the sensitivity of the managers' beta to the private market timing signal is measured by δ_p. The amended Merton–Henriksson test is

$$R_{pt} - r_f = \alpha_p + b_d(R_{mt} - r_f) + B'_d z_{t-1}(R_{mt} - r_f) + \delta_c(R_{mt} - r_f)^+ + \Delta' z_{t-1}(R_{mt} - r_f)^+ + \eta_{pt} \quad (13.9)$$

where:

$$(R_{mt} - r_f)^+ = (R_{mt} - r_f)^* \max[0, R_{mt} - r_f - E(R_{mt} - r_f | Z_{t-1})]$$

and

$$\delta_c = b_{up} - b_d \quad \Delta = B_{up} - B_d$$

The significance of market timing is represented by the significance of δ_c. In all cases these market timing and conditional performance evaluation techniques may be extended to the three factor benchmark.

13.4 DATA

The data used in this study was provided by Combined Actuarial Performance Services Ltd (CAPS). It consists of quarterly returns on UK equity portfolios of 2,175 UK pension funds from March 1983 to December 1997. In addition for each fund-quarter the manager of the fund and the size of the fund is provided. CAPS provide a performance measurement service for about half of all segregated pension fund schemes in the UK. There is one other major provider of pension fund performance: WM Ltd. Chart 13.1 shows the distribution of pension fund assets across asset categories in the general CAPS database. Typically a UK pension fund invests about 57% of assets in UK equities, and it is the returns on UK equity portfolios which is examined in this study. The market return in this study is taken to be the quarterly return on the FT All Share Index, and the risk-free rate is the quarterly return on the three month Treasury bill rate.

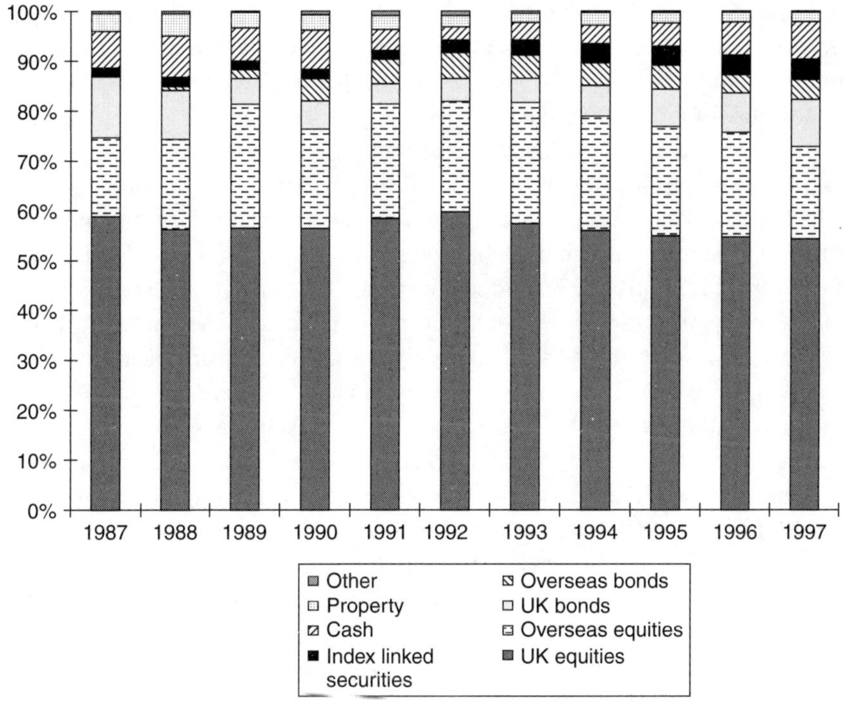

Source: CAPS (1999)

Chart 13.1 Average asset distributions of UK pension funds 1987–1997

Our dataset consists of a total of 59,509 observations on quarterly returns and fund size, and the maximum number of quarters is 56. Table 13.1 illustrates the distribution of fund quarters over the dataset, and shows that 50% funds have 24 or fewer observations, and the average life of a fund in the data is just less than seven years. This high attrition rate is partly explained by the closure of funds due to the sponsoring companies merging, or becoming insolvent, and also due to the fund switching to alternative performance measurement services.

Table 13.1 Descriptive statistics on pension fund-quarters

Fund-quarters						
No. of funds		2,175		No. of quarters		59,509
Distribution of fund-quarters						
min	5%	25%	50%	75%	95%	max
1	4	12	24	41	56	56

Table 13.2 provides some descriptive statistics on the returns to the UK equity portfolios of the pension funds in our dataset. The average discrete quarterly return over all funds over all quarters is 4.32%, compared with an average discrete return of 4.38% for the FT All Share Index. The overall standard deviation of these returns is 8.67%, and the distribution of returns also emphasizes the variability in returns. But these pooled measures disguise an important statistic, which is that the between funds standard deviation is much less than the within fund distribution. This implies that for a particular quarter the distribution of fund returns is tightly packed around the mean, but that over time the variability of returns is much higher. In fact the correlation between the time series values of the FT All Share Index and the average return each quarter across the pension funds is 0.995. The contrast in the within and between standard deviations might be indicative of the herding behaviour of pension funds suggested by Lakonishok, Shleifer and Vishny (1992).

Table 13.2 also reports on the distribution of returns weighted by the value of the fund at the beginning of each quarter. The value weighted average return of 3.80% implies that small funds have a higher return than large funds and this is an issue we will return to later. In the subsequent regression analysis, we require a minimum number of observations to undertake a meaningful statistical analysis, and we impose the requirement that time series fund parameters are only estimated when there were 12 or more quarterly returns for that fund. This cut-off value of three years accords with the typical fund mandate. Table 13.2 reports the distribution of returns of the subsample of 1,724 funds with at least 12 time series observations, and this may be checked with the distribution of returns across the whole sample, to check that the subsample is indeed representative. Similarly Table 13.2 also reports the distribution of returns of those 284 funds that remained in existence over all 56 quarters in our dataset.

In panel B of Table 13.2 we report statistics of the size of the equity portion of the pension funds in our sample. The size distribution is highly skewed with a large number of very small funds. For example, in 1997 the median size fund had an equity portfolio of £28 million. Whereas the largest fund had an equity portfolio of over £9 billion.

In this study we use data on all UK pension funds irrespective of whether they change manager, though normally we think of abnormal returns as being due to fund manager skills, and indeed this is the motivation in the Brown, Draper and McKenzie (1997) and Blake, Lehmann and Timmermann (1999) studies. But survivorship bias is likely to be more of an issue in same manager funds. In addition pension funds may be inherently different, for example due to a different mix of contributors/pensioners. Further concentrating on the same fund manager condition ignores movement in personnel between fund

Table 13.2 Descriptive statistics on fund returns and fund size

Panel A: Returns across quarters and funds

	Returns				FT-All Share returns
	All	Weighted by smv	>= 12 Quarters	= 56 Quarters	
Mean	0.0432	0.0380	0.0428	0.0444	0.0438
Std. dev.	0.0867	0.0814	0.0867	0.0858	0.0834
Overall					
Between funds	0.01652		0.0092	0.0030	
Within funds	0.08628		0.0864	0.0857	
Distribution of returns:					
5%	−0.0725	−0.0689	−0.0727	−0.070	
10%	−0.0543	−0.0537	−0.0543	−0.0536	
25%	0.0016	0.0016	0.0015	0.0021	
50%	0.0463	0.0441	0.0459	0.0469	
75%	0.0896	0.0747	0.0885	0.0926	
90%	0.1525	0.1346	0.1527	0.1511	
95%	0.1825	0.1693	0.1825	0.1823	
Obs.	59,317	59,314	56,403	15,842	56
No. of funds	2170	2170	1724	278	

Panel B: Fund size across funds

	Size at start of quarter (£m)		
	March 1983	Dec. 1990	Dec. 1997
Mean	25.02	50.24	102.27
Std. dev.	85.01	194.45	387.30
Between			
Distribution of fund size:			
Min	0	0.018	0.17
5%	0.307	0.92	3.95
10%	0.441	1.36	6.02
25%	1.06	3.31	12.39
50%	3.20	8.35	28.12
75%	14.25	27.36	70.14
90%	51.64	102.88	221.90
95%	111.30	174.89	356.03
Max	1,113.4	3,823.63	9,108.62
Obs.	833	1131	1004

The table shows discrete returns, and computes arithmetic averages.

management companies. Pension fund trustees may switch fund managers after movement in personnel.

13.5 RESULTS

In the first row of Table 13.3 we report the average parameter estimates from regressing equation (13.1) across 1,714 funds, where the single factor benchmark return is specified as the excess return on the market. It can be seen that the average α is slightly positive but is insignificantly different from zero. We also report the distribution of these parameter values and the t-statistics across funds, and the distribution of the Jensen alphas and the associated t-statistics are plotted in Figures 13.1 and 13.2. It can be seen that both distributions are symmetrically distributed around the mean. Just over half of the alpha statistics are positive, and about 10% are significantly different from zero. The explanatory power of the individual time series regressions is very high, with the average coefficient of determination being 0.95. In addition the fund betas are typically close to unity: 80% of the funds have betas between 0.95 and 1.08, which is consistent with our earlier finding that the distribution

Table 13.3 Performance evaluation with CAPM benchmark

	No. funds	α	α t-stat	β	β t-stat	R^2
Panel A: All funds						
Average values	1714	0.00017	0.966	1.018	1,280.0	0.953
Distribution of parameters						
10%		−0.0047	−1.4833	0.9525	14.4449	0.9146
25%		−0.0021	−0.7167	0.9911	20.8745	0.9510
50%		0.0002	0.0570	1.0218	30.5056	0.9692
75%		0.0023	0.8101	1.0508	39.8608	0.9796
90%		0.0046	1.4554	1.0802	48.3085	0.9861
No. coeffs > 0(* > 1)		898		1173*		
No. of signif. coeffs			165		1714	
Panel B: Small Funds (<40% smv)						
Average values	731	−0.00002	−1.5600	1.018	750.26	0.950
Panel C: Large funds (>80% smv)						
Average values	302	0.0001	0.2092	1.014	685.9	0.967

For each fund we regress the single factor model (CAPM) $R_{pt} - r_{ft} = \alpha_p + \beta_p(R_{mt} - r_{ft}) + \varepsilon_{pt}$. In the first row of the table we report the average parameter estimates from these regressions, and the relevant overall t-statistic for the average value of each parameter is computed as in equation (13.3) in the case of the αs, and similarly for the other parameters. The cross-fund distribution of the parameter estimates and corresponding t-statistics are displayed in the remaining rows. The final row counts the number of cross-fund parameter estimates that are greater than zero (greater than unity in the case of the β coefficient).

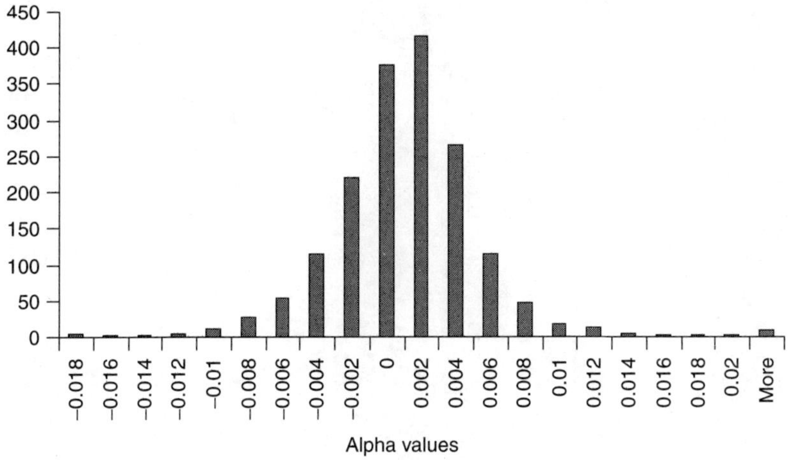

Figure 13.1 Distribution of Jensen alphas using CAPM model

of returns in any quarter is highly correlated with the market index. It would appear that the funds in the sample are 'closet-trackers' since they all invest in similar well-diversified portfolios, which mimick the market index.

We then divided the funds into two groups on the basis of fund size. This classification was determined as follows. Over the whole sample we computed the distribution of fund size, over time and across funds. We identified the fourth and eighth deciles of this distribution. Then for each fund we computed the average fund size over the fund's life. Those funds whose average size was less than the pooled distribution's fourth decile were classified as small funds;

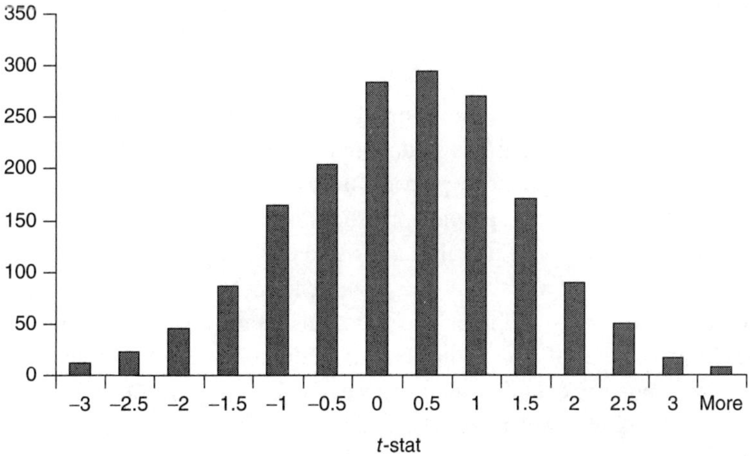

Figure 13.2 Distribution of Jensen alpha t-statistics using CAPM model

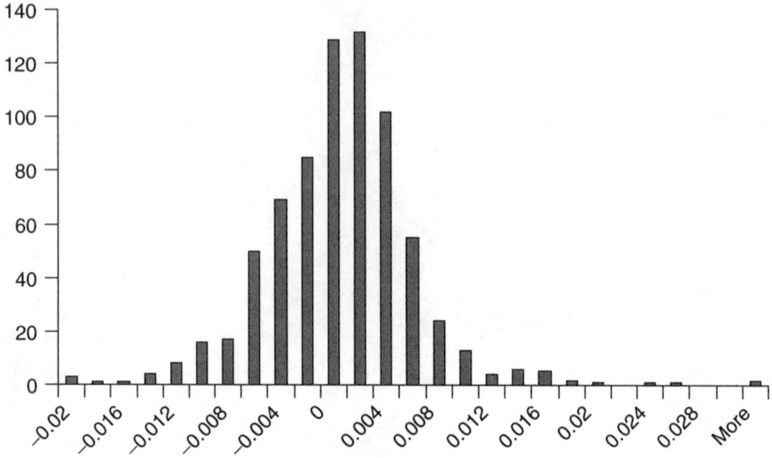

Figure 13.3 Distribution of Jensen alphas for small funds using CAPM model

those funds whose average size was greater than the pooled distribution's eighth decile were classified as large funds. This classification resulted in 731 small funds and 302 large funds. This classification was clearly arbitrary, but the reason for the asymmetric use of deciles reflected the skewed size distribution in the sample as evidenced in Table 13.2, panel B.

In panels B and C in Table 13.3 we report the results by fund size. Surprisingly, the average alpha coefficient for the 731 funds in the small fund sample is negative, though insignificant. The average alpha coefficient for the 302 large funds is positive, but also insignificant. The interpretation of these results in comparison with the descriptive statistics in Table 13.2 is that once an adjustment is made for the fund's risk, the outperformance of small funds is less than for large funds. In Figures 13.3 and 13.4 we plot the cross-section distributions of the fund alphas for large funds and small funds separately. These results contradict a recent finding by Blake, Lehmann and Timmermann (2000) that large pension funds underperform small funds. But their sample consists of a smaller number of pension funds over a shorter time period, and it is likely, given that their sample construction of funds maintaining the same fund manager, that only relatively large funds are included in their sample.

In Table 13.4 we report the results of extending the single factor model to include an additional size factor and a default factor. The inclusion of a size factor allows for the fact that historically, small companies have outperformed their larger counterparts, though in the early 1990s this outperformance by small companies was reversed. The small firm effect has been shown to be important in the computation of appropriate benchmarks for studies of UK stock returns (Dimson and Marsh, 1986). The returns on the size factor that we

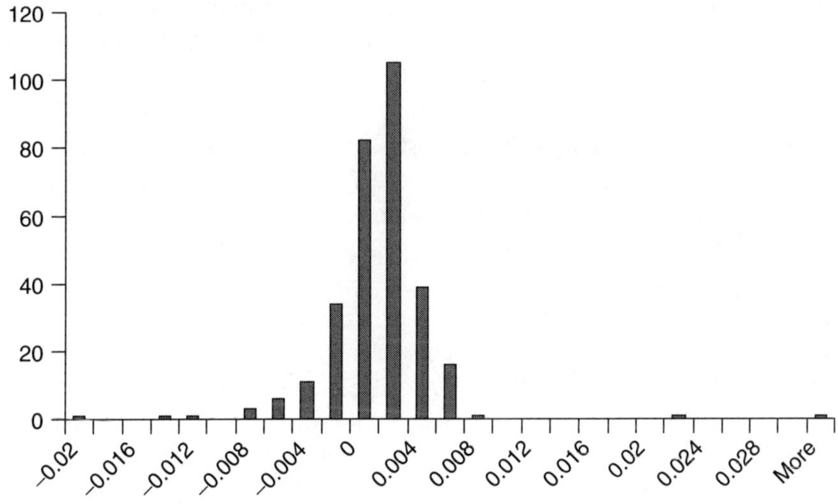

Figure 13.4 Distribution of Jensen alphas for large funds using CAPM model

Table 13.4 Performance evaluation with three factor benchmark

	No. funds	α	α t-stat	γ	γ t-stat	λ	λ t-stat	R^2
Panel A: *All funds*								
Average values	1714	0.0001	4.526	0.0838	54.668	−0.0612	−6.614	0.962
Distribution of parameters								
10%		−0.0052	−1.3562	−0.0430	−0.6004	−0.8646	−1.3545	0.9335
25%		−0.0019	−0.5536	0.0204	0.3002	−0.4228	−0.7883	0.9588
50%		0.0004	0.1277	0.0725	1.2825	−0.1049	−0.1893	0.9733
75%		0.0025	0.8426	0.1386	2.3182	0.2840	0.4783	0.9827
90%		0.0047	1.4657	0.2261	3.2436	0.7376	1.0925	0.9883
No. coeffs >0		940		1392		725		1714
Panel B: *Small funds (<40% smv)*								
Average values	731	−0.0003	−0.0969	0.0973	34.0003	−0.0471	−3.5815	0.9608
Panel C: *Large funds (>80% smv)*								
Average values	302	0.0004	3.5756	0.0580	21.6615	−0.1224	−5.4803	0.9718

For each fund we regress the three factor model $R_{pt} - r_{ft} = \alpha_p + \beta_p(R_{mt} - r_{ft}) + \gamma_p(R_{mt} - R_{HGt}) + \lambda_p(R_{dt} - r_{ft}) + \varepsilon_{pt}$. In the first row of the table we report the average parameter estimates from these regressions, and the relevant overall t-statistic for the average value of each parameter, computed as in equation (13.3) in the case of the αs, and similarly for the other parameters. The cross-fund distribution of the parameter estimates and corresponding t-statistics are displayed in the remaining rows. All standard errors are robust.

use are the difference between the return on a small firm index (Hoare–Govett Small Companies Index) and the FT All Share Index. In fact in the early 1990s this premium was negative. The first row of Table 13.4 shows that the coefficient γ_p on the size premium was positive on average and significant, meaning that funds had a positive exposure to the size premium. In Table 13.4 we can see that the value of the average Jensen alpha is similar to the single factor case, but this time, this small outperformance measure is significantly positive. This is an important finding, since it means that the measure of abnormal performance is sensitive to the specification of the benchmark: a three factor benchmark yields small but significant outperformance by the average pension fund. The average coefficient γ on the size factor is positive and significant, and the coefficient λ on the default factor is negative and significant. In panels B and C we again split the sample into small and large funds. It can be seen that the performance of the small funds is insignificantly different from zero, but the Jensen alpha for the large pension funds is significantly positive, implying outperformance on average. Looking at the coefficients of the other factors, it appears that the small funds are more sensitive to the size factor, and both groups of pension funds are negatively related to the default factor, with the large funds being more sensitive to this factor.

In Table 13.5 we apply the two tests for market timing, for the single factor CAPM benchmark. The two tests are the Treynor–Mazuy test from equation (13.4) and the Merton-Henriksson test outlined in equation (13.5). Both tests produce similar results. The Jensen–alphas reported in Table 13.3 can be decomposed into a selectivity alpha, and a market timing delta. The results in Table 13.5 show that the selectivity alphas for both the Treynor–Mazuy and the Merton–Henriksson tests are significantly positive, but that the timing coefficients are significantly negative, meaning that funds appear to be very poor market timers: they increase the betas of their portfolios at the wrong times. These funds appear to increase the beta of their portfolios when the market index is going down, and reduce the portfolio beta when the market index is increasing. These perverse market timing results are consistent with the findings of Coggin, Fabozzi and Rahman (1993). The distribution of the selectivity alphas and the market timing delta are illustrated in Figures 13.5 and 13.6.

In Table 13.6 we extend the timing tests to the three factor case, and we test for timing effects with respect to the market index, the size premium and the default premium. The logic behind these tests rests on the idea that in a multi-factor environment, a fund manager may be able to ‘time’ any one of the factors: that is if the size effect is positive, a skilled fund manager may adjust the portfolio to have additional exposure to the size factor. Similarly, a fund manager may be able to ‘time’ the default risk in the economy. The

Table 13.5 Performance evaluation for CAPM with market timing: all observations

	No. Funds	α	α t-stat	β	β t-stat	δ (market timing)	δ t-stat	R^2
Panel A: Treynor–Mazuy method								
Mean parameter	1714	0.0008	11.055	1.012	1,310.1	−0.0013	−21.152	0.956
10%		−0.0042	−1.1350	0.9431	12.5994	−0.3816	−2.2391	0.9185
25%		−0.0012	−0.4001	0.9847	20.9055	−0.2395	−1.4136	0.9528
50%		0.0009	0.2918	1.0170	30.4643	−0.1068	−0.5497	0.9709
75%		0.0031	0.9912	1.0489	40.1341	0.0859	0.3593	0.9808
90%		0.0055	1.5914	1.0777	50.1130	0.5032	1.1716	0.9872
No. coeffs > 0(* > 1)		1054		1099*		93		
Panel B: Merton–Henriksson								
Mean parameter	1714	0.0018	19.412	1.044	1,107.6	−0.0493	−27.14	0.956

For each fund we regress the single factor model augmented by a market timing term. The Treynor–Mazuy test in (13.4) is $R_{pt} - r_{ft} = \alpha_p + \beta_p(R_{mt} - r_{ft}) + \delta_p(R_{mt} - r_f)^2 + \varepsilon_{pt}$, and the relevance of market timing is represented by the significance of the δ_p coefficient. The Merton–Henriksson test in (13.5) is $R_{pt} - r_f = \alpha_p + \beta_p(R_{mt} - r_f) + \delta_p(R_{mt} - r_f)^+ + \eta_{pt}$ where $(R_{mt} - r_f)^+ = \max(0, R_{mt} - r_f)$, and the relevance of market timing is again given by the significance of the δ_p coefficient. Panel A reports the results of the Treynor–Mazuy test, including the distribution of the individual fund estimates. Panel B reports only the mean parameter values of the time series estimates. The relevant overall t-statistic for the average value of each parameter is computed as in equation (13.3) in the case of the αs, and similarly for the other parameters. All standard errors are robust.

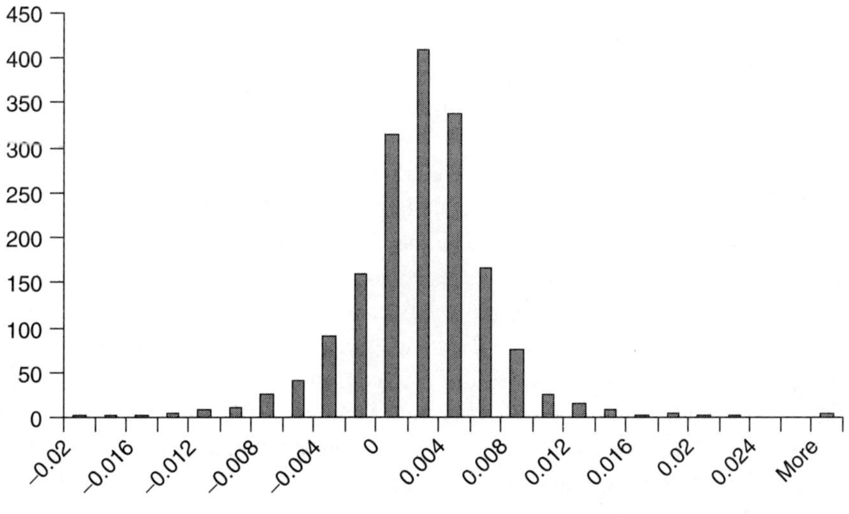

Figure 13.5 Distribution of selectivity alphas in CAPM single factor market timing regression

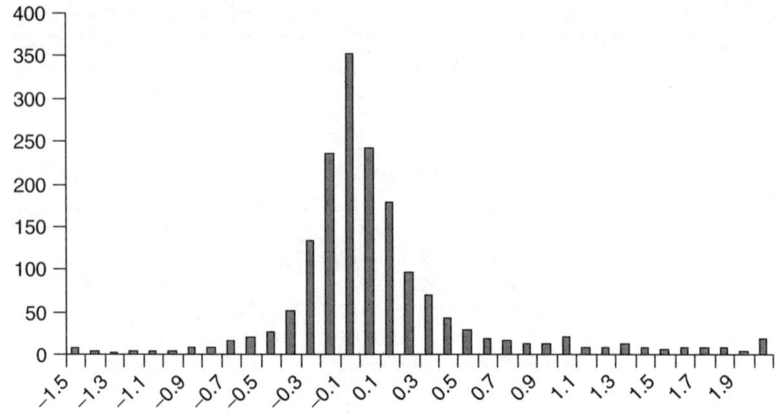

Figure 13.6 Distribution of deltas (market timing coefficient) in CAPM single factor market timing regression

δ_p coefficient reports the market timing effect, the κ_p coefficient the effect of size timing, and the η_p coefficient the effect of default timing. For the sample overall, from the first two rows of Table 13.6, panel A, we can see that according to both the Treynor and Merton tests, the average selectivity alpha is significantly negative, and the average market timing parameter is also significantly negative. These results imply that funds are both poor at selectivity and market timing. However, in the case of the Treynor measure the positive exposure to the size premium is accompanied by a positive average size timing κ_p parameter. This implies that funds are good at timing the size premium. The Merton test is slightly odd because of a negative coefficient on the size factor. For both the Treynor and Merton tests the coefficient on the default factor is negative, but the default timing coefficient is significantly positive.

The remaining panels in Table 13.6 investigate these issues further by examining whether there is a difference in parameter estimates by size of fund, and also over different subperiods. Panel B shows that it was also the case that both large and small funds had a positive exposure to the size premium, and the sensitivity of the small funds was greater: 0.072 rather than 0.038. For both subgroups of funds, selectivity was significantly negative, market timing was poor, but size and default timing was significantly positive. The average size timing coefficient of 1.15 and default timing coefficient of 13.12 for the small fund sample was greater than that for the large funds, and implies that the small funds are more able to time both the size and default premia. This is consistent with the idea that small funds are able to invest in small companies, whereas large funds are unable to take advantage of movements in the size premium, because it is more difficult for them to invest in small companies on account of their larger size.

Table 13.6 Performance evaluation for three factor benchmark with market timing

No. funds	α	α t-stat	γ	γ t-stat	λ	λ t-stat	δ	δ t-stat	κ	κ t-stat	η	η t-stat	R^2
Panel A: All funds (with more than 20 observations)													
Treynor–Mazuy test:													
1299	−0.0011	−10.303	0.039	44.24	−0.035	−7.019	−0.052	−20.706	0.922	45.251	17.235	6.160	0.968
Merton–Henriksson test													
1299	−0.0017	−10.582	−0.007	−1.442	−0.222	−11.022	−0.043	−20.591	0.160	34.429	0.358	32.694	0.9671
Panel B: By fund size													
Treynor test small funds (<40% smv)													
486	−0.0015	−7.072	0.072	29.772	0.006	3.158	−0.044	−10.671	1.1508	28.269	13.123	2.803	0.965
Treynor test large funds (>80% smv)													
256	−0.0007	−4.022	0.038	19.160	−0.008	−4.071	−0.107	−16.111	0.995	25.056	9.840	1.512	0.976
Panel C: By time subsample													
Treynor test: 1st Q 1983–3rd Q 1987													
594	−0.0022	−11.818	0.142	29.666	−0.428	−12.223							0.976
594	0.0008	20.801	−0.232	−30.341	0.622	12.507	−0.230	−49.197	5.113	50.672	−94.354	−20.801	0.983
Treynor test: 4th Q 1987–2nd Q 1992													
773	0.0026	20.970	0.086	32.669	−0.539	−18.926							0.972
773	0.0002	1.764	0.078	32.258	−0.530	−22.173	−0.088	−11.005	0.844	34.634	19.038	2.291	0.978
Treynor test: 3rd Q 1992–4th Q 1997													
806	−0.0008	−8.917	0.084	37.475	0.426	28.348							0.957
806	−0.0030	−26.323	0.089	46.018	0.240	14.248	0.506	26.619	−0.133	−6.233	63.637	23.441	0.968

For each fund we regress the three factor model $R_{pt} - r_{ft} = \alpha_p + \beta_p(R_{mt} - r_{ft}) + \gamma_p(R_{mt} - R_{HGt}) + \lambda_p(R_{dt} - r_{ft}) + \varepsilon_{pt}$, with additional quadratic terms for market timing, size premium timing and default premium. The Treynor–Mazuy test becomes $R_{pt} - r_{ft} = \alpha_p + \beta_p(R_{mt} - r_{ft}) + \gamma(R_{HGt} - R_{mt}) + \lambda_p(R_{dt} - r_{ft}) + \delta_p(R_{mt} - r_{ft})^2 + \kappa_p(R_{HGt} - R_{mt})^2 + \eta_p(R_{dt} - r_{ft})^2 + \varepsilon_{pt}$. The relevance of market timing is represented by the significance of the δ_p coefficient, size timing by the significance of κ_p and default timing by η_p. The relevant overall t-statistic for the average value of each parameter is computed as in equation (13.3) in the case of the α's, and similarly for the other parameters. All standard errors are robust.

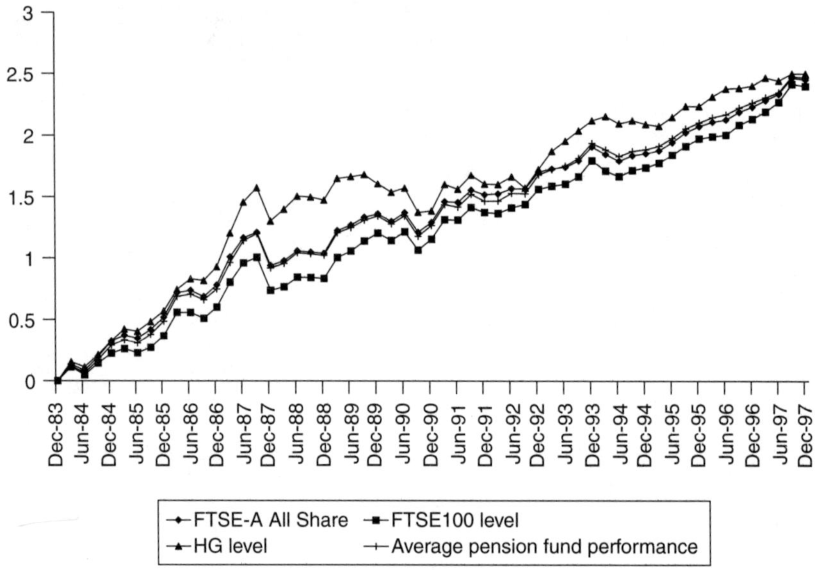

Chart 13.2 Level of FTSE100/FT All Share/Hoare–Govett Indices and Index of Equity Portfolios of UK Segregated Pension Funds, 1984–1997 (all indexed at zero on 31 December 1983)

Chart 13.2 shows the movement in a number of market indices over the whole period 1984–1997. We can identify three distinct periods. The mid-1980s were characterized by a steep bull market, which ended after the stock market crash in the fourth quarter of 1987. There followed a period of slow and not very volatile growth in the indices up to the middle of 1992 when the UK exited the Exchange Rate Mechanism. The third period is identified by a continuation of the steady growth trend but with increased volatility.

Panel C in Table 13.6 reports the results of the three factor model for each of the three subperiods with and without the inclusion of the timing variables. In the initial bull market phase and the last subperiod there is significant underperformance on average, though in the middle subperiods on average funds significantly outperform relative to the three factor benchmark. The exposure to the size factor is always positive and significant. The exposure to the default premium is negative up to 1992 and positive thereafter. The inclusion of the timing variables shows a clear pattern between the first two subperiods as distinct from the final subperiod. In the first two subperiods up to 1992 selectivity is positive. Market timing is negative and size timing is positive. In contrast in the last subperiod, selectivity is significantly negative, market timing is positive and size timing is negative. It appears that the outperformance in the middle subperiod is explained by the slight positive selectivity, and the positive size and default timing, even though the market timing in that period is negative. Summarizing the results in panel C it appears that measures of portfolio performance are critically dependent on the time period of study.

Table 13.7 expands on the results in Table 13.6, by examining portfolio performance jointly split by fund size and time period. Over the first subperiod 1984–1987 both large and small funds underperformed the three factor benchmark. The decomposition of this underperformance shows that large funds had positive selectivity, but small funds had negative selectivity. For both small and large funds there is positive and significant size timing, negative market timing and negative default timing. In both cases the addition of the quadratic size premium means that the coefficient on the linear size premium becomes negative. In the middle time period 1987–1992, both small and large funds display outperformance. Both small and large funds display insignificant selectivity, negative market timing, but with strong size timing in both groups. Hence the implication is that most of this outperformance is driven by significant size timing. In the final subperiod 1992–1997, both small and large funds underperform the benchmark. Both types of funds exhibit significantly negative selectivity, positive market timing and default timing, but negative size timing over this subperiod, particularly for large funds.

In Table 13.8 we re-examine the question of portfolio performance using conditional performance evaluation techniques for the single factor case only. Applying the conditional estimation to the three factor model is difficult to implement, because of the lack of degrees of freedom: adding an extra factor loses five degrees of freedom. Comparing the results in Table 13.8 with the single factor case in Table 13.4, it can be seen that in the case of the Treynor test, the conditional estimation does not greatly alter the unconditional results: significant selectivity, but perverse market timing. Though for the Merton test, the conditional tests result in both significant selectivity and market timing.

13.6 CONCLUSIONS

We have investigated the performance of the UK equity portfolios of 2,175 segregated UK pension funds over the period 1983–1997 using alternative specifications of the benchmark portfolio. This is longest set of UK pension fund data analysed to date, and with such a long dataset we have been able to examine performance over three distinct subperiods.

We noted at the outset the similarity between pension fund returns and the returns on the FT All Share Index, and most of the pension funds in our sample had an equity beta close to unity, implying that their returns were very close to the returns of the FT All Share Index. Any measures of outperformance were

Table 13.7 Performance evaluation by time and size subsamples with three factor benchmark and market timing

No. funds	α	α t-stat	γ	γ t-stat	λ	λ t-stat	δ	δ t-stat	κ	κ t-stat	η	η t-stat	R^2
Panel A: Treynor test: 1st Q 1983–3rd Q 1987, small funds													
223	−0.0024	−7.140	0.160	19.328	−0.407	−6.421							0.972
223	0.0003	−0.464	−0.201	−14.409	0.581	5.917	−0.211	−26.580	4.966	27.792	-87.343	−10.119	0.980
Panel B: Treynor test: 1st Q 1983–3rd Q 1987, large funds													
147	−0.0022	−6.942	0.110	13.495	−0.409	−6.811							0.982
147	0.0019	2.166	−0.276	−21.770	0.804	10.037	−0.289	−34.819	5.190	31.093	−115.063	−15.366	0.988
Panel C: Treynor test: 4th Q 1987–2nd Q 1992, small funds													
260	0.0026	10.517	0.098	19.810	−0.414	−8.091							0.970
260	−0.0002	−0.153	0.088	19.844	−0.428	−10.083	−0.068	−5.157	0.829	18.632	32.378	2.810	0.977
Panel D: Treynor test: 4th Q 1987–2nd Q 1992, large funds													
181	0.0028	12.242	0.073	15.744	−0.595	−11.666							0.979
181	0.0007	1.945	0.068	15.439	−0.554	−12.911	−0.115	−6.992	0.966	21.054	1.066	−0.912	0.984
Panel E: Treynor test: 3rd Q 1992–4th Q 1997, small funds													
191	−0.0007	−3.547	0.101	18.014	0.383	11.345							0.946
191	−0.0028	−10.780	0.105	20.892	0.221	6.068	0.439	9.540	−0.062	−0.283	56.637	9.052	0.957
Panel F: Treynor test: 3rd Q 1992–4th Q 1997, large funds													
190	−0.0007	−4.303	0.069	19.294	0.403	15.737							0.972
190	−0.0029	−14.411	0.074	24.783	0.184	6.390	0.594	18.332	−0.295	−7.117	71.866	15.054	0.979

For each fund we regress the three factor model $R_{pt} - r_{ft} = \alpha_p + \beta_p(R_{mt} - r_{ft}) + \gamma_p(R_{mt} - R_{HGt}) + \lambda_p(R_{dt} - r_{ft}) + \varepsilon_{pt}$, with additional quadratic terms for market timing, size premium timing and default premium. The Treynor–Mazuy test becomes $R_{pt} - r_{ft} = \alpha_p + \beta_p(R_{mt} - r_{ft}) + \gamma(R_{HGt} - R_{mt}) + \lambda_p(R_{dt} - r_{ft}) + \delta_p(R_{mt} - r_{ft})^2 + \kappa_p(R_{HGt} - R_{mt})^2 + \eta_p(R_{dt} - r_{ft})^2 + \varepsilon_{pt}$. The relevance of market timing is represented by the significance of the δ_p coefficient, size timing by the significance of κ_p and default timing by η_p. The relevant overall t-statistic for the average value of each parameter is computed as in equation (13.3) in the case of the α's, and similarly for the other parameters. All standard errors are robust.

Table 13.8 Performance evaluation with conditional estimation for CAPM with market timing

	No. funds	Average α	α t-stat	Average β	β t-stat	Average δ	δ t-stat	R^2
Treynor all ($n > 12$)	1714	0.0018	19.38	1.041	811.7	−0.405	−21.39	0.967
Teynor all ($n > 20$)	1299	0.0020	19.85	1.025	847.0	−0.2583	−20.697	0.964
Teynor small funds ($n > 20$)	486	0.0016	8.4993	1.019	430.03	−0.1507	−7.874	0.961
Treynor large funds ($n > 20$)	256	0.0021	11.443	1.0176	499.9	−0.2903	−14.638	0.974
Merton–Henriksson ($n > 20$)	1299	0.0016	16.466	1.003	517.3	0.1593	2.003	0.970

For each fund we regress the conditional single factor model augmented by a market timing term, where each of the time series regressions is restricted to those funds having a minimum of 20 quarters, since the parameters in the amended Merton–Henriksson regressions require 11 degrees of freedom. The Treynor–Mazuy test in (13.8) is $R_{pt} - r_f = \alpha_p + b_p(R_{mt} - r_f) + B'z_{t-1}(R_{mt} - r_f) + \delta_p(R_{mt} - r_f)^2 + \varepsilon_{pt}$ where the sensitivity of the manager's beta to the private market timing signal is measured by δ_p. The amended Merton–Henriksson test is $R_{pt} - r_f = \alpha_p + b_d(R_{mt} - r_f) + B'_d z_{t-1}(R_{mt} - r_f) + \delta_c(R_{mt} - r_f)^+ + \Delta' z_{t-1}(R_{mt} - r_f)^+ + \eta_{pt}$ where $(R_{mt} - r_f)^+ = (R_{mt} - r_f)^*$ max$[0, R_{mt} - r_f - E(R_{mt} - r_f|Z_{t-1})]$; and $\delta_c = b_{up} - b_d$; $\Delta = B_{up} - B_d$. The signifiance of market timing is represented by the significance of δ_c. The reported coefficients are the mean parameter values of the time series estimates from the individual fund regressions. The relevant overall t-statistic for the average value of each parameter is computed as in equation (13.3) in the case of the α's, and similarly for the other parameters.

therefore bound to be small. We also investigated the sensitivity of the fund returns to the addition of a size premium, which we found to be significant, and important for the smaller funds in our sample.

Over the whole period and across all funds the outperformance was insignificant when measured by a single factor benchmark. However, when we applied a three factor benchmark we were able to detect slight but significant average outperformance. However, during the subperiods there was significant average underperformance during the strong bull market of the mid-1980s, but significant outperformance since 1987. In particular in the period 1987–1992 the average outperformance across pension funds was a percentage point per year.

Decomposing this abnormal performance we found that most of it could be explained by the ability of both large and small funds to time the size premium. On the whole there were negative returns to both selectivity and to market timing.

ACKNOWLEDGEMENTS

The data used in this study was provided by CAPS Ltd, and we are grateful for the assistance of Alan Wilcock and Ian Ibbotson. This chapter has benefited from comments made at seminars at the University of Bristol, Lancaster University, London School of Ecnomics and Said Business School, Oxford. We are particularly grateful to comments made by David Ashton, Tim Jenkinson, and John O' Hanlon.

REFERENCES

Blake, D. and Timmermann, A. (1998) The birth and death processes of mutual funds, *European Finance Review*, **2**, 57–77.

Blake, D., Lehmann, B. and Timmermann, A. (2000) *Performance Clustering and Incentive in the UK Pension Fund Industry*, Pensions Institute.

Blake, D., Lehmann, B. and Timmermann, A. (1999) Asset allocation dynamics and pension fund performance, *Journal of Business*, **72**, 429–461.

Brown, S. and Goetzmann, W. (1995) Performance persistence, *Journal of Finance*, **50**, 679–698.

Brown, G., Draper, P. and McKenzie, E. (1997) Consistency of UK pension fund performance, *Journal of Business Finance and Accounting*, **24**, March, 155–178.

CAPS (1999) *CAPS Pension Fund Review*, Combined Actuarial Performance Services Ltd, CAPS.

Carhart, M. (1997) On persistence in mutual fund performance, *Journal of Finance*, **52**, 57–82.

Coggin, T.D., Fabozzi, F.J. and Rahman, S. (1993) The investment performance of US equity pension fund managers: an empirical investigation, *Journal of Finance*, **48**, 1039–1055.

Consumers' Association (1997) *A Blueprint for Better Pensions*, Consumers' Association.

Daniel, K., Grinblatt, M. Titman, S. and Wermers, R. (1997) Measuring mutual fund performance with characteristic based benchmarks, *Journal of Finance*, **52**, 1035–1058.

Department of Social Security (1998) *A New Contract for Welfare: Partnership in Pensions*, HMSO.

Dimson, E. and Marsh, P. (1986) Event study methodologies and the size effect, *Journal of Financial Economics*, **17**, 113–142.

Fama, E. and French, K. (1993) Common risk factors in the returns on stocks and bonds, *Journal of Financial Economics*, **33**, 3–56.

Fama, E. and French, K. (1996) The CAPM is wanted, dead or alive, *Journal of Finance*, **51**, 1947–1958.

Ferson, W.E. and Schadt, R.W. (1996) Measuring fund strategy and performance in changing economic conditions, *Journal of Finance*, **51**, 425–462.

Financial Services Agency (1999) *Comparative Information for Financial Services*, Financial Services Agency.

Grinblatt, M. and Titman, S. (1992) Persistence in mutual fund performance, *Journal of Finance*, **47**, 1977–1984.

Grinblatt, M., Titman, S. and Wermers, R. (1995) Momentum investment strategies, portfolio performance and herding: a study of mutual fund behaviour, *American Economic Review*, **85**, 1088–1105.

Gruber, M. (1996) Another puzzle: the growth in actively managed mutual funds, *Journal of Finance*, **51**, 783–810.

Hendricks, D., Patel, J. and Zeckhauser, R. (1993) Hot hands in mutual funds: short run persistence of relative performance, 1974–1988, *Journal of Finance*, **48**, 93–130.

Ippolito, R.A. and Turner, J.A. (1987) Turnover, fees and pension plan performance, *Financial Analysts Journal*, **43**, 16–26.

Jensen, M.C. (1968) The performance of mutual funds in the period 1945–64, *Journal of Finance*, **23**, 389–416.

Lakonishok, J.A., Shleifer, A. and Vishny, R.W. (1992) The structure and performance of the money management industry, *Brookings Papers on Economic Activity*, 339–391.

Malkiel, B.G. (1995) Returns from investing in equity mutual funds 1971 to 1991, *Journal of Finance*, **50**, 549–572.

Office of Fair Trading (1997) *Report of the Director General's Inquiry into Pensions*.

Thomas, A. and Tonks, I. (2001) Equity performance of seggregated pension funds in the UK, *Journal of Asset Management*, **1**(4), 321–343.

Index

(n = footnote)